New York New Amsterdam

Broadway
PALACE
VALENTINE TO TIMES SQUARE
ZALES
CHICAGO
W 46 ST
ONE WAY
ONE WAY
WEST SIDE STORY
FUEL
McDonald's
Restaurant
OPEN 24 HOURS
TIMES SQUARE INFORMATION CENTER
TIMES SQUARE INFORMATION CENTER
TIMES SQUARE ALLIANCE
TIMESSQUARENYC.ORG
OPENING NIGHT
Espresso

A Story of Pride

The relationship between New York, or New Amsterdam as it was called in the seventeenth century, and Amsterdam, the capital of the Netherlands, is like that of a child who found its own way, without its mother, and went far in this world. Four hundred years ago, when the Englishman Henry Hudson on commission from the Dutch East India Company (Verenigde Oost-Indische Compagnie, or VOC) sailed up the river that would later bear his name, this child had yet to be born. The earliest account of Hudson's journey tells of a desolate place and of unspoiled nature along the river.
The New Amsterdam colony had an exciting youth under Dutch custody. The most frequent contacts were with Amsterdam, and trade interests were promoted by the VOC's Amsterdam Chamber. The enterprising Amsterdammers helped the fledgling settlement blossom and flourish. We are proud that the letter of 1626 confirming Dutch possession of the island of Manhattan is preserved in our National Archives. Though not a deed of purchase in the modern sense of the word, the letter nevertheless symbolizes the beginning of a settlement that would become one of the world's most important cities.
The official relationship between Amsterdam and New Amsterdam ended in 1667, when New Amsterdam was ceded to the English during a European summit conference. The Dutch Republic kept Suriname, which it had conquered shortly before. This meeting, attended by the Netherlands, England, France and Denmark, was held in the city of Breda. The Treaty of Breda – a document that likewise is part of our cultural heritage – marks a second milestone in the Dutch-American story. It would be followed by many more important moments. One of the most memorable of these occurred in 1782 when the Dutch government and the "newborn" United States entered into diplomatic relations. The official envoy in Amsterdam and The Hague was no one less than John Adams, who would later become America's second president.
Jubilee years must be commemorated. And so too 2009, the 400th anniversary of Henry Hudson's arrival in the New World and thus the advent of New Amsterdam. Such a celebration reminds us that what now exists did not grow up overnight, but is the product of a long and rich history.

Mr. M.J. Cohen
Mayor of Amsterdam

A Story of Courage and Daring

Four hundred years ago the Englishman Henry Hudson set sail on his ship the *Halve Maen* (Half Moon) in a westward direction. He had been hired by the Dutch East India Company (Verenigde Oost-Indische Compagnie, or VOC) to find a northern passage to Asia. Nowadays traveling is a common occurrence and a round trip to New York is no longer anything special, and so it is almost impossible to imagine just how much courage, drive and adventurousness it took for those hardy individuals to undertake such a journey back then. To be sure, the existence of America and the traveling distance to the new land were known, but it was totally unclear just how large this continent was, who inhabited it and what its waterways were. And then there were the risks of the journey itself: storms, powerful and treacherous currents, cold and damp, illness, and the discontent of the crew. On the other hand, the unenviable uncertainty of those who stayed behind must have been considerable: they waited months, sometimes years, for news....

It is a remarkable fact that an Englishman chartered by a Dutch trading company traveled to the New World, where he laid the foundations for today's great metropolis, New York City. The English and the Dutch would encounter each other quite a few more times in the following years! Once the New Amsterdam settlement had taken shape and become economically and strategically significant, the colony became a plaything of the Dutch and the English. More than half a century after Hudson's arrival, New Netherland was ceded to the English and Dutch rule came to an end.

Since then countless books have been written on this period. However, the history of the Dutch colonization of present-day New York comes most distinctly alive in the archives. The old documents and maps provide surprisingly rich and vivid insight into the time in which Henry Hudson, Adriaen van der Donck, Peter Minuit and Peter Stuyvesant lived.

Those interested in the history of New York should start in the New York city and state archives, and will invariably wind up in Amsterdam and The Hague as well. Through careful study of the original sources preserved there and spirited storytelling, historians can flesh out the past of New Amsterdam and New Netherland for us in the twenty-first century.

In the colony sheer courage and drive proved decisive. At the same time, the very existence of the settlement on Manhattan was threatened by disputes, opportunism and favoritism. New York's short yet riveting Dutch period comes to life in this book. It could have happened yesterday...

This publication could never have been realized without the boundless energy of Martine Gosselink. I should like to express my gratitude to the author, the editing team and the publisher for their determination to tell this impressive story with utmost eloquence.

Martin Berendse

Director, Nationaal Archief (National Archives of the Netherlands)

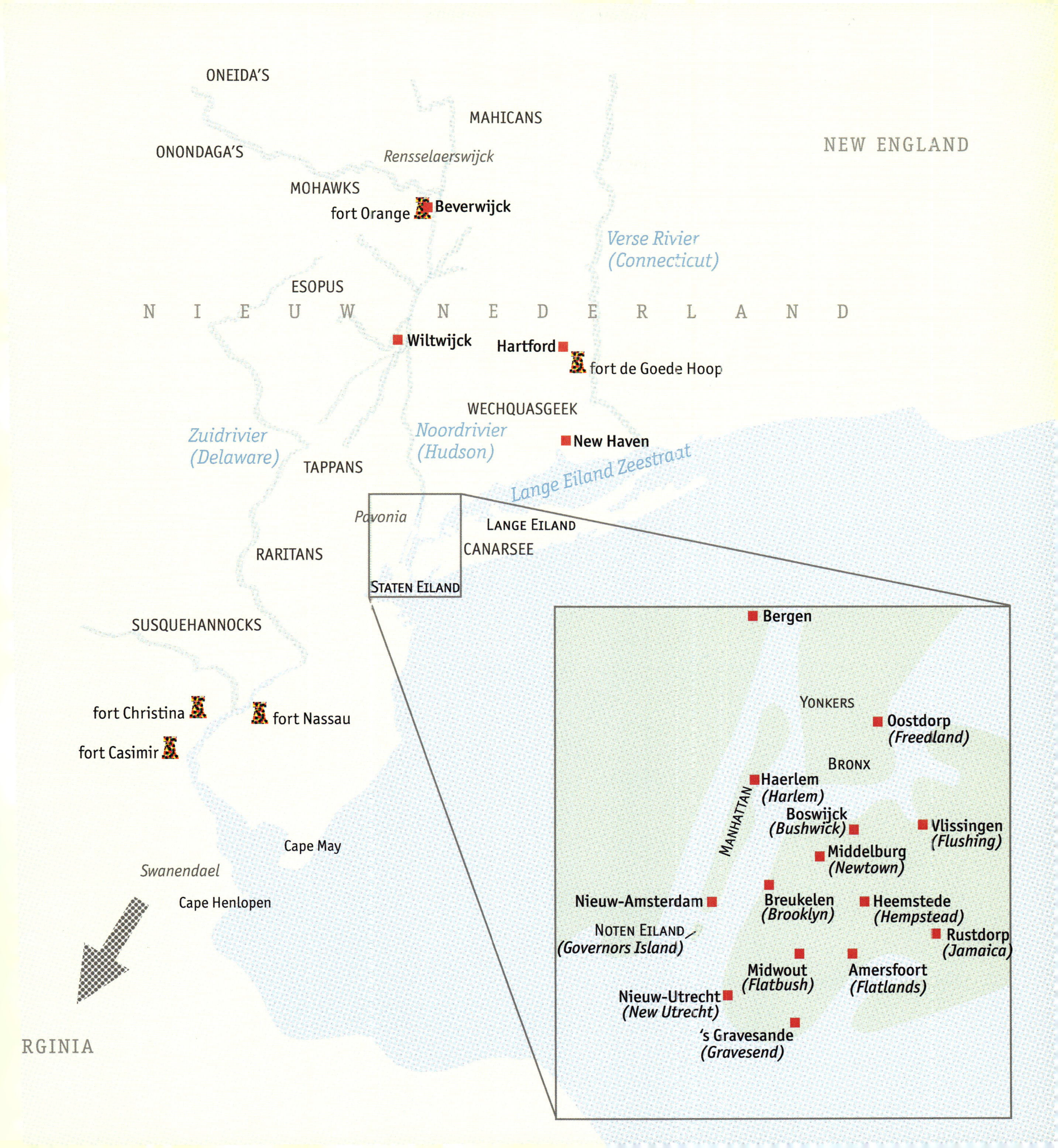

ONEIDA'S
MAHICANS
ONONDAGA'S
Rensselaerswijck
NEW ENGLAND
MOHAWKS
fort Orange
Beverwijck
Verse Rivier
(Connecticut)
ESOPUS
N I E U W N E D E R L A N D
Wiltwijck
Hartford
fort de Goede Hoop
WECHQUASGEEK
Zuidrivier
(Delaware)
Noordrivier
(Hudson)
New Haven
TAPPANS
Lange Eiland Zeestraat
Pavonia
LANGE EILAND
CANARSEE
RARITANS
STATEN EILAND
SUSQUEHANNOCKS
Bergen
YONKERS
Oostdorp
(Freedland)
BRONX
Haerlem
(Harlem)
MANHATTAN
Boswijck
(Bushwick)
Vlissingen
(Flushing)
Middelburg
(Newtown)
Nieuw-Amsterdam
Breukelen
(Brooklyn)
Heemstede
(Hempstead)
NOTEN EILAND
(Governors Island)
Rustdorp
(Jamaica)
Midwout
(Flatbush)
Amersfoort
(Flatlands)
Nieuw-Utrecht
(New Utrecht)
's Gravesande
(Gravesend)
fort Christina
fort Nassau
fort Casimir
Cape May
Swanendael
Cape Henlopen
RGINIA

Introduction

I will resist resorting to cliché and stating the number of words any given picture is worth. I'll start instead with the observation that the story of the Dutch founding of the colony of New Netherland – with its capital of New Amsterdam, which later became New York City – becomes that much richer in the mind when it is tricked out with images of the period.
New Netherland was one of many outposts of the Dutch empire in the 17th century. Those outposts spanned the globe, from Malaysia to Brazil to Japan to Indonesia. But none of the colonies of the Dutch Republic would have the impact of the one centered on the island of Manhattan.
History is big, messy, hard to define, yet it does have lines within it that can be traced. Because Henry Hudson charted the Middle Atlantic region of North America on behalf of the Dutch, and because the Dutch colony that grew up in the aftermath of that voyage borrowed features from the home country – most notably the Dutch invention of "tolerance" and the Dutch commitment to free trade – New York City became a very different place from, say, Boston, or Hartford, or anywhere else in the British colonial world. New York, thanks in large measure to its Dutch roots, grew into the archetypal modern society: a mixed society, in which people from all parts of the world jostled together, sought a better life, and did so alongside one another thanks to the underlying notion of tolerance. And because New York became what it did, the influence of that long-ago Dutch colony spread farther still, across the American continent, helping to shape nothing less than the American consciousness.
You can experience the roots of that originating society in books, that is to say in scholarly arguments. But you can also see it: in maps, charts, paintings, drawings, bricks.
To me as a historical researcher, perhaps nothing brings the past to life so vividly as the written word: letters in faded ink, crafted by a human being three or four centuries before I lived, detailing and preserving a moment, describing a precarious life eked out on the edge of wilderness.
The letters link to a pen, which links to poised fingers, which links to a particular human heart that once beat as surely as mine does, a particular human mind flush with intensions and dreams.
Henry Hudson, Emanuel van Meteren, Adriaen Block, Johannes de Laet: these are just names, until we find ways to attach the names to the work and deeds of the people.
History only matters when it matters – when it works its way into the minds of individuals in the here and now.
So we come at it from many angles: books, exhibits, websites, timelines. History is a room, a house, and for entry sometimes one key works better than another.
The great historian Johan Huizinga once wrote something that, for me as a miner of the past, has illuminated my own impulses. The wellspring of all historical inquiry, he said, is "our perpetual astonishment that the past was once a living reality."[1] These people lived as we live; they changed their world, and bequeathed to us our world. Here, in these pages, is ample evidence of their lives, their impact, how they did what they did, and gave us what we have.

Russell Shorto

[1] From: Johan Huizinga, *Nederland's beschaving in de zeventiende eeuw*, (Haarlem 1941).

THE WORLD NEW YORK WAS BORN INTO

I

Around 1600 the Dutch Republic of the United Provinces emerges as one of the leading players on the maritime stage. Its fiercest adversaries are Portugal, Spain and England. They all essentially have the same objective, namely to amass wealth through trade in exotic plants and products. Spain and Portugal are seasoned colonial powers, but England, the Republic as well as France are just embarking on this grand undertaking. Through trial and error, private trading companies establish the first overseas contacts. Diplomatic relations are entered into with princes and other rulers along the coasts of Asia and Africa. The first Dutch trading posts and forts appear around 1605. When there are no suitable authorities – in the eyes of the Dutch that is – with whom to close contracts, they simply seize the land and put it to their own use.

Competition between trading companies and with other countries is the order of the day.

At times this leads to minor problems: disputes about the asking prices of products or the best anchorage in the harbors. Larger issues are settled with arms. Under the States General, the Republic's governing body, the Dutch trading enterprises decide to join forces to curb competition among themselves and present a stronger front against the foreign companies.

The Dutch East India Company (Verenigde Oost-Indische Compagnie, or VOC) sees the light of day in 1602 and the company that will occupy itself with the western hemisphere, the Dutch West India Company (West-Indische Compagnie, or WIC), is founded in 1621.

By 1630 the Republic has become a force to be reckoned with. Various Portuguese and Spanish strongholds have been conquered by then. The Republic assumes the leading role, and dominates the scene in Europe for a long time. The Republic reaches its apex as a colonial power in the mid-seventeenth century. Countless trading posts around the world become subject to Dutch administrators and merchants.

One of these places is New Amsterdam, the capital of the colony of New Netherland, where beaver and otter pelts come from. The English, too, have their eye on this territory. The WIC has to be careful and protect New Netherland to its utmost, for England is persistently trying to knock the legs out from under the Republic.

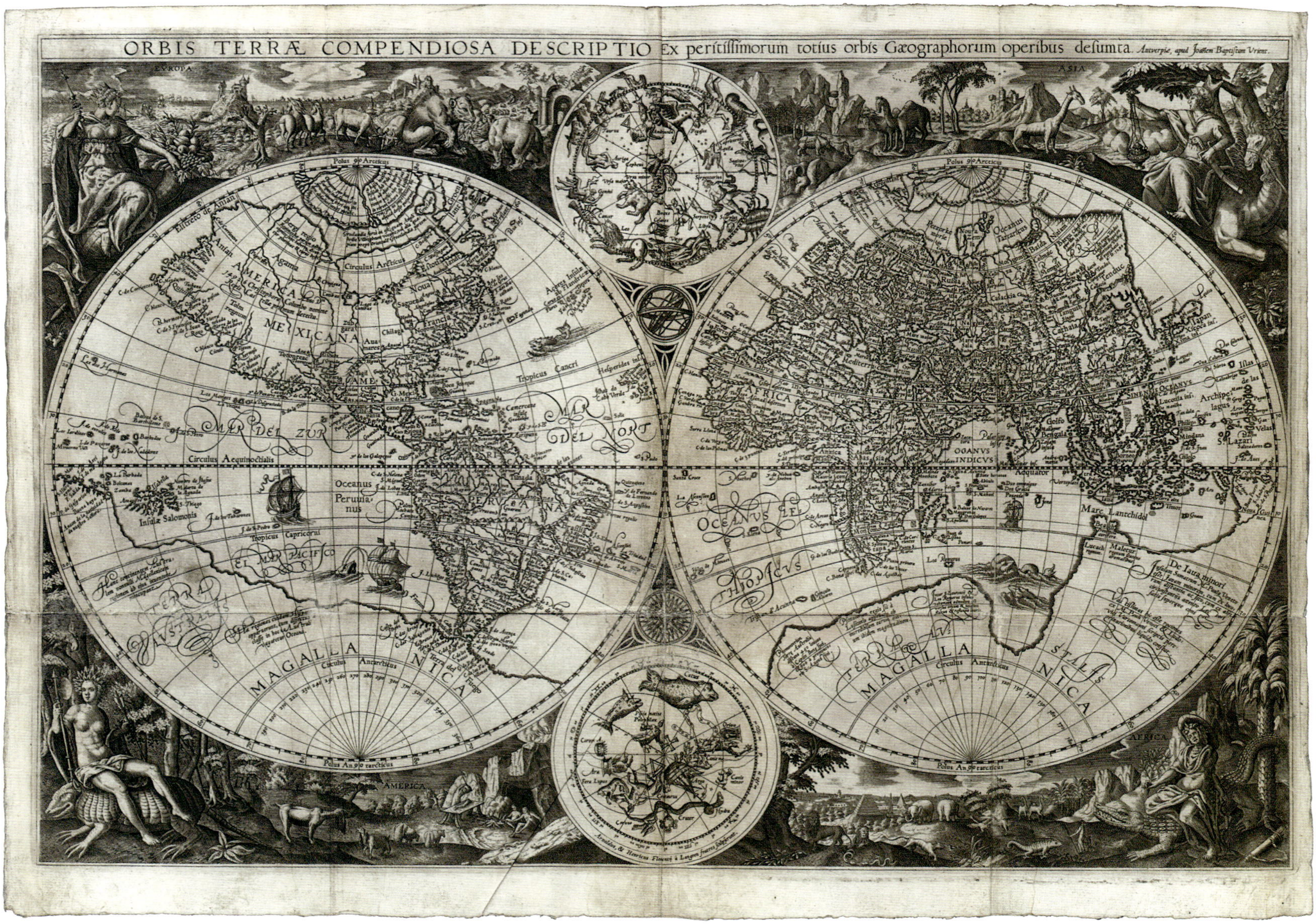

"Orbis Terrae Compendiosa Descriptio Ex peritissimorum totius orbis Gaeographorum operibus desumta"
Petrus Plancius and Jan Baptist Vrients, 1596
Nationaal Archief (National Archives of the Netherlands), The Hague
Library 393 G 12
59 x 42 cm

The World According to Plancius

At first sight this looks like a "classic" map of the world divided into an Eastern and a Western hemisphere. But upon closer inspection of this 1596 map by the Antwerp geographer Pieter Platvoet (Flat Foot), or Petrus Plancius as he was called in Latin, a world opens up, the world as it was known, or thought to be known around 1600.

In the corners are engravings of four allegories representing the continents. At the upper left is the "mother continent" Europe, with a cornucopia, ships, a high-rising castle, horses, cattle and bears. At the upper right is a figure with a censer, sword and turban, which stands for Asia. Here, too, we see a castle on a cliff, as well as a fantastical creature with a long neck, dromedaries and elephants. At the lower right is Africa wearing a sunhat and riding on a crocodile. Again we see elephants and dromedaries, this time accompanied by iguanas, snakes, lions and pyramid-shaped buildings.

America, the youngest offspring, closes the ranks. Her mount is a strange creature that most closely resembles an armadillo. She holds a spear in her right hand and an arrow in her left one. Her feather headdress, as well as the scene with three Native Americans at her right, makes it abundantly clear that the lady personifies America. To her right is a scene with three Indians.

Detail of "Orbis Terrae Compendiosa..."

This depiction of American Indians presents them in a stereotypical fashion. The man and woman seated before a cliff are roasting a human leg that has just been hacked off by a third Indian standing behind a table. His ax raised above his head, he is about to chop the limb on the table into smaller chunks. These kinds of gruesome details were frequently included in depictions of Indians. The travel accounts with illustrations of American natives eating, scalping or sacrificing people were very popular. Indigenous peoples of both South and North America were known to commit acts of cannibalism. In these cultures eating human flesh was a way of assimilating the spiritual power of a vanquished valiant foe. Eyewitnesses of cannibalism recounted their experiences in Europe, where artists then interpreted these stories in a highly personal fashion. Not only were the alleged cruelties of the Indians underscored, the ways in which the Spanish interacted with the indigenous peoples were also highly exaggerated. Books with these kinds of illustrations were in great demand and can be seen as anti-Spanish propaganda. However, often their contents simply did not tally with the facts. For one, the engravers had never even been to the countries they were depicting. In making their drawings they relied on but a single source, their own imagination.

In addition to the engravings there is another striking detail in the map itself. According to Plancius' calculation it was possible to sail to Asia via the North Cape, past Nova Zembla, a passage he discussed with Henry Hudson prior to the latter's trip in 1609. Following the passage from the Republic to Japan indicated in the map, you could indeed sail straight to Asia.

The International Players around 1600

At the end of the sixteenth century, the Dutch Republic's curiosity and interest in cities, coasts, ports and rivers in other parts of the world broadened. At the time, this tiny country along the North Sea was at war with mighty Spain, fighting for its independence. Spain was not only lord and master of the Netherlands, but also of various overseas colonies. More than a century earlier, in 1492, the Spanish had sent Columbus in search of new lands, and he discovered the coast of America. Peoples in various parts of the world were introduced – by force if necessary – to the Spanish language and Catholicism. The country had the capital and the manpower to found a sprawling colonial empire in America, a new Spain across the seas. By 1600 Spain was already trading in profitable regions in Asia and in Central and South America.

Portugal did not lag behind. In 1497, five years after the discovery of America, Vasco da Gama sailed around the Cape of Good Hope to Asia for the first time. While Spain concentrated on colonizing the country and founding a massive overseas imperium, Portugal focused on small-scale commercial activities in Asian, African and South American coastal towns, where the country regularly set up its own trading posts. Portuguese captains fetched cinnamon from Ceylon, sugar from Brazil and spices from the islands of the Malay Archipelago. Pepper and fabrics such as cotton and silk were bought in India. Both nations of the Iberian Peninsula long held sway over the seas unchallenged.

This situation gradually changed in the second half of the sixteenth century, when the English, the Dutch and to a lesser degree the French and the Danish emerged on the world stage. At first they explored hesitantly and cautiously, but once the newcomers discovered what the earth had to offer there was no stopping them. Trading companies popped up like mushrooms throughout Western Europe. Now the wealth of plants, minerals and products had to be divided among many more parties. The countries along the North Sea were not planning to send their merchants solely in search of these items. They were swept up in the surge to expand, the desire to own land elsewhere. Naturally this raised some serious problems: the Spanish and Portuguese were not about to give up their position!

There were many fertile regions well worth fighting for. To mention just a few: silver was mined in Peru and Mexico; sugar cane plantations were maintained on the island of São Tomé along the coast of Africa and in Brazil; pepper was cultivated throughout Asia; young men dove for pearls along the coasts of India and the Arabian peninsula;

Spanish Cuba

We see a warship in Havana Bay, the Cuban city founded by the Spanish as early as 1515. The flag flying from the ship's stern displays the characteristic Catholic cross of Burgundy, and the escutcheon bears the arms of the Spanish king. The Spanish had dominated Central America and the Caribbean for centuries. They discovered and took over Mexico, Cuba, Hispaniola and Puerto Rico, among other places. The silver ships from Mexico, Venezuela and Honduras gathered in Havana Bay for their joint crossing to Europe. However, around 1600, French, English and Dutch ships appeared in the region. They circled their prey – the richly laden silver fleets – like sharks. Sometimes their efforts paid off and they raked in the money. Spanish islands were also the targets of attacks by the vying Europeans. Nevertheless Spain ruled the Caribbean for a long time, partly thanks to the sturdy forts and defenses along the coast. As can be seen in the map, Havana, too, was heavily fortified: the city was flanked by forts on either side of the bay.

"De Stadt ende Bay van Havana geleegen op 't Eylandt Cuba" (The City and Bay of Havana on the Island of Cuba)
Johannes Vingboons, third quarter of the seventeenth century
Nationaal Archief (National Archives of the Netherlands), The Hague
4.VELH 619-57
Watercolor on paper, 42 x 54 cm

shiploads of cheap cotton cloth came from the Coromandel Coast in India; cloves grew on Ambon; nutmeg trees were cultivated on the southern islands of the Moluccas; Africa's coasts abounded in gold, ivory and the fuel of the day: slaves.

The Republic Follows Suit

What motivated the Dutch ships at the end of the sixteenth century to venture beyond their own borders? What occasioned them to go in search of the unknown in the hope of forging lucrative commercial ties with foreign merchants?

The Republic had been waging war with Spain since 1568. As a result, the supply of various goods from the Iberian Peninsula came to an end. The harbors of Portugal, which had entered into a union with Spain in 1580, became less accessible to the trading ships from the Republic coming there in search of products. Consequently the cost of the commodities – cotton, pepper, sugar, salt and spices, such as cardamom, cloves, nutmeg and mace – that Dutch households had become so used to in the course of the sixteenth century skyrocketed. While demand for luxury goods rose, the supply from Asia lagged behind. This applied mainly to pepper. The trading houses in the Republic's larger towns were excluded from the most important pepper contracts in Europe. Dutch merchants, therefore, had even more difficulty obtaining the coveted commodity.

Several merchants took the initiative to organize their own commercial trips to Asia in pursuit of pepper. This required capital. And there was plenty of it: the Netherlands had prospered in the preceding decades partly by trading in wood and grain with the Baltic region. Its geographic location on the coast guaranteed the Republic's position as an important entrepot. A great deal of money was earned and there were plenty of investors with the necessary means to finance expeditions to Asia.

With funds to invest and enough drive to ensure the favorable outcome of this grand project, the entrepreneurs were already more than halfway there. They were in a position to fit out and man fleets of ships. Yet one more ingredient was crucial for ensuring the success of a shipping industry to the East: science. Precisely this field had reached new heights in the last 20 years of the sixteenth century. Antwerp had fallen to the Spanish in 1585 and countless merchants, artists and scientists sought refuge in the cities of the Republic. The scientists included astronomers, printers and cartographers who catalyzed Dutch cartography and navigation. The globes, maps and navigation instruments vital to intercontinental shipping could now be produced. Cartographers helped the captains with calculations to plot clear routes to the desired regions. In the meantime, the trade passage to Asia had also become known in the Republic and now had to be charted as accurately as possible.

The Republic, which had managed to assume a prominent position within the sphere of European trade and shipping in the sixteenth century, now set out on commercial journeys to the East. With record speed, the country emerged as one of the greatest players in the Asian waters.

Dutch Trade in the East

The First Trading Expeditions

Dutch ships made their first scouting expeditions to Asia in 1595. Not all of the ships made it back, and less than half of all of those on board survived the journey. Nor did the goods they had brought with them immediately yield the envisaged profit, but a start had been made nonetheless. In stark contrast, the second trip in 1598 was most fortuitous. In the next few years Dutch entrepreneurs deployed 65 ships spread over 15 fleets. The ships collected pepper and other spices from Bantam on Java, Banda (Banda Aceh) on Sumatra and the Moluccan Islands.

However, the independently operating private entrepreneurs failed to see one important consequence of their success: their rivalry caused the prices of the coveted trading items to skyrocket. The States General was alarmed at the situation. The grand-pensionary of Holland, Johan van Oldenbarnevelt, and Stadholder Maurits thought that the merchants should work together. If they could join forces and operate as a single commercial organization, adverse competition could be eliminated. After many heated arguments, investors and other interested parties finally agreed that this was, indeed, a good plan. The uniting of the companies could take place.

Document granting the VOC its monopoly,
1602
Nationaal Archief (National Archives
of the Netherlands), The Hague
Archive VOC, 1.04.02, inv. no. 1
Ink on parchment, 33.5 x 28.5 cm

VOC Charter in 1602

On 20 March 1602 the States General granted the VOC the monopoly for trade and shipping to Asia. The world's first capital trading partnership was born. A few articles in the charter afford insight into the structure of the VOC.

The Participants

The six cities that had earlier had substantial private companies were now the six Chambers of the VOC: Amsterdam, Zeeland, (Middelburg), Rotterdam, Delft, Hoorn and Enkhuizen. The Chambers counted a total of 60 representatives: "The Chamber of Amsterdam at 20 people, that of Zeeland 12, that of Delft 7, that of Rotterdam 7, that of Enkuizen also 7, and that of Hoorn the same number".

Meetings

The directors of the Chambers chose representatives from their midst who participated alternately in Amsterdam and Middelburg in the meetings of the highest governing body. A total of 17 seats were established and this gathering became known as the *Heeren XVII*, or Lords Seventeen. Amsterdam was designated eight seats; four were allocated to Zeeland and one each to the remaining Chambers. To prevent Amsterdam from gaining the upper hand, the 17th representative came from Zeeland or one of the smaller Chambers in rotation.

Investments

The trading partnership needed starting capital to build ships, hire crews and buy goods that could be traded for Asian products. This capital was invested by private individuals who bought shares. In Amsterdam at least 1143 people invested a total of 3,679,915 guilders. This was more than half of the total starting capital of 6,424,588 guilders. Middelburg had 264 investors, each one on average investing larger amounts than their Amsterdam counterparts. The amounts varied from 50 to 85,000 guilders.[1]

Return

The shareholders' money was to be returned after ten years; this was laid down in the charter. In reality, however, this never happened. What was meant as a temporary investment kept on being reinvested. The money was crucial to defray the costs of the voyages, trade and military expeditions. Only in 1610 did the Company pay out the first dividends, that is in kind: mace, pepper and later also nutmeg. The investors thus did not get their money back, as agreed upon, but were compensated in another way. The VOC changed from an occasional undertaking into a permanent one. Later, dividends were in fact paid out. In the years up to 1622 investors received an average ten percent interest annually, far less than was initially thought. But thereafter the VOC's situation steadily improved: the dividends were paid out regularly, and as of 1630 almost annually.

The Founding of the Dutch East India Company (VOC)

And so it came to be. In 1602 the companies merged to become the Dutch East India Company. With the charter of the States General the VOC could conduct trade in the region to the east of the Cape of Good Hope. Capital was raised in the amount of 6,424,588 guilders. The venture was the first public corporation in the world, disposing over capital that was divided in shares. Previous companies had been set up as occasional undertakings. However, in the case of the VOC, when the fleet returned the fleet the capital was not given back to the investors, but reinvested instead.

The initiative rapidly proved successful. Even though not all of the ships by a long shot returned from Asia, many crewmembers died en route and the first dividends were only paid out in 1610, the Republic agreed that the country benefited from the existence of the VOC!

Now, the Dutch could sail, trade and fight to their hearts' content. The latter should not be underestimated. Had the VOC not received permission to attack trading posts, lodges, ships and forts belonging to other European powers, it would not have amounted to much.

Ambon Taken from the Portuguese

One of the VOC's first military operations was the conquest of the Moluccan island of Ambon from the Portuguese. Until 1606 Fort Victoria in the port of Ambon provided sufficient protection from the Dutch, who had already had their eye on the island for some time. Ambon and the surrounding islands yielded cloves, which in the meantime had become a favorite ingredient in European cuisine. The VOC wanted to establish a base on Ambon from where other expeditions in the area could be undertaken. When Admiral Steven van der Hagen occupied Fort Victoria in 1606, the 600 Portuguese stationed there offered little resistance. After the occupation, close to 46 Portuguese families decided to continue living on the island.

With this first victory in the bag, the confidence and bellicosity of the Dutch admirals grew. The Portuguese strongholds of Malacca (Melaka, now in Malaysia) and Mozambique were attacked in 1606, but the Portuguese did not yield. The Dutch admiral Cornelis Matelief besieged Malacca for a few months until Portuguese infantry drove him out.

"Afbeeldinghe van Amboina" (View of Ambon)
Johannes Vingboons, third quarter of the seventeenth century
Nationaal Archief (National Archives of the Netherlands), The Hague
4.VELH 619-16
Watercolor on paper, 44 x 67 cm

Ambon Taken from the Portuguese

Cloves from Ambon and the neighboring Moluccan islands were the bait the Dutch traders were so tempted by around 1600. After a successful attack on Ambon in 1606, the Portuguese on that island and surrounding area were effectively cut out. It was paramount that the clove trade on the islands be safeguarded from other European trading vessels; particularly the English ones that were beginning to arrive there as well. To prevent the islanders from trading with their rivals, the Dutch burned their clove trees. A few well-guarded plots were left, the harvest from which was reserved for the Dutch alone. In this way the VOC acquired the monopoly on this spice.

In Search of a Permanent Base

In the following years the commercial center of gravity remained in the Moluccas. Voyages from the motherland followed in increasingly rapid progression. When the VOC had been in existence for around 10 to 15 years plans were drawn up to gain a foothold elsewhere as well. This was imperative, for competition with the other countries was ruinous and tensions were mounting. Malacca and Bantam were obvious choices. Both were known for their international trading status; dealers from China, India and Persia had already been living and working there for centuries. In addition, from these ports the VOC would be in a position to control the rival shipping to the easternmost spice islands: from Bantam you had a view of Sunda Strait, and from the Strait of Malacca you could catch sight of Malacca. If the VOC were able to establish its headquarters in either one of these places, this would be a fantastic trump card vis-à-vis the competition. In 1615 a Spanish-Portuguese fleet was defeated off the coast of Malacca, but once again this had no lasting consequences. The Dutch would not succeed in conquering Malacca until 1641, thereby driving out the Portuguese after a presence of 128 years.

Initially Bantam, on the western tip of Java, seemed to be a good second choice; after all, the VOC already had a trading lodge there. But on closer reflection, this port was less suitable: the English sat firmly in the saddle and the local Javanese rulers were not particularly fond of the Dutch. Jan Pietersz. Coen, who was appointed governor-general by the VOC in 1618, devised another plan. He disbanded the Dutch lodge in Bantam and annexed the somewhat more southerly Jacatra (Jakarta). The village was razed to the ground and became the site of the Company's administrative center in Asia. It was named Batavia in 1619.

Consolidation in Asia

In the same year, the English East India Company and the VOC concluded the Treaty of London to protect the oversea spice trade. The Dutch government, the States General, exerted considerable pressure on the directors of the VOC to consent to this. The VOC, however, was not intent on splitting up the trading regions; everything was going so well. But the authorities of both countries had other ideas. By entering into a treaty the competitive hostilities between the two countries would cease and the trading companies could concentrate on commerce rather than warfare. Moreover, both parties could then jointly resist Spain and Portugal.

The non-attack treaty with England lasted less than four years. Nevertheless, a certain division remained in effect: the English focused more on India, the Dutch on the Malay Archipelago. In addition, the Company tried to expand its network in East Asia, the result of which were permanent settlements on the Japanese island of Dejima and on Taiwan.

BATAVIA OPT EYLANDT

Batavia: A Dutch City on Java

The Dutch tricolor dominates the multitude of flags flying here. The ships at either side of the composition draw the viewer's eye via the series of poles in the water, indicating the roadstead, to the coastal town looming on the horizon rising in the distance. The most striking building is the Castle of Batavia, where the governor-general and his councilors lived and ran their offices. The huge fort also housed the barracks for the workmen and soldiers and offices for the merchants and clerks. Next to it are warehouses, workshops and a church. The church spire rises up to the left of the pier.
With its little bridges spanning the canals and the warehouses along the water, the city made a very Dutch appearance. The goods shipped in by the Republic were distributed from the harbors and the depots. In turn, Batavia was the entrepot for all kinds of spices and products coming from the trading posts and settlements in Asia, from the southern Moluccas to Dejima in Japan.

View of Batavia
Anonymous, ca. 1665
Nationaal Archief (National Archives of the Netherlands), The Hague
4.VELH 619-28
Engraving, 37 x 48 cm

"Aldus Verthoont hem de Tafel Bay Geleegen aen Cabo de Bona Speranca" (Represented here is the Tafel [Table] Bay at the Cape of Good Hope)
Johannes Vingboons, third quarter of the seventeenth century
Nationaal Archief (National Archives of the Netherlands), The Hague
4.VELH 619-36
Watercolor on paper, 42 x 61 cm

The Cape of Good Hope: An Outpost

As of 1619, the year in which the governor-general and the Council of the Indies established themselves in the new headquarters in Batavia, a plan was conceived in the Dutch Republic and Asia to set up a staging post at the Cape of Good Hope. The bay had already served for some years as a way station for ships en route to more eastern destinations. Portuguese, Spanish, Dutch and English ships regularly rested at anchor there. It was a pleasant bay: the ships were safe, there was always fresh drinking water from the mountain streams, and the Tafelberg (Table Mountain) was an unmistakable beacon for the captains.

The expense of building a fort and maintaining a garrison would not be offset by the profits, for virtually no trade could be conducted. In the following decades Dutch ships continued to make use of the safe bay at the Cape. The crews could recuperate and trade tobacco and alcohol for fresh meat from the local Khoikhoi. Shifts in the European balance of power at mid-century, caused the VOC to reconsider. Rivalry with England was only growing. Establishment of a secure provisioning halt would give the Dutch a significant advantage. The time for this was ripe in 1652. Jan van Riebeeck, the first governor of the Cape, claimed the land at the foot of Table Mountain for the VOC.

Dutch Trade in the West

To South America for Sugar and Salt

For the Dutch the war with Spain was partly the reason for organizing regular crossings to Asia. The same applied to the shipping traffic to the Atlantic region. The war had led to a severe shortage of sugar in the Republic. As a rule merchants of the Republic procured their sugar from dealers in Antwerp, who processed it in their refineries. This came to an end in 1585, when the Spanish captured Antwerp. The Dutch were now compelled to go in search of this commodity themselves. A number of Antwerp merchants who had emigrated to Amsterdam after the fall of their city simply took up where they had left off. They started new refineries and sent ships to sugar producing regions, such as Brazil and the African island of São Tomé. Dutch entrepreneurs followed their example and so began the first phase of trade in the Atlantic Ocean.

A shortage of salt had also arisen. A continuous supply of salt was needed for the fisheries and the herring catch in the Republic. Portugal had long been the supplier of salt to the more northern European countries. But since it had been taken over by Spain in 1580, the Portuguese harbors were no longer accessible. In 1585 the Spanish king Philip II had confiscated all the Dutch vessels in the Spanish and Portuguese harbors. In addition, in 1598 he placed an embargo on exporting products to the Republic. Dutch ships could no longer drop anchor in Portuguese harbors, and Portuguese products could no longer be shipped to the Republic. Nevertheless, trade between Portugal and the Republic did not grind to a complete halt. After all, dealers from the south depended on their confreres in the north primarily for the provision of grain. However, the embargo caused such a shortage that in the same year the Dutch took the initiative to seek out the salt regions on the other side of the ocean. Even before 1600, every year close to 100 Dutch ships set sail for the saltpans along the coast of Venezuela.[2]

The Spanish were disinclined to tolerate these newcomers in their territory. Upon the appearance of the Dutch ships, short-lived yet violent hostilities ensued. A rather more harsh approach in 1605 had adverse consequences for the Dutch. The ruthless Spanish policy led the Dutch captains to lose interest in ever trying their luck again on the Venezuelan coast. But there were frictions elsewhere as well. Along the coasts of Africa and Brazil, Dutch ships ran into stiff competition and aggression from the Portuguese.

To Africa and North America for Ivory and Fur

Shortages of sugar and salt were not the only stimuli for trade in the Atlantic Ocean. The products from Africa's west coast also gave the entrepreneurs from the Republic cause to equip ships. The ships sailed along the entire west coast of Africa, from Senegal to Angola. Notwithstanding regular clashes with the Portuguese, who had erected a dozen forts along the coast, the Dutch were fairly successful in making the return journey with holds laden with "grein" (a kind of pepper), ivory and gold.

In addition to the west coast of Africa and the north coast of South America, there was yet another area in the West that the Dutch regularly sailed to. This region was known for the North River, as the Dutch called the waterway which had been discovered more or less accidentally in 1609 by the Englishman Henry Hudson on a trip he made at the behest of the Republic. New Netherland was the name given to the region by private dealers in 1614, five years after Hudson's discovery. They bought otter and beaver pelts from the local population on Manhattan and primarily in the surrounding area. Semi-permanent trading posts were built on the banks of the North River, which only much later would become known worldwide as the Hudson River. In less than 20 years Dutch dealers, captains and investors managed to establish a network in the Atlantic Ocean with which all of the bordering continents were allied.

Setting Course for a Single Company

The VOC was a smart move for trade in the East, but how was the future development in the West viewed? Why, after the proven success of the VOC in the early years of the seventeenth century, had no comparable enterprise been set up for the Atlantic Ocean? The answer to this question is not so simple.

First, in the Republic, praise for the VOC was accompanied by the necessary criticism, chiefly of the Company's monopoly position. Adversaries believed that the Company would be unable to cover the entire area for which the charter had been granted. As a result, it was argued, fine opportunities remained unused, ones that – had there been no monopoly – could have been taken by other Dutch enterprises. Consequently, foreign dealers made off with the goods which the VOC left untouched.

Willem Usselincx Makes Plans

In his youth, the Calvinist economist Willem Usselincx had spent some time in Spain and Portugal as well as the Azores. He witnessed the potential afforded by trade with the East and the West. He was also highly intrigued by the idea that the Protestant Republic could dispose over real colonies. His commercial plans, thus, were firmly coupled to religious ideals. Nothing would have made him happier than to see the rise of overseas colonies whose inhabitants would practice and spread Calvinism.
When the WIC was finally founded in 1621, Usselincx realized that the Company would not develop along the lines of his ideology and that it was solely interested in establishing trading posts. He decided to back other endeavors instead and invested in the Beemster, a region in the Dutch province of Noord-Holland that had just been drained. However, Usselincx does not seem to have been suited to be a landowner and he went bankrupt. In Sweden he was offered the chance to found a South Sea Company entirely in keeping with the ideals he had fostered for the WIC. Unfortunately for Usselincx luck was against him and he failed to find enough investors. The initial champion of the WIC died around 1647, destitute and virtually forgotten.[3]

Portrait of Willem Usselincx
Anonymous, dated 1637
Rijksmuseum, Amsterdam
SK-A-1675
Oil paint on panel, 17.5 x 14 cm

These negative views notwithstanding, ideas for a consortium for the West were circulating. Voices, mostly on the strict Protestant side, were raised calling for joint action against the Spanish supremacy. One of them was that of the arch-Calvinist Willem Usselincx, an Antwerper who after the fall of the city in 1585 had chosen the Republic as his port of refuge. Arguing for the foundation of such a company, he suggested that the possession of overseas colonies was crucial for acquiring primary goods and other products. The motherland would become strong and independent as a result. The Republic could expand its own market by supplying the colonized territories. And, a not to be overlooked added advantage, according to Usselincx, was that the new colonies afforded a wonderful opportunity for disseminating the "true" faith, namely Calvinism. All in all the Republic would stand more firmly in its shoes and offer greater resistance to "perverse" Catholic Spain and other European rivals.

Usselincx won many supporters, though not everyone was quite as eager to found colonies based on a Protestant ideal. Usselincx had already divulged his plans for a West India Company around 1600. He presented them to the States General, deliberated on them with the town councils of leading cities and discussed them with various influential individuals. The Dutch provinces of Holland and Zeeland were positive, as indeed were some merchants with substantial capital. The States General reacted more cautiously; it first wanted to know more about the state of affairs in the Atlantic Ocean. Usselincx's plans were put on hold.

They were dusted off only in 1606. Interest in a company oriented on the West increased in that year. In fact, the States of Holland drew up a draft charter. Unfortunately for Usselincx no articles were included addressing the idea of large-scale agricultural colonies. Attention was aimed solely at trade, not on founding settlement colonies or expanding Dutch territory overseas. The draft was a pendant for the charter of the VOC, but then for the West. Everything seemed to be settled, the foundation of the WIC was virtually in the bag.

The Republic, however, had one other concern: peace with Spain. Fed up with the war a large group of Dutchmen were clamoring for a truce. Under Grand Pensionary Johan van Oldenbarnevelt, representatives of the two nations negotiated a cease-fire in secret locations. During the talks, Van Oldenbarnevelt tried to safeguard the Republic's trading interests in the East, but in concession to Spain he relinquished the plans for the WIC. The founding of the WIC was subject to delay yet again.

In 1606, Spain and the Republic arrived at a truce that was to last 12 years. In many ways this Twelve Years' Truce was a victory for the

Dutch. Foremost, Spain acknowledged that the Republic of the United Netherlands was a more or less independent nation. The fact that Spain, the most powerful country in Europe, recognized the Republic as such was fairly significant for a country which – without the presence and statesmanship of a sovereign ruler – had proclaimed itself an independent nation only a few decades earlier.

Peace had favorable consequences for commerce as well, for the Dutch dealers were now in a position to begin shipping on a grand scale in and outside of Europe. Spanish and Portuguese harbors were opened and the Mediterranean was once again in calm water. The sugar ships sailing to Brazil now also returned with profitable cargos. Because the struggle with Spain had subsided, a lot of personnel became available that had formerly sailed with the navy. The increasing availability of work forced wages to go down. And, because the seaways were now safer the high costs of insurance decreased whereby the dispatching of ships became much less expensive.[4]

Despite the truce, hostilities between Spanish and Dutch ships did not cease entirely. Primarily in the East, the armed trade ships from the Republic and the Spanish galleons made life difficult for one another. In the Atlantic Ocean the struggle between the two nations played out more quietly.

The truce with Spain certainly had advantages, but these were cancelled out only a few years later with the appearance of other players: the English, French, Danish and Swedes had arrived on the scene. Not only in the East, but also on the coasts of West Africa, Brazil and the Caribbean the struggle for power among the European nations sharpened. This adversity spelled trouble for the Dutch merchants overseas and their investors. The curtailment of trade in the East caused the VOC shares to plummet on the Amsterdam stock market.

In the meantime the champion of a company for a grandly conceived organization in the West was still actively trying to realize his dream. Between 1614 and 1617 Usselincx repeatedly petitioned the States General to set up the WIC. Grand Pensionary Van Oldenbarnevelt, the architect of the cease-fire with Spain, thwarted his plans once more. But Van Oldenbarnevelt had to watch his own step as well. A growing national conflict had arisen whereby opposition to the grand pensionary gradually grew. In 1618 Van Oldenbarnevelt was even accused of favoring Holland over the other provinces of the Republic. Van Oldenbarnevelt could no longer plead his case and in 1619 he was charged with high treason and beheaded.

The most fearsome adversary of the WIC was no more and the year 1621, the end of the truce, was nearing. Was the time finally ripe for the

Murder of Van Oldenbarnevelt brings the WIC closer

The execution of Johan van Oldenbarnevelt
Claes Jansz. Visscher, 1619
Atlas van Stolk, Rotterdam
Inv. no. 15479
Engraving, 19.3 x 36.7 cm

The young Republic was governed by Johan van Oldenbarnevelt as its political leader and by Prince Maurits as its commander-in-chief. This combination worked well for a long time. However, against Maurits' wishes, in 1609 Van Oldenbarnevelt concluded a truce with Spain. The grand-pensionary was convinced that temporary peace was in the nation's best interest. Maurits opposed the truce, but got the short end of the stick. In the eyes of the grand-pensionary the war was too expensive and obstructed trade. This difference of opinion degenerated into a protracted dispute when a religious issue became involved. In 1617 Van Oldenbarnevelt ratified a resolution passed by the States of Holland allowing the cities in Holland to use mercenary troops to quell riots. In so doing Van Oldenbarnevelt was undermining Maurits' authority as the supreme commander of the national army. Maurits refused to be mollified and staged a coup d'état. On 29 August 1618 he had Van Oldenbarnevelt arrested on charges of high treason. In 1619 Maurits manipulated the political situation such that a court was set up with 24 judges who condemned the 71-year-old to death. The execution took place in the Binnenhof in The Hague on 13 May 1619.
With Van Oldenbarnevelt's decapitation, Usselincx's fiercest opponent was eliminated. The foundation of the WIC, which Van Oldenbarnevelt had opposed for so long, was imminent.

new company? Rumors of skirmishes with Spanish in Asia abounded. The States General became convinced that a lasting peace with Spain was not feasible. Where possible the English, too, tried to obstruct Dutch trade. Nevertheless, the States General decided to deal softly with England; after all, it could be an indispensable ally against Spain.

The Founding of the West India Company

The Twelve Years' Truce ended in 1621. This meant that the war with Spain could be resumed and that the West India Company would finally see the light of day. On 3 June 1621 the States General issued a charter for trade in the Atlantic Ocean. In so doing, as co-author of the important document and responsible organ, the States General obtained a say in the WIC's administrative framework. On page 54 of this book is discussed how the Company's administration was structured and how this influenced the realization of the colony of New Netherland in general and New Amsterdam in particular.

It would take a while before the enterprise would yield actual results, but the first step had been taken. While Usselincx was delighted with the new Company, it was not the business enterprise he had imagined it would be. Nothing was left of his plans for colonization in the foundation statutes. "His" WIC would have been the founder of extensive and productive agricultural colonies. The harvest would have been shipped to the Republic and in turn the new territories would have been a great market for the motherland. In his eyes, now the Company was only a strategic answer to the presence of European nations competing for the lucrative trade in the West.

The WIC's primary mandate was to protect and promote the existing Dutch trade in the Atlantic Ocean. In a certain sense though Usselincx's ideas would become reality: in the course of the seventeenth century the Company founded a colony on the coast of North America. In Brazil, the Caribbean, Suriname and West Africa it would be limited to the foundation of several trading regions. In the end, the West India Company's charter territory would encompass all of the Atlantic Ocean.

Attacks on Spanish and Portuguese Territory

The WIC lacked sufficient investors and it took two years to raise the necessary capital. In part this had to do with the complex relationship between the shareholders and the governors of the VOC, which was a kind of "big brother" role model for the WIC. The hesitation of the prospective investors was also related to the bellicose language of proponents of military operations in the charter territory.

Salt traders from the towns of Hoorn and Enkhuizen constituted yet another obstacle. They opposed WIC's intention to include the salt trade in the charter, which had been their source of income for all these years. Initially the WIC had agreed to leave the salt trade to Hoorn and Enkhuizen, but after its foundation the directors nevertheless wanted to incorporate it into the monopoly. Investors were then expected to quickly jump on board – after all, great profits were to be made in the salt trade. These expectations would fall short.[5]

It took two years after the company was established before enough financiers had been won over and enough money collected to be able to speak of a substantial work capital. This was necessary in order to actually commence the tasks for which the Company had been founded in the first place: freeing the Atlantic region for trade, if necessary with acts of war. In addition to being a commercial enterprise, the Company was also an instrument of the state with political goals: running interference with Spain and other dealers where possible.

The WIC had three mandates: trade, territorial expansion and privateering. The first is obvious and was the most important. After all, the charter gives "shipping, dealing, the commerce in the quarters of West Indies and Africa" as the main duties. But battle also had to be done with the other powers in the West. Attacks on Spanish and Portuguese strongholds on the Atlantic coast could – finally – be waged.

Privateering was a lucrative undertaking and a proven means of eliminating the ships of hostile nations, that is Spain and Portugal. Plundering, destroying or taking over their ships fundamentally weakened them. Moreover, privateering afforded an important source of income for the WIC. Holds laden with silver and sugar could be seized from enemies. The years 1625-30 marked the Dutch heydays of privateering. Many profited from the take. Part of it landed directly in the coffers of the WIC, but the lion's share went to the stockholders.

With a well-lined purse military expeditions could be fitted out. In 1624 the first squadrons were sent to Bahia in Portuguese Brazil and Luanda in Angola, the largest Portuguese slave depot. Both attacks failed. At a massive offensive on the Portuguese city of Elmina on the Gold Coast, the present Gulf of Guinea, the Dutch suffered a painful defeat. Other tactics, though, proved effective: by striking up friendships with African rulers on the Gold Coast, the admirals of the WIC were able to bring about a pact against Portugal.

The 1630s were good years for the WIC. In 1630 the Company annexed a vast area in Brazil, the rich Portuguese sugar province Pernambuco (Recife). Various forts along the coast of Africa were conquered; the attempt to take Elmina in 1637 proved successful. Now that

Attacks on Puerto Rico

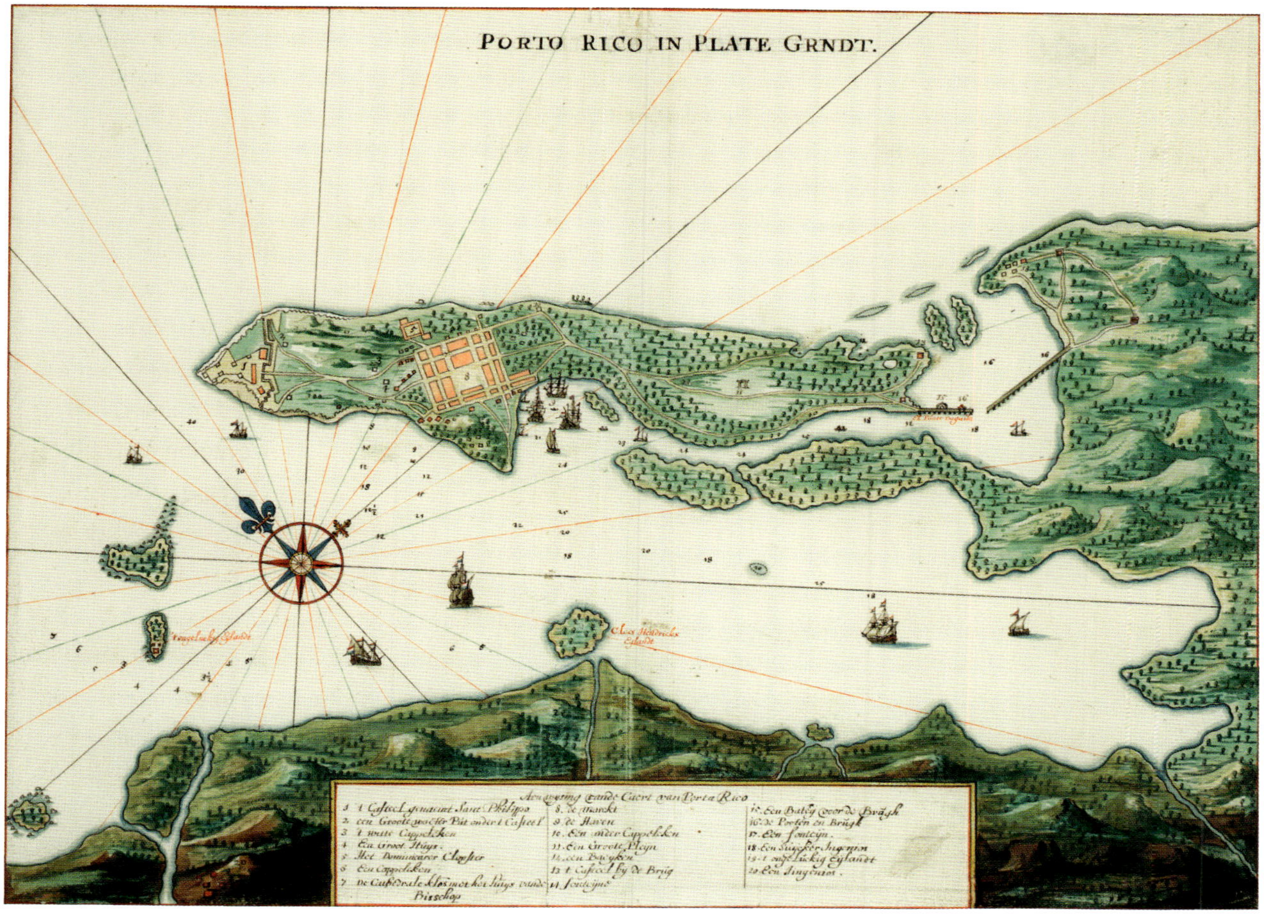

"Porto Rico in plate grndt" (Map of Puerto Rico)
Johannes Vingboons, third quarter of the seventeenth century
Nationaal Archief (National Archives of the Netherlands), The Hague
4.VELH 619-87
Watercolor on paper, 42 x 56 cm

The city of San Juan on the Spanish island of Puerto Rico was home to the strongest fort in the Caribbean, El Morro. In the legend to the map the fort is indicated as "called Saint Philip Castle" ('t Casteel San Philippo genaemt). The fort had earlier withstood French and English attacks. However, there was a reversal of fortune in 1625. The Spanish were challenged by Boudewijn Hendriksz., who appeared before San Juan in September of that year with a fleet of eight ships. To force the Spanish to surrender he threatened to set fire to the city. The Spanish refused and the city was reduced to ashes in no time. Hendriksz., though, made no further progress, for the Spanish immediately called in their reinforcements and retained control of the island.

Even though the Dutch failed to occupy Puerto Rico, the attack was nevertheless a modified success – the city and its indomitable fort had been razed to the ground. Any damage that could be inflicted on Spanish possessions counted as a victory, at least in the eyes of the Republic.

The Capture of Portuguese Pernambuco

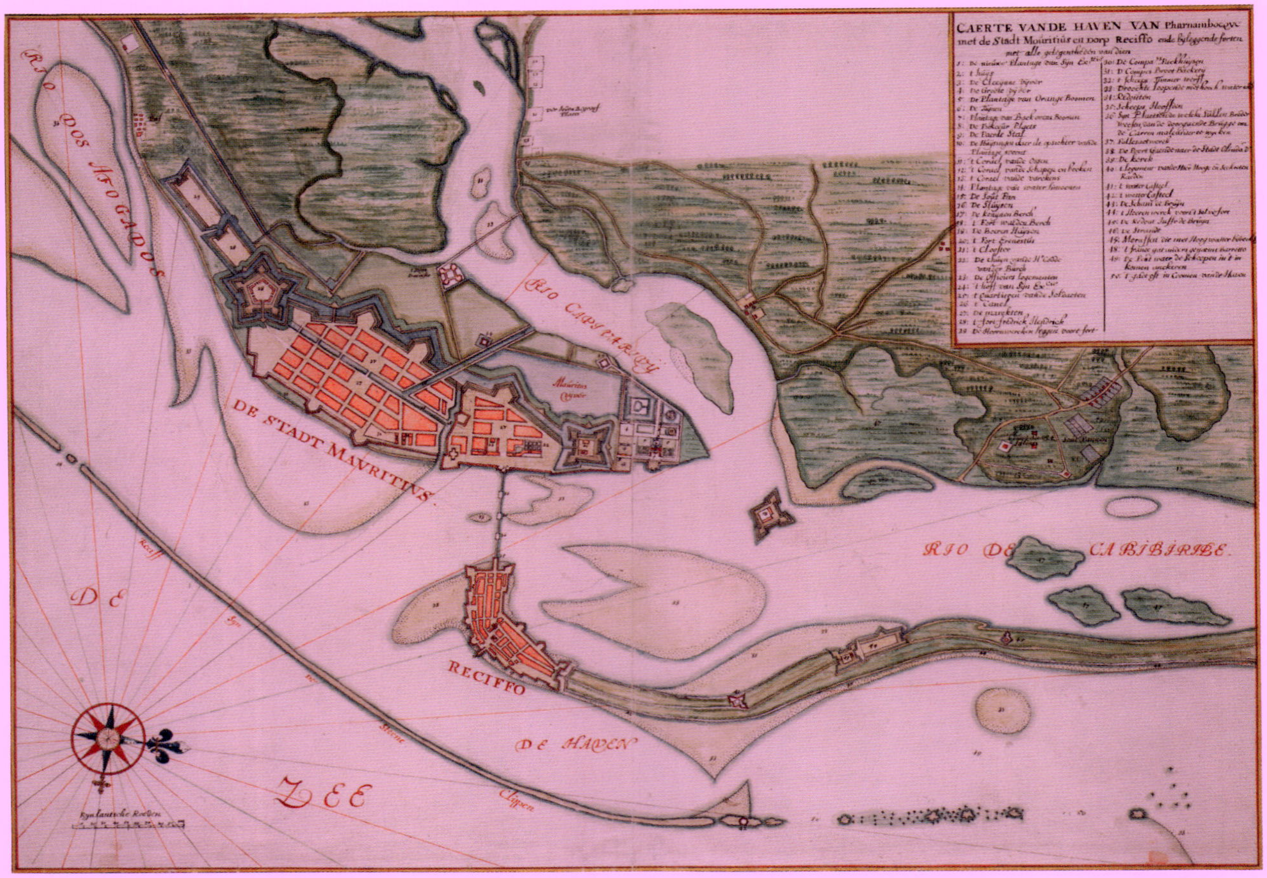

"Caerte van de haven van Pharnambocque, met de Stadt Mouritius en dorp Reciffo ende bijleggende forten met alle gelegentheden van dien" (Map of the harbor of Pernambuco, with Mauritsstad and the village of Recife with the nearby forts and all their facilities)
Johannes Vingboons, third quarter of the seventeenth century
Nationaal Archief (National Archives of the Netherlands), The Hague
4.VELH 619-74
Watercolor on paper, 45 x 64 cm

Pernambuco was Portugal's overseas treasure chest. The Brazilian province had at least 137 sugar mills producing 35,000 to 40,000 crates of sugar annually. Pernambuco gradually became an obsession for the WIC. When the WIC was founded in 1621 plans were already being hatched to occupy the region, but only in 1630, when Piet Hein had seized the Silver Fleet, was there sufficient capital to fit out a war fleet large enough to annex the region.

Olinda, north of Recife and just off this map, was stormed first in 1630. And then it was Recife's turn, where a town arose fairly soon after the Dutch conquered it. Recife became overpopulated just a few years later and a second town had to be founded, which was called Mauritsstad after Johan Maurits van Nassau-Siegen who was governor-general of Dutch Brazil, or New Holland, from 1637 to 1644. The map shows Recife and Mauritsstad connected by a bridge.

Pernambuco, with its hundreds of sugar plantations, was in Dutch hands, supplying this region with slaves was suddenly crucial. With the appropriation of coastal Elmina, this problem was solved. The former Portuguese stronghold was an important assembly point for slaves who were brought to the coast from the interior.

Mid-Seventeenth Century: A Mid-Term Review

Around the middle of the seventeenth century, the Republic could look back on a long period of fruitful and less fruitful conquests in countries nowadays known as India, Sri Lanka, Taiwan, Indonesia, South Africa, Ghana, Senegal, Angola and Brazil. Countless regions that had earlier belonged to other seafaring powers had in the meantime come under the control of the VOC or the WIC. Moreover, several regions where Europeans had never before established themselves had also been drafted into the domain of the Companies, for instance New Netherland in North America. Some were in Dutch possession for only a brief period before having to be relinquished with.

Naturally, there were also countries and regions where the Republic traded without conquests, such as Japan, Thailand, India and West Africa. There, trading offices or estates were rented from local authorities. Commanders, merchants and other functionaries protected the Companies' interests. Of course, these administrators and high-placed merchants were not without their own rivalries fueled by jealousy and corruption. But the majority of them were none the poorer for it: on the contrary. Numerous servants of the VOC and WIC came home wealthier than when they had left. Nor was the motherland lagging behind. In fact, the Republic was prospering.

The WIC was especially successful in one respect: the necessary damage had been inflicted on Spain. In the period 1623-1635 alone, 600 Spanish ships were captured or scuppered. Spain ran up a 70 million-guilder loss through the Republic's actions alone. In the subsequent years the war with Spain would abate.[6]

As an enterprise, the WIC's financial situation was less rosy. The costly overseas wars had almost brought the Company to the brink of bankruptcy more than once. The charter would run out in 1645. Would the States General renew it? Propagandists of free trade opposed this. Why should the monopoly be exclusive to an institution unable to properly organize the seaborne trade and expansion? Voices were also raised calling for the fusion of the VOC and the WIC. Primarily the directors of the WIC were interested in joining forces, and they tried to convince their VOC confreres. Hadn't the VOC profited from the sharp blows the WIC had dealt Spain? The enemy could be weakened even more if the two Companies were to join forces in the battle.

The directors of the VOC had little faith in the plan: the WIC's coffers were almost empty and the losses in the West too great. In addition they were not interested in becoming saddled with the high debts of their sister enterprise. Fusion was excluded as far as they were concerned. The States of Holland's response to this was to ask the VOC to meet the WIC with financial support. The VOC wanted none of this. Only when its charter was threatened with non-renewal – it too was running out – did the VOC see no other choice than to pay the WIC an amount of one and half million guilders.

English Virginia

The title of this map "Map of the Powhatan River in New Netherland" is misleading. It may have been the product of wishful thinking on the part of the mapmaker, or the person who commissioned it. Whatever the case may be the inscription is incorrect. The Powhatan – now the James River – lay in the English part of Virginia.

At the time, what was called Virginia covered a much larger territory, which included the New Netherland colony. However, the region we see in this map had nothing to do with New Netherland. In 1607 English colonists had sailed up the Powhatan River, the name of which was derived from the Native Americans living there. They dropped anchor near a peninsula and settled in what they called Jamestown, after the English king James I. They dubbed the river the James River. Jamestown would be the first permanent English settlement in America. On the map the location is indicated as "Bloc house Jamestown."

The map was probably copied from a drawing by David Pietersz. de Vries, who had sailed the James River in 1633 and charted Virginia and its plantations. On 11 March 1633 he arrived at what he called "Jems-Toin." He evidently forged good ties with the English. Upon his departure on 18 March, the English governor gave him a half dozen "Goats to take on board, also honoring our governor with a ram, as he had understood that there were no goats at Fort Amsterdam in New Netherland".[7]

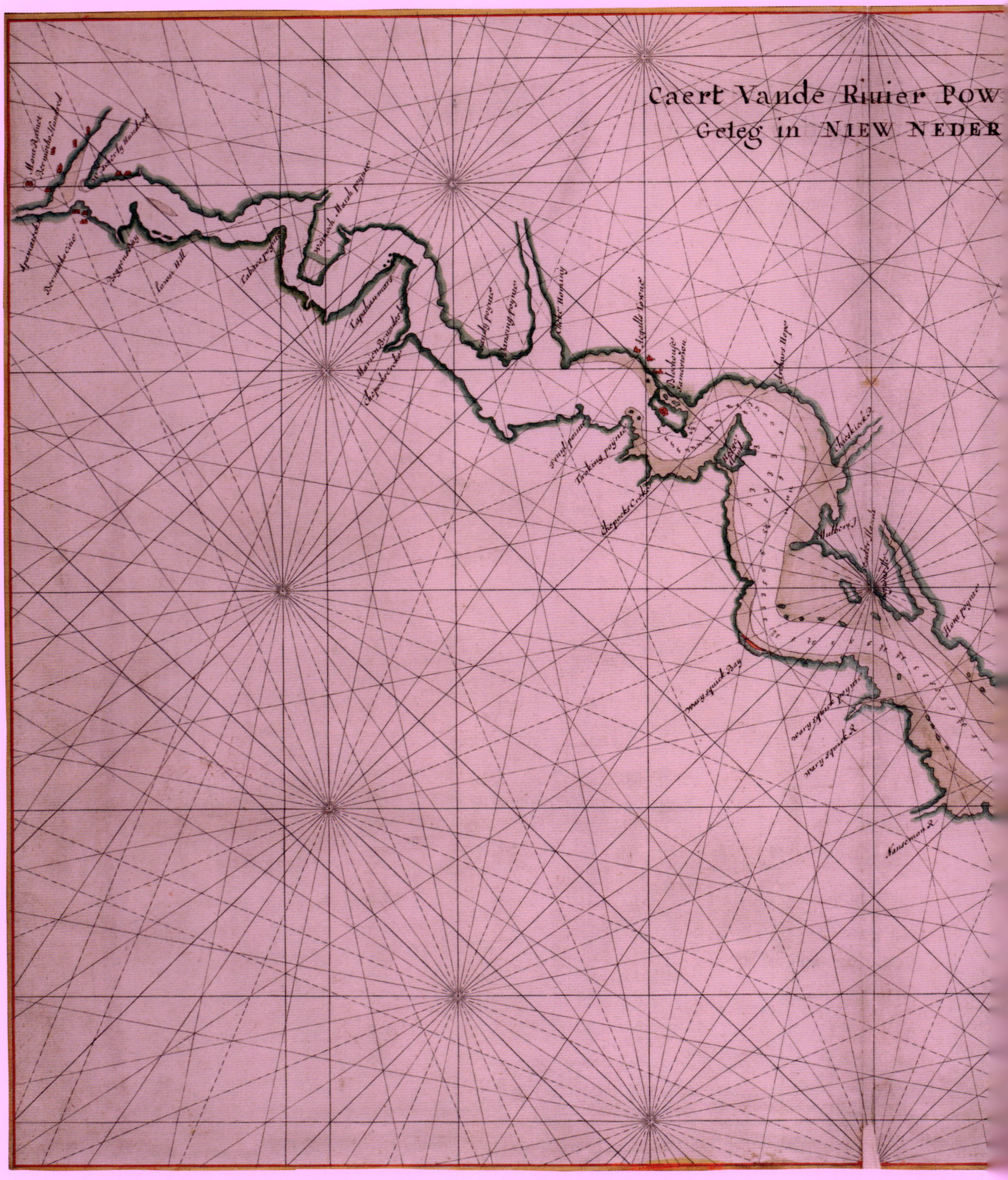

"Caert van de Rivier Powhatan geleg in Nieuw Nederlandt"
(Map of the Powhatan River in New Netherland)
Johannes Vingboons, third quarter
of the seventeenth century
Nationaal Archief (National Archives of the Netherlands),
The Hague
4.VELH 619-89
Watercolor on paper, 48 x 69 cm

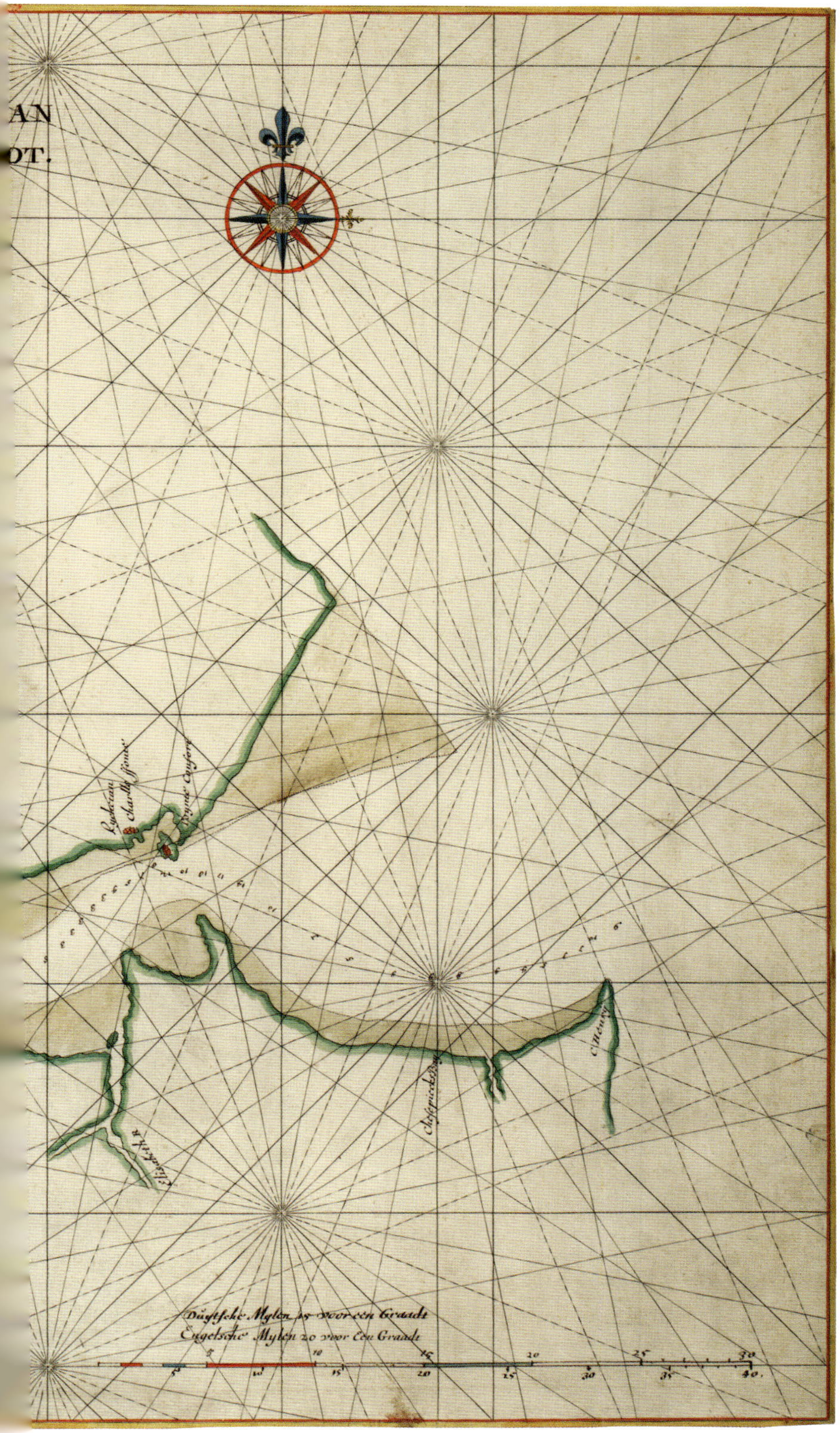

The Waning Power of the WIC

In 1647 the States General renewed the charters of both the WIC and the VOC. This time it would be valid for 25 years. The financial boost of the VOC was to no avail and the WIC went downhill. The Company had to relinquish Luanda in Angola in 1648, and then Brazil in 1654. The money-guzzling defense of Brazil cooked the WIC's goose. After these losses the Company was unable to once again make the profits needed to pay off the ruinous debts.

The WIC had as much as run its course by the end of the 1660s. After a few convulsions it ceased to be in 1674; the Company was bankrupt. Its mandate was carried on with the foundation of the second WIC, which came into existence in the same year as the first WIC was dissolved.

From then on, the triumvirate of the English, Spanish and Portuguese called the shots in the West, with the exception of Suriname and Curaçao. With respect to New Netherland it was the English who delivered the coup de grace to the Dutch. Exerting pressure from surrounding regions and even England itself, they brought the Dutch to a stalemate. The curtain would fall on the WIC's only colony settlement, New Netherland, in 1664.

[1] Gaastra, *De geschiedenis van de VOC*, pp. 21-34.
[2] Den Heijer, *De geschiedenis van de WIC*, p. 17.
[3] Israel, *The Dutch Republic*, p. 326.
[4] Israel, *Dutch Primacy*, pp. 80-120; Rink, *Holland on the Hudson*, p. 55.
[5] Rink, *Holland on the Hudson*, pp. 64-65.
[6] Den Heijer, *De geschiedenis van de WIC*, p. 98.
[7] De Vries, *Korte historiael ende journaels aenteyckeninge*, p. 170.

THE ISLAND AND ITS HINTERLAND

II

CHAPTER 1

Manhattan: "Discovered" and Navigated 1609-1625

The history of "Dutch Manhattan" begins with Henry Hudson's voyage under the authority of the Dutch East India Company (VOC). The Company commissions the English explorer to find a sea route leading to Asia via a northeast passage. The reason for this is that on the standard southerly route, via the Cape of Good Hope, Dutch ships are too often confronted with violence. The Republic has been at war with Spain since 1568, and this struggle is also being fought out in the Atlantic Ocean. To avoid unnecessary confrontations and to reach Asia in a shorter time, the VOC is intent on discovering an alternative sea route, via the North Cape.
Hudson is appointed captain of the ship the *Halve Maen* (Half Moon) and sets out northwards in April of 1609. Having reached the Cape he deviates from the agreed-on route and sails west towards North America. He explores the coast until dropping anchor in a bay on 2 September 1609. There he spies the entrance to the river that will later bear his name, and sails upstream. The inhabitants who come to greet him offer him a variety of furs. Hudson thus has discovered a territory replete with great commercial opportunities for his masters.
Although Hudson is unable to pass on the crucial information about the route to the river of furs to his masters, his reports of the territory's commercial potential do reach the Republic. The Dutch estimate that the fur trade is promising enough to them to embark on a regular traffic to the region. The first trading post, Fort Nassau, is founded upstream in 1614. At the same time they think "New Netherland" is not worthwhile enough to establish a permanent colony there. Initially little changes with the founding of the Dutch West India Company in 1621. Some years have to pass before the settlement in Manhattan truly assumes significance. In this period, too, the first colonists venture the crossing to New Amsterdam.

What the Dutch Knew about America in Hudson's Time

Waerachtige
Historie en beschrijvinge eens Landts in America ghelegghen / wiens inwoonders Wilt/ Naect/ seer godtloos/ ende wreede Menschen eeters zijn.
Beschreuen door Hans Staden van Hamborch wt lant te Hessen/ die welcke seluer in persone het lant America besocht heeft.
Nu niews wt den Hoochduytschen overgheset.
Ghedruckt t'Amstelredam / door Cornelis Claesz/op t'Water by d'Oude Brugge int Schrijf-boeck, Anno 1595.

Title page of *Waerachtige Historie en beschrijvinge eens Landts in America gheleghen, wiens inwoonders Wilt, Naect, seer godtloos ende wreede Menschen eeters zijn* (True history and description of a land situated in America, the inhabitants of which are savage, naked, most heathen and cruel cannibals), 1595
Royal Library, The Hague
1703 C 54
15 x 10 cm

In the period of Hudson's voyage to North America, little was known in the Dutch Republic about this continent. This small, bound pamphlet contains one of the earliest descriptions of America. The title predicted that not much good could be expected from any future contacts with the Indians who were "savage, naked, most heathen and cruel cannibals."

What Did the Dutch Consul Emanuel van Meteren and Henry Hudson Talk about over Dinner?

Emanuel van Meteren, *Historien* (Histories), 1663 (first edition, 1614)
Nationaal Archief (National Archives of the Netherlands), The Hague
Library 401 F 3, 28th book, fol. 572
41 x 27.5 cm

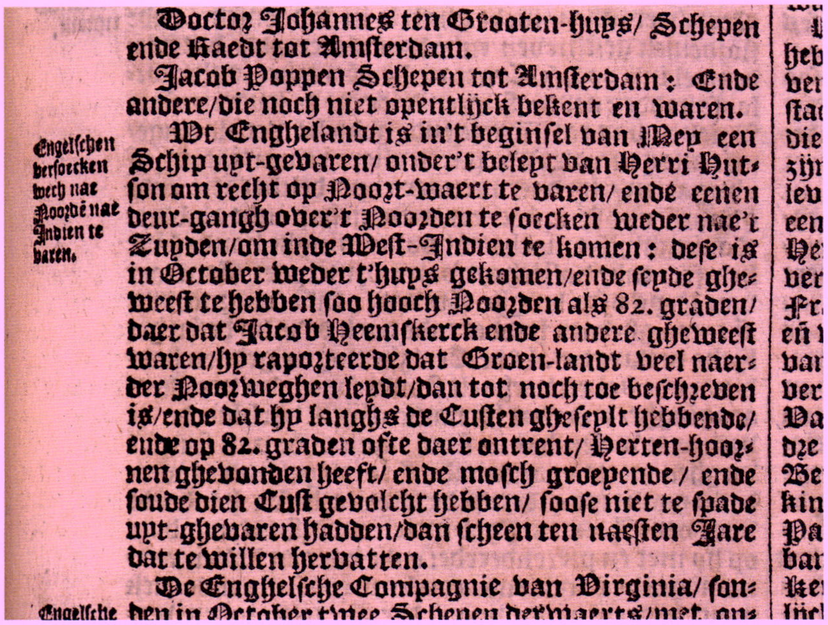

Doctor Johannes ten Grooten-huys/ Schepen ende Raedt tot Amsterdam.
Jacob Poppen Schepen tot Amsterdam: Ende andere/die noch niet opentlijck bekent en waren.

Engelschen versoecken wech nae Noorde nae Indien te varen.

Wt Enghelandt is in't beginsel van Mey een Schip uyt-gevaren/ onder't beleyt van Herri Hutson om recht op Noort-waert te varen/ ende eenen deur-gangh over't Noorden te soecken weder nae't Zuyden/om inde West-Indien te komen: dese is in October weder t'huys gekomen/ende seyde ghe-weest te hebben soo hooch Noorden als 82. graden/ daer dat Jacob Heemskerck ende andere ghe-weest waren/hy rapoorteerde dat Groen-landt veel naerder Noortweghen leydt/dan tot noch toe beschreven is/ende dat hy langhs de Custen ghe-seylt hebbende/ ende op 82. graden ofte daer ontrent/ Herten-hoornen ghevonden heeft/ ende mosch groepende/ ende soude dien Cust gevolcht hebben/ soose niet te spade uyt-ghevaren hadden/dan scheen ten naesten Jare dat te willen hervatten.
De Enghelsche Compagnie van Virginia/ son-

Emanuel van Meteren is known as the writer of *Historien* (Histories), a sizable work various versions of which were published after his death in 1612. In the context of Hudson's journey, Van Meteren's other activities should also be mentioned for it was he who arranged contacts between Hudson and the directors of the VOC. Without him Hudson might never have made the voyage of 1609, or else he would have done so, but not with the Dutch as his patrons.

As the Dutch consul and representative of the VOC in London, Van Meteren set up a meeting with the ship's captain. Over dinner the two discussed the possibilities of a journey to Asia by way of the North Cape. In the last months of 1608 Van Meteren negotiated an agreement between the explorer and the directors of the VOC. At one of these meetings, on 8 January 1609, the contract between the VOC and Hudson was signed. During the same period Hudson met the cartographer Petrus Plancius with whom he planned the charts and the routes for the journey.

Van Meteren wrote in the 1663 edition of his *Historien* (Histories) shown here about the voyage Hudson had previously made for the English in 1607. In the left margin we read: "In the beginning of May a ship sailed from England under the captaincy of Henry Hudson to sail northwest and to seek a northern passage in order, sailing south once more, to reach the West Indies."

The VOC Draws Up a Contract with Henry Hudson

On 8 January 1609 the VOC signed a contract with Hudson, by which he undertook to "seek a passage through the north around the north of Nova Zembla."[1] In the resolutions of the VOC the decision to go to sea with the Englishman is recorded as follows:

"On today 8 January in the year of our Lord one thousand six hundred and nine, the Directors of the East India Company of the Amsterdam Chamber on the one side and Mr. Henry Hudson, Englishman, advised by Jodocus Hondius on the other, have agreed and decided in the following way, namely: the above Directors will first of all equip a ship or yacht, of about 30 last, in which the above mentioned Hudson on about the first of April...will sail to seek a passage through the north to the north of Nova Zembla...and if it is possible to return the same way, to give the Directors a faithful report and account of his journey, and to hand over his journals, routes, charts and everything that befell him during the journey, without withholding anything..."

Hudson was to receive 800 guilders for the entire voyage. On 19 January 1609, the VOC paid him 150 guilders "as an advance on his wage." An advance usually amounted to two months wages. It enabled Hudson to purchase provisions and clothing for the crew. Financial terms were also agreed with his family in case he did not return within a year. Prior to the voyage Hudson was expected to come and live in the Republic with his family. With this clause the VOC aimed to ensure that he returned there after the voyage. Or did the VOC think that as long as Hudson's family was in the Republic the information that he gathered would be better kept secret? It was a clever idea, but it seems that his family did not comply with this requirement.

The VOC's notes shown here were preparatory to the contract to be drawn up with Hudson. Not everyone was apprised of all the details; for instance, the clerk wrote his name on 19 January 1609 as "Tomas Hutson" (see bottom resolution).

First two resolutions, 29 December 1608:
"To draw up a contract with the Englishman, and to make a draft of the letters to be sent to the Chamber, Mr. Dirck van Os, Jan Poppe and Arent ten Grotenhuijs.

Mr. Marcus de Vogelaer and Mr. Jan Hermansen agree, together with the boatswain, Dirck Gerritsen to provide a seaworthy ship of between 25 and 35 last for the Englishman to sail in"

Second resolution, 19 January 1609:
"It is resolved that Master Tomas Hudson contracted to undertake the voyage to the North shall be given the sum of 150 guilders as an advance on his wage"

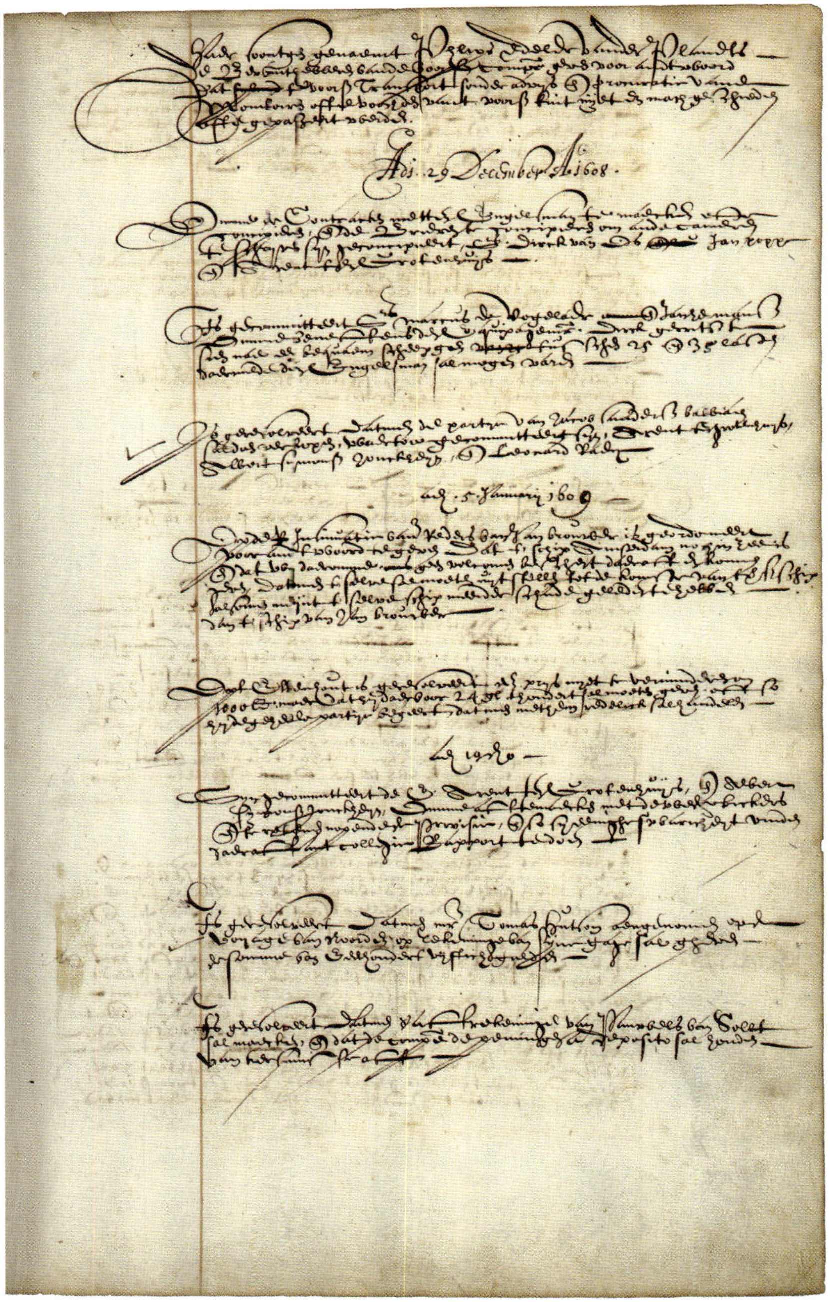

Book of Resolutions of the Amsterdam Chamber of the VOC, 1608
Nationaal Archief (National Archives of the Netherlands), The Hague
VOC Archives, 1.04.02, inv. no. 226
36 x 25.5 cm

The *Halve Maen* (Half Moon) Sets Sail from Amsterdam

THE HALF-MOON LEAVING AMSTERDAM.2

#304 (c1892)

ead of returning to Holland when the peltry
be more advantageous to remain in America.
ade in furs would obviously be very much
permanent settlement were established on
ng the Great River. The Indians could
ed to bringing their skins to a fixed locality
would thus acquire more regularity, and

-to ed.).
tes the spot
re for long
"Schreyers
here leave
who were

usually in a tearful condition as the ship proceeded on her way out of the harbor into the Zuyder Zee. It is unquestionably at this point that the Half-Moon cast off her moorings and began her eventful journey in 1609.

The "Halve Maen" at the Schreierstoren
New York Public Library, New York
ID: 814706

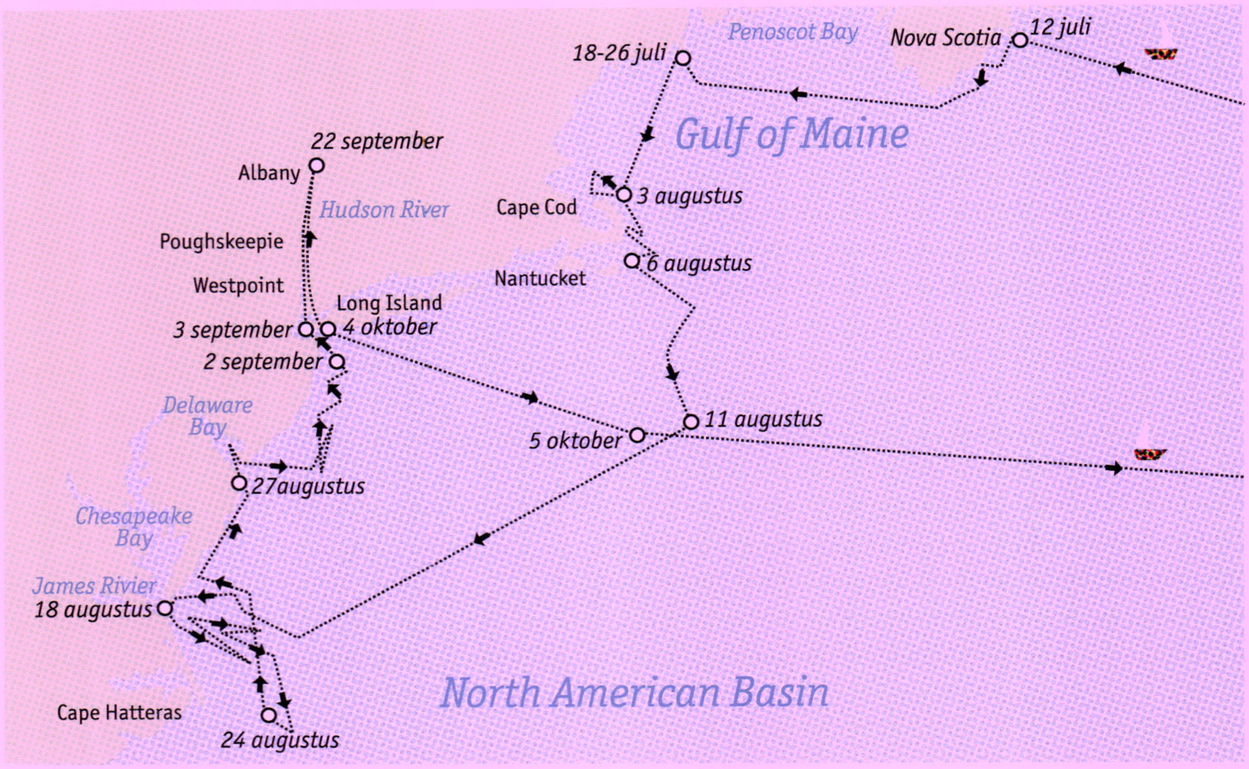

Hudson's Route in 1609
Bibian Harmsen, 2009

In this late-nineteenth century print we see the *Halve Maen* (Half Moon) sailing from Amsterdam. In the background is the "Schreierstoren," or weepers' tower, said to have been the place where wives bade sad farewells to their husbands when they went to sea. Whether the tower was actually named after the weeping ladies is not sure, but it makes a nice story. Years after Hudson's voyage a spot was also designated in New Amsterdam where lovers could take leave of each other. This was the "Schreiers Hoeck," or weepers' corner, at the southern tip of Manhattan.

The *Halve Maen* (Half Moon), the ship in which Hudson carried out his voyage for the VOC, was a yacht with a cargo capacity of 80 tons. The VOC later undertook more voyages with this ship. One of the best known was to Solor in 1613, an island in the Indonesian Archipelago, a Portuguese-owned territory. The assault on the island was launched from the *Halve Maen* and two other ships.[2]

The *Halve Maen*
Model of the *Halve Maen* (Half Moon), nineteenth century
Amsterdam Historical Museum, Amsterdam
KA 13684

The First Voyages, 1609-1614

Hudson's Journey of 1609

The VOC contacted Henry Hudson in 1608 to sound out if he was interested in undertaking an expedition for the Dutch. The voyage's goal was to determine whether a northern passage to Asia existed. The Englishman consented and agreed with the VOC on a date of departure and his fee. He hastened to make ready, selecting his crew personally, and set sail in April 1609.

Other explorers had preceded him in exploring the route around the North Cape in the years 1596-1597, but without success. Willem Barentsz. and Jacob van Heemskerck, captains reputed to be skilled professionals, had been unable to find a northern passage to Asia. Cold winters and icy seas had mocked their endeavors. Would Hudson succeed where they had failed?

When the Englishman accepted the commission he already had some years experience as an explorer. The seventeen-member board of the VOC (the Lords Seventeen) hoped that with a man like Hudson in command the desired route to Asia would be discovered. With the aid of the best cartographers of the age, a route was worked out "to find a northern passage to the north of Nova Zembla".[3] The voyage via the northeast passage had to take place in the summer when the seas would be free of ice.

Hudson completed the initial stage, to the North Cape, according to plan. All too soon, however, the ship was battered by a heavy storm with snow, hail and bitter cold and he was forced to change course. Hudson had been specifically instructed by the Lords Seventeen to return to Amsterdam should this prove to be case. But what did he do? He decided to sail in the opposite direction, westwards. He was convinced of the existence of a route that would take him right across North America to Asia and was determined to be the one to discover it. The charts he had received from his fellow countryman, John Smith, would guide him to the desired passage.[4]

On 12 July 1609, Hudson arrived at today's Nova Scotia on the northeast coast of North America (ill. on p. 38). Six days later he reached the coast of Maine. After the storm-stricken ship had been repaired, he sailed southwards along the coast. Leaving Cape Cod behind him, he sailed still further south, until he reached the latitude of Cape Hatteras in today's North Carolina on 24 August. He sailed on the following week, only northwards this time, to explore the coastline from Chesapeake Bay to Long Island, a part of the coast that had already been navigated by others.[5]

He sailed near the estuary of Chesapeake Bay, where Jamestown, the English settlement in Virginia, was located a little further inland. His fellow countrymen had founded the settlement two years earlier, in 1607. He did not land in Jamestown, however, no doubt sensitive to the fact that he was sailing under Dutch orders. Moreover, he was looking for something he knew he would not find in Virginia – the western sea route to Asia.

Hudson Discovers the Hudson, 2 September 1609

On 28 August 1609, Hudson might well have imagined he had discovered the promised waterway to the west. He was at the mouth of the Delaware River. He soon found out, however that, due to shallows, this river was difficult to navigate and so sailed on further north. A few days later, on 2 September 1609, he anchored in a bay. Here he saw the entrance to the river that would later bear his name. It had already been navigated in the sixteenth century by other Europeans up to the passage known today as the Narrows, but it was Hudson who has gone down in history as the discoverer of the river.[6]

On 11 September he sailed up the river, calling it "as beautiful a river as one could imagine." The captain encountered Native Americans, whom he described as "brave and able-bodied." Further inland he found the people "friendly and polite." They provided him with victuals "and many hides and furs." Sometimes ceremonial receptions were held. On these occasions the Indians gave the captain otter and beaver pelts. In return he handed over metal artifacts that his crew had brought with them. Not all the contacts he had as he sailed upstream were friendly, however. Violence was resorted to on three occasions, with deaths on both sides. It is unclear what events preceded these skirmishes. The aggression must have originated mainly through ignorance and fear of the stranger.[7]

Hudson continued upstream until 22 September 1609; on that day he decided to sail no further. Part of his crew traveled another 20 miles in a longboat, returning with the news that the river was too shallow. It was clearly not the passage to the west he had so fervently hoped for. The present city of Albany was the last stop on Hudson's journey. He turned around and went back again downstream. On 4 October 1609, he left the region and returned to Europe empty-handed. Nevertheless, his encounters with the Indians would represent a radical change both for his Dutch masters and for the inhabitants of the region he had explored.

Hudson's Discovery as Described by a Contemporary

Johannes de Laet, *Nieuwe Wereldt ofte Beschrijvinghe van West-Indien*
(New World or Description of the West Indies), Leiden, 1625
Nationaal Archief (National Archives of the Netherlands), The Hague
Library 399 B 7
33 x 32 cm

Indian with Club and Bow
From: De Laet, *Nieuwe Wereldt* (New World), p. 114

Johannes de Laet wrote about Hudson's "discovery" in his *Nieuwe Wereldt* (New World). De Laet had obtained Hudson's logbook, and quoted from it frequently: "Hendrick Hudson who was the first to discover this river...tells us of the manners and nature of the people there / whom he encountered in the bay: When I came to land / all the Black people sung in their fashion..." . Hudson admired the beautiful trees growing there and described the Indians who apparently sang to him as he went ashore.[8]

De Laet was not just the author of the *Nieuwe Wereldt* (New World). He was also a director of the WIC, which comes to the fore now and again in his descriptions of New Netherland. After all, he was rather eager to convince the reader of the justice of Dutch claims to the territory. His book was published in 1625, by which time it had become increasingly important to know for sure who the territory belonged to: after all, it was also being claimed by the English. That De Laet, as a director of the WIC, was eager to promote the Company's interests is evident from this passage: "The territory was first explored at the expense of our Dutchmen and a few years later it was navigated by others and provided with some forts and settlements of the Dutch, under a special charter and under the authority of the High and Mighty Members of the States General of the United Provinces." The next sentence contains a hidden message: "... They did not hear of any Christians having been up this river before them."

De Laet tried to persuade his readers that the Dutch had met with all the requirements for a proper claim to the territory. It was first discovered by Dutchmen and not by other Christians. Later the Dutch exploited it and then took up residence there. These were the rules, and in the correct order, that were adopted in the Dutch Republic for taking possession of newly discovered land.

The Return to Europe

After his journey of seven and a half months Hudson did not sail back directly to Amsterdam, where the directors of the VOC were eager to hear about his voyage. When he was off the English coast, his crew – consisting largely of Englishmen – forced him to enter the harbor of Dartmouth. Once there most of them left the ship. While awaiting the funds to finance a replacement crew that would sail the ship back to the Dutch Republic, Hudson wrote a letter to the Lords Seventeen in Amsterdam describing the region he had explored as a land of milk and honey.

The English authorities came on board a short while later. The captain must have known the risk he had taken in dropping anchor in Dartmouth. After all, he had sailed to North America for a Dutch patron, thus transgressing an important English charter that claimed a large part of the continent for the English crown. Hudson was arrested and his logbooks, charts and other travel documents were confiscated by the English.

Emanuel van Meteren was the Dutch consul in London at the time. According to various sources, he had visited the *Halve Maen* (Half Moon) prior to Hudson's arrest. During the consul's visit Hudson may have passed on essential information, but the map with the precise route to the river he had discovered never came into the hands of his employers.[9]

Hudson was admonished to remain in England and forbidden to correspond with the VOC any more. He would never visit the Republic again, but went to work instead for the English Muscovite Company for which he had previously undertaken voyages. In 1610 the VOC brought the *Halve Maen* back from England. The English, now fully informed of the river visited by Hudson, sent an engineer to further explore the surrounding region and the south coast of Long Island.[10]

Hudson went on a final voyage from England to seek a passage through North America; an expedition that ended in tragedy. The last we know of him is that he was lowered overboard in a longboat by his own mutinous crew in 1611 and abandoned in a bay.

Who Was Henry Hudson?

Henry Hudson's greatest wish was to go down in history as the man who discovered the northern passage to Asia.[11]

In fact, he never got close to this, but his four voyages of discovery were remarkable in and of themselves. He was spurred on by the theory of Robert Thorne that in the summer months the sun was so close to the North Pole that the ice would melt, making it possible to sail in a straight line over the North Pole to China.[12]

In 1607 Hudson went on his first voyage in the pay of the English Muscovite Company. He was charged with exploring the northern route to Asia, across the North Pole. Due to massive quantities of drift ice he was forced to stop near Spitsbergen Island. A second attempt in 1608, this time between the North Pole and Nova Zembla and further east along the top of today's Russia, also ended in failure. Hudson took this route a second time, under the orders of the VOC, and once again found his way blocked by ice. He then decided to head off in a westerly direction. Whether he had planned this beforehand, we do not know. During this journey he would sail up the river that today bears his name, the Hudson, but once more he found no through route to Asia.

At the outset of his final expedition (1610-1611), he set sail straight for North America, once again in search of the northwest passage. Robert Juet was a member of the crew as he had been on two of Hudson's previous voyages. Juet's logbooks are among the most important sources for Hudson's journeys. The expedition went via Iceland, Greenland and the Hudson Straits directly to Hudson Bay. Poor weather forced the crew to winter in Penobscot Bay.

Driven to despair by scurvy, hunger and frostbitten limbs, the men mutinied in the spring of 1611 when Hudson wanted to sail on again. Possibly under the captaincy of Juet, the crew set sail for England. Hudson, his son and a few of the men who had remained loyal, were left behind in a longboat in the bay and were never heard of again.[13]

Hudson died in Hudson Bay, which he had discovered.

The Soft, Snug Fur of the North American Beaver

The North American Beaver, ca. 1700
Wonderen der Natuur: in de menagerie van Blauw Jan in Amsterdam, zoals gezien door Jan Velten rond 1700 (Wonders of nature: In the menagerie of Blauw Jan in Amsterdam, as seen by Jan Velten around 1700)
Digital version: Royal Library, The Hague
Signature: AEL 204

The American beaver (Castor Canadensis) has a flat tail and webbed hind feet, which explains why this rodent was categorized in the seventeenth century as belonging to the fish family. Its powerfully developed rodent incisors allow it to gnaw through tree trunks. With branches, leaves and tree trunks they build enormous dams, or forts, up to 100 meters long and 3 meters high. We know of beaver dams that are 50 years old. The beavers themselves for that matter have a long history; the species originated five million years ago. The beaver has been hunted for its russet brown, occasionally brownish-black waterproof fur in Asia, North America and Europe.

The "Fort of Nassoueen"

In this detail of Adriaen Block's map (see ill. on p. 47) we see a small island, today's Castle Island in Albany. Block ordered a fort to be built there on his journey in 1614 and called it "Nassau." When the trading season was over, he decided to post Jacob Eelkens, one of the members of his crew in the fort. Johannes de Laet's reported the following: "In 1614 a small fort on an island far upstream...and occupied by 10 or 12 men under Hendrick Christiaens or, in his absence, Iaques Eelckens". Eelkens and his men wintered there and were ordered to continue buying beaver pelts when Block and his (Fortune) returned to the Republic.[14] Eelkens and his men may have been the first Dutchmen to spend a longer period of time in this region.[15]

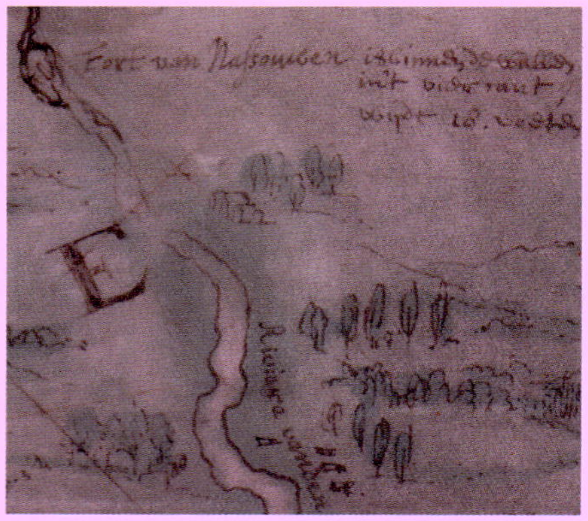

Detail of the "Figuratieve caerte" (Figurative Map), Adriaen Block, 1614 (see p. 47)

The Next Expeditions, 1610-1614

Trading Furs from on Board Ship

Hudson did not succeed in passing on the crucial information about the route to the river to his Dutch patrons.[16] His reports about potential trade with the Indians in the region, though, did reach the Dutch Republic. His voyage had shown what the area between Virginia and Cape Cod had in store for the young Republic – the luxurious fur of the North American beaver, offered to the sailors on the riverbank by American Indians. This tantalizing news whetted the appetites of Dutch entrepreneurs, making them eager to return, and in the years after Hudson's voyage several different traders founded private companies to this end. Their goal was simple, namely to buy beaver pelts in bulk for the European fur market.

One of these private companies was the Van Tweenhuysen Company, founded by Lambert van Tweenhuysen. The Company's first ship, the *St. Pieter* (St. Peter), undertook a voyage to Hudson's river in 1611.[17] Van Tweenhuysen did not operate alone, but involved various influential partners in his project. One of them was Adriaen Block, the man who would explore the region systematically over the next few years.

On this initial voyage of the Van Tweenhuysen Company, Block most likely traveled as a supercargo, the term used for the functionary directly responsible for trading. Before he could do business with the Indians, however, he had to locate Hudson's river for himself. Which he did, and upon arriving there he soon found both Indians and fur. The traders traveled up and down the river in their longboats, in search of offers of skins and pelts. Block traded from his ship and the voyage was a huge success. A year later he made another expedition to the land of furs, this time as captain of the *Fortuyn* (Fortune).

Others followed Block's first two voyages. In the winter of 1612-1613, on the third voyage of the Van Tweenhuysen Company, he was suddenly faced with competition in the form of fellow countrymen, who lay at anchor with the *Jonge Tobias* (Young Tobias) in the river bay at the same time as Block's ship. The *Jonge Tobias* had been sent by the Hans Claesz. Company, under Captain Thijs Volckertsz. Mossel. The supercargo of this expedition was Hans Jorisz. Hontom. To take the wind out of Block's sails, Hontom offered the Indians twice the price for the beavers. Block was furious and did not shirk a confrontation with Hontom, pointing out that they should not allow the Indians to drive a wedge between them by pushing up the prices. The purchasers agreed on a fixed price per beaver. Two-thirds of the pelts would go to Block and the rest would be Hontom's share. Apparently the prevailing principle was that the newcomer had the least rights.[18]

Increased Competition

The following year the Van Tweenhuysen Company decided to equip a second ship under Hendrick Christiaensz., a captain from Germany. Block's ship got there a month later than that of his colleague. In the meantime the crew of their competitors had also arrived. Yet again a quarrel broke out between the supercargoes. This time too the conflict was resolved by adopting a formula: Block and his colleague Christiaensz. received three-fifths of the beavers, while the remaining two-fifths went to Hontom.

Block thought it wise to leave the trade on the river to Christiaensz. and Hontom; he would travel further upstream in search of new suppliers of furs. At least that was his plan, until his ship accidentally caught fire! Hontom offered to come to his aid, but at a price; in exchange for his assistance he demanded a more favorable share. Block would not hear of it and responded by building a new ship, the *Onrust* (Restless).

The companies that employed Block and Hontom had already acquired plenty of experience in undertaking voyages to North America by the time the third player, the Witsens Company, appeared on the scene. Once more terms had to be settled about the allocation of the spoils. When a fourth company showed up, a firm from the town of Hoorn, the supercargoes could no longer take the bickering. It dawned on them, and also on the captains and their crews and above all on the shareholders back home, that the situation had become unmanageable. With more and more new companies appearing, unsound agreements, incalculable risks and rising prices for the beavers, little profit remained for the traders. The shareholders of the different Dutch cities batted the matter back and forth. Why not join forces?

Jan Rodrigues

Manhattan's First Mulatto?

Jan or Juan Rodrigues is variously recorded in the sources as "Spaniard," "mulatto" and "black". No one knows with certainty where exactly he came from or whether he was in fact Spanish, mulatto or black. It is clear, however, that Rodrigues came from Santo Domingo, on the Caribbean island of Espanola, otherwise known as Hispaniola. This island, with its many sugar mills and plantations, was one of the most important Spanish strongholds in the region. It is not particularly surprising that Rodrigues came into contact with the Dutch merchants who eventually became his employers. By the late sixteenth century despite wars between Spain and the Dutch Republic skippers from Dutch Zeeland had formed trading links with this Spanish city. During the Twelve Years' Truce (1609-1621) it became easier to sail in what till recently had been troubled waters, and trade flourished. Rodrigues came into contact with the Dutch in these years.

He was the first fur trader to spend lengthy periods living among the Indians. We cannot be sure whether that was on Manhattan or in surroundings districts, but a plaque in Riverside Park commemorates Jan Rodrigues as the first merchant and non-American to live on Manhattan.

His employer provided him with 80 axes, several knives, a musket and a sword. All summer Rodrigues remained among the Indians, presumably exchanging these items for furs and finding out more about the natives and their language. He must have communicated with them about the buying and selling of furs, particularly prices, weights, types and quality of fur. To begin with there was probably a good deal of gesturing and talking, as the Dutch expression has it, "with hands and feet" – literally, since when Indians wished to indicate the number 20 they first held up their ten fingers and then pointed to their ten toes.

Santa Domingo
Johannes Vingboons, third quarter of the seventeenth century
Nationaal Archief (National Archives of the Netherlands), The Hague
4.VELH 619-051
Watercolor on paper, 45 x 62 cm

Rodrigues was probably initially employed by Captain Thijs Volckertszoon Mossel and the supercargo Hans Joriszoon Hontom, who were trading on the Hudson River in the spring of 1613. In the month of May or June that year, when Mossel expressed a desire to return to the Dutch Republic, Rodrigues refused to accompany him. It is not clear whether he resigned of his own accord, but it is known that he then started working for Hendrick Christiaenszoon, Mossel's rival. Not surprisingly, Mossel was infuriated by Rodrigues' decision to change masters. At one time, Mossel and his men decided tried to vent their rage on Rodrigues, who had to be rescued by Christiaenszoon's crew.[19]

Photo Riverside Park at 80th Street
where Jan Rodrigues lived

Block's Map of "New Netherland," 1614

During his expeditions to the coasts of Connecticut, Long Island Sound, Rhode Island, Boston, Plymouth Bay and many other inlets, islands and bays along the coast between the 40th and 45th latitudes, Adriaen Block made drawings and sketches that formed the basis for this map on parchment. Cornelis Doetsz, from Edam, drew the basic outlines in red on the map.[20]
Let us follow Block's discoveries, starting at the lower left, where we find the estuary of Chesapeake Bay. Above it is "Virginia." Further north we come to the mouth of the Delaware, which the Dutch named the South River. In the hinterland we see the names of different Indian tribes, with "Aquamachykes" (Aquamachukes) being the most legible. A few rectangles indicate Indian settlements. Staten Island is shown in dark red. Above it we see a neck of land with the tribe of "Sangicans" marked.
To the right, triangular in shape, is the island of "Manhates," referring to the tribe that lived there. Block was the first cartographer to depict Manhattan as an island. He sailed via the bay up the Hudson, along which he has written: "Riviere vander vorst Mauritius" (Prince Maurice River), today's Hudson, which was usually denoted by the Dutch as the "North River." On both sides of the river is the name of the tribe of the "Mahicans," the Mohicans.
At the upper left of the map is written that – if one had understood the words and gestures of the "Maquaas" (Mohawks) correctly – the French were sailing to the north of their country in pursuit of trade. At the very top on the left is a sentence referring to the house inside the grounds of Fort Nassau: "the house is 36 feet long and 26 wide inside the fort." Upstream, at the fort, we read, "Fort Nassau is 58 square feet wide within [the ramparts?], while the moat is 18 feet wide." On the left of the map the names of a few tribes are written in a barely legible fashion, including "Sennecas" (Senecas) and "Maaquaas" (Mohawks).
Returning downstream we come to Long Island, with the name "Nahicans" written on it. Above Long Island to the left, in the East River in New York City, we see "Hellegatt," or Hell's Gate, so called due to its dangerous currents. As far as is known Adriaen Block was the first European to navigate this stretch of water. He then entered Long Island Sound and navigated the Connecticut River, here named "Versche rivier" (Fresh River). Block explored this river up to today's city of Hartford.[21]
On leaving the sound he discovered a stream on the left that he called "Oester riviertjen" or Oyster stream.[22] He must then have sailed past today's Block Island, before the coast of the present state of Rhode Island. This was an islet to the right of Long Island, which we can still decipher, though written very indistinctly on the map, as "Adrian Bloxeyland."
Further east we see the "Zuijder zee" and the island with the names "Texel – Vlielant" (Texel and Vlieland are two of the Dutch Wadden Islands). Below Texel is a small islet, "Walvisch eijland / Hendrick Christiaanse eyland" (Whale Island / Hendrick Christiaanse Island). To its right is present-day Cape Cod Bay, denoted here with the name "Staten Baij."
The entire coast northeast of Cape Cod is rendered in detail as far as "Nova Franciae" (Nova Scotia). At the moment when Adriaen Block arrived at Cape Cod, a peninsula on the Massachusetts coast, he met up with the ship of Hendrick Christiaensz., which was part of the same expedition. Not long afterwards he decided to return to the Republic, where this map was made in the same year.[23]
Block's map includes several new features: by sailing around both Manhattan and Long Island he discovered that they were islands, and showed them as such. It remains uncertain whether he made these discoveries in 1614 or earlier.
Finally, one striking feature of the map is the diagonal caption, "Nieu Nederlandt," the first time the name of the region between the South (Delaware) River and the Fresh (Connecticut) River was recorded on a map. These letters, in capitals, make clear the trading ambitions of Block and his colleagues: with this map, they hoped to be granted a charter for the beaver trade.

Manhattan as an Island
Detail "Figuratieve caerte" (Figurative Map), Adriaen Block, 1614

"Figuratieve caerte" (Figurative Map),
Adriaen Block, 1614
Nationaal Archief (National Archives of the Netherlands), The Hague
4.VEL520
Parchment, 64 x 49 cm

Block Builds the *Onrust* (Restless)

The *Onrust* (Restless)
MDC-deWeerdt, 2008
www.theonrust.com

A Joint American-Dutch Project to Rebuild the *Onrust* (Restless)
MDC-deWeerdt, 2008
www.theonrust.com

Competition on the North (Hudson) River forced Block to search for more northerly coastal reaches where the Indians would offer him their beaver pelts. He did not get very far, as the frozen seaways forced him to call a halt to his voyage in late January 1614. He ended up bivouacking in the bay of the North (Hudson) River. When time came for the return voyage to the Republic his ship, the *Tijger* (Tiger) caught fire and went down with its cargo of furs.

Block did not let either the fire or the bitter weather defeat him. He gave orders for a smaller ship to be built, naming it *Onrust* (Restless): "... and he built a yacht...and sailed in it through the *Helle-gat* (Hell's Gate) in the bay and explored all the surrounding places..."[24]

Even with the certainty of a new ship, peace and quiet had not returned.

It was as if Block was born under an unlucky star: no sooner was the *Onrust* (Restless) seaworthy than a mutiny broke out. A group of the crew boarded the *Nachtegael* (Nightingale), the ship of their competitors, the Hans Claesz. Company. The men sailed off with it and went on to make their living as pirates in the Caribbean.

The *Onrust* is one of the first European ships to have been built in North America. In the same period the Dutch built another small ship, the *IJzeren Varcken* (Iron Pig). It was probably deployed for expeditions southwards, while the Onrust was reserved for those to the north.[25]

The Charter of the New Netherland Company, 1614

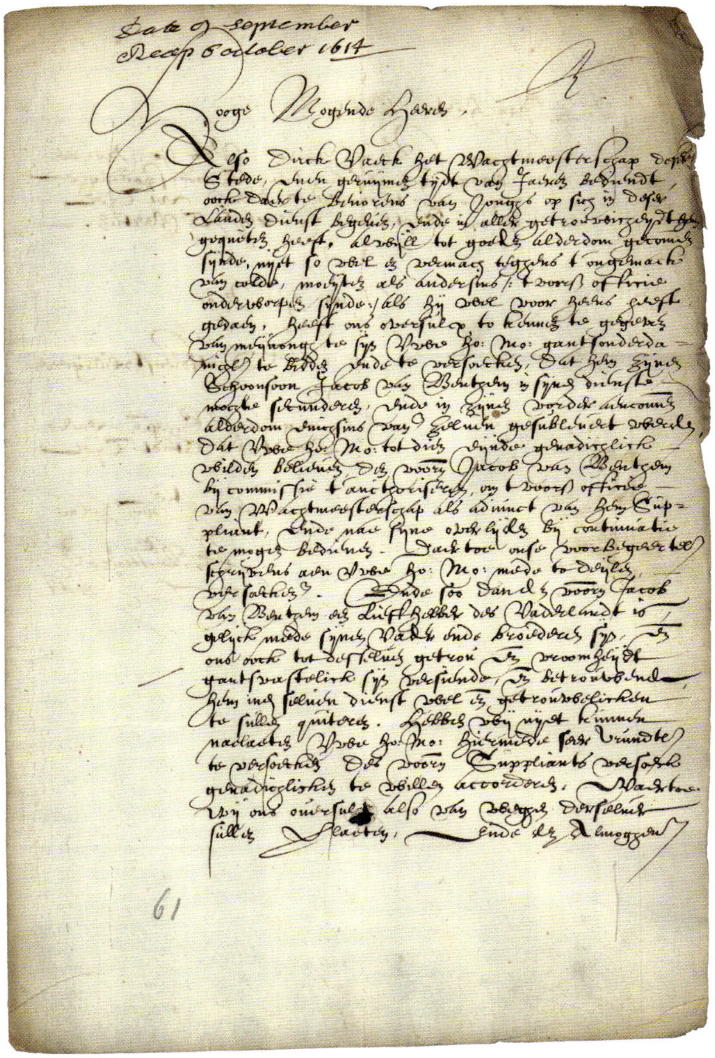

Charter in the Book of Statutes 1614-1616
Nationaal Archief (National Archives of the Netherlands), The Hague
States General, 1.01.06, 12301, 11 oct, folio 80
23.5 x 34 cm

This is the charter the States General granted to a group of merchants allowing them to trade in New Netherland. The applicants were mainly Amsterdam traders and their names appear on the first page of the charter.
The legislation for issuing this charter was drafted in the spring of 1614.[26] The monopoly was to come into force on 1 January 1615 and was valid for three years. The merchants were permitted to make four voyages to New Netherland. The trade monopoly extended from the 40th to the 45th latitude. Block's explorations in the winter and spring of 1613 and 1614 cover exactly the same territory as that which the Company wanted to exploit for trade. The charter for the Company also mentions Block's "Figurative Map," which was submitted as an appendix to the application.[27]

The Companies Unite to Form the New Netherland Company, 1614

The plans to form a cartel began making sense to the various parties. Negotiations followed and in 1614 the New Netherland Company was founded. The new company took the name of the region in question – New Netherland. However, it needed a charter to give it a proper foundation. Only an official monopoly would prevent new competitors from appearing on the scene.

The application for a charter was carefully prepared. One of the appendixes was a map (ill. on p. 47) that Block had made during his voyages of discovery.[28] It shows the full extent of the territory that the company would claim for its commercial activities.

The States General granted the charter to the New Netherland Company on 11 October 1614. All the document really signified was that no other Dutch trading organization was allowed to sail to this region. The charter did not amount to any appropriation or claim on the territory of New Netherland; it was just a monopoly.

Even though the New Netherland Company had been operating for three years now, we know few details of the voyages or of the enterprise as a whole. However, clearly the shareholders wanted to expand their activities in New Netherland, because in 1616 they requested a charter for another territory. This second request was based on information obtained on a number of expeditions led by Captain Cornelis Hendricksz. In the years 1614-1616 Hendricksz. set sail on the *Onrust* (Restless), the ship Block had left behind in the colony after his own expeditions. Hendricksz. had thoroughly explored the surroundings of the Delaware River; the region definitely had potential for the fur trade. One of the appendixes to the request for the new charter was a map showing the desired trading area (ill. on p. 51).

The New Netherland Company's request was not granted. This probably had to do with plans circulating in the Republic to found an even larger company, but one in which the state had a stake – the Dutch West India Company, or WIC.

Having failed to obtain an additional charter, the applicants now turned their attention to obtaining an extension to the existing charter, which would expire in 1618. Once again the States General were unhelpful, probably due to the plans for founding the WIC, the Dutch company that would control both shipping and trade throughout the Atlantic Ocean.

The decision not to extend the charter of the New Netherland Company meant that the trade in beavers was once again open to all comers. And so it is hardly surprising that the same problems surfaced

Cornelis Hendricksz. Explores the Delaware

On page 48 we saw that prior to his return to Amsterdam in 1614, Captain Adriaen Block left behind the *Onrust* (Restless), which he had built in America. Block's colleague, Cornelis Hendricksz., made a number of voyages in it. This ship's captain from Monnickendam explored the Hudson and Delaware Rivers with the aim of mapping them. In spring 1616 he sailed in the *IJzeren Varcken* (Iron Pig) up the Delaware, which was first named the South River on this occasion. As Hendricksz. realized that this new river fell outside the original territory covered by the charter, he decided to sail as quickly as possible in the *IJzeren Varcken* to the Republic. Upon his return in 1616, the New Netherland Company presented the States General with a map on which the newly discovered territories were drawn. The Company tried to obtain a supplementary charter allowing it to trade in the region below 40 degrees latitude. This request was a sequel to the charter of 1614.[29]

The map of the new discoveries presents both the North (Hudson) River and the South (Delaware) River in detail, but without mentioning their names. Fort Nassau, built in 1614, is visible on the upper reaches of the North (Hudson) River. Some branches of the river are indicated with the names Hudson had given them seven years earlier. One of them is the Esopus, which is still called so today.[30] Another striking feature is the mention of the numerous Indian tribes, which we encounter for the first time on this map. The maker of the map, Hessel Gerritsz., made use of the details provided by Cornelis Hendricksz.

The text on the map gives the following information: "Kleijntjen and his companion have informed me of the location of the rivers and the settlements of the peoples they have found on their voyage beginning with the Mohawks and heading inland and downstream along the new river to the Ogehage, which is the enemy of the northerly nation and I can presently not find other than two drafts of these maps with regard to the one that is partially a fair copy. And while I think the one with the drafts denoting the locations to be the most reliable, I find that the settlements of the tribes of the Senecas, Gachoos, Capitannases and the Jottecas should be shown as being a good deal further west in the country."

Kleyntjen and two other Dutchmen had let themselves be persuaded to go with a group of Indians on the warpath. They became involved in a war of the Mohawks against the Susquehannas, with the latter capturing three of their men. Hendricksz. ransomed them when he was exploring the Delaware in the *IJzeren Varcken* (Iron Pig). The mapmaker Hessel Gerritsz, who appears to have spoken with Kleyntjen, states here that he only had two partial plans of this territory at his disposal in making his map. Upon comparing these maps with Kleyntjen's account he comes to the conclusion that the settlements of the Indians should have been located further to the west. The quotation was thus added to the map at a later stage.

In any case Hessel Gerritsz. had a number of sources, including both the oral account of Kleyntjen and the maps of the New Netherland Company, which he obtained from Cornelis Hendricksz.[31]

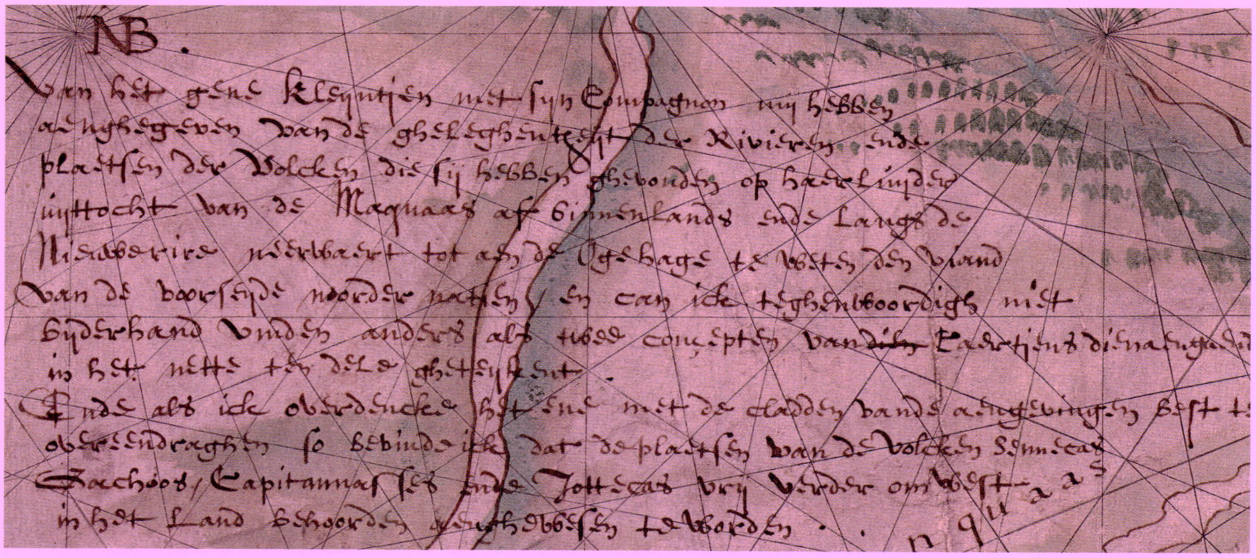

"Rivieren ende plaetsen der Volcken" (Rivers and settlements of indigenous peoples)
Detail of the map by Hessel Gerritsz., ca. 1616

Attributed to Hessel Gerritsz., ca. 1616
Nationaal Archief (National Archives of the Netherlands), The Hague
4.VEL519
Manuscript on paper, 101.50 x 33.50 cm

as before 1614, albeit on a somewhat smaller scale. With or without the charter, the New Netherland Company largely preserved its share in the trade. The investors made sure that their company would continue to dominate the business; after all they disposed of the greatest amount of both capital and experience. Some newcomers did operate in the region with varying success, usually in partnership with the New Netherland Company.

The Dutch West India Company and New Netherland

Willem Usselincx, who had devoted himself to the founding of the Dutch West India Company (WIC) for many years, has already been discussed on page 24. He first raised the idea around 1600. At the time New Netherland was not on anybody's drawing board and Hudson had yet to discover Manhattan and its river. In 1606, too, when various parties had hashed out the draft plan for the WIC's charter, there was still no trade in this region. It was only in 1609 that Hudson made his crucial voyage and the potential benefits of the region became known. In the same year Spain and the Dutch Republic signed a truce, which lasted until 1621. The WIC was founded almost directly after the truce ended.

The States General granted the new company its charter on 3 June 1621. Because it was first required to raise some starting capital, the WIC could not immediately embark on the fur trade in New Netherland. The New Netherland Company, therefore, asked the States General permission to continue its operations for the time being. The States General agreed that it would be a shame were the territories to remain unexploited until the WIC was ready and granted a temporary dispensation.

The traders of the former company were thus allowed to continue trading for up to two years after the founding of the WIC. The beginning of the end of the free trade was proclaimed in a verbal report by Captain Adriaen Jorisz. Thienpont to the Company's Lords Nineteen on 3 November 1623. He asked leave to bring back the last traders of the private company. The last captain of the New Netherland Company only left Manhattan Bay in 1624.[32]

Charter of the Dutch West India Company

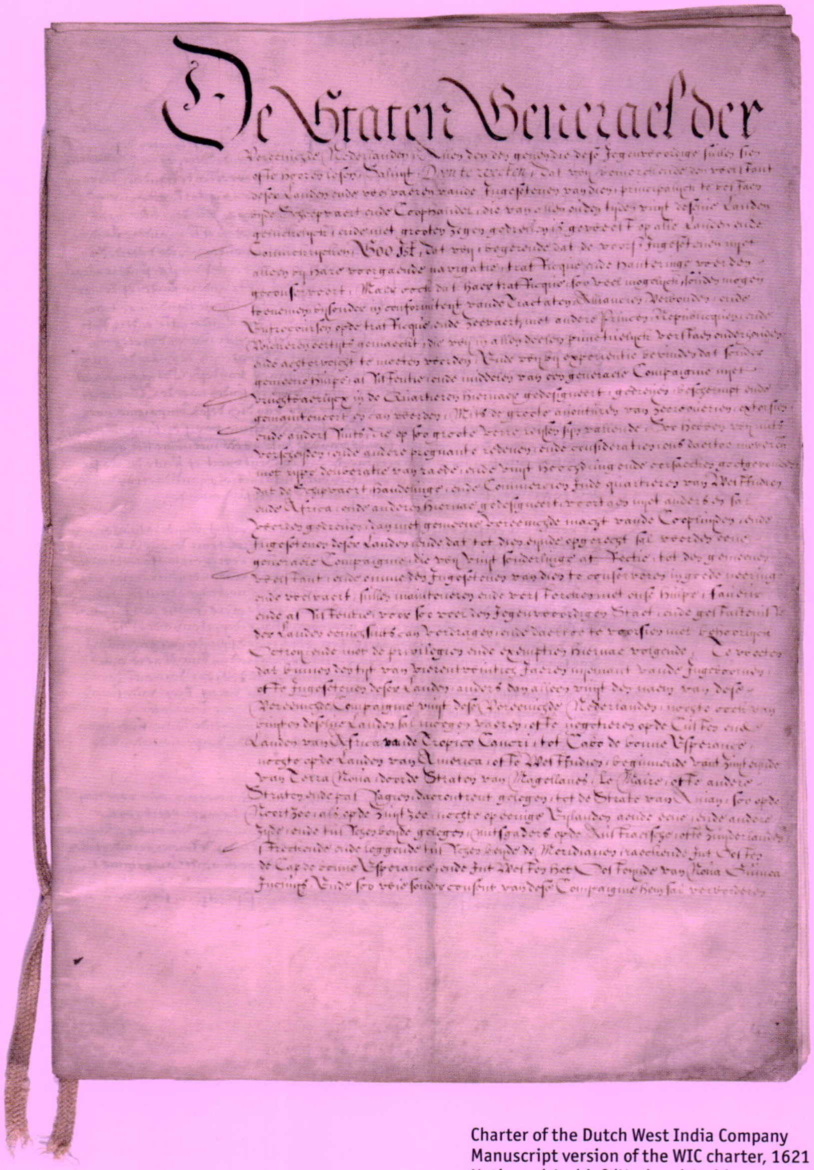
De Staten Generael der

Charter of the Dutch West India Company
Manuscript version of the WIC charter, 1621
Nationaal Archief (National Archives
of the Netherlands), The Hague
WIC, 1.05.01, inv. no. 13
Ink on parchment, 40.5 x 27.5 cm

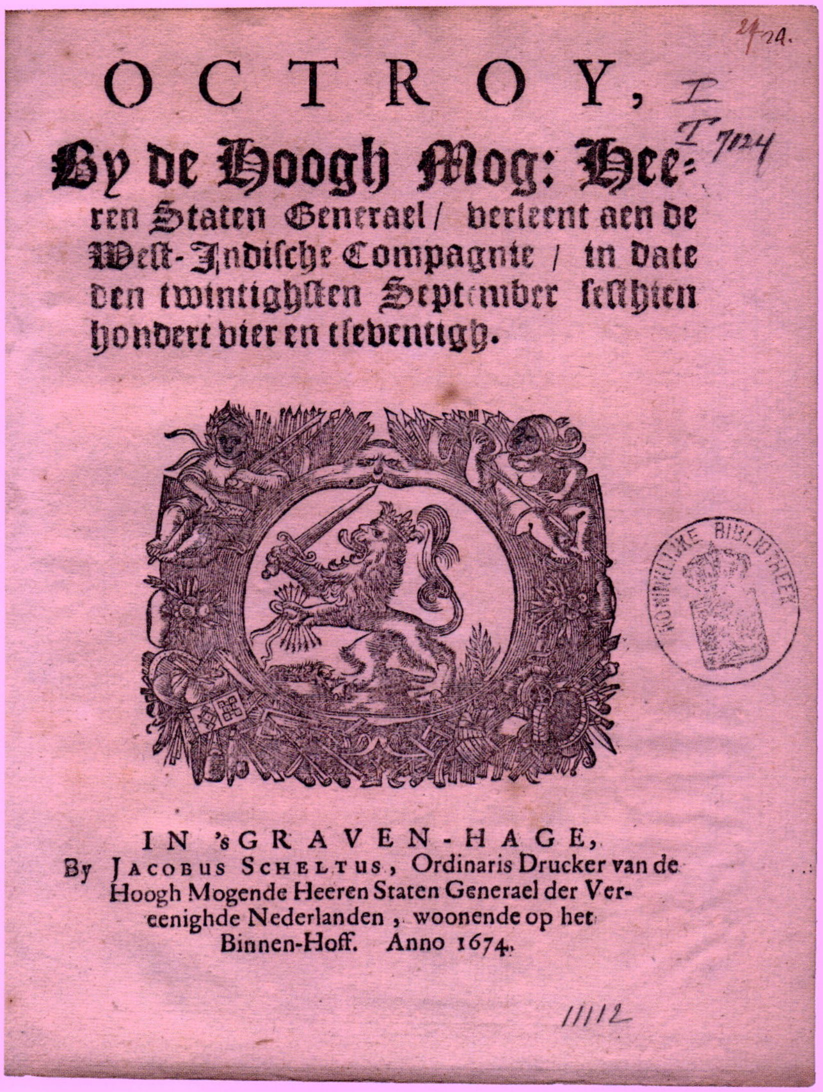
OCTROY,

By de Hoogh Mog: Heeren Staten Generael/ verleent aen de West-Indische Compagnie / in date den twintighsten September sesthien hondert vier en tseventigh.

IN 'sGRAVEN-HAGE,
By JACOBUS SCHELTUS, Ordinaris Drucker van de Hoogh Mogende Heeren Staten Generael der Vereenighde Nederlanden, woonende op het Binnen-Hoff. Anno 1674.

Charter of the West India Company
Printed version
Royal Library, The Hague
Pflt 11112
19 x 27.5 cm

Once the States General had granted the West India Company its charter on 3 June 1621, it was able to get down to business. The charter contained 45 articles, one of which stipulated that the charter would be valid for 24 years. Throughout that period the Company would have a monopoly on trade in the Atlantic Ocean. After that the States General would decide whether to renew it. The precise definition of the region covered by the monopoly included the west coast of Africa south of the Tropic of Cancer, the coasts of North and South America, the islands in the Atlantic Ocean and the eastern part of New Guinea.

From Log Cabin to Trading Post

New Netherland embraced Manhattan, Long Island and some small settlements along the South (Delaware) River, the North (Hudson) River and the Fresh (Connecticut) River. A handful of trading posts were built on the authority of the former companies. These premises were generally nothing more than simple log cabins that were occupied on a semi-permanent basis.[33] Even after the charter went into effect the WIC could not immediately make any claim on the territory. The previous companies had not officially owned the land either. Nonetheless, the founding of the WIC meant the end of the straightforward navigation to and from the territory. It was now possible for a new concept of the distribution of power in the Atlantic Ocean to be developed, one that would have no small implications for New Netherland. People had to be sent there straightway to claim the region before the English intervened. Sir Dudley Carleton, the English ambassador in The Hague, had started proceedings in 1622 to prevent the Republic from settling there permanently.[34] To be ahead of the English, the new land had to be occupied by at least 50 colonists. This first step towards claiming the territory would have great consequences. A fort was built to protect the trading post. This was occupied by colonists to stabilize the territory and offer better resistance both to English political machinations and to the neighboring English colonies. The WIC's charter provided for this. The second article stated that the WIC was permitted to promote the occupation of "fruitful and uninhabited quarters" in the territories it was to navigate.

At first little changed with respect to the Company's official occupation of the territory. On the same day that Thienpont had submitted his request to bring back the last employees of the private companies, however, the directors of the WIC decided on 3 November 1623 to send a ship to transport several families "to plant a beginning."[35] Only by sending people was it possible to "continue the business," which was after all what the WIC had been set up to do.

The decision of the Lords Nineteen to establish a small trading post in New Netherland was intended to foster trade, while protecting it against competition. When the WIC was launched it entrusted decisions concerning New Netherland to a special committee of its Amsterdam Chamber. After some time this committee was also put in charge of the management and supervision of the colony. It was not long before differences arose among the directors of the Chamber who sat on this committee. For instance, they disagreed about how New Netherland should be organized. What structure should a trading post be given?

There were two factions. The first had an agricultural colony in mind and was headed by Kiliaen van Rensselaer, who later founded a colony of this sort in New Netherland himself. The other faction believed that the sole emphasis should be on the trade in beaver pelts. They were called the monopolists or trading faction. The struggle between the two largely determined the early history of New Netherland. Was the trading post destined to grow into a highly developed colony with a center such as Batavia in the East Indian archipelago? Or would contacts between the Dutch Republic and New Netherland amount to nothing more than Dutch ships sailing back and forth and returning to dock in the mother country at the end of every season?

But, first of all a trial voyage to the territory had to be made. The first WIC ship to reach the colony must have been the *Mackreel* (Mackerel), which sailed from Texel on 16 July 1623.[36] The *Mackreel* landed in New Netherland on 12 December. It was late in the season. The captain, Daniël van Crieckenbeeck had chosen to sail to the Caribbean first to hunt down some Spanish ships. He then traveled on to the Hudson River, where he spent the whole winter stocking up furs, and returned to the Republic in the summer of 1624.[37]

The First Ship with People on Board: "V or VI Families of Colonists"

The first ship to transport colonists to New Netherland was the *Eendracht* (Unity), with Captain Adriaen Jorisz. Thienpont at its helm. It probably left harbor in January 1624.[38] There were not many newcomers, as conveyed by the tally recorded in the minutes of a meeting of the Lords Nineteen of "V or VI families of colonists." Even though the identity of these pioneers is unknown and they are only described as people who had applied to emigrate, it is assumed that they were five or six families of Walloons.[39]

A second shipload of colonists followed two months after the *Eendracht* docked. With the *Nieu Nederlandt* (New Netherland) under Captain Cornelis Jacobsz. May, 30, mainly Walloon families set foot on dry land. These Protestant Walloons were refugees from the Spanish Inquisition and had fled to northwest Europe for this reason. They emigrated to the Dutch colony via the Republic (see also p. 181).[40] On arrival they were distributed over the trading posts on the Fresh (Connecticut) River, the South (Delaware) River, on Noten (Governors) Island and on the upper reaches of the North (Hudson) River.

Just before the *Nieu Nederlandt* (New Netherland) returned to the Republic, the WIC decided to send further shiploads of colonists, this time including some cattle as well. The following year, a total of

West India House in Amsterdam
Photo: David Cohen de Lara, 2009

The Organization of the WIC

The WIC's charter regulated both the organization of the board and the powers of its members. Its structure was virtually identical to that of the VOC. The board consisted of directors from five Chambers: Amsterdam, Zeeland, Maze (Rotterdam, Dordrecht, Delft), the Northern Quarter (Hoorn and Enkhuizen) and City and Country (Groningen). In the Amsterdam Chamber, for instance, there were seats for 20 directors, who in turn were appointed by the major shareholders. To become a major shareholder one had to have deposited at least 6000 guilders in capital.

The directors of the five chambers elected the central managing board, in which 19 men had seats, the "Lords Nineteen" as they were known. The directors in the Amsterdam Chamber provided eight of them, the Zeeland Chamber four and the other Chambers two each. The 19th vote was reserved for a representative of the States General. In this way the state was represented at the highest level in the Company, which gave it considerable influence.

The chairmanship of the board alternated between the Chambers of Zeeland and Amsterdam. When the Lords Nineteen convened in Amsterdam, they gathered at the West India House, which remained the WIC's headquarters from 1623 to 1656. While the States General was the highest administrative authority over the colonies, they gave the Company extensive powers, over "directors, soldiers, and magistrates, and over the other essential services, over the upkeep of the locations, the maintenance of order, police and justice, in short to the furtherance of trade." Appointments and the descriptions of the functions of the higher officers of the Company had to be approved of by the States General.[41]

Because the voyages to New Netherland were generally organized by Amsterdam entrepreneurs, it was self-evident that the Amsterdam Chamber was responsible for the execution of policy with regard to New Netherland. A separate committee was set up for this purpose. Each Chamber had its own committees, each with its own controlling and administrative functions, such as the upkeep of the docks, the equipping of the ships and the purchase and sale of merchandize.

six vessels set sail with new settlers on board. The extra man- and womanpower was sorely needed to stake out, as it were, the fairly extensive territory – without a permanent settlement the WIC would have no legal claim to the territory.[43] A whole region had to be populated if one were to have permanent rights to it. And this was necessary because the presence of the French and English, who had colonized parts of North America prior to the founding of the WIC, formed a threat to the Dutch Republic's trade and settlement ambitions. English colonists had settled in Virginia and New England, with Jamestown and Plymouth as their main bases, both on the southern and northern borders of New Netherland.[44] Given that England had previously claimed the whole region for itself, including New Netherland, the WIC had to tread carefully and to populate the colony as quickly as possible.

In sending all those people one would think that of the two warring factions in the Amsterdam Chamber, it was the colonizers who had won the day. Nonetheless, this early attempt at colonization should be seen more as a way of providing a minimum of protection for the trade in pelts. It was precisely the difference between founding a colony and sending just enough settlers to safeguard trade that would prove to be a key factor in the role New Netherland played in the first years of its existence.

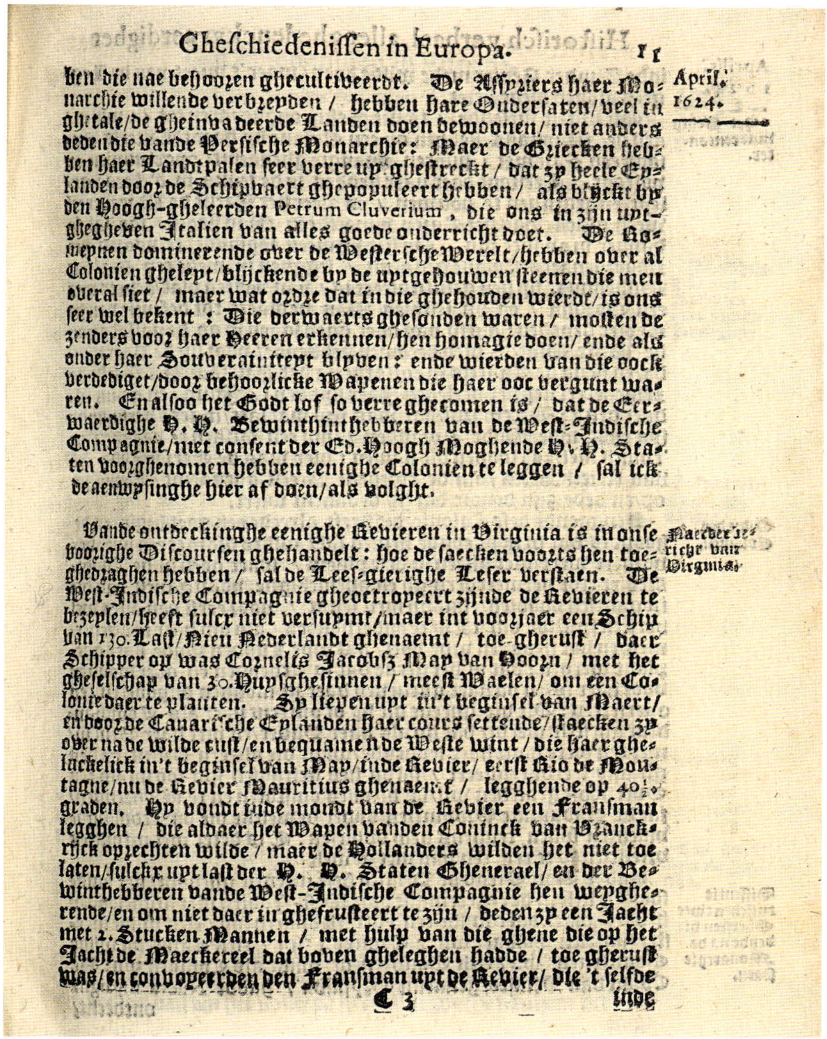

Gheschiedenissen in Europa. 11

ven die nae behooren ghecultiveerdt. De Assyriers haer Monarchie willende verbreyden / hebben hare Ondersaten / veel in ghetale / de gheinvadeerde Landen doen bewoonen / niet anders deden die vande Persische Monarchie: Maer de Griecken hebben haer Landtpalen seer verre uyt gheſtreckt / dat zy heele Eylanden door de Schipvaert ghepopuleert hebben / als blijckt by den Hoogh-gheleerden Petrum Cluverium, die ons in zijn uytghegheven Italien van alles goede onderricht doet. De Romeynen domineerende over de Westersche Werelt / hebben over al Colonien ghelept / blijckende by de uytgehouwen steenen die men overal siet / maer wat ordre dat in die ghehouden wierdt / is ons seer wel bekent: Die derwaerts ghesonden waren / mosten de zenders voor haer Heeren erkennen / hen homagie doen / ende als onder haer Souverainiteyt blyven: ende wierden van die oock verdediget / door behoorlicke Wapenen die haer ooc vergunt waren. En alsoo het Godt lof so verre ghecomen is / dat de Eerwaerdighe H. H. Bewinthhintheb[b]eren van de West-Indische Compagnie / met consent der Ed. Hoogh Moghende H. H. Staten voorghenomen hebben eenighe Colonien te leggen / sal ick de aenwysinghe hier af doen / als volght.

April. 1624.

Vande ontdeckinghe eenighe Revieren in Virginia is in onse voorighe Discoursen ghehandelt: hoe de saecken voorts hen toegedraghen hebben / sal de Lees-gierighe Leser verstaen. De West-Indische Compagnie gheoctroyeert zijnde de Revieren te bezeylen / heeft sulcx niet versuymt / maer int voorjaer een Schip van 130. Last / Nieu Nederlandt ghenaemt / toe-gherust / daer Schipper op was Cornelis Jacobsz May van Hoorn / met het gheselschap van 30. Huysghesinnen / meest Waelen / om een Colonie daer te planten. Sy liepen uyt in't beginsel van Maert / en door de Canarische Eylanden haer cours settende / staecken zy over na de wilde cust / en bequamen de Weste wint / die haer ghelückelick in't beginsel van May / inde Revier / eerst Rio de Montagne / nu de Revier Mauritius ghenaemt / legghende op 40½. graden. Hy vondt inde mondt van de Revier een Fransman legghen / die aldaer het Wapen vanden Coninck van Vranckrijck oprechten wilde / maer de Hollanders wilden het niet toelaten / sulckx uyt last der H. H. Staten Gheneraael / en der Bewinthebberen vande West-Indische Compagnie hen weygherende / en om niet daer in ghefrusteert te zijn / deden zy een Jacht met 2. Stucken Mannen / met hulp van die ghene die op het Jacht de Maeckereel dat boven gheleghen hadde / toe gherust was / en convoyeerden den Fransman uyt de Revier / die 't selfde

Maeckerie ... richt van Virginia.

C 3 inde

30 Families to Plant a Colony
Historisch Verhael (Historic Story) by Nicolaes van Wassenaer
Historisch Verhael (seventh volume; printed in 1625 and beginning in April 1624), p. 11
Nationaal Archief (National Archives of the Netherlands), The Hague
Library 405 D 13
Parchment, 19.5 x 17 cm

The seventeenth-century chronicler Nicolaes van Wassenaer summed up the arrival of the Walloon families in 1624 as follows:
"In our previous discourses the discovery of some rivers in Virginia was discussed: the interested reader will have learned there how the events occurred. The West India Company, having been granted a charter to navigate the river, did not waste any time but fitted out a ship of 130 last in the spring named *Nieu Nederlandt* (New Netherland). Its captain was Cornelis Jacobsz. May from Hoorn and it sailed with a company of 30 families, mostly Walloons to settle a colony there."[42]
Van Wassenaer's book is the first printed source in which the name New Netherland appears. It occurred previously in written form in Block's map of 1614 and in the charter of 1614.

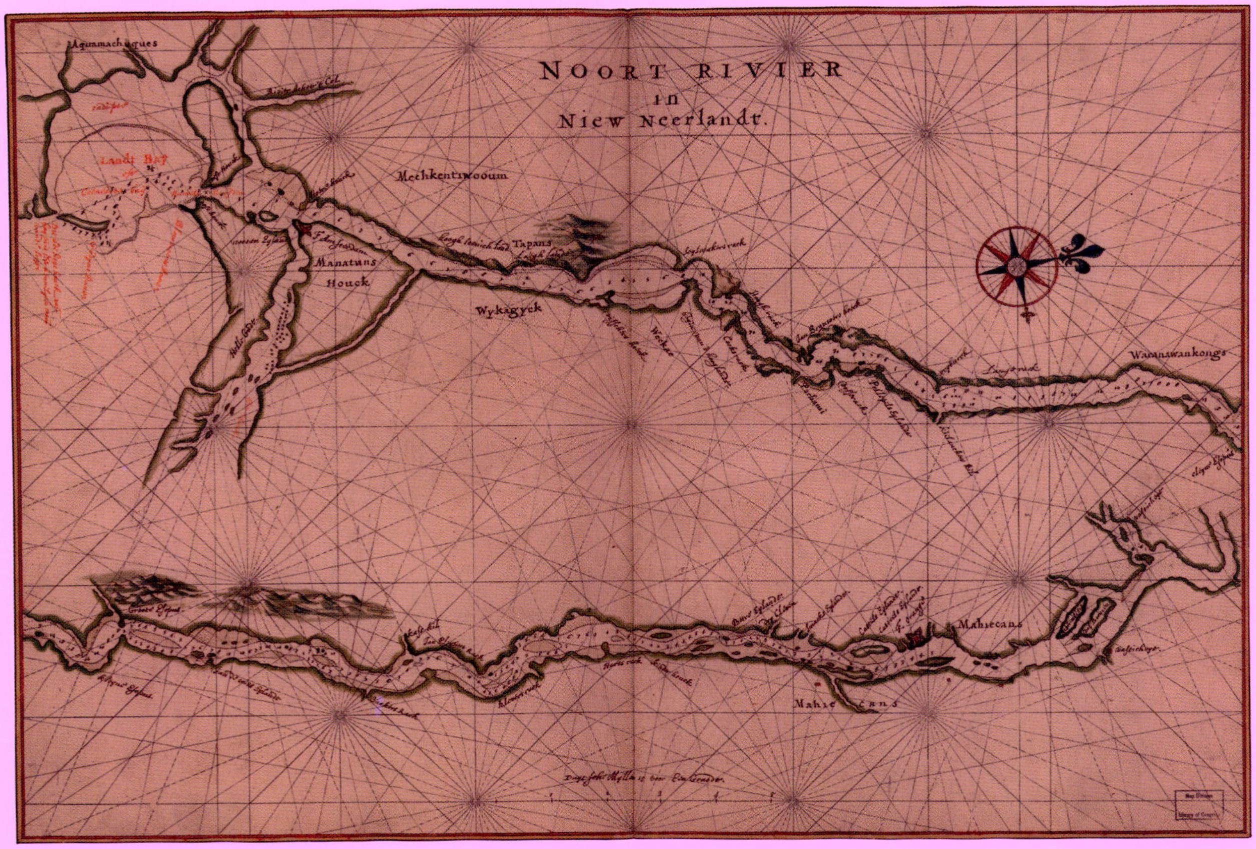

"Noort Rivier in Niew Neerlandt" (North River in New Netherland)
Johannes Vingboons, third quarter of the seventeenth century
Library of Congress, Washington, D.C.
G3291.S12 coll .H3 Vault: Harr vol. 3, map 13
Paper, 47 x 67 cm

Sailing up the North (Hudson) River to Albany

From 1610 onward the North (Hudson) River was navigated almost solely by Indians and Dutchmen. This map gives a survey of the entire North (Hudson) River, from the "Landt Bay" to Fort Orange, today's Albany.

The bay into which the river flows was described as so large that "more than a thousand fully laden ships" could lie at anchor there.[45] Between the "Hamelshoofden," or the Narrows between Staten Island and Long Island, indicated in red ink here, one could sail upstream to today's Albany. This was also the final point on Hudson's voyage of discovery. On the orders of Block the first tiny Dutch trading post, Fort Nassau, was built on this site. It was erected on Castle Island, also shown on this map as "Casteels Eylandt."

The trading route up the North (Hudson) River begun at the estuary and ended in Albany. The river was subjected to a dramatic ebb and flow, so that the flow of the tide could still be observed as far as Albany and beyond. To the north of Albany there was a confluence with a westerly river. There was a waterfall there, which is known today as the Cohoes Falls.

This map is in fact the first large-scale map of Manhattan and the North (Hudson) River. Manhattan is indicated here as "Manatans Houck," and is triangular in shape. On it we can also see Fort Amsterdam. Noten (Governors) Island is shown here to the left.

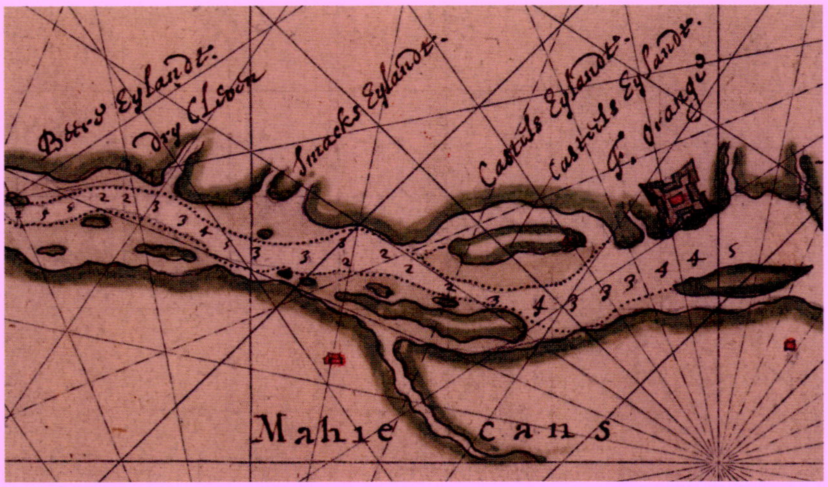

Detail of the map "Noort Rivier in Niew Neerlandt"

New Amsterdam

Few documents have come down to us regarding the period from 3 November 1623, the day the Lords Nineteen decided to found a small trading post in New Netherland, and the moment the settlement on Manhattan took shape. One cannot say with any certainty what the events were leading up to it. Accordingly, the following is no more than a brief reconstruction.

It is likely that Cornelis Jacobsz. May was instructed to distribute the immigrants, after their arrival, over the entire territory. Even though he remained on board ship, May was the highest authority in New Netherland, and as such he can be regarded as the first director of the colony.[46] He was probably responsible for ordering the building of Fort Orange on the upper reaches of the North (Hudson) River to replace Fort Nassau built in 1614.[47]

On the *Nieu Nederlandt*'s return to the Republic in the fall of 1624, May was able to inform the board of the WIC that yet another fort had been built, Fort Wilhelmus on the South (Delaware) River. The territory now boasted a number of fortified places: besides Fort Wilhelmus, there was Fort Orange on the North (Hudson) River (1624), Fort Nassau on the South (Delaware) River (1624) – not to be confused with the one of 1614 on the North (Hudson) River – and a fort on Noten (Governors) Island (1624).[48]

The fort on Noten (Governors) Island was the early colony's seat of government. Willem Verhulst was appointed May's successor as director and he was already resident in New Netherland when he took on the post. He received the instructions issued in January 1625 by the Amsterdam Chamber in the summer of that year. The next set of instructions, dated April 1625, reached him a little later. These documents reveal that the Chamber felt that the colony should be able to feed its own residents. Seeds, plants and trees, dispatched with the orders, were to be planted in the proper season. Several ships also arrived with horses, sheep and cattle. Special stables were built for the animals on two of them, the *Griffioen* (Griffin) and the *Swarte Paert* (Black Horse). Other ships brought yet more colonists as well as the first Company employees.

A striking feature of Verhulst's orders is that the board of the Company instructed him to give priority to organizing the trade. In contrast to the previous idea of occupying as much land as possible by dispersing the inhabitants throughout the region, the director was now requested to bring them back to a single location.[49]

This order seemed intended to solve a dilemma. Initially the Company's goal was to spread the inhabitants to the furthest corners of the trading region as a means of laying claim to it. However, due to the great distances between the central trading post on Noten (Governors) Island and the other posts, it was difficult to protect the latter against Indian raids. Disturbing rumors were circulating in the Republic about English colonists in neighboring Virginia being murdered by Indians.[50] This was never to be allowed to happen to the people living in and around Fort Orange. Protecting the colonists went hand in hand with controlling their activities, because individual dealings ran counter to the Company's interests. The colonists were obliged to sell the beaver pelts to the Company for a fixed price. Soon enough, though, some of the colonists were starting up their own fur trade and selling the pelts on to others. To put a stop to this illicit trade the WIC revoked its decision, made less than a year previously, to encourage extensive colonization. The more distant trading posts would continue to exist, but with a minimum of personnel.

The Chosen Site

All the colonists would be summoned to live together once again. Which site would Verhulst select for this future village? The instructions from Amsterdam were quite clear. The director was expected to find an attractive spot and while Verhulst, in theory, was free to make his choice, the instruction stated that the southern tip of Manhattan would be suitable: "... to choose the most ideal spot for its dwellings, pastures and lands... on the tip of Manhattan, to the north of Noten (Governors) Island, or some other ideal place... taking heed that the place selected should dispose of water and wood for fire and for building houses, and that the river in the region should be abundant in fish."[51]

And so it transpired. "The tip of Manhattan" seemed the most advantageous site, and a fort was built there to protect the village. As director, Verhulst was not the right person to design it. The engineer Crijn Fredericksz. was dispatched to New Netherland, with ground plans in his pocket.[52] All that was needed now was a name, but the board of the WIC had already come up with one. The briefing stated that, "... Director Verhulst assisted by the Board should take charge of the fort according to the concept No C. which shall be named Amsterdam."[53]

Crijn Fredericksz. arrived in June and took up residence in the fort on Noten (Governors) Island where Verhulst and his board held their sessions. He sat at the table with the director, discussing the plans for the fort of Amsterdam at the tip of Manhattan Island.[54] A month later, in July 1625, the first drawings were ready. The board made the decision to move the headquarters from Noten (Governors) Island permanently to Manhattan. Hence the fort became the governing seat of New Netherland.

"The Fort of New Amsterdam on Manhattan"

Nieuw Nederlandt. 9

spruytende is. Dit soude het Lack der Iracoysen wesen / soo groot als een Middelandtsche zee/ van by de veertigh mijlen wijdt/ geen gesicht kan daer over dragen/ al is men daer midden in: het heeft oock heel veel groote Valleyen/ met Riet en Broeck-landen/ soo wijdt en breedt dat mede niet te oversien zijn / en by somer-tijde seggense komter veel water-gevogelte droepen: maer als de Wilden het over moeten varen/ soo wetense eenige Eylanden/ die daer in leggen/ waer te nemen/ ende gaen soo met dagh-reysens van het eene Eylandt op het ander/ tot drie ofte vier toe/ souden anders niet te recht konnen komen/ doch dit stellen wy maer na de onderrichtinge der Wilden/ andere seggen oock / dat men met kleyn vaertuygh van de Noort-Rivier tot in de Rivier van Cannada soude komen varen door het selve Lack/ maer dat dunckt my heel onwaerschijnelijck. De andere arm van de Noordt-Rivier / loopt/ als ghesegt is / door vier spruyten tot de groote Afval van de Macquas-kil, de Wilden noemense Chahoos, ende onse natie noemense de groote Afval; boven de Afval is de rivier weder eenige 100 treden wijdt/ende de Water-val is na gissinge hondert vijftigh of twee hondert voeten hoogh / en daer stort het water soo glat af / als of het langhs een effen muyr neer viel/ daer het af valt/ daer het langhs valt/ en daer het op neer komt/ is niet anders als een hechte blaeuwe Klip-steen; daer dichte by om laegh staen oock noch eenige ronde Klippen heel speculatijf/in 't water/ als groote Hoy oft Turf-hoopen/ de sommige van acht / sesthien/ ofte dertigh voeten hoogh/ seer plaeysierigh om aen te sien: soo daer omtrent veel Anticque Poëten verkeerden/ sy souden

B

"'t Fort Nieuw Amsterdam op de Manhatans"
(The Fort of New Amsterdam on Manhattan)
From: Van der Donck's *Beschryvinge van Nieuw-Nederlant* (A Description of New Netherland), 1655
Royal Library, The Hague
343 J 2
Print, 8.2 x 12.4 cm

This bird's eye view is probably the first survey of Manhattan to be made. In the center we see the first fort of New Amsterdam, built in 1625. The building is not correctly depicted; there are too many bastions and it looks as though it were built of stone, which was not the case. The image itself is misleading, moreover, because the island is depicted in reverse. The print originally dating from 1626-1628 was published 20 years later in Van der Donck's *Beschryvinge van Nieuw-Nederlant* (A Description of New Netherland) of 1655. It had previously been shown in Joost Hartgers' *Beschryvinghe van Virginia, Nieuw Nederlandt / Nieuw Engeland* (A Description of Virginia, New Netherland / New England) in 1651, which explains why it is known as "The Hartger View."

The Founding of New Amsterdam?

The flag of New York City is highly unusual. The colors of the three stripes are the same as those of the House of Orange in the sixteenth and seventeenth centuries – orange, white and blue – which were originally worn by the supporters of the Orange family during the Eighty Years' War against Spain. Even more remarkable is the centrally placed seal. On the coat of arms we see two windmill sails, two barrels of corn and two beavers. The escutcheon is crowned by an eagle and flanked by an Indian on the right and a European on the left. Below them is inscribed the year – 1625.

July 1625 is often given as the date when New Amsterdam was founded. In that month the decision was made to transport the occupants of the fort on Noten (Governors) Island and their possessions to Manhattan.[55] Either then or shortly thereafter the first stone of the fort was laid, or rather the first spade load was dug, because the fort was built of earth and not stone. And so the summer of 1625 does seems highly plausible as the birthday of New Amsterdam.

But other moments, such as the day when the men moved into the new fort on Manhattan, could also do the honor. While it would take years before the fort was completed, the quarters for the director and the Board will have been ready much sooner. We do not know exactly when, though, and there is nothing in the sources to help us.

Other authors have proposed an earlier date for the foundation of the city, in 1624, when the administration of the colony took up its seat in the fort on Noten (Governors) Island, thus making the island part of the later urban territory of New York City. While some agree with the dating as 1624, they dot not regard it as the year when the city was founded, seeing it instead as marking the founding of the colony. There are two more possibilities – the day in the summer of 1626 when Pieter Minuit bought the island of Manhattan from the Indians and 1653, the year when New Amsterdam was granted its city rights.

How can one decide on the exact date of Manhattan's foundation? That depends firstly on one's definition of the notion itself and then, of the territory one has in mind – the colony of New Netherland and with it the future state of New York, or New Amsterdam and with it the future city, New York City. Actually, one should take into account the time that the witnesses themselves thought appropriate. The question that then arises is whether they consciously experienced such a moment as being the foundation of New Amsterdam. In this context one can do little more than fantasize about the event. Maybe once upon a time on a fine summer evening the colonists downed a bottle of Dutch gin and toasted the future.

Flag of New York City
Photo: Richard Koek, 2009

Crijn Fredericksz. also drafted plans for roads and farms outside the fort and houses for the inhabitants. Now that the foundations of New Amsterdam had been laid, Verhulst set to work in building up the colony. He was not to remain director for long, however. Apparently he falsified the books and may even have drawn on Company funds for his own gain. His colleagues blew the whistle on him, and in the first half of 1626 he was replaced by Pieter Minuit. This colonist had previously sounded New Netherland for the presence of precious metals and other valuable raw materials, which could be profitably exploited. His explorations had lasted a year and he knew the country better than anyone. In this early stage of the colony's development he was one of the few who was familiar with the original occupants of the region, even picking up something of their languages.[56]

It was probably Minuit who purchased the island of Manhattan from the Indians early in the summer of 1626, during the first year of his directorship. Some authors claim that Verhulst, his predecessor, negotiated the transaction.[57] As mentioned, no deeds have been preserved that confirm the purchase. There is, however, an at first sight rather modest-looking document that mentions the purchase of Manhattan.

Griet Reyniers and Anthony "The Turk" van Salee

A Remarkable Pair: The First Muslim and the First Prostitute in Manhattan

The most astounding tales are told about Anthony, or Antoni, van Salee and Griet Reyniers. Sorting truth from fiction is a far from simple matter, but there is no doubt that they were one of the most colorful couples of New Amsterdam.

Anthony was the son of a Dutch father and a Moroccan mother. His father was a pirate who landed on the North African coast, where Anthony was born around 1607. There he grew up and lived until he set off for the Dutch Republic.[58]

The story goes that Anthony's father converted to Islam and thereafter developed a great hatred for Christians. Anthony too became a Muslim but it is doubtful whether his aversion to Christendom was as great as his father's. He is, however, remembered as the first Muslim of Manhattan and is said to have brought the first Koran to the island.

Anthony sailed to New Netherland in 1630 and it seems he married Griet Reyniers on board the ship. In Amsterdam she had worked as a "waitress" in a tavern but rumors circulated in the colony that she had been dismissed because of her scandalous behavior: it was said that her employer had discovered her with her petticoat pulled up to her knees.[60] Between the two of them, the couple caused quite some commotion in the colony. Anthony, who soon acquired the nickname "The Turk," apparently wandered drunk through the streets of New Amsterdam, firing his weapon and cursing the heavens.[61] He also summoned his neighbors before the judge – on one occasion claiming that they had poisoned his dog, another time because of a presumably drunken brawl.[62]

And there was much more talk about Griet. Was she a prostitute? And was it really true that back in Amsterdam she used to stretch out her clients' penises against a broomstick to measure the length?[63] From time to time Griet would call herself a whore and she certainly had the reputation of being one, so we should not be surprised by the story of midwife Lysbet Dircks, who claimed that on one occasion, after she had assisted her in labor, Griet had inquired who the newborn baby resembled: Andries Hudde or her husband, Anthony? Lysbet replied: "If you don't know who the father is, how on earth should I? But the child's skin is certainly somewhat brown."[64]

Despite the many wild stories that circulated, the couple did surprisingly well. They owned a farm north of the Singel, present-day Wall Street and they may have had a house on Brugh Straat (Bridge Street).[65] After they moved away from New Amsterdam – allegedly because of Grietje's scandalous behavior – Anthony bought a plot of land near Gravesend on Long Island. He continued to deal in real estate in the city. Their four daughters, Annica, Cornelia, Eva and Sarah, married ambitious businessmen in New Amsterdam.[66]

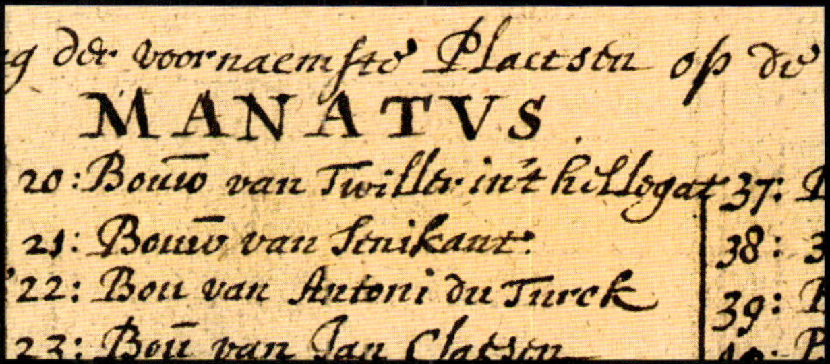

Detail of the "Manatus Map" (see pp. 190-191)
Listed at number 22 is the farm of "Antoni de Turck"
(Anthony "The Turk")

Photo of Broad Street near Bridge Street, where Griet Reyniers and Anthony "The Turk" van Salee lived

Cordula Hahn
Born 1942 Utrecht
In New York since 1974

[1] For Henry Hudson's contract, see: Van Dam, *Beschrijvinge*, pp. 38-39.
[2] Bruijn, *Dutch-Asiatic Shipping*, p. 765.
[3] Van Dam, *Beschrijvinge van de Oostindische Compagnie*, pp. 38-39.
[4] Wieder, 'Onderzoek', p. 255.
[5] L'Honoré Naber, "Hudsons reize," with *The third Voyage of Master Henry Hudson... written by Robert Juet of Lime-house* printed at the back, 1626, p. 9 ff.
[6] Jacobs, *Een zegenrijk gewest*, p. 55; Phelps Stokes, *The Iconography*, vol. 2, pp. 29-30: Jehan Alfonse de Saintonge (1541-1542) and Jehan Cossin (1570).
[7] Otto, *The Dutch-Munsee Encounter*, pp. 39-43; Spinoza Catella Jessurun, *Kiliaen van Rensselaer*, p. 4; Van Meteren, *Belgische ofte Nederlantsche oorlogen*, fol. 347 right.
[8] De Laet, *Nieuw-Nederlandt*, pp. 106-107.
[9] Emanuel van Meteren, in Asher, *Henry Hudson*, p. 150; Wieder, "Onderzoek naar de oudste kaarten," p. 237; De Laet, *Beschryvinge*, also quotes from Hudson's journal.
[10] Wieder, "Onderzoek naar de oudste kaarten," p. 7.
[11] Edwards, *Last Voyages: Cavendish, Hudson, Ralegh*, p. 125.
[12] Rink, *Holland on the Hudson*, p. 25.
[13] Edwards, *Last Voyages: Cavendish, Hudson, Ralegh*, p. 127.
[14] Jacobs, *Een zegenrijk gewest*, p. 56; Condon, *New York Beginnings*, p. 30; De Laet, *Nieuvve wereldt ofte Beschrijvinghe van West-Indien*, p.106.
[15] It is possible that Dutch people may have spent the winter there at an earlier date: Muller, *May*, p. xlviii-xlix, shows a quotation suggesting that the admiralty of Amsterdam had dispatched two ships in 1611 under Captain May, once again to search for the northern passage and that he was explicitly instructed to sail afterwards to the coast of America. Both ships spent the winter there from November 1611 to February 1612, but the crew must have spent most of that time on board ship.
[16] Hart, *The prehistory*, p. 20.
[17] According to some authors, the St. Pieter was not the first ship to follow Hudson's route to the region. L'Honoré Naber, *Henry Hudson's reize*, p. LXX, believes that LeMaire had already purchased the three-master Vos from the admiralty in 1610 and had undertaken a voyage with it to this territory.
[18] Jacobs, *Een zegenrijk gewest*, p. 56; Hart, *The prehistory*, pp. 22-23.
[19] Condon, *New York Beginnings*, p. 30; Hart, *The prehistory*,p. 21, 23, 26, 75; *de Halve Maen* 71 (1998) 4, p. 75.
[20] De Laet, *Nieuvve wereldt ofte Beschrijvinghe van West-Indien*, p. 107 [Third Book, chapter 10].
[21] I am grateful to Jaap Jacobs for this information. It is in any case certain that the Delaware was explored by the *IJzeren Varcken* early in 1616. The ship was then sent to Amsterdam with a report of the voyage, so that rights could be claimed for the newly discovered river.
[22] Instead of the "Oester riviertje" (Oyster River) this could also by the "Ooster riviertje," or East River. De Laet, p. 103, describes it as follows: "On the mainland in the bay is a curved point of land / behind which there is a small river or inlet / which is called Ooster river by us, since it flows eastward" (Aen't vaste landt recht binnen de baye light een krom punt / achter 't welck een kleyn rievierken ofte inwijck is / welck by de onse word genoemt 't Ooster-rivierken doordien 't oostwaert streekt).
[23] Jameson, *Narratives of New Netherland*, pp. 50-51.
[24] Zandvliet, *Mapping for Money*, p. 59; Wieder, "Onderzoek naar de oudste kaarten," p. 253.
[25] De Laet, *Johannes de, Beschryvinge van West-Indie*, 2nd ed., Leiden, 1630, ch. 8, pp. 101-104.
[26] Hart, *The prehistory*, p. 33; Engelbrecht and Van Herwerden, *De ontdekkingsreis van Jacob Le Maire*, pp. 34, 37, 38.
[27] Condon, *New York Beginnings*, p. 23.
[28] Jacobs, *Een zegenrijk gewest*, p. 59, erroneously dates the map as from around 1615-1618 and states that it is one of the maps that the New Netherland Company showed to the States General in their request for the charter to be prolonged in 1618, by which he meant the charter request of 1614; Hart, *The prehistory*, pp. 33-35; Cohen, *Manhattan in Maps*, p. 22; Schilder, "Van Nieuw-Amsterdam naar New York in kaarten"; Zandvliet, *Mapping for Money*, p. 57, note 5.
[29] Schilder, "Van Nieuw-Amsterdam naar New York in kaarten," p. 10.
[30] Wieder, "De Stichting van New York," p. 8.
[31] Cornelis Hendricksz. negotiated with the Indians in person, as can be seen in: NA 1.01.07 (States General) 5484, Ingekomen stukken / Lias Admiraliteiten 1620, 11-4: Report of Cornelis Hendriks of Monnikendam of August 1616 who negotiated with the natives of Minauman and bought 3 people from them: "That he also negotiated with the natives of Minquas / and purchased from them at least three / people being of this company of people / which three people he had allowed them to use / at the service of the Maquas and the Machicans, / giving them in return some corals, and / articles of trade" (Dat hij oock mette Inwoonderen van Minqunas / gehandelt ende haer affgecocht heeft seeckere drije / Persoonen weesende van dese Compaignie volck / welcke drije persoonen haer hadden laeten gebruijcken / ten dienste vande Maquas ende Machicans, daer / voor gevende eenige Letelen [sic], Corallen, ende / Coopman schappen); Kees Zandvliet, Mapping for Money, p. 187.
[32] Wieder, "Onderzoek naar de oudste kaarten," p. 11.
[33] Den Heijer, *De geschiedenis van de WIC*, p. 81; Wieder, "Onderzoek naar de oudste kaarten," p. 13.
[34] Rink, *Holland on the Hudson*, p. 69.
[35] Wieder, "Onderzoek naar de oudste kaarten," p. 11.
[36] Wieder, *Monumenta cartographica*, p. 10 says of the Mackreel that it "apparently did not belong to the WIC".
[37] Jacobs, *Een zegenrijk gewest*, p. 63; Wieder, *Monumenta cartographica*, p. 10.
[38] Jacobs, *Een zegenrijk gewest*, p. 63.
[39] Rink, *Holland on the Hudson*, p. 76, Rink incidentally makes no mention of the *Eendracht*.
[40] Wieder, *De stichting van New York*, p. 4: reference to Nicolaes Wassenaer and document A of Van Rappard. Like Rink Wieder does not mention the *Eendracht*.
[41] Jacobs, *Een zegenrijk gewest*, p. 105.
[42] Wassenaer, *Historisch verhael*, 7th vol. [printed in 1625 and beginning in April 1624], p. 11. NB: the volume here is bound incorrectly. After folio 8 comes 9, followed by 6, followed by 11, followed by 12.
[43] Rink, *Holland on the Hudson*, p. 73. From a report of the Lords Nineteen for 1624 (National Archives, via Liassen, West-Indische Compagnie, 5751: 22 April 1624])we learn that the notion in the Republic was that the discovery of the North River on the order of the Republic (the VOC) was not in itself sufficient to give the Dutch any right to ownership of the territory. The clearly stated view was that for a nation to have any exclusive claim on a territory, it was necessary for the cities and forts in a region to be populated by at least 50 people dispatched by a kingdom or country.
[44] Rink, *Holland on the Hudson*, pp. 70-74.
[45] Jacobs, *Een zegenrijk gewest*, p. 36.
[46] Jacobs, *Een zegenrijk gewest*, p. 481 calls Adriaen Jorisz. Thienpont the first director and Cornelis Jacobsz. May the second in 1623; Wieder by contrast writes in, De Stichting van New York, p 12: "Wassenaer tells us that it was the captain of the Nieuw-Nederland Cornelis Jacobsz May van Hoorn, who was appointed by him as first director of New Netherland in 1624."
[47] Jacobs, *Een zegenrijk gewest*, note 140, p. 416, refers to Zabriske and Kenney, "The Founding of New Amsterdam," but does not state when the fort was built, or which one. He does state that 'shelters' were built in 1614/15, and that the WIC decided in the spring of 1625 that the three trading posts should be merged to form a single settlement. Van Nierop, *Rensselaerswijck*, p. 1.
[48] Wieder, *De Stichting van New York*, pp. 12-13; Jacobs, *Een zegenrijk gewest*, pp. 63-64.
[49] Wieder, *De Stichting van New York*, p. 5: the Walloons who had first settled in Fort Orange and Delaware had to return to Manhattan.
[50] Sainsbury, *Calendar of State Papers*, pp. 31-33.
[51] Wieder, *De Stichting van New York*, p. 136-137.
[52] Jacobs, *Een zegenrijk gewest*, note 143: p. 416; Zabriske and Kenney, *The Founding of New Amsterdam*, p. 12; Wieder, *De Stichting van New York*, pp. 149-59
[53] See Wieder, *De Stichting van New York*, p. 155: Van Rappard, Document E, Fol. 11.
[54] In this context Menno Leenstra's account is interesting: "In the meantime the cattle for the various settlements round the mouth of the Hudson, the central trading station, had arrived. The arrival of the cargo ships with cattle must have forced the Company to exploit in the short term a larger area of pasturage than just Noten Island. The cattle after all could not be distributed to the various settlements, but had to be accommodated in one place. In all likelihood this was originally the main reason for the purchase of the island of Manhattan. Whether this idea ad been mooted before the arrival of the cattle remains a question."
[55] Wieder, "De Stichting van New York," p. 14; Wassenaer, *Historisch verhael*, see November 1626.
[56] Wieder, *De Stichting van New York*, Briefing for Willem Verhulst (January 1625), p. 124.
[57] Jacobs, *Een zegenrijk gewest*, p. 416, note 144; Weslager, "Did Minuit Buy," pp. 5-6; Wieder, *De Stichting van New York*, p. 140. According to Wieder, Verhulst departed for the Republic in September 1623 with Crijn Fredericksz.; Rink, *Holland on the Hudson*, p. 85, note 34: Verhulst departed for the Republic in 1625; Gehring, "Peter Minuit's Purchase," p. 6; Kammen, *Colonial New York*, p. 30; Zabriske and Kenney, *The Founding*
[58] Jacobs, *New Netherland*, p. 449.
[59] Vrijman, *Kaapvaart en zeerooverij*, p. 219.
[60] Shorto, *Nieuw Amsterdam*, pp. 107-108.
[61] Shorto, *Nieuw Amsterdam*, pp. 107-108.
[62] Van Laer, *Council Minutes*, 1638-1649, I: 5, 6.
[63] Van Laer, *Council Minutes*, 1638-1649, I: 80.
[64] Van Laer, *Council Minutes*, 1638-1649, I: 49.
[65] Phelps Stokes, *The Iconography of Manhattan Island*.
[66] Shorto, *The Island at the Center of the World*, p. 337.

II

CHAPTER 2

A Real Colony? 1626-1640

In 1626 Pieter Minuit, the trading post's new director, purchases the exclusive rights to Manhattan Island from a group of local Indians. This will allow the island to serve as the operating base for the fur trade along the rivers in the region. The directors of the Dutch West India Company (WIC) do not see eye to eye about the organization of the colony. The Amsterdam Chamber, in charge of running it, is divided on the question of whether or not to start up an extensive agricultural enterprise.

The dispute among the directors has long-lasting consequences. Shifts in power within the Chamber automatically impact the colony. As a result, there are different responses to questions such as whether colonists should be sent out or not; who should be appointed director; and how much should be invested?

The changing policy destabilizes the colony and limits its population growth. Consequently, in 1629 the WIC decides to partially open up the fur trade to stimulate investment in the colony. The Company envisages having patroons, or patrons, that is wealthy Dutch men, invest their own money to attract settlers and develop large plantations in New Netherland. And, indeed, some financiers sign on as patroons for the farmlands granted by the WIC. However, because this plan does not exactly take off, in 1640 the Company opens up the fur monopoly, the definitive green light to make New Netherland attractive to investors, dealers and farmers.

The Island of Manhatten Bought from the Savages

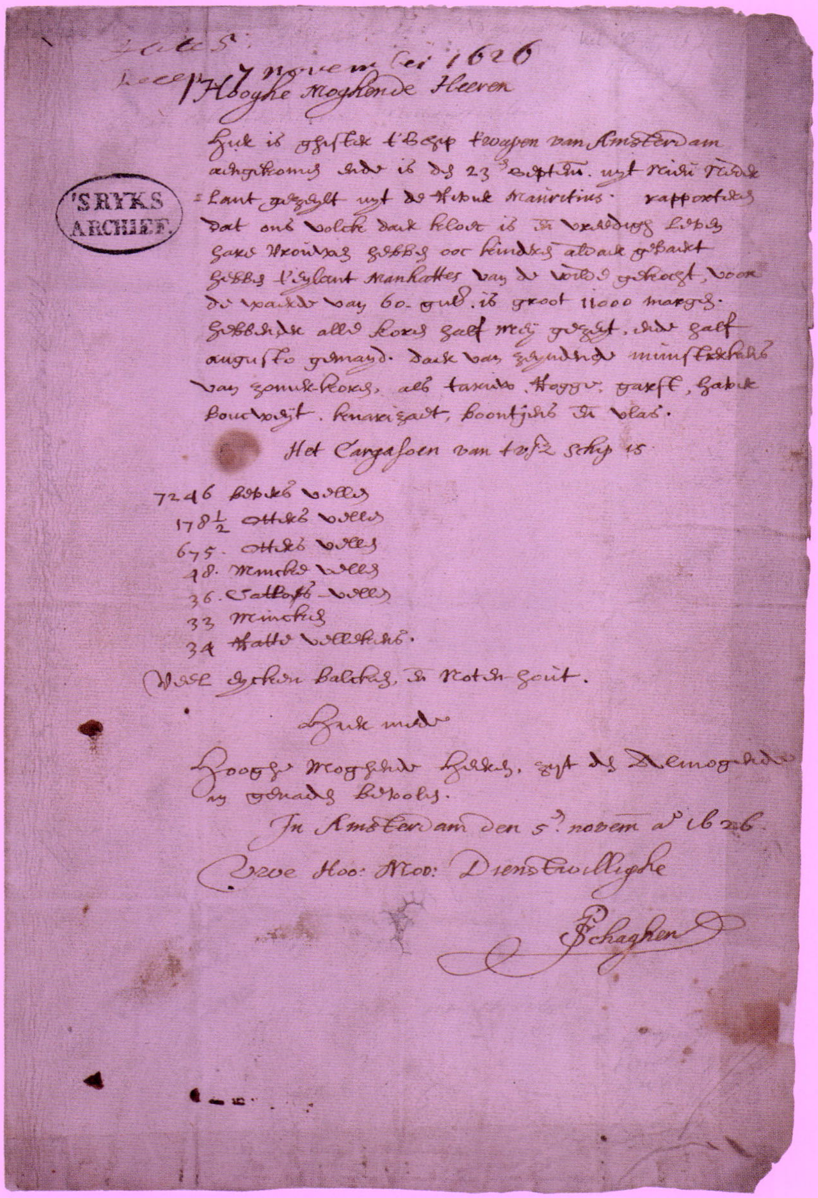

The Schagen Letter, 1626
Nationaal Archief (National Archives of the Netherlands), The Hague
VOC, 1.01.04, inv. no. 5751 II
Ink on paper, 32.5 x 21.5 cm

Date 5 November 1626
Received 7 November 1626

High and Mighty Lords,
Yesterday the Ship the Arms of Amsterdam arrived here. It sailed from New Netherland, out of the River Mauritius, on the 23rd of September. They report that our people are in good spirit and live in peace. The women also have borne some children there. They have purchased the Island Manhattes from the Indians for the value of 60 guilders. It is 11,000 morgens in size [app. 22,000 acres]. They had all their grain sowed by the middle of May, and reaped by the middle of August. They sent samples of these summer grain; wheat, rye, barley, oats, buckwheat, canary seed, beans and flax.

The cargo of the aforesaid ship is
7246 Beaver skins
178 1/2 Otter skins
675 Otter skins
48 Mink skins
36 Wildcat skins
33 Minks
34 Muskrat skins

Many Oak timbers and Hickory.

Herewith,
High and Mighty Lords, be commended to the mercy of the Almighty.
In Amsterdam, The 5th November Ao. 1626.
Your High Mightinesses' obedient,
P. Schaghen

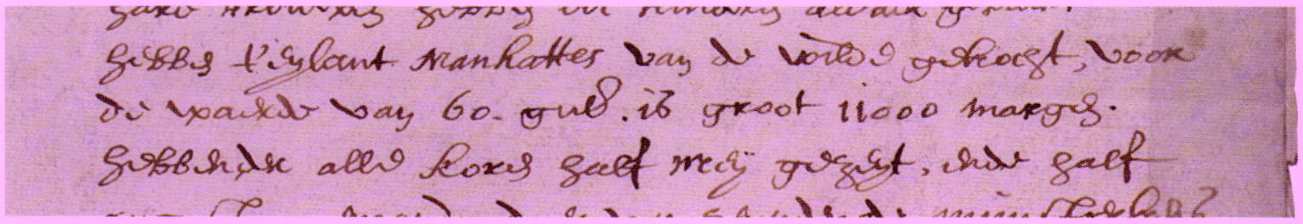

Detail of the Schagen Letter, 1626

The Purchase of Manhattan

When Pieter Schagen wrote his letter to the States General, he could not have fathomed the value that would come to be attached to his missive. This document is prized like a crown jewel because it describes the purchase of one of the most magnetic places in the world: Manhattan. This is highly exciting. Our imagination runs wild picturing a verdant island inhabited by Indians and where there was little to experience. Certainly when we compare it to that same strip of land now, with all of its skyscrapers. The difference is so great, so difficult to comprehend, that anyone reading Schagen's letter cannot help but be captivated by the idea that such a purchase was ever even possible.

Yet the letter has so much more to tell us, for instance about daily life in the colony. Children had been born, grain had been sown and the harvests were good. For the Lords of the Company in the Republic the rest of the letter was far more valuable; after all, they wanted to know the kind and number of pelts that had arrived with the ship. Legends have grown up around Schagen's letter, which is certainly understandable. The acquisition of a piece of land that would later become so important simply calls out for mythologization.

Accordingly, a fair amount of misinformation exists with respect to Pieter Schagen. For instance, it is claimed that he was actually present at the purchase of Manhattan, that he was in the service of the VOC and that he was standing on the quay in Amsterdam when the ship arrived with the news.

Some authors do not so much twist the truth, as give it their own interpretation. One claims that the sale was effected in Lower Manhattan. Others assume that the transaction actually transpired in the far north, in Inwood Hill Park. It is all guesswork, for no one knows where the sale actually took place.

The magazine Fortune once dubbed the purchase of Manhattan, understood by the Indians as a treaty of friendship, as "the best business deal ever." The idea that the Indians would have understood the sale as a "friendship treaty" is debatable. They gave their land to the Dutch on loan in exchange for goods. In other words, the agreement was not a purely altruistic affair for the Indians either. The "best business deal ever" is true only with today's knowledge. This claim would only have held water had the land already been so valuable back then. However, the island was worth no more or less than the surrounding region. Moreover, the two parties did not interpret "the deal" the same way. For the Indians it was a matter of giving the land on loan, not an outright sale. Had the Indians actually sold their land then we could speak of an equal interpretation and of a "deal".

Was the purchase price of goods valued at 60 guilders reasonable? In the eyes of the Dutch it will not have been an enormous amount of money. In 1628 Reverend Michaëlius wrote that at that time the Dutch could buy large tracts of land for relatively low prices. Perhaps he was also referring to the purchase of Manhattan.[1]

The Schagen Letter: The "Deed of Purchase" of Manhattan?

The "Schagen letter" is often referred to as the deed of purchase of Manhattan. While a truly remarkable document, it is in no way a deed of purchase. It was written by Pieter Jansz. Schagen, who represented the States General at the meeting of WIC's directors, the Lords Nineteen, in Amsterdam at the end of 1626. Schagen never went to New Netherland and therefore did not actually witness the transaction. He included an interesting bit of news he had picked up from a ship, the *Wapen van Amsterdam* (Arms of Amsterdam), which had just arrived from New Netherland, namely the purchase of a piece of land, Manhattan. Schagen most likely penned his letter in the West India House in Amsterdam and addressed it to his colleagues in the States General in The Hague.

Schagen's letter, thus, is not a deed of purchase. With the sentence: "...our people are in good spirit and live in peace. The women also have borne some children there. They have purchased the Island Manhattes from the Indians for the value of 60 guilders; it is 11,000 morgens in size [about 22,000 acres]," Schagen was referring to the purchase of Manhattan for goods worth 60 guilders. Perhaps the captain of the *Wapen van Amsterdam*, Adriaen Jorisz. Thienpont, brought the official deed with him. Whether it actually still exists and, if it does, where it might be found is unknown. We do know with certainty that a copy of the deed was once made.[2] The phrase "for the value of 60 guilders" gave rise to yet another misunderstanding. The letter was discovered in the nineteenth century in the archives of the States General, a logical place to find it since it was addressed to this governing body. The amount of 60 guilders was converted to the dollar rate of the day, giving rise to the myth that Manhattan was bought for 24 dollars.
The payment to the Indians, in reality a number of objects worth 60 guilders at that time, will have consisted of cauldrons, knifes, axes, hoes, wampum or cloth. At the time of the purchase, 60 guilders were equal in value to 30 beaver pelts.[3] To gain some perspective of this sum, it is useful to compare it to the wages of a common soldier, which were eight or nine guilders a month; Manhattan was bought for an amount equivalent to seven or eight month's worth of a soldier's salary. As another example, the 60 guilders can be measured against the value of the load of beaver and otter pelts brought back on the ship, which was close to 45,000 guilders.[4]

"The best business deal ever"

This twentieth-century print depicts the purchase of Manhattan. It is an amusing interpretation of the event, but whether or not it transpired this way is up for debate. The goods shown for barter in the print will have been different in reality. Here fabric and beads are being offered, but more likely these were items of everyday use such as axes, hoes, cauldrons and knives.

Pieter Minuit Buying the Island of Manhattan
New York Public Library, New York
ID: 808099
Engraving

Who Actually Owned Manhattan?

The American natives interpreted the concept of "purchase" differently than the Dutch. The Indians considered the transaction as an agreement, in which in exchange for goods the other party would be free to do as they pleased in the agreed upon region: a kind of non-exclusive loan. Land ownership as understood by the Europeans was unknown to the Indians. From their point of view, no one actually owned land. Like water or air, land could not be possessed. Indians used the land to fish, to hunt, for cultivation or habitation. The "purchase" was more like an exclusive use rights. The newcomers were permitted to move there, and reclaim and cultivate the land. This did not mean, that the Indians were actually giving up their rights, for they simply took back the land once the Dutch temporarily abandoned it. This emerges from the repeated "sale" of the rights. An example of this is Staten Island, which the Munsee Indians "sold" more than once.[5]

For the Dutch, however, the purchase meant something very different indeed. It guaranteed the safety of New Amsterdam and the surrounding farmsteads. After all, the Company could produce the deed if challenged by the Indians or other European nations. The Dutch had been ordered by the Amsterdam Chamber not to drive the Indians from land they wished to use, certainly not with force or against their will. Nor were private individuals allowed to buy land from the Indians, this was the prerogative of the WIC directors. The Company clearly stipulated that contracts were to be drawn up.[6]

In other words, the "buyers" of the land would have assumed that they officially owned it after the "purchase." But, there were others who contested the Dutch territory; in the previous years the English had claimed a territory to which Manhattan, according to them, also belonged.

A Difficult Start and Exodus, 1626-1628

When Pieter Minuit "bought" Manhattan from the Indians in 1626, the first settlers had already been living there for some time. New Amsterdam finally began to take shape in the fall of that year. The village had a fort, and 30 wooden houses for the settlers had been built along "The Strand." The village had but a single stone building. This was the comptoir, or office, the WIC's headquarters in the colony, where the furs were stored and prepared for transport to the Republic. Finally, there was a mill, the upper storey of which was used for religious services.[7] This short description would seem to sketch a peaceful image of the budding community. Nothing could be farther from the truth. These were turbulent times for New Amsterdam's early inhabitants. They had experienced first hand Verhulst's short-lived tenure as director of the colony. His anything but cooperative attitude towards the colonists, who tried to acquire as many pelts as possible to sell to the WIC, had stirred up a lot of ill will. His harsh policy in dealing with the colonists who refused to work on the Company's farms had also backfired.

Verhulst's singular lack of administrative skills was reported by the Company's secretary, Isaac de Rasière, in a letter of 22 September 1626 to the directors in the Republic. He wrote that the director and his advisors did not see eye to eye. Worse, his bookkeeping was sloppy and unsound and Verhulst had even had the audacity to use Company money for his own gain! Matters reached such a head that Verhulst threatened to go work for the English or French. He was subsequently dismissed and replaced by Minuit. Verhulst was ordered to await the arrival of the ship the *Wapen van Amsterdam* (Arms of Amsterdam) that would subsequently convey him back to his fatherland. Upon docking in Amsterdam, the ship not only delivered Verhulst, but also De Rasière's letter spelling out his policy and the above-discussed reference to the purchase of Manhattan.[8]

Tall Stories[9]

Minuit's years as director were riddled with problems between the Indians and the colonists. The Indians complained about the abuse they suffered at the hands of the servants of the WIC. If they were not left alone, they would drive out the Dutch – with violence if need be, at least that is what they threatened to do. At the same time there were increasing reports of war among the various Indian tribes issuing from Fort Orange (now Albany) at the headwaters of the North (Hudson) River.

In the spring of 1626 the Dutch in Fort Orange were embroiled in a conflict between the Mahicans and the Mohawks, two tribes living nearby. The Mahicans asked the commander of the Fort, Daniel van Crieckenbeeck, whom we already encountered in 1623 as a customs officer on the ship the *Mackreel* (Mackerel), for help in their battle with the Mohawks.

Their number was large, that of Van Crieckenbeeck and his men small. There was little else they could do but agree to their request. With six of his men Van Crieckenbeeck took up arms against the Mohawks. His intervention flew in the face of the Company's injunction to remain impartial in intra-tribal disputes. Van Crieckenbeeck and his men headed west into Mohawk territory. Betrayed by the sudden partisanship of the

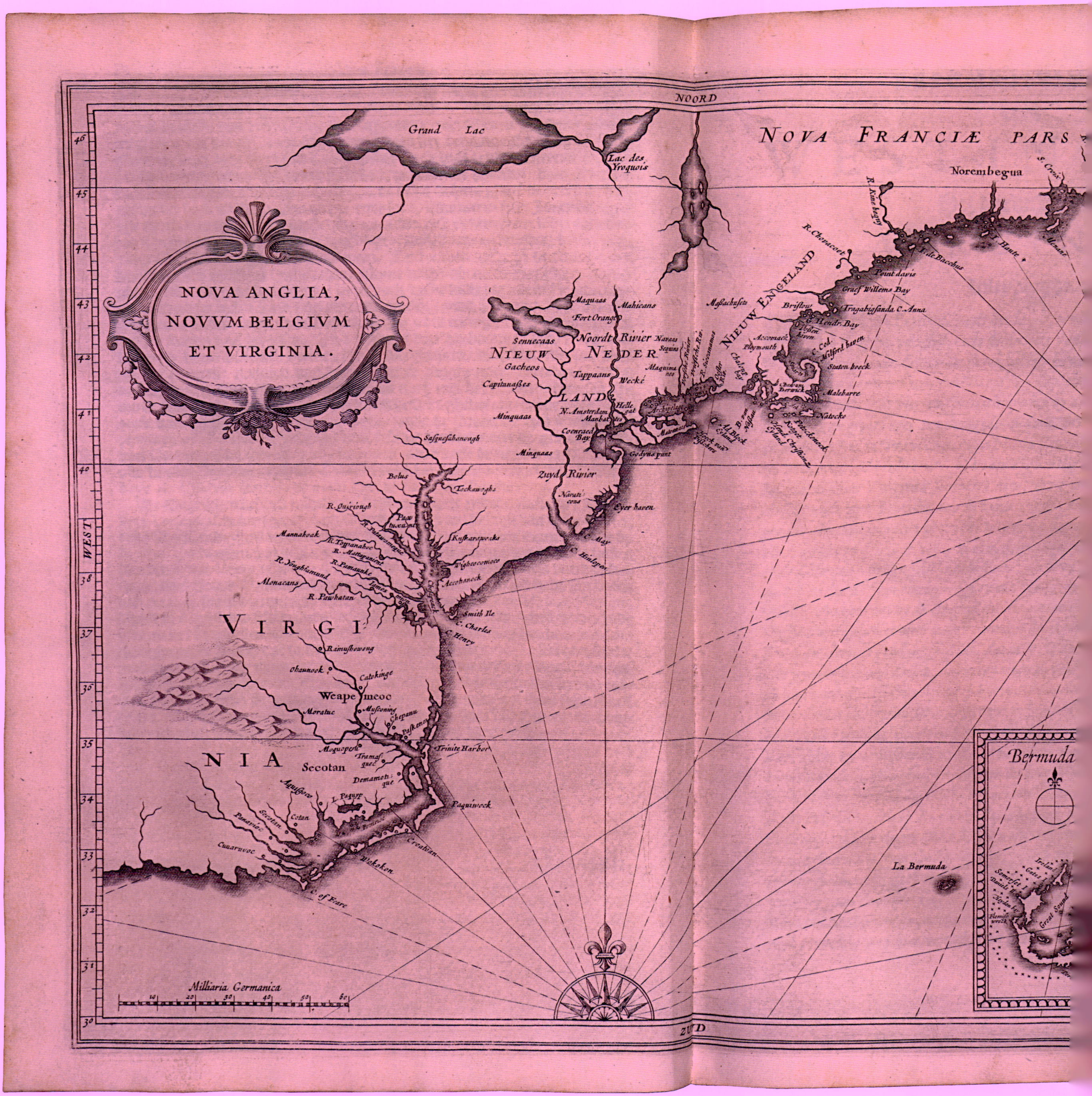
NOORD
ZUYD
WEST
NOVA ANGLIA, NOVVM BELGIVM ET VIRGINIA.
NOVA FRANCIÆ PARS
Grand Lac
Lac des Yroquois
Norembegua
NIEUW ENGELAND
NIEUW NEDER LAND
Noordt Rivier
Zuyd Rivier
Fort Orange
Maquaas
Mahicans
Sennecaas
Gacheos
Capitanasses
Tappaans
Wecké
Minquaas
N. Amsterdam
Godyns punt
Ever haven
C. Hinlopen
Massachusets
Plymouth
Staten hoeck
Malebarre
Natocke
Hendr. Bay
Point davis
Sasquesahanough
Tockwoughs
Kuskarawacks
Smith Ile
C. Charles
C. Henry
VIRGINIA
Weapemeoc
Secotan
Trinité Harbor
Paquiwock
Croatoan
Wokokon
C. of Feare
R. Pawhatan
Monacans
Mannahoak
Bermuda
La Bermuda
Milliaria Germanica

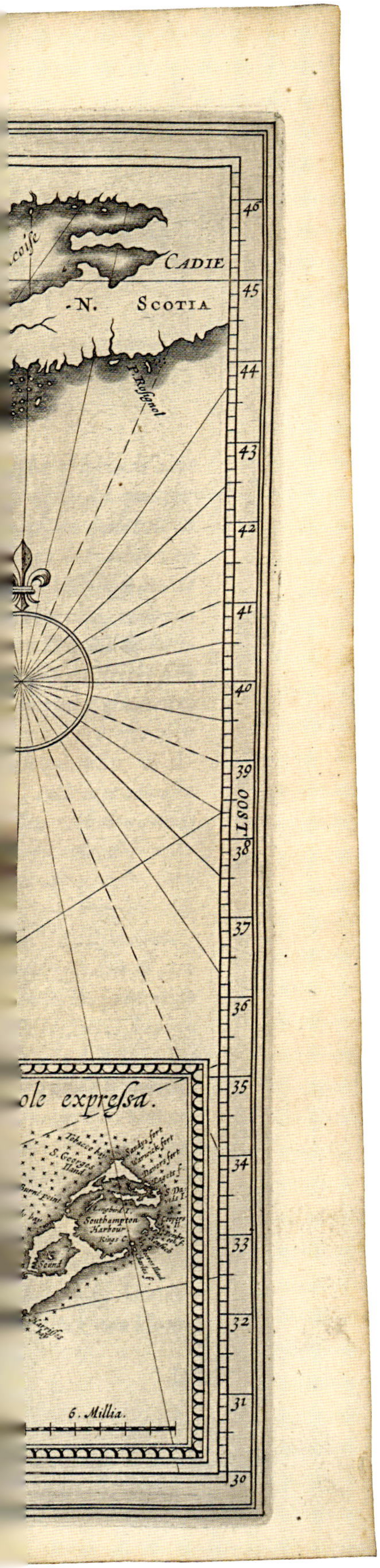

"Novum Belgium" or "New Netherland"

The first time the name Manhattan features in a printed map is on this one in Johannes de Laet's *Nieuwe Wereldt* (New World). The island is spelled "Manbattes." The following names are also included for the first time: "N. Amsterdam." "Fort Orange," "Noordt Rivier," "Zuyd Rivier" and "Massachusetts."[10]
The map was published by Hessel Gerritsz. in 1630, 21 years after Henry Hudson sailed up the North (Hudson) River. In addition to being a publisher Gerritsz. was a cartographer, an engraver and a chief map-maker in the service of the VOC. Fourteen of his maps appeared in the second edition of Johannes de Laet's *Nieuwe Wereldt* of 1630.

"Novum Belgium" or "New Netherland"
"Nova Anglia, Novum Belgium et Virginia" (New England, New Netherland and Virginia)
Hessel Gerritsz., 1630
In J. de Laet, *Nieuwe Wereldt ofte Beschrijvinghe van West-Indien* (The New World or Description of the West Indies), 1630
Nationaal Archief (National Archives of the Netherlands), The Hague
Library 399 B 7
Paper, 32.5 x 22 x 5.5 cm

Dutch, these Native Americans retaliated in no uncertain terms: they killed and burned Van Crieckenbeeck and three of his men. One of them, Tymen Bouwensz., was roasted and partially eaten. The other three, two Portuguese and a man from Hoorn, just managed to escape. [11]

After the Van Crieckenbeeck incident, Minuit decided it was high time to strengthen the bonds with the Mohawks. First he sent the trading agent Pieter Barentsz. to talk with them. Barentsz., who was familiar with several of the Indian languages, investigated the commander's death. He discussed the matter with the Mohawks and tried to convince them that Van Crieckenbeeck had acted on his own initiative. Barentsz. explained to the Mohawks that the Company strictly censured partisanship. To lend weight to his words Minuit himself sailed upriver. He realized that the wars in these remote regions posed too great a threat to the colonists. He could ensure their safety only by relocating them. It is also possible that the Mohawks insisted Minuit take the colonists, leaving only a handful of trading agents behind at Fort Orange.

In his aforementioned letter, Isaac de Rasière noted that he had missed Director Minuit when he dropped anchor in Manhattan: "Having arrived here I did not find Minuit as he had sailed to Fort Orange to investigate the accident resulting from Van Crieckenbeeck's bold enterprise."[12]

De Rasière also wrote that Minuit had appointed a new head at Fort Orange: Bastiaen Jansz. Krol. He mentioned that Krol was well versed in the language of the Indians. Minuit had fully understood just how important it was to use people who could communicate with the Indians, first by allowing the trading agent Pieter Barentsz. to make peace with the Mohawks and later by putting Bastiaen Jansz. Krol in charge of Fort Orange. Krol had headed to New Netherlands as a lay minister in 1624. He was the first to be authorized to baptize and marry the inhabitants of the colony.[13] Years later, when Minuit was recalled the Dutch Republic in 1632, Krol took his place as director for the space of a year.

How to Get a Colony Up and Running

While Minuit was busy trying to find solutions to restore the bond with the Indians, carpenters were hard at work building Fort New Amsterdam. One of Minuit's first decisions in this respect was to radically alter the building plans drawn up by the Dutch engineer Cryn Fredericksz. The latter had planned to erect a pentagonal fort in which everyone could live. However, there was hardly enough manpower to raise such a large structure. Hence, its size was reduced and it was provided with four rather than five bastions. The fort would have been enhanced with a

A Letter Loaded with Information

Isaac de Rasière, secretary of the New Netherland colony, set foot on Manhattan on 27 July 1626 only to discover that Willem Verhulst had been dismissed and Pieter Minuit appointed director by the Board.[14] De Rasière returned to the Republic in 1628. His letter is addressed to Samuel Blommaert, director of the WIC, though it is not entirely clear whether he still held that position when he received it. Most likely, Blommaert, who intended to found a patroonship in New Netherland, had asked De Rasière for the most recent news about the colony. Any useful information was more than welcome. Knowing which grounds were fertile and which areas safe would enable Blommaert to take the necessary measures from the Dutch Republic in preparation of his new enterprise. It is entirely possible that thanks to De Rasière's indications he knew exactly which region he would choose when he purchased his land.
De Rasière's letter to Blommaert is an account of his observations of New Netherland, which commences with his arrival in the colony on 27 July 1626. He mentions that work had begun on building a fort, for instance, and continues with a description of the island of Manhattan and the Indians. Below is a sample of some of the more interesting passages in the letter:

On the 27th of July, Anno 1626, by the Grace of God, I arrived with the ship, the *Arms of Amsterdam*, before the bay of the great Mauritius River, sailing into it about a musket shot from Godijn's Point, into Coenraet's Bay because there the greatest depth is...."

The land is in many places good, and fit for plowing and sowing. It has many fine valleys, where there is good grass. Their form of government is like that of their neighbors, which is described hereafter."

"...the Mauritius River in the highlands, thus making the northwest land opposite to Manhatas [Manhattan], an island 18 leagues long. It is inhabited by the old Manhatesen, about 2[00?] to 300 strong, women and men, under different chiefs, who they call Sackimas [Sachems]."

"The six farms, four of which lie along the River Hells' Gate, stretching to the south side of the island, have at least 60 morgens of land ready to be sown with winter seed...The two hintermost farms, Nos. 1 and 2, are the best; the other farms also have good earth, but not so much, and more sandy; so that they are best suited for rye and buckwheat."

"The small fort, New Amsterdam, commenced to be built, is situated on a point opposite to Noten (Governors) Island..."

"Up the river the east side is high, full of trees, and in some places there is a little good land, where formerly many people have dwelt, but who for the most part have died or have been driven away by the Wappenos. These tribes of savages all have a government. The men in general are rather tall, with well proportioned limbs, and of an orange cast like the Brazilians; very inveterate against those whom they hate; cruel by nature, and so inclined to freedom that they cannot by any means be brought to work...."

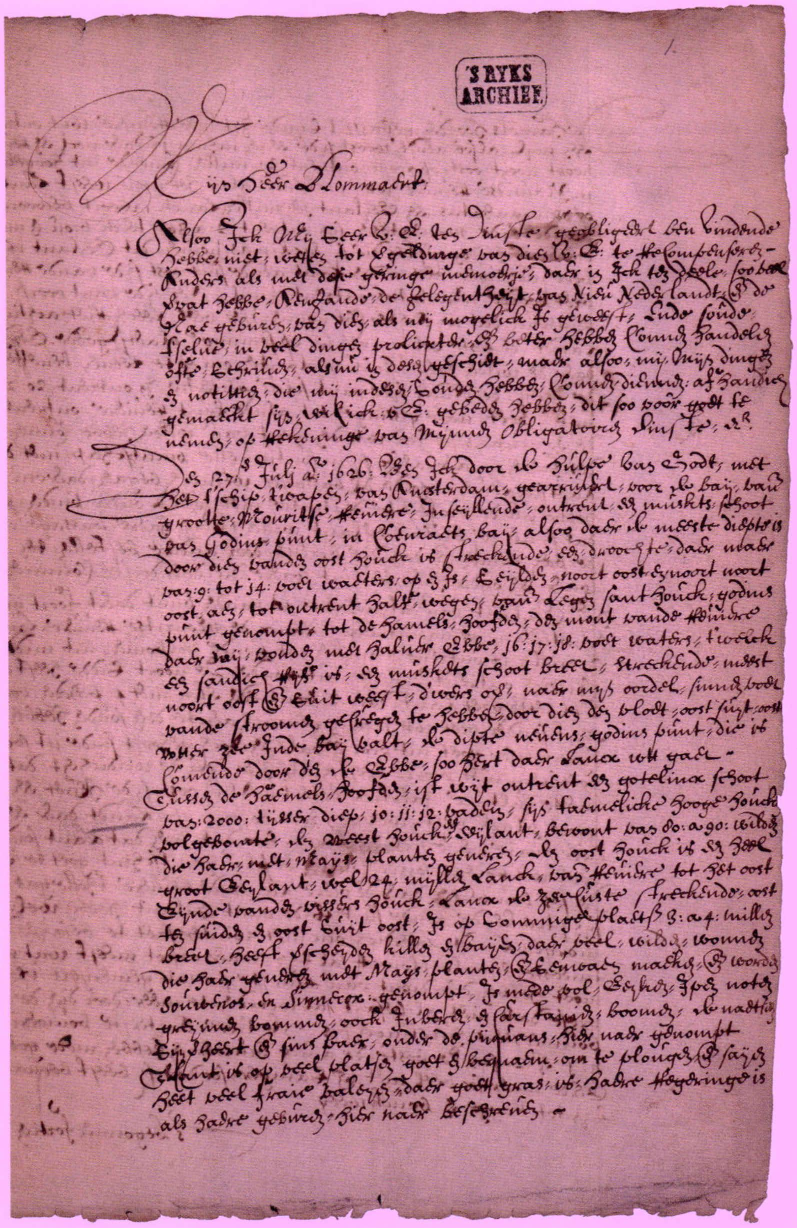

Letter from Isaac de Rasière to Samuel Blommaert, ca. 1628
Dutch National Archive, The Hague
Verspreide Westindische Stukken, 1.05.06, inv. no. 2
Ink on paper, 33.5 x 22 cm

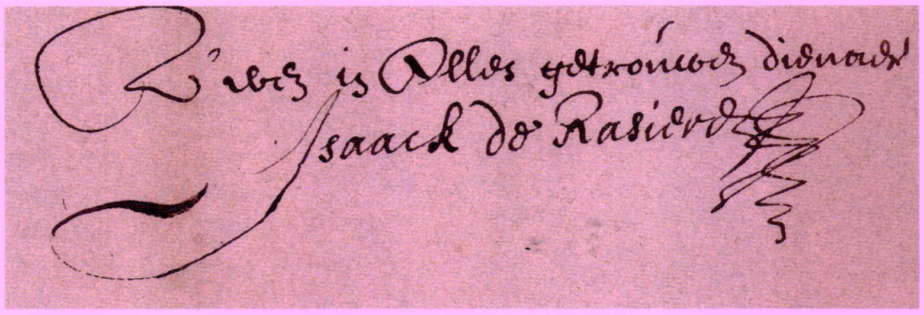

Detail of the Letter from Isaac de Rasière to Samuel Blommaert, ca. 1628

handsome commanders quarters and other delights had Minuit not seen to it that the expensive building materials were used for other purposes, namely housing for the colonists. And this was sorely needed, for there was a serious shortage of solid dwellings for Manhattan's first inhabitants. By cutting back on the fort in favor of housing construction, Minuit had the inhabitants of New Amsterdam eating from the palm of his hand.[14]

With the new dwellings for the colonists Minuit had earned some credit and solved a pressing problem. This, however, did not spell the end to all their worries. Verhulst's legacy included dubious bookkeeping, the pilfering of goods from the Company's warehouse and disappointing profits from the fur trade. In addition to the volatile situation with the Indians, the directorship had its hands full with its own people. The agreement between the Company and the Flemish Walloon settlers was that they would work as a community to get the colony off the ground. Their contribution in this respect fell miserably short. The Walloons could not have been less interested in the work the Company offered them. Other hired workers were also difficult to motivate, as emerges from a passage in De Rasière's letter. For instance, the laborers in the service of Cornelis van Vorst could only be kept working by means of violence, De Rasière groused: "The people of Cornelis van Vorst do not amount to much as they are rough and must be persuaded to work through force."[15] For the colonists the trade in beaver fur was much more attractive for the simple reason that it generated more money and was easier than the physical labor the colony required of the men.

Then there were any number of other start-up problems plaguing the small community: people were caught smuggling, fires had broken out and livestock had perished. The storerooms were full of goods that could not be traded for the otter and beaver skins. Iron cauldrons, which initially had been so popular with the Indians, were no longer in demand because they were too heavy to transport on foot over long distances. And what to do with the many damaged cauldrons: "110 damaged cauldrons were sent over, which cannot be sold here because they are broken and leak," De Rasière wrote to the Amsterdam Chamber. He advised his superiors to send duffels – warm woolen blankets produced in the Southern Netherlands – instead of the cauldrons from then on.

The Dutch could exchange the duffels for *sewant*, or wampum, beads made from shells that were coveted by the Indians. There was a shortage of this commodity in various regions occupied by the Indians. There the Dutch could use the wampum they had received in exchange for the duffels to obtain beaver skins.[16] The Amsterdam Chamber, charged with overseeing New Netherland, met the secretary's plan with reserve. His proposal would mean that even more capital would have to be pumped into the region, and this while the colonization had already cost so much and yielded so little profit.

The beaver furs fetched a reasonable price in Amsterdam, but the effort it took to acquire them called for substantial investments. In 1627 four ships were sent to the colony to collect the pelts. Not one returned with a full hold. Therefore, in the following year only two ships were sent out. Even this cost-reducing measure of 50 percent did not yield a profit for the company.[17] The homeward bound vessels of 1627 and 1628 brought cargo back to the Dutch Republic which differed greatly from a shipment turning a profit or at least breaking even: namely, the first colonists to return.

The Walloons Pack it In

It is not difficult to understand why a large number of settlers gave up their pioneer's existence and returned to the Dutch Republic upon the termination of their contract. The population struggled with the Indians, with the management and with each other. The work was grueling and there was little diversion. Primarily, though, there was hardly any community spirit in the young town. "The church," led by New Amsterdam's first Dutch Reformed minister Jonas Michaëlius, was unable to instill a sense of belonging in its congregation. Michaëlius was sent to the colony to establish the first Dutch Reformed Church by the classis of Amsterdam on 7 January 1628. The colonists living in the island's far-flung farms rarely went to church. They were mostly Walloon and spoke French, Dutch or another European language. Michaëlius' command of French was limited and he had difficulty making contact with "his" people.[18] He specially adapted the Eucharist for the Walloons. Naturally, this then raised consternation among the congregation. It was a matter of give and take; the church could only continue to exist by making compromises.[19]

His difficult personality – he was known as a fractious, sullen man – will also have contributed to the atmosphere. Writing to an Amsterdam colleague on 11 August 1628, Michaëlius complained about the settlement's poverty, the colonists' coarse nature and the Indians' devil worship. In the same letter the Reverend also mourned the loss of his wife. He felt inconvenienced now that he had to carry on on his own. He missed butter and milk, bread and fruit. He felt that many more farmers should come in order to facilitate their production.[20] De Rasière also elected to leave behind his life in New Netherland. After only two years as secretary for the Company he returned to Amsterdam.

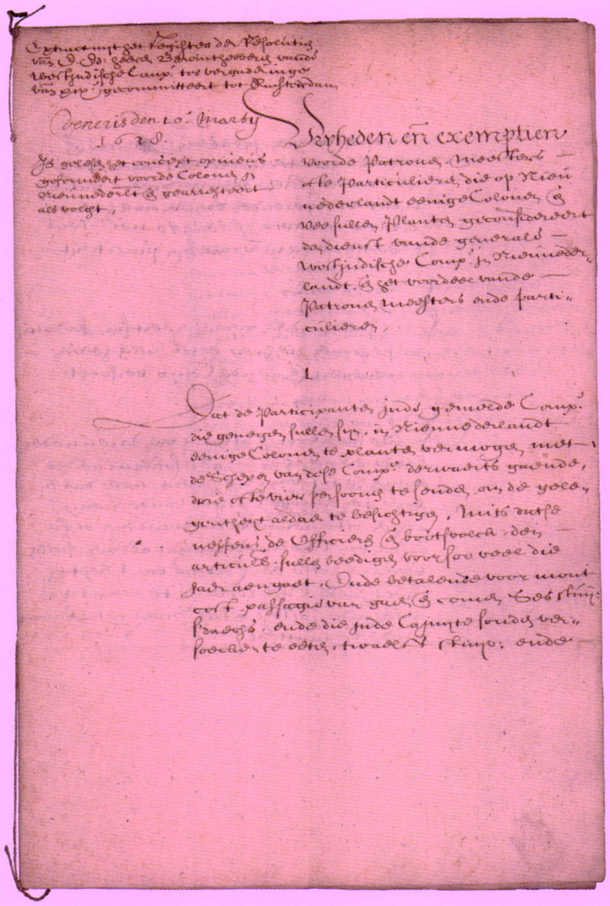

Vryheden en exemptien

Vryheden en Exemptiën (Charter of Liberties and Exemptions) 1628
Nationaal Archief (National Archives of the Netherlands), The Hague
Wassenaer van Duvenvoorde, 3.20.87, inv. no. 2052[21]
Ink on paper

Vryheden ende Exemptien voor de Patroonen / Meesters ofte Particulieren / die op Nieu-Nederlandt eenighe Colonien ende Vee sullen planten / gheconsidereert ten dienst van de generale West-Indische Compagnie in Nieu-Nederlandt / ende het voordeel van de Patroonen / Meesters ende Particulieren.

I.

Vryheden en Exemptiën
Royal Library, The Hague
Signature: pflt 4000
Printed pamphlet, 15 x 20 cm

New Rules for the Colony

The fur trade was thrown open, and the free entrepreneurs from the Dutch Republic could finally begin to profit from the overseas colony. The new rules were laid down in *Vryheden en Exemptiën* (Charter of Liberties and Exemptions). According to these regulations, fur traders who went to work for the patroons no longer had to first hand over their beaver pelts to the Company, but could sell them themselves. The WIC, though, did excise duty on the beavers at one guilder per skin. However, as the free fur trade applied to only a part of New Netherland, namely those areas where the Company had no customs officers, the WIC still largely retained control of this trade. And so the new prospects for the fur trade did not really amount to much: in reality the partially deregulated trade was merely a carrot. The WIC wanted to engineer a situation to entice patroons to join in the agricultural enterprises and the partial free trade. If they took the bait, the colony could become populated more rapidly.

The *Vryheden en Exemptiën* dictated that the Company would impose duties on the import and export of other goods. In return, the WIC would assume responsibility for the protection of the patroons and the colonists against all enemies, both domestic and European. Manhattan continued to function as a staple market for the goods and still belonged to the WIC. The patroons were entitled to buy the land in New Netherland from the Indians and were free to set up the estates as they saw fit. As a result the patroonships became independent entities with their own juridical authority and administrators. The patroonships, thus, were similar to the domains in the Republic to which seigniorial rights were attached. The lords who “lent” the estates to third parties also extended a package of privileges, which varied from manor to manor. Those receiving the manors on loan had, just like the patroons of the patroonships, certain privileges varying from the collection of tithes, tolls and rents to fishing and hunting rights.

The future patroons would be the rightful owners of all of the fruit trees, flora, minerals, rivers and springs on their parcels. In addition, they would be permitted to conduct trade all along the east coast. Finally, the patroons were entitled to tax the farmers on their land up to a maximum of ten percent of all of the products ensuing from agriculture, mining and fishing.[22]

The most important duty the WIC imposed on the patroons was that they set up within four years a settlement populated by at least 50 souls, upwards of 15 years old. They could be farmers, smiths, carpenters, bakers and other craftsmen, people who would be transported to New Netherland with the Company’s ships. The new plan thus comprised a combination of a partial opening up of the market and the establishment of patroonships.[23]

Back home he complained bitterly to the directors about the colony's lawless state of affairs. In his eyes, because of the Board's lack of authority he had been forced to look on helplessly as others mocked the administration and flouted all of the rules. De Rasière made a career change and became a merchant in Brazil.[24]

A Colony, Now with Inhabitants

Minuit is still known as one of New Netherland's better directors. Was he blessed with the character traits necessary for running the disjointed community? Did he retain his composure when at the end of their contract period the Walloons abandoned Manhattan and he witnessed "his" colony drain away? Could he convince the settlers, not to mention the Company's servants, not to repatriate? Ultimately Minuit was also dependent on instructions from the Dutch Republic, which he received only a few times a year. Those of 1629 would alter the course of the colony in a way Minuit had little control over.

Back in Amsterdam it was becoming patently evident that despite the steady supply of beaver and otter furs, maintaining the colony was only going to lose money. In the years 1624-1625 alone 100,000 guilders had been spent on the colonization. The exodus from the colony in the years 1627-1628 – more people returned to the Republic than left for New Netherland – had not contributed to a healthy situation. How to get out of debt? The old debates between the Amsterdam trading and colonization factions flared up again.

One of the directors, Kiliaen van Rensselaer, steadfastly championed maintaining the colony and promoting large-scale emigration, as was discussed in the preceding chapter. His arguments gained ground and it was decided that the colony's appeal could be enhanced by permitting agricultural enterprises.

The WIC Partially Permits Free Trade

And so a new rule was devised for the colony. With investments from the Republic, patroonships – estates where farmsteads would be established – could be set up in the colony. The financiers of these agricultural ventures were patroons, or patrons, operating from the Republic. In addition to the possibility of exploiting agricultural activity, the patroons also received the opportunity of becoming involved in the fur trade, albeit on a small scale.

The new colonial structure was laid out in the *Vryheden en Exemptiën* (Charter of Liberties and Exemptions), a document ratified by the Lords Nineteen on 7 June 1629. At first sight it seemed as though the Amsterdam colonization faction had made the greatest headway with this regulation. Yet the opponents, supporters of the trade faction, were not displeased with the outcome: the WIC still had control of most of the fur monopoly. What was not known at the time was that the patroonship system would not succeed. What had seemed to be a healthy step in the direction of privatization, would wind up in disagreements regarding the interpretation of the released rights.[25]

Pieter Minuit Leaves the Colony

The new rule was devised around the conference table in Amsterdam. But how were the new plans received in New Amsterdam? There too opinion was divided: Director Pieter Minuit favored the new patroonship system, while Reverend Michaëlius and Secretary Jan van Remunde sided with the Amsterdam trade faction. However, another, unsolvable conflict had arisen between Pieter Minuit and Michaëlius. Both gentlemen were on the church council. Other members included the lay minister Bastiaen Jansz. Krol and Minuit's brother-in-law Jan Huygen. At first everything seemed to go well, until the Reverend began expressing concern about the lack of balance in the church council. In his view the religious side was underrepresented and the political side too conspicuous, which entailed confusion and conflicts of interest. Though dissention arose as a result, at that time the quarrel did not amount to much. However, matters came to a head when he voiced his criticism of Minuit as director. Michaëlius made public the fact that Minuit had attempted to take financial advantage of the Company, and the swords were as good as drawn.[26] Minuit, Michaëlius and Secretary Van Remunde were recalled to the Republic to account for their actions in 1623. The directors wanted to replace the entire administration of New Nederland. The three men embarked on the ship the *Eendracht* (Unity), an ironic name in light of their situation.[27]

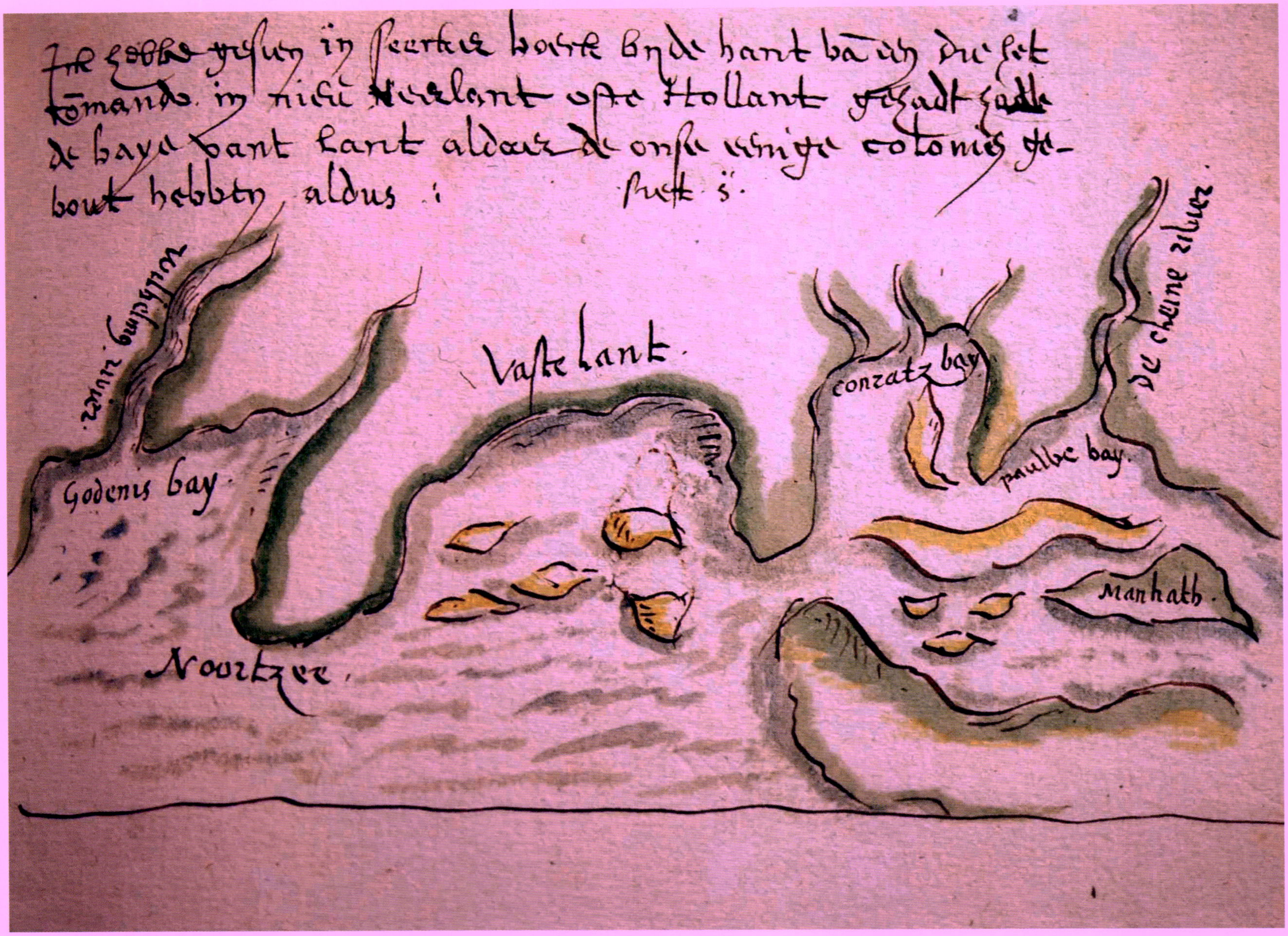

Map of the Area South of Manhattan
Diary of Buchelius, ca. 1635
Nationaal Archief (National Archives
of the Netherlands), The Hague
Aanwinsten Eerste Afdeling, 1.11.01.01,
inv. no. 256, fol. 126
Watercolor and ink on paper, 30.5 x 19.5 cm

The Land around Manhattan Carved Up and Parceled Out

Arnoldus Buchelius, or Arend van Buchel, was a director of the VOC from 1619 to 1621. As of the foundation of the WIC in 1621, he was one of the most prominent and influential shareholders of the Company. The directors of the WIC regularly consulted him. That he was entirely up to date on matters relating to the colony emerges from his diaries, which are now in the Nationaal Archief (National Archives of the Netherlands) in The Hague. One of them bears on East India and New Netherland. The descriptions of the latter colony contain a great deal of information, which he received from his family in New Netherland. A map of New Netherland was included, which was probably copied from a map owned by Pieter Minuit.[28]

The map contains the following annotation: “I have seen some work by one who was in command of New Netherland or Holland, who built our own colonies in the bay of the land there.” This is followed by the map itself.

Above the island of Manhattan lies “Pauw Bay,” which bordered on the patroonship of Michiel Pauw founded in 1630 and which was not granted a long life.[29]

The map was thus made after 1630. This date agrees with the period in which Buchelius wrote his diaries, namely from 1634 to 1641. To the left of “Pauw Bay” lies “Conratz Bay.” It, too, is named after a patroon, Albert Coenraetsz. Burgh, the owner of a patroonship that would also be short lived. At the far left we read “Godenis Bay,” referring to the bay bordering the patroonship of Swanendael located on the west bank of the South (Delaware) River (in the map called the Wilhelmus River). Swanendael was founded in 1630 by WIC director Samuel Godijn. “Godenis” is a Latinized version of his name.

The map refers to three patroons who launched their enterprises as of 1630. Therefore, the situation recorded in the map cannot date earlier than 1630, and probably not much later than 1634, given that Pauw already sold his patroonship again in that year. Pieter Minuit is thought to have been the maker of the map. It is entirely possible that he sketched it upon his return to the Dutch Republic in 1632. While this remains speculation, the German spelling “Conratz” rather than “Coenraetsz.” could betray Minuit’s hand given his German origins.[30]

Patroonships: Mini Colonies in the Colony

After the *Vryheden en Exemptiën* (Charter of Liberties and Exemptions) were issued several candidates interested in starting patroonships presented themselves. The estates to be developed were not only in North America, but also in the Caribbean.[31] The privileges for the tracts of land were generous, also by seventeenth-century standards.

Five patroons put in their bid. Kiliaen van Rensselaer, the fervent champion of colonization could finally found his own colony, Rensselaerswijck. He chose the area near Fort Orange, at the upper course of the North (Hudson) River. Just like patroon Samuel Godijn, Van Rensselaer had already dispatched scouts to New Netherland in January of 1629 to pick out the best plots of land. Samuel Godijn established his patroonship, Swanendael, on the west bank of the South (Delaware) River. The third patroon was a director of the Company, Samuel Blommaert. He set up two estates, both on the Fresh (Connecticut) River. A fourth patroon, Albert Coenraetsz. Burgh, began his settlement on the east bank of the South (Delaware) River.

It did not take long for these four gentlemen to join forces as a means of spreading the risks. Even though the agreements they reached were clear – each one retained two-fifths of the shares of his own estate and received one-fifth of the shares of the other three patroonships – the experiment failed. Burgh and Blommaert’s patroonships foundered relatively quickly. Godijn saved himself by drawing in more shareholders, helped by David Pietersz. de Vries and others.

There was a fifth patroonship. Michiel Reyniersz. Pauw had reserved a piece of land for his estates along the North (Hudson) River, facing Manhattan, which he called Pavonia. Pauw established his American estates from the Republic. He lost a fortune, sinking it into a bottomless pit.

The Rensselaerswijck Patroonship Remains Standing

The only patroonship to function fairly well was that of Kiliaen van Rensselaer. He stayed in the Republic, but had appointed someone to look after his interests on site. His estates stretched out around the upper course of the North (Hudson) River. Patroon Van Rensselaer bought the land from five Indian chiefs in August 1630. The deed was drafted in Dutch, raising the question of whether the Indian chiefs actually grasped its significance. Van Rensselaer could not have cared less: he was now the owner of an immense tract of land and would remain so until his death, after which his enterprise was managed by his sons.[32]

Rensselaerswijck gradually developed into an independently operating organ that administered its own justice. Van Rensselaer

Van Rensselaer: A Financier from the Fatherland

Kiliaen van Rensselaer was born in Hasselt, in the Province of Overijssel, around 1580. The Amsterdam jeweler Wolfert van Bijler employed his young nephew Kiliaen as a "koopmansdienaer," or merchant's servant. He learned how to trade and negotiate on his business trips throughout Europe. He also became versed in a range of political relations. We have the letters he wrote his uncle on a trip to Prague in which he discusses the absolutism in Eastern Europe versus the freer political movement in Amsterdam. When his uncle retired, Van Rensselaer started up his own commercial establishment. In 1614 he would go into business with his relative Johan van Wely. Not only did Kiliaen seek his associates within his family, but also his wife: he married his cousin Hillegond van Bijler in 1616. They had two sons, Hendrik and Johan. The first died young, and the second took over Rensselaerswijck after his father's death. In the same year Kiliaen's business partner, Johan van Wely, was killed. Van Rensselaer subsequently worked for four more years in the partnership they had set up. He developed into a successful and multi-faceted entrepreneur, as a broker in jewelry and precious metals and as a land developer. His investments varied from clearing moors for agriculture to land reclamation by means of drainage. When the WIC was founded in 1621, Van Rensselaer also detected new possibilities. He was directly active in the WIC as director of the Amsterdam Chamber. Within the Chamber Van Rensselaer was known as a supporter of colonization. After the death of his wife, Hillegond, he married Anna van Wely, the daughter of his former associate Johan, in 1627. Four sons and four daughters issued from this union. Three of the boys later became directors of Rensselaerswijck, the fourth became a clergyman. Van Rensselaer retired as director of the Amsterdam Chamber of the WIC in 1631. From then on he devoted himself to the further development of the new colony that bore his name. Kiliaen van Rensselaer died in October 1643.[33]

Plaque Commemorating Kiliaen van Rensselaer, 1643
Oude Kerk, Amsterdam
Photo: David Cohen de Lara, 2009

invested vast sums of money in his colony; livestock had to be transported from the fatherland, supplies had to be stockpiled and workers had to be contracted from every corner of the earth. Achieving all of this required boundless stamina. Workers were difficult to find and a regulated transport of livestock to the colony was virtually impossible: the ships could hardly spare any space for this and the Company refused to build stables below deck. The resourceful patroon devised his own solution to the problem. He began breeding cattle at a farm in Manhattan and paid for its transportation to Rensselaerswijck himself![34]

1640, Free Trade at Long Last

With Rensselaerswijck as the only remaining patroonship, New Netherland still did not develop into the prosperous well-populated colony envisaged by the colonization faction. In reality the patroonship plan had failed, the colony remained seriously dependent on the fatherland for its survival. Why was the Company unable to effect a healthy economic situation? Evidently the Company's offer had not been attractive enough for such a risky undertaking as setting up a patroonship. People simply could not stomach the high taxes levied on every single pelt that was brought in.

In addition, the undertaking received insufficient support from the Amsterdam Chamber, and of those who had initially suggested the plan, too few were left who could take on the opposition. Finally, the agreements with the Company were too exacting: there were too many rules, for example compulsory use of the Company's ships and the payment of levies to the Company. Perhaps the most important reason for the failure was that the Company itself had not invested a single penny! The colony's infrastructure remained substandard. If the WIC wanted to retain the area, it would have to relinquish its monopoly. And, indeed, in 1640, when a new version of the patroonship system was introduced, it abandoned the fur monopoly entirely.[35]

Free trade was appealing to trading houses and merchants. Less advantageous was the regulation requiring extant patroonships to pay a tenth of the yield from the land in taxes. The new regulation deviated the most from that of 1629 on these two points. Now that the WIC had bid farewell to its monopoly on the fur trade new patroons were free to take the bait in large numbers. Except that they didn't. The number of new investors could be counted on one hand. Godard van Reede and Cornelis Melijn had chosen Staten Island as the location for their patroonship, which became a successful enterprise. All of the other initiatives bit the dust in no time. Despite the new regulations and liberties Rensselaerswijck once again remained standing.

While the number of new patroonships fell far short of expectations, the number of private merchants – mostly operating on a seasonal basis – grew.

Consensus at a Remove

The survival of New Netherland depended on the compromises reached between the two factions of the Amsterdam Chamber. It should also be noted that at times one faction was stronger than the other. This politic of compromise and rapidly alternating balance of power determined the advent and development of New Netherland. By the time a new director of the colony – after much worry and a long journey – was finally appointed and installed, an entirely new faction could have gotten the upper hand back in Amsterdam. This problem recurred with virtually all of the appointments of directors, the legislation of the colonization and the patroonships.

In addition we must not forget that both the directors of the WIC and the directors in the Amsterdam Chamber could have had personal and economic interests at heart when making their decisions. This loomed large primarily in the run-up years of the patroonships. The investors, that is board members, continually scored legally and economically off of one another. Private interests conflicted with the interests of the WIC. For instance, former directors suddenly became patroons with their own investments. To obtain the best land the new patroons tried to get the better of one another. Yet right after establishing themselves they entered into some form of cooperation to successfully run their colonies, being unanimously hindered in this by those trying to allow the WIC to make a profit. The sitting WIC directors appointed people whom they hoped would promote their interests, but by the time they actually arrived in New Netherland, the constellation of the administration in the Republic had changed and the wrong man for the new interested parties was now in New Netherland.

Map of Rensselaerswijck
Gillis van Scheyndel, 1630-1632
New York State Library, Albany
Parchment, 58 x 179 cm

The WIC and Rensselaerswijck: A Troubled Marriage

The patroonship of Rensselaerswijck covered a large tract of land along the Hudson River, as can be seen in this undated and unsigned map. The first rough sketches for this map are thought to have been made by Gillis van Scheyndel of around 1630, while the actual map originated one or two years later in the Dutch Republic. Van Rensselaer himself lived and worked in the Dutch Republic, from where he ran his patroonship. Initially, Van Rensselaer, and the other patroons as well, received little cooperation from the trade faction in Amsterdam, which in the beginning of the 1630s gained ever more power. In no time at all a fierce difference of opinion arose between the Chamber and the patroons. According to the *Vryheden en Exemptiën* (Charter of Liberties and Exemptions), the patroons were allowed to trade in fur only in those regions where the WIC had not stationed a customs officer. The patroons assumed this meant those areas that were designated at the time that the *Vryheden en Exemptiën* were proclaimed. The Company disagreed. After the proclamation of the *Vryheden en Exemptiën* they had appointed customs officers all over the place, assuming that the patroons' trading range had thus been contained. A deadlock ensued. Aside from this there was no consensus about the borders of the territories mentioned in the Vryheden en Exemptiën. The patroons felt that no matter what they were permitted to conduct trade in their own patroonships and inland. Pelts acquired in these regions were free of excise duties, in their view.

All hell broke loose between the Company and the patroons. The Company defended itself by making it widely known which areas belonged to it, and where the fur trade was prohibited to unauthorized persons, even in regions belonging to the patroons. The latter did not take kindly to this. A protracted court case followed in the Republic. There was but one solution: the Company would have to buy out the patroons. Which is exactly what they did. Van Rensselaer made it clear that he would go along only if the bid was high. The Company did not comply, and Van Rensselaer stood his ground. The battlefront between Van Rensselaer and the Company settled down for some years. At times they even collaborated, though sooner out of necessity than friendship. When it became known that a new *Vryheden en Exemptiën* would appear in 1640 and that the patroonship system would be altered, Van Rensselaer was wary, and rightly so. The Company did not prove to be a trustworthy partner. It had kept the definitive text of the new regulation secret until the States General had approved the concept. For Van Rensselaer this was "an outrageous perversion and a venomous Italian trick" (was dat 'een schandelijcke verdraijinge ende eenen vergiftigen Italiaenschen streeck).[36]

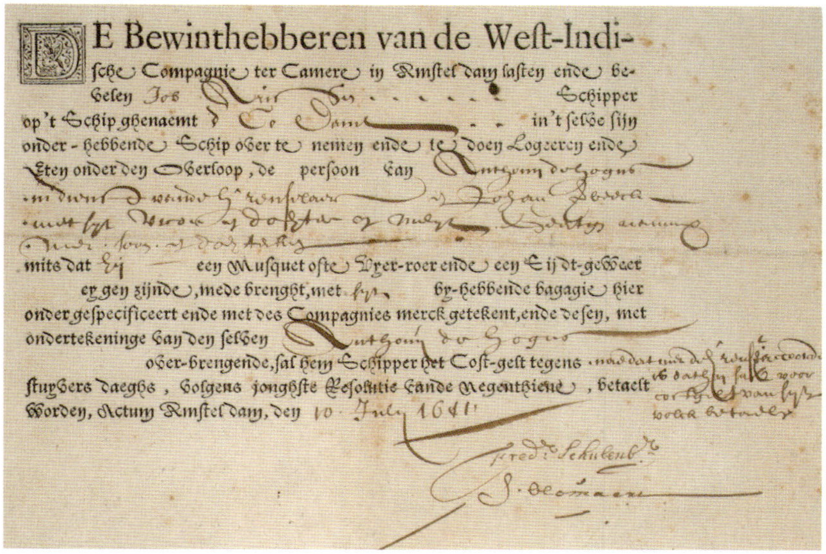

DE Bewinthebberen van de West-Indische Compagnie ter Camere in Amsteldam lasten ende bevelen Job [illegible] Schipper op't Schip ghenaemt [illegible] in't selve sijn onder-hebbende Schip over te nemen ende te doen Logeeren ende Eten onder den Overloop, de persoon van Anthony de Hooges [illegible]
mits dat hij een Musquet ofte Vyer-roer ende een Sijdt-geweer ergen zijnde, mede brenght, met hy by-hebbende bagagie hier onder gespecificeert ende met des Compagnies merck geteekent, ende desen, met onderteeckeninge van den selven Anthony de Hooges over-brengende, sal hem Schipper het Cost-gelt tegens [illegible] stuyvers daeghs, volgens jonghste Resolutie vande Negenthiene, betaelt worden, Actum Amstelдam, den 10 July 1641

[illegible]

Fred. Schulenb.

J. [illegible]

Agreement between the Compagnie and Captain Job Arisz., 1641
National Maritime Museum, Amsterdam
Ink on paper

People for the Crossing

Attracted by the free fur trade, after 1640 increasing numbers of pioneers came to New Netherland. Usually they worked in the colony only in the trading season. Transportation had to be arranged for these passengers. This was done in all kinds of ways, with ships of the WIC, as well as private vessels. Once in a while, the WIC gave permission to passengers to travel to the colony with specific ships. For example, on 10 July 1641, Captain Job Arisz. was asked whether he could organize the crossing for several passengers on his ship the *Coninck David* (King David).

PEARL ST
PHANTOM

Annetje Jans

From King's Daughter to Matriarch of Millions

Annetje Jans, sometimes known as Anneke, is considered the matriarch of the Dutch population of the United States of America. The story goes that she was the granddaughter of William the Silent, Prince of Orange and Stadholder of the Dutch Republic. Her father was supposedly an Amsterdam merchant named Wolfert Webber, her mother Anna a daughter of the Stadholder. Anneke was brought up in the royal palace in The Hague where, in the palace pleasure gardens, she fell in love with a gardener named Roelof Janszoon. Because he came from a low social class, the couple had to marry in secret. When grandfather William of Orange (referred to in the story as King rather than merely Stadholder) discovered this, he banished Anneke from the royal residence and disinherited her. He was generous enough to invest her inheritance share in the Bank of Holland, with the proviso that Anneke's heirs would have a right to it only after seven generations. By the nineteenth century Anneke's descendants numbered in the tens of millions.

An intriguing tale, but it contains scarcely a word of truth. There are few New Amsterdammers around whom so many myths have built up. Who exactly was Anneke? She was born in 1604 or 1605 in the Norwegian town of Fleckerøy. Her parents moved to Amsterdam where, at the age of about nineteen, she married Roelof Janszoon. This Roelof seems to be virtually the only non-fabricated person in the fable.

Three daughters were born to the couple in Amsterdam. At some point the family left for New Amsterdam. From there they traveled on to Rensselaerswijck, where Roelof went to work as a tenant farmer on the farming estate of De Laetsburch. During those years the couple had three more children, one of whom was a son. In 1634 Roelof lost his job, probably because of a small independent business that Anneke had set up with her sister and mother, thereby violating the rules.

The family moved to New Amsterdam, where Roelof became foreman of one of the farms belonging to the WIC. In 1636 he acquired the farm and the land around it, which covered about 26 hectares. He died in 1637, just three years after the family's arrival in Manhattan. The following year his widow married Everadus Bogardus, a minister in the Dutch Reformed Church. They had four sons. The farm that Roelof had

Photo of Pearl Street near State Street, where Annetje Jans lived

Gabri Christa, dancer, born 1963 Curaçao
Idea Viola Reid, born 2003 Staten Island
In New York since 1993

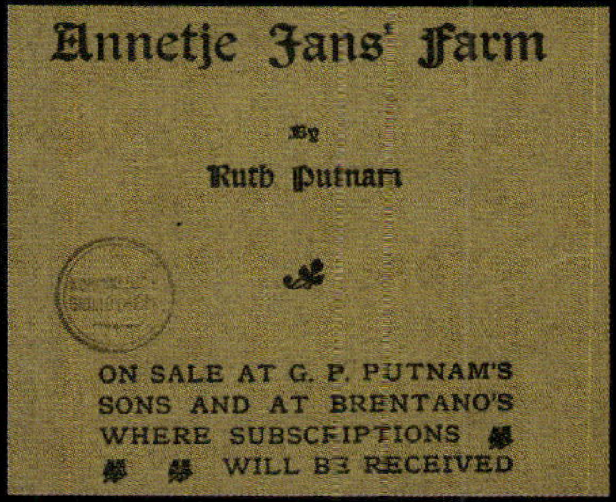

Annetje Jans' Farm
Ruth Putnam, 1897
Royal Library, The Hague
788 J 30
14 x 21 cm

acquired was renamed after the minister, the Dominie's Bouwerij, Preacher's Farm. It lay outside the city to the northwest of the Singel (Wall Street). Anneke and Everadus rented out the farm as well as a patch of land on Long Island that became known as Dominee's Hoek, or Preacher's Corner.

Everadus Bogardus was a Protestant minister who cared greatly about social issues. He made sure the schoolteacher included black children in his classes. The present-day New York Collegiate School for Boys claims direct descent from the school where those pupils were taught, over 300 years ago. Bogardus preached impassioned sermons against Director Kieft's anti-Indian war policy (p. 94). Neither man could abide the other. When the war was over, Kieft was summoned back to the Dutch Republic to answer for his deeds. Bogardus sailed home with him, to explain his side of the story. But neither ever saw the Dutch Republic again. They drowned together in September 1647 when their ship was wrecked on the jagged coast of Wales.

For the second time Anneke had lost a husband though she still had all nine of her children. In 1642 her oldest daughter, Sara, had married Hans Kierstede, who worked for the West India Company as a surgeon. Sara was a remarkable character. The archives describe her as a "good woman," and today we might call her a mediator. She was frequently asked to arbitrate conflicts in New Amsterdam and she acted as an interpreter in some native American languages, which she had apparently learned as a child in Rensselaerswijck.

Accompanied by her seven younger children, Anneke returned to the neighborhood of Rensselaerswijck. She bought a plot of land in Beverwijck (Albany) and became a trader in beaver skins. She was clearly a woman of considerable means; in 1654 she became owner of the Dominee's Bouwerij (Preacher's Farm) estate on Manhattan and acquired the dwelling at the corner of Paerl Straet (Pearl Street) and Stuyvesants Hoeck (State Street).[37] She sold the house in 1657 to her brother-in-law Govert Loockermans. Anneke died in 1663. Today a plaque at 63 State Street in Albany marks the house where she once lived.[33]

[1] Otto, *The Dutch-Munsee Encounter*, p. 95, note 72.
[2] Shorto, *The Island at the Center of the World*, p. 54.
[3] Otto, *The Dutch-Munsee Encounter*, p. 95.
[4] Jacobs, *Een zegenrijk gewest*, p. 181.
[5] Otto, *The Dutch-Munsee Encounter*, p. 97.
[6] Wieder, *New York*, p. 126.
[7] Rink, *Holland on the Hudson*, p. 87.
[8] Wieder, p. 162. According to the notes in Wieder, pp. 162-163, Minuit arrived in New Netherland in May 1626 on the Meeuwtje (Sew Mew).
[9] A source publication with this title by Kees Waterman, Charles Gehring and Jaap Jacobs will be published by the Walburg Pers in 2009.
[10] Van Bracht and Schilder, "The Origins of New York," p. 9.
[11] Jameson, *Narratives*, pp. 84-85.
[12] Wieder, *New York*, p. 162.
[13] Eekhof, "Bastiaen Jansz. Krol"; Wieder, *New York*, pp. 11, 13.
[14] Rink, *Holland on the Hudson*, pp. 83-85.
[15] Laer, *Huntington Documents* 204, F 17.
[16] Wieder, *New York*, pp. 172-173.
[17] Rink, *Holland on the Hudson*, p. 91.
[18] Rink, *Holland on the Hudson*, p. 92.
[19] Rink, *Holland on the Hudson*, p. 92.
[20] Eekhof, *Jonas Michaëlius*, p. 3.
[21] Rink, *Holland on the Hudson*, p. 98. The version of 1628 is a precursor of the definitive *Vryheden en Exemptiën* of 1629. The copy on view here is from the archive of the Van Wassenaer van Duvenvoorde archive.
[22] Rink, *Holland on the Hudson*, p. 99.
[23] Jacobs, "Dutch Proprietary Manors in America," p. 38.
[24] Shorto, *The Island at the Center of the World*, p. 62; Jameson, *Narratives of New Netherland*, p. 100.
[25] Jacobs, *Een zegenrijk gewest*, pp. 118-121; Rink, *Holland on the Hudson*, pp. 94 ff.
[26] Jacobs, *Een zegenrijk gewest*, pp. 239-240.
[27] Shorto, *The Island at the Center of the World*, p. 65; Jacobs, *Een zegenrijk gewest*, p. 115.
[28] Wieder, *De Stichting van New York*, p. 106.
[29] Rink, "1629 A Year of Decision for New Netherland," p. 88.
[30] Jameson, *Narratives of New Netherland*, pp. ix-xiii.
[31] De Roever, *Rensselaer*, p. 38.
[32] Den Heijer, *De geschiedenis van de WIC*, pp. 84-85.
[33] Rink, *Holland on the Hudson*, pp. 192-196.
[34] Rink, *Holland on the Hudson*, p. 111.
[35] Rink, *Holland on the Hudson*, pp. 115-116.
[36] Jacobs, *Een zegenrijk gewest*, p. 429, note 98. *The Vryheden en Exemptiën* (Charter of Liberties and Exemptions) of 1640: NA, SG, LWI, inv.no. 5755 II, ingekomen 1640, C.1047 ff; *The Vryheden en Exemptiën* of 1650: JJ p. 430, note 99: SG, Loketkas WIC, inv.no. 12564.30A; Jacobs, *Een zegenrijk gewest*, p. 126.
[37] Phelps Stokes, *The Iconography of Manhattan Island*.
[38] Venema, *Beverwijck*; Zabriskie, "Anneke Jans in Fact and Fiction," pp. 157-164.

II

CHAPTER 3

Internal and External Conflicts

New Amsterdam is in the starting blocks. The Company has introduced measures to open the colony to emigrants. But threats inside and outside its territory are preventing the colony from really taking off. There are constant problems on the borders with English territories. On the northern border in particular, along the Fresh (Connecticut) River, the Dutch colony is being put under great pressure. The director of the colony, Wouter van Twiller, has difficulty protecting the land from English incursions.

His successor, Willem Kieft, suffers more from problems with the indigenous inhabitants. Native American and European cultures increasingly clash. There is a lack of understanding on both sides and the American natives become more and more irritated by Dutch rule. Minor conflicts about land, trade and old injuries escalate into a disastrous war. Kieft seeks support from the people and establishes two advisory councils, the Board of Twelve, then the Board of Eight. After the war Kieft is blamed for causing the trouble and the community turns against him.

With the arrival of Peter Stuyvesant in 1647 peace seems to return to the colony. Stuyvesant also creates an advisory committee, the Board of Nine. The early years of his rule as director-general are characterized by the Board's resistance to his authority and that of his advisors. One of these advisors is the lawyer Adriaen van der Donck, who collaborates with the Board of Nine on a pamphlet against Stuyvesant's government, the 1650 *Vertoogh van Nieu Nederland* (The Remonstrance of New Netherland). Will the colony's citizens manage to bring down Stuyvesant?

The English Surround New Netherland

This map shows Virginia, the English colony founded in 1607. Here several English investors were granted land to exploit by royal charter. The Virginia Company organized and financed the colonizing expeditions without further government involvement.

The capital of the territory, Jamestown, was named after King James I of England and situated on the Powhatan River. Dutch traders visited it, just as English traders called in at New Amsterdam. Relations between the English and the Dutch were generally good. It was not the people of the English colonies, nor initially their governors, who threatened New Netherland but England itself. During the 1620s, however, there was hardly any sign of threat, for the dispute between England and the Dutch Republic amounted to little more than bickering about their respective titles to the region of New Netherland.

This changed in the early 1630s as the English presence in the area gradually became evident. Around 1630 English Puritan colonists began to flood into North America. They mainly settled in New England and annexed lands, which the Dutch Republic claimed belonged to New Netherland. The Dutch started to feel increasingly hemmed in.[1]

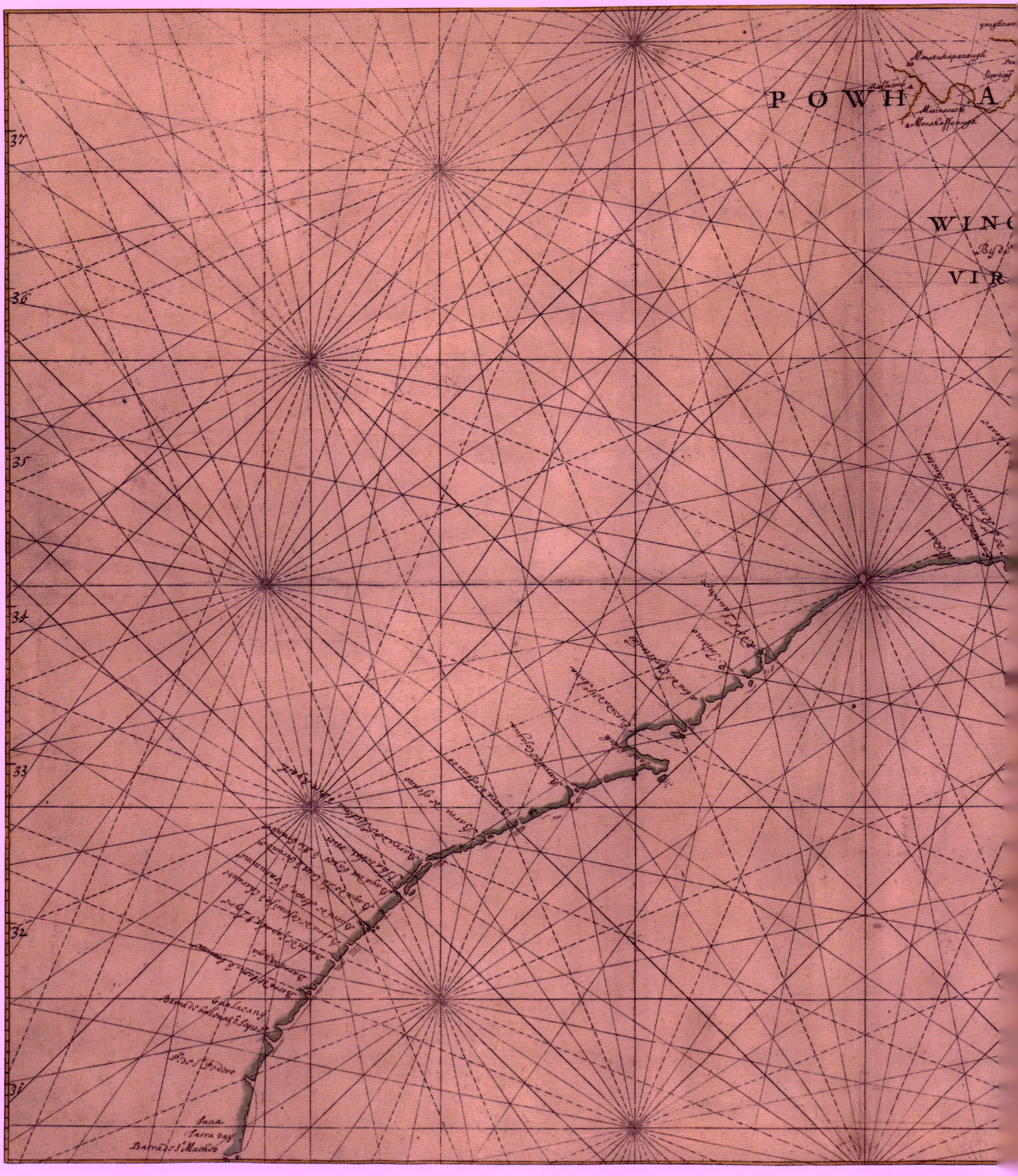

Map of the Atlantic Coast of North America, from Chesapeake Bay to Florida
Johannes Vingboons, third quarter of the seventeenth century
Library of Congress, Geography and Map Division, Washington, D.C.
G3291.S12 coll .H3 Vault: Harr vol. 2, map 8
Paper, 50 x 71 cm

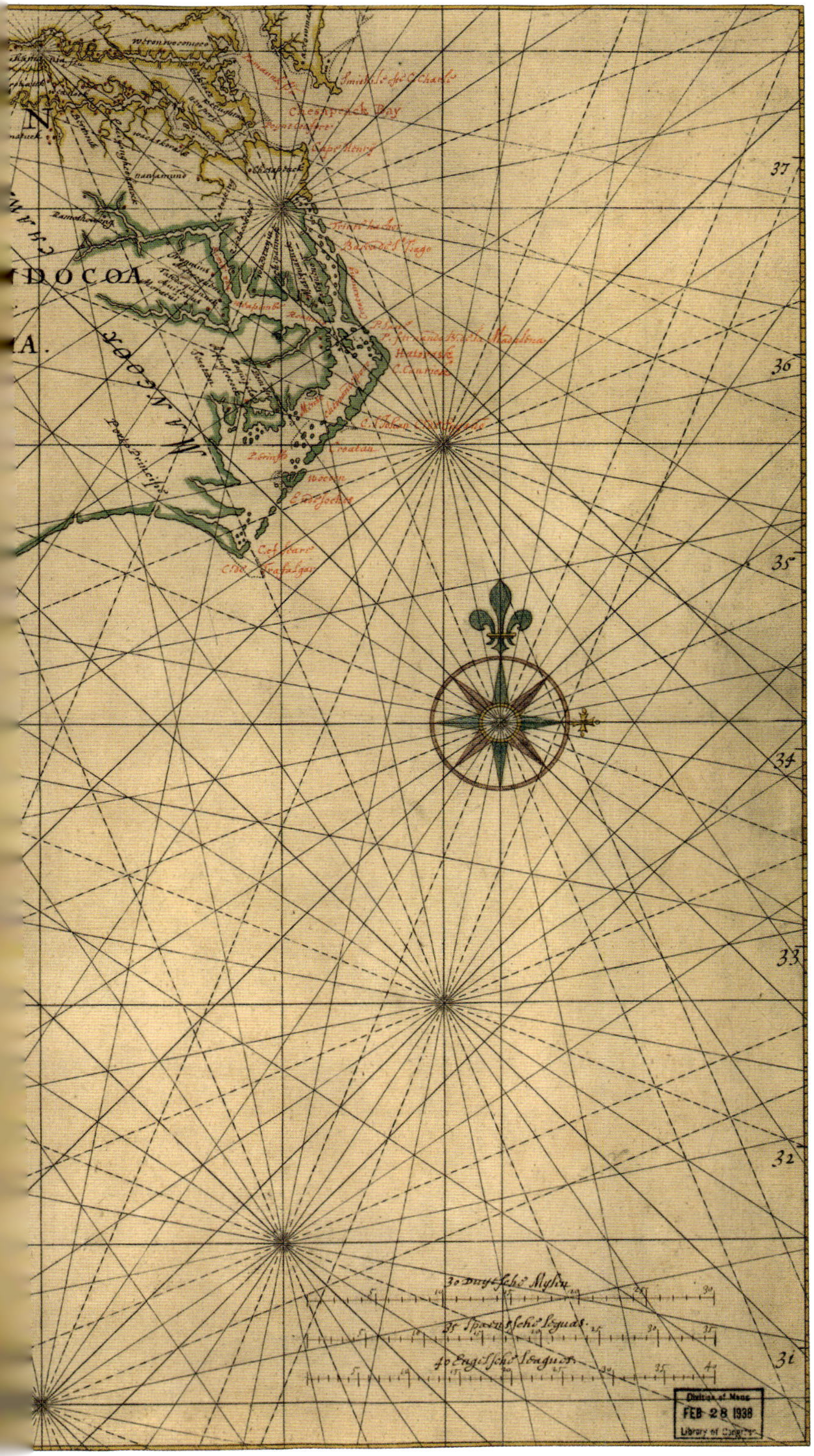

The 1630s: Will the English Take New Amsterdam?

During the 1630s the Dutch colony was increasingly threatened by rising numbers of English settlers, especially on New Netherland's northern border. New England was in the ascendant and armed conflict with the colony's English neighbors was a distinct possibility. The Dutch West India Company decided that the administration of New Netherland should show its teeth. Minuit had been forced to relinquish his post as director in 1632 and Bastiaen Jansz. Krol was temporarily doing the honors. A new, forceful director was required. Wouter van Twiller, married to a relative of Kiliaen van Rensselaer, was the man chosen to protect the colony from the English. However, the new director, like his predecessors, had little experience in governing.

Van Twiller arrived in Manhattan on the *Soutberg* (Salt Mountain) in the spring of 1633. The ship's cargo did not consist of the usual goods, for it was carrying 104 soldiers, 52 sailors, weapons and ammunition. Everyone was ready to resist their English neighbors.

Van Twiller immediately became embroiled in an incident involving the captain of an English ship, the *William*, which had put in at New Amsterdam on 18 April 1633. The captain, a Dutchman, Jacob Eelkens, had been one of the first Dutch people to spend the winter in the region, during the early years of New Netherland (see p. 42). The incident was described by David Pietersz. de Vries, who was an eyewitness. According to De Vries, Van Twiller made a complete fool of himself when he allowed Eelkes to sail up the North (Hudson) River, without ordering him to stop, then opened a vat of wine and proclaimed that everyone who loved the Prince of Orange and himself should do the same and apprehend the Englishman immediately; everyone present laughed at him for this misplaced bravado, for the captain had already sailed far up the river.[2]

De Vries, who was present in the Dutch fort when the *William* sailed straight up the North (Hudson) River, then recounted that he had advised Van Twiller to capture the ship anyway, which the director proceeded to do. The conflict ended with the goods on the English ship being confiscated. So Van Twiller eventually did show his teeth, though he had not proved the resolute leader the colony required, at least in De Vries' opinion.[3] Nevertheless the events described by De Vries should be taken with a pinch of salt, for his book is renowned for its passages in which the author likes to lay it on thick and beat his own drum.

Who Was David Pietersz. de Vries?

David Pietersz. de Vries was born around 1593 in the French port of La Rochelle, where his father worked as a trader. He followed in his father's footsteps and became an adept businessman throughout the Mediterranean and Newfoundland. At the age of about 30 he decided to travel to America to see if he could set up a trade in beaver pelts and fish. However, he was refused permission by the Dutch West India Company on the grounds that such an undertaking would breach their shipping monopoly. De Vries then worked for the Dutch East India Company for a time until he felt the pull of the West again.

De Vries made three trips to New Netherland. In the years 1632-1633 he visited the Delaware region; in 1634-1636 his itinerary included Staten Island. On his third trip, from 1638 to 1643, he stayed somewhat longer in the colony. He established two patroonships, both of which were destroyed by Indians. Back home in the Republic, in the little town of Hoorn, De Vries wrote an account of his travels that was published in 1655. His book features several engravings of American natives, in whom De Vries was exceptionally interested. These images are adapted from illustrations in Samuel de Champlain's *Voyages et Decouvertes* (Voyages and Discoveries) from 1620. De Vries died in 1655.

In: David Pietersz. de Vries, *Korte historiael ende journaels aenteyckeninge van verscheyden voyagiens in de vier deelen des wereldts-ronde, als Europa, Africa, Asia ende Amerika gedaen* (Brief history and journal notes of diverse voyages undertaken in the four parts of the globe, to wit Europe, Africa, Asia and America), 1655
Royal Library, The Hague
1394 CB
Engraving, 10 x 13.6 cm

David Pietersz. de Vries: Joint Patroon of Swanendael

Samuel Godijn founded the Swanendael patroonship on the bank of the Fresh River (in Delaware) in 1630. Not long thereafter, a ship, the *Salm* (Salmon), arrived there with timber and farmers. The *Salm* had originally been bound for the island of Tortuga in the Caribbean where Godijn also had a patroonship. However, the crew of the *Salm* had found the Tortuga patroonship in a terrible condition, for the colony had been attacked by the Spanish.

Crew and passengers had resolved to sail on to Godijn's second colony, Swanendael, where Godijn's men built a small fort. The captain of the *Salm*, Pieter Heyes, chose to return to the Republic with an empty cargo hold, a decision that was not appreciated. Heyes was dismissed and David Pietersz. de Vries took his place for the return trip to Swanendael. When De Vries arrived at the settlement in December 1632, he discovered that it too had been destroyed. Indians had ravaged the place. No one had survived.[4]

The map shows Godins Bay (now Delaware Bay), named after Samuel Godijn, and the location of the small fort. It is quite feasible that De Vries drew it when he arrived in the colony, for he is known to have worked as a draftsman and to have been skilled at charting rivers.

De Vries probably supplied the chart, which served as the model for Vingboons' map of the Powhatan River in Virginia (ill. on p. 30).

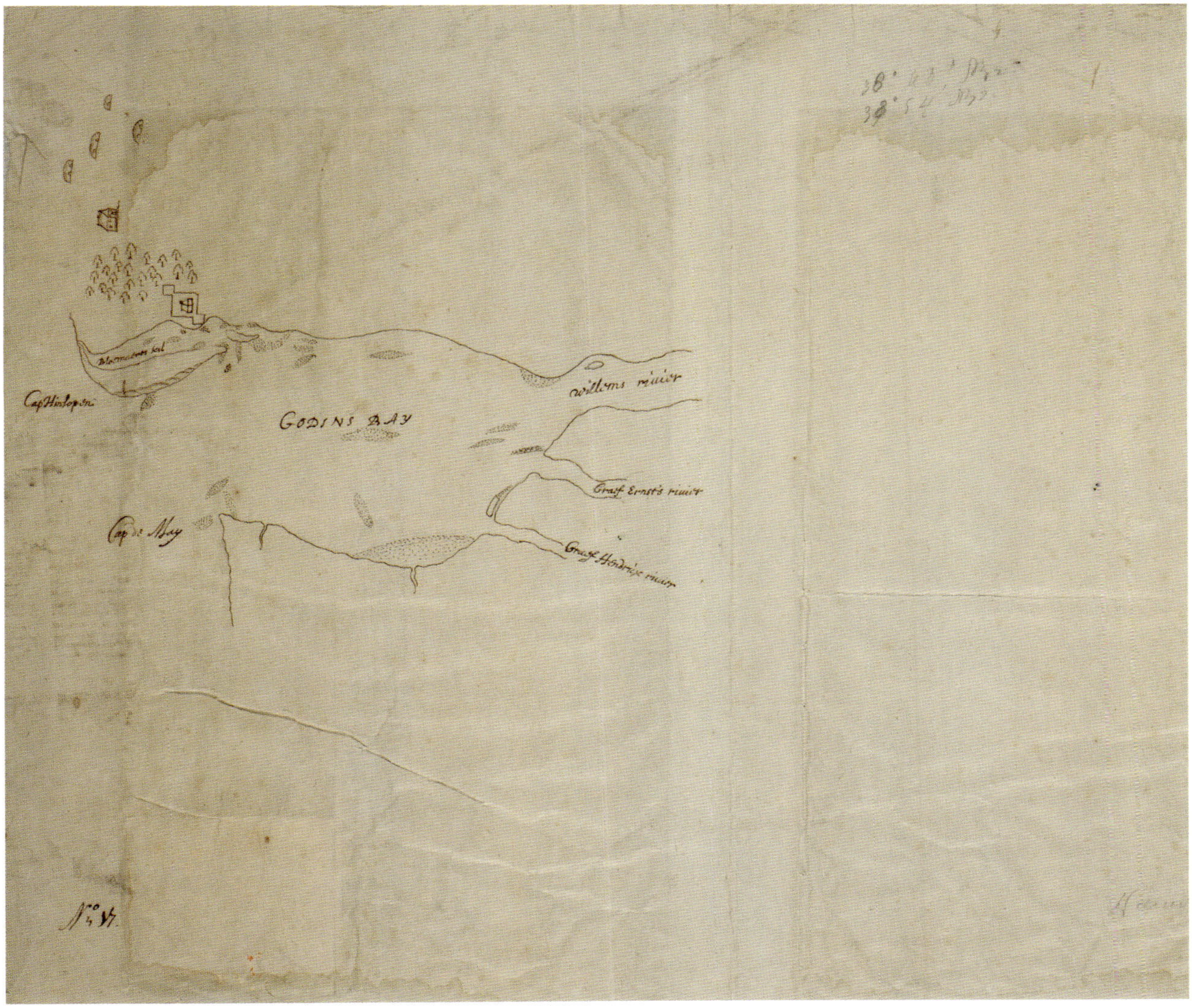

The Swanendael Patroonship of Godijn and De Vries
Anonymous, ca. 1630
Nationaal Archief (National Archives of the Netherlands), The Hague
4.VEL 518
Manuscript map, 32 x 42 cm

Was New Netherland a Dutch Possession?

This memorandum contains a number of questions posed by the members of the States General to the governors of the Dutch West India Company. The key issues become clear once all eight questions have been read. What territory does the Republic actually possess? How can the Republic's title to this be improved? And is the best use being made of this territory? The answers to these questions, provided by Cornelis Musch, secretary to the States General, are given in italics.

The Hague 30 April 1638

Since the lords States General receive uncertain report of the affairs pertaining to New Netherland that the same are deteriorating more and more to the detriment of this State and the inhabitants thereof it must be asked,
in the year 1614 (?) given by their High Mightinesses by private patent to Jonas Witzen and Twenhuijsen, and on expiration of the same to the West India Company of Virginia to whit from Ciçapoa to Terra Nova along the sea coast.

I How far do the boundaries of New Netherland extend along the sea coast here (Hoe verre de limiten van Nieu-Nederlant langs de zee custe haer sijn streckende),

II Whether the same boundaries are still possessed at this time by the West India Company and the inhabitants of these lands,
We possess Mauritius or the North River on which are two forts Orangien and Amsterdam and there is another house built by the Company and there is the most population

III And in the case of no [being the answer], what nations have seized these and with what right and under what pretext,
the right is who the strongest is, the English come from the North East from New England up to the Fresh River

IIII Whether the Company will be able to maintain the other boundaries and by what means,
if they have people they can maintain the others and from the North River they can go as deep into the land as they wish.

V What Christian nations are its [the colony's] neighbors above and below,
the English enclave us from Virginia to New England and have come so much closer to us.

VI Whether the Company has made profit or loss since the populating of New Netherland,
loss made, but could give profit, principally from corn.

VII And in the case of loss that their High Mightinesses find it expedient to conserve the boundaries of New Netherland and regarding the population to contrive an improved and permanent base,
the Company cannot populate it because there is no understanding amongst the Company, but a base of opening [up the colony] must be contrived.

VIII And whether therefore it would be inexpedient to transfer the district of New Netherland to the disposition of the Generality,
have no intention in this regard provided that they derive some advantage from this, but hope that now an order has been made regarding Brazil that in time it will turn out well: the most fear is for the English striking before they are willing to give them the trade with the savages or something else.

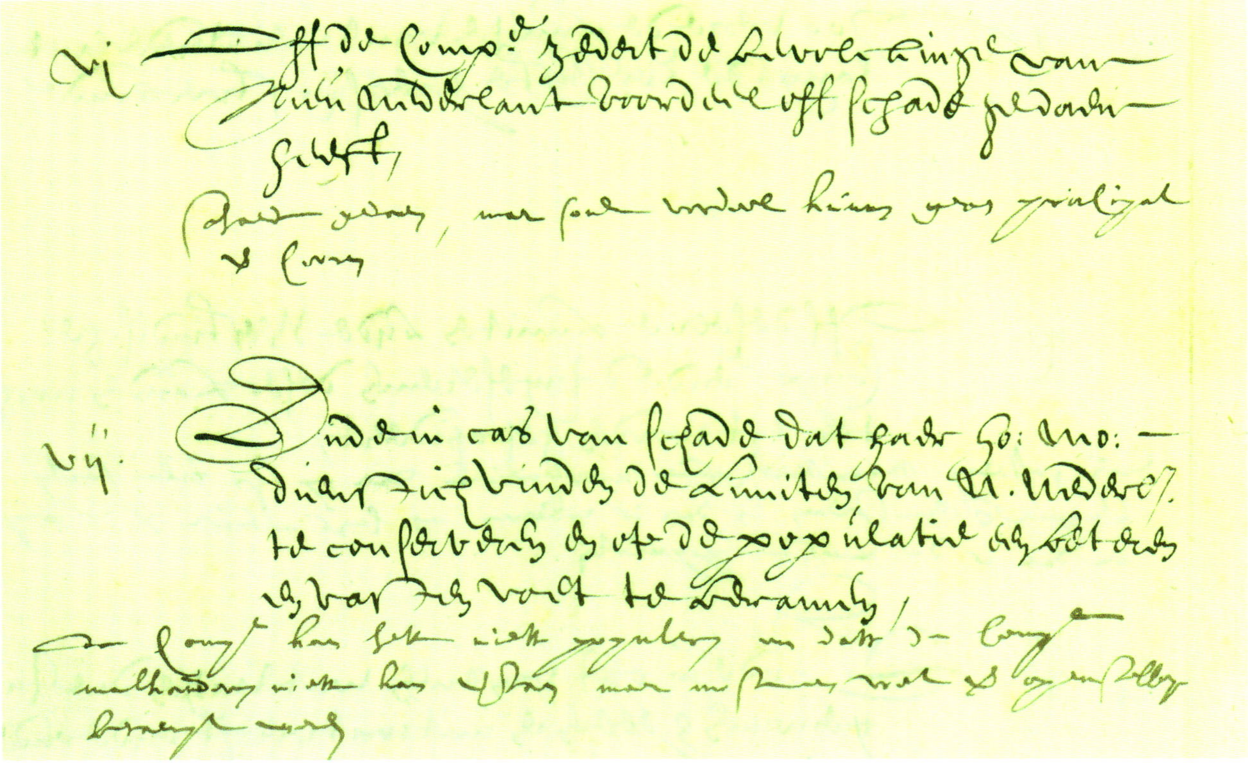

"Memorandum of questions regarding the borders, the neighbours, the population etc. of New Netherland, posed by the States General to the governors of the West India Company, with the answers to these", 1638
Nationaal Archief (National Archives of the Netherlands), The Hague
States General, 1.01.07, inv. no. 12564.6, marked "eerste afd. 5" (first sect. 5)
Ink on paper, 19.5 x 31.5 cm

John Winthrop, Governor of the Massachusetts Bay Colony

Governor Winthrop wrote to Director Van Twiller to inform him that England had assigned the Connecticut Valley to subjects of the English crown. His intention with this letter was to stop Dutch building activities in the valley. Van Twiller replied that the Dutch had acquired the land legally by purchasing it from the Indians; moreover his compatriots had already erected a building there with a view to populating the region. Van Twiller's correspondence with Winthrop had little effect. The Dutch quickly vacated the scene, while the English brought their first permanent base in the valley into operation. This was Hartford, which was populated by emigrants from Massachusetts. The first church and the first court were established there in the years 1635-1636.

Portrait of John Winthrop
Jarvis Griggs Kellogg, 1805-1873
New York Public Library, New York
ID: 478593

He probably also wanted Van Twiller's job. The new director of New Netherland was certainly not going to have an easy time of it. Without a careful plan it would be impossible to resist the English who were infiltrating the colony on all sides.[5]

Although Van Twiller has a reputation as a weak director, he cannot be accused of never having shown a willingness to fight. One of the ways in which he endeavored to intimidate the English was through official sequestration of the upper reaches of the Fresh (Connecticut) River, by purchasing the land in the region from the Indians. The latter subsequently claimed that they had only given the Dutch permission to use the land to set animal traps, but this was irrelevant to Van Twiller, who was solely interested in creating a buffer against the English. He purchased the land in the same year in which he arrived in the colony, and immediately ordered that a fortified trading post be built there, appropriately named Fort Good Hope (*de Goede Hoop*).[6]

The fort was intended to act as a deterrent but achieved the opposite effect, for the English instantly made their presence felt in the area. Van Twiller then proposed that he and the English governor, John Winthrop, jointly seek a solution that would satisfy both parties. However, his initiative produced no sign of conciliation: the English replied to Fort Good Hope by simply building their own trading post, a few miles away. When the Dutch soldiers in the region were uncertain how to react to this development, their lack of response gave the English courage, for it showed them that they could do what they liked with impunity. From this moment onwards the WIC had lost its de facto power over the region. The English trading post drew settlers like a magnet and subsequently grew into the little town of Hartford. Increasing numbers of English colonists chose to settle in the area, effectively ruining the Company's fur trade on the Fresh (Connecticut) River. Around 1640 there were more English than Dutch living in the valley.[7]

Van Twiller had cherished strategic intentions with the building of Fort Good Hope but his plan had not achieved its aim. Now Dutch colonists were at risk, a fact for which he was blamed by the New Netherlanders. Van Twiller's character also repelled the colony's inhabitants. He is said to have been ridiculed for his public drunkenness more than anything else. He also did not enjoy the support of the minister Everardus Bogardus, successor to Michaëlius, or the public prosecutor Lubbert van Dincklagen. Van Dincklagen had even accused the director, and other councilors, of acting against the Company's interests.[8]

The directors of the Company's Amsterdam Chamber were not pleased by the reports coming from the colony. Moreover, everything they learned was hearsay for Van Twiller barely corresponded with them.

Lady Deborah Moody

From Religious Warrior to City Planner

Deborah Moody, widow of Sir Henry Moody, was a London aristocrat who converted to Anabaptism and became one of its most fervent champions. She is said to have been willing to give up her life for the right to administer adult baptism. She and her fellow Anabaptists believed that people should be baptized only when they were able to understand what baptism meant. She felt it was wrong, indeed sinful, to baptize babies who could not know its significance.[9] Across the Atlantic in New England, Lady Deborah was soon made unwelcome for of her outspoken views; in 1642 she was excommunicated by the Puritan Church of Salem "to avoid further difficulties."[10] Governor John Winthrop even described her as "a most dangerous woman."

So Lady Deborah and her son Henry, together with other Anabaptists, set out for New Netherland. WIC director Willem Kieft granted Moody and her group permission to found a colony as well as the right to practice their particular religion behind closed doors.

Moody and her co-religionists settled in the southwest of Long Island where they established a small community. The group organized its own day-to-day affairs but on Kieft's orders had to nominate a number of magistrates half of whom he would select.[11] The new colony of Gravesend,[12] probably named after the village of 's Gravenzande in South Holland province lay where Brooklyn stands today – named after the village of Breukelen, in the Dutch province of Utrecht. Lady Moody herself drew up the street plan for Gravesend. Her farm suffered badly in 1643, during Kieft's War against the Indians, when she managed to defend her property with the help of a group of 40 armed men.[13]

She and her son Henry were prominent within the colony until her death in 1659. Henry then moved to Virginia where he died not long after his mother, in 1662.[14]

Plaque Commemorating Lady Deborah Moody
Photo: Richard Koek, 2009

Photo taken in front of the supposed residency of Lady Moody on Gravesend Neck Road

Frank Jump, born 1960 Queens
Willy Broekveldt Jump, born 1936 Amsterdam
In New York since 1958

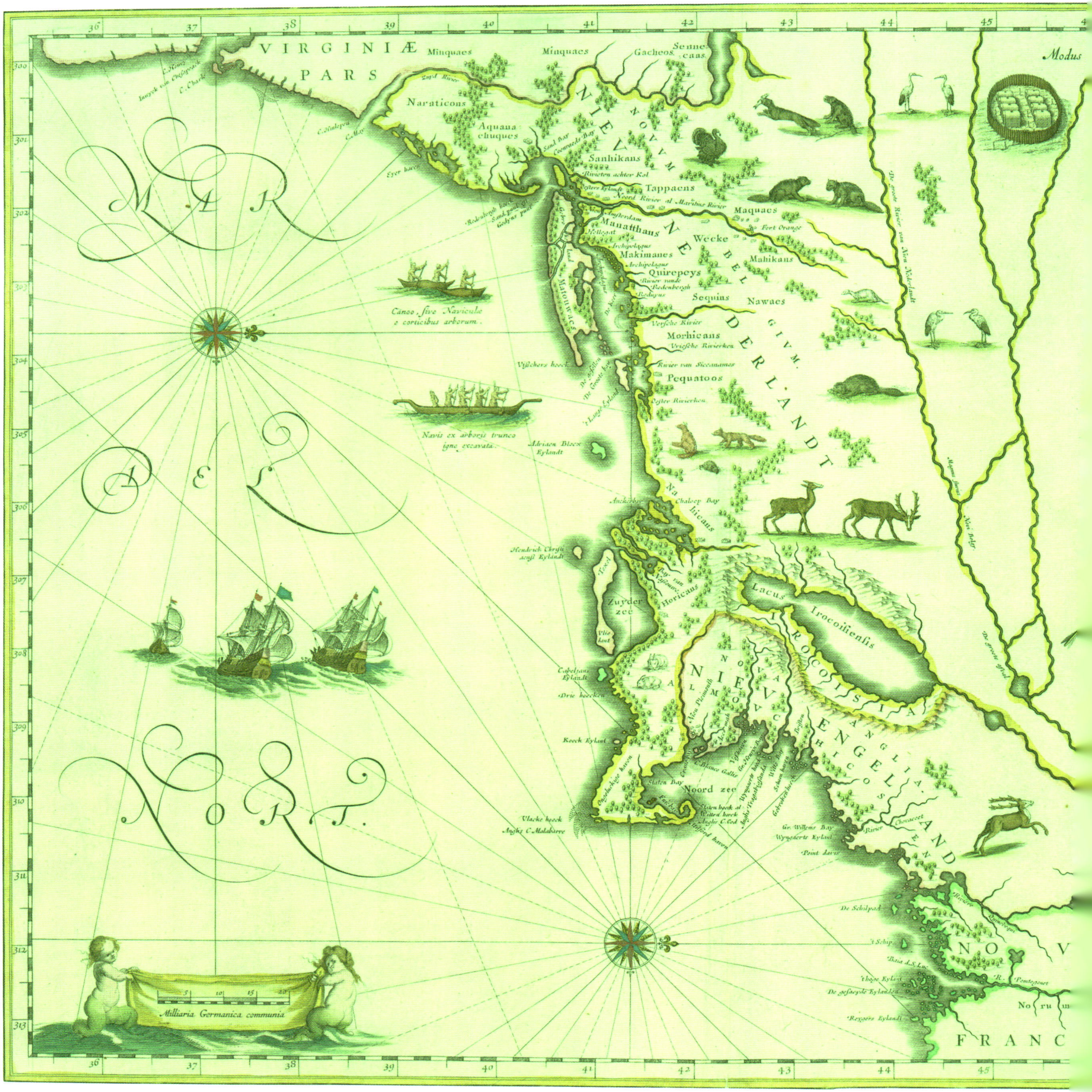
VIRGINIÆ PARS
Minquaes
Minquaes
Gacheos
Senne caas
Modus
Naraticons
Aquana chuques
Sanhikans
Tappaens
Maquaes
Fort Orange
Manatthans
Wecke
Makimanes
Mahikans
Quirepeys
Sequins
Nawaes
Morhicans
Pequatoos
NIEUW NEDERLANDT
NOVUM BELGIUM
MAR DEL NORT
Canoa, five Naviculæ e corticibus arborum.
Navis ex arboris trunco igne excavata.
Adriaen Blocx Eylandt
Visschers hoeck
Anckerbay
Chaloop Bay
Horicans
Zuyder zee
Lacus Irocoisiensis
Cabelyau Eylandt
Drie hoecken
Roeck Eylant
Noord zee
Vlacke hoeck
NIEU ENGELANDT
NOVA ANGLIA
De Schilpad
't Schip
Milliaria Germanica communia
FRANC

New Netherland and New England

This map by Blaeu, entitled "Nova Belgica et Anglia Nova," was published in 1635 in Blaeu's two-volume atlas *Toonneel des Aerdrycks, ofte Nieuwe Atlas* (Stage of the World, or New Atlas). The Latinized name Nova Belgica has nothing to do with the modern state of Belgium: it was a term commonly used to denote New Netherland.

There are considerable similarities between this printed map and the manuscript map by Block from 1614 (ill. on p. 47). However, it has been rotated 180 degrees and there are cartographic improvements to the coast south of Manhattan. These adjustments were taken from Hessel Gerritszs' map from 1630, for which see the illustration on page 69.

When "Nova Belgica et Anglia Nova" was published in 1635, it represented the most recent geographic and cartographic knowledge of the colony of New Netherland.

To the south of New Netherland – upper left on the map – is "Virginiæ Pars," the English colony of Virginia. To the north of the Dutch colony lies "Niev Engeland," or New England. The Fresh (Connecticut) River, disputed by the English and the Dutch from 1633, still lies in the midst of territory marked "Niev Nederlandt." In other respects, particularly the details, the Blaeu map is very different in appearance from Block's 1614 work. There are ships out to sea, plus a finely rendered, colorful cartouche decoratively flanked by American natives. Closer to shore Indians are canoeing in hollowed-out tree trunks. On the land, upper right, are two Indian villages enclosed by palisades. There are also meticulously drawn animals; storks, otters, foxes, a turkey, a weasel, bears and deer. It is unclear if these creatures were based on original drawings from the New World, for they could just as easily have been drawn, with the exception of the American turkey, from similar European species.[15]

"Nova Belgica et Anglia Nova"
Willem Jansz. Blaeu, first edition 1635
Nationaal Archief (National Archives of the Netherlands), The Hague
4.AKF 2.11.
Engraving, 39 x 50 cm

When a rumor circulated that Van Twiller intended to buy a tract of land using Company money, they decided that enough was enough. In 1637 the Amsterdam Chamber ordered Van Twiller to return to the Republic and designated Willem Kieft as his promising successor.

Kieft Appears on the Scene

When Willem Kieft[16] took up his post as director of New Netherland, in 1638, he had no more experience of governing a colony than Wouter van Twiller. He had never even been outside Europe, nor traveled further than France where he had worked as a businessman. Yet he retained his office for a comparatively long time, for Peter Stuyvesant would not replace him until nine years later, in 1647. The number of years he spent in this post says nothing about his qualities as a leader, however.

Kieft would become known as the man who entangled the colony in a seemingly endless and bloody conflict with the Native Americans. The war, which was fought from 1643 to 1645, even bears his name, "Kieft's War." Historians are divided by the question of the extent to which Kieft may be regarded as the instigator and sponsor of the war, and as to whether he was indecisive and simply did what others encouraged him to do, or conversely failed to act through his lack of forcefulness.

This war and its consequences for the Indians and colonists are described in greater detail on page 171 of this book. More than 1600 American natives would die in the conflict, including a number of tribal chiefs and leaders. Their deaths caused the Indians to regroup and enter into new alliances.[17]

There were considerably fewer deaths on the colonists' side: the farmers' losses mainly took the form of burned buildings, dead livestock and trampled crops. As a precautionary measure the colonists sought each other out, moving their homes closer together on the southern point of Manhattan. Several returned to Europe, disillusioned. The people who remained were no longer able to find any common ground with their director.

The Colonists Begin to Hate Kieft

Before the war with the Indians, Kieft had established a Board of Twelve, an advisory committee that was supposed to represent the people and assist the colonial government. One issue he put before the Board was the raid on a group of Indians to avenge the killing of a Dutch colonist. Kieft wanted the committee to advise him solely on this single matter but he had miscalculated, for the Board of Twelve had other issues on their agenda. To their frustration Kieft forbade them to meet again. His disbanding of the Board of Twelve marked the beginning of the dispute between Kieft and the citizens of New Amsterdam, whose demands for local government along the lines customary in the Republic grew increasingly loud.

While the war was still in progress Kieft instituted a new committee, the Board of Eight. Although he created this to serve as an advisory body, he also gave the Board the task of encouraging the citizens of the colony to recruit as many men as possible for the war. Kieft did not allow the members of the Board of Eight to meet on their own initiative, and he summoned them with decreasing frequency. This angered the Board of Eight, who began to accuse the director of allowing the war to smolder on, while the people suffered.

In the midst of this turmoil, as the Eight grew progressively more discontent, Kieft convoked them on 18 June 1644. He brought a handful of soldiers to this meeting at which his loyal and obedient secretary Cornelis van Tienhoven would certainly have been present too. Kieft had an unwelcome message for the Board of Eight: he informed them that as the colony's coffers were empty, he would have to levy taxes.

After this meeting the Board of Eight wrote a letter to the general directors of the Amsterdam Chamber in which they expressed their opinion of Kieft in no uncertain terms, reviling the man and his conduct, and claiming that his war had laid waste to everything that had been achieved in the years before the conflict. They also condemned Kieft's attitude to them, for he had barely made use of their services as an advisory body, and called for a radical restructuring of the colony's administration and the director's dismissal. Although the Amsterdam Chamber proved indifferent to their complaints, the States General, who had also heard reports of the brutal warfare in the colony, put pressure on the Chamber to take appropriate measures.

The Amsterdam Chamber decided to institute an investigation into the situation in New Netherland. Any future action would be dependent on its findings. The investigation, conducted by the WIC's Audit Office, was completed in December 1644. The final report stated that Kieft was clearly no longer functioning and the colony's government required a radical overhaul; moreover the Indians had also been calling daily for Kieft to leave. So Kieft had played out his part. A new name was now being whispered in the corridors of the West India House in Amsterdam, that of Peter Stuyvesant.

An Inauspicious Send-Off

In the Dutch Republic it was decided that Kieft should be replaced. Stuyvesant was appointed director of New Netherland in May 1645, although his term of office would not officially commence until two years later. The year in which Stuyvesant finally succeeded Kieft, 1647, was also the year in which Kieft set sail to return to the Republic. The former director of New Netherland and his adversaries had been recalled to the Republic to explain themselves to the States General. Kieft's chief opponents were David Pietersz. de Vries, the minister Everardus Bogardus and the colonists Cornelis Melyn and Jochem Pietersz. Kuyter.

Kuyter had returned to New Netherland in 1639 and started a farm to the north of Manhattan, in what is now Harlem. Five years later, in March 1644, an Indian fire arrow had struck his farmhouse: he lost all of his possessions in the resulting inferno. A year later Kuyter had discovered that the fire arrow had not been shot by Indians but supporters of Kieft whom, he alleged, had taken advantage of the war with the Indians to intimidate him. It was then that Kuyter had declared war on Kieft.

In 1643 Kuyter had been chosen to serve on the Board of Eight, together with Cornelis Melyn. In October 1644 they had signed a letter to the States General in which they requested that an investigation be conducted to establish who was responsible for the war with the Native Americans. Although Kieft had initially been unaware of this letter, the States General later apprised him of it. He responded by having Melyn prosecuted for illegal trade.

Once Peter Stuyvesant had taken up his post, Melyn requested that the members of his Council be questioned for the purpose of gathering testimonies against Kieft. His request was a direct response to Kieft's attempts to have the Board of Eight interrogated. Stuyvesant, however, regarded Melyn's action as an overt act of resistance to the authorities and thus a form of treason. He therefore instituted legal proceedings against Melyn and Kuyter, which resulted in both men being banished from New Netherland.[18]

Melyn and Kuyter set sail for the Republic with minister Bogardus and Kieft on board the *Prinses Amelia* (Princess Amelia). However, the ship was wrecked and did not complete the voyage. Melyn and Kuyter survived the disaster, but Kieft was killed and all his personal possessions and records, including the papers for his defense before the States General, sank to the bottom of the ocean. De Vries' words to Kieft on the latter's departure from the colony had become reality: "I said in my leave-taking of Willem Kieft to him, that the murder he had had committed on so much innocent blood, that the same would yet be wreaked on him, and thus took leave of him".[19]

A New Wind

The Last Dutch Director-General, Peter Stuyvesant

After Peter Stuyvesant was appointed director-general of New Netherland, in May 1645, he had to wait another two years before he could assume the post. Internal differences of opinion regarding the execution and financing of the colony's reorganization delayed the processing of his appointment.

How did Stuyvesant prepare himself for this troublesome task? For troublesome it certainly was: none of his predecessors had escaped unscathed with their reputations intact. It would have been easy for Stuyvesant to have used the colonists' dissatisfaction with Kieft as a way to win their allegiance and as a tool in his own political game. Kieft had become unpopular, not only with the American natives but also with the colonists and the guardians of the church. He was hated both by the people who had suffered losses in the war with the Indians and those individuals who had attempted to acquire a greater degree of self-government under his regime.

After Stuyvesant's arrival in the colony in May 1647, several changes were made to the advisory committee. Henceforth the new body was to comprise nine men from New Amsterdam, who were collectively to be known as the Board of Nine or the "councilmen" (gemeentsmannen). They were not allowed to assemble on their own initiative, nor offer unsolicited advice, which was also the custom with similar boards in the Republic. A conspicuous change from the advisory boards created by Kieft was the composition of the new body. The Board of Nine was to comprise three farmers, three traders and three burghers, chosen by Stuyvesant and his Council from a preliminary selection of 18 men. Stuyvesant used measures such as the succession procedure, which required two-thirds of the Board of Nine to be replaced on an annual basis, to ensure these advisors did not acquire too much authority. However, he did accord the Board of Nine a role in the civil justice system.[20]

The Board of Nine Versus Peter Stuyvesant

Less than two years after Stuyvesant had taken up his appointment, there was again disagreement between the colony's administration and its people. In December 1648 the members of the Board of Nine were partially replaced, in accordance with agreed procedure. One of the new members was Adriaen van der Donck who had previously worked as *schout* (a kind of bailiff) for the Rensselaerswijck patroonship. With his legal training Van der Donck would become the inspiring force behind the Board of Nine, taking the lead in a range of initiatives such as organizing a delegation to the States General. Although

Who Was Peter Stuyvesant?

Stuyvesant[21] was not a soldier, although it is often thought he was on account of his leg being shot off. Over the centuries his wooden leg, and his intemperate character, have been a target of ridicule, both in writing and prints and drawings. Most images of Stuyvesant depict him as an irate, stubborn man who quickly flew into rages. His adversaries loved to represent him in this manner.

Stuyvesant studied literature and philosophy at the University of Franeker for a time. In his fraternity register he inscribed a text by St. John Chrysostom:

"Trust in God, mistrust yourself, mistrust protectors,
Mistrust your father and kings.
Trust only in God, for when all hope is gone
And people finally desert you,
Your trust in God will still be there, and He will begin
And give a happy deliverance."

The scrawled entry betrays Stuyvesant's origins, his family's strict Calvinist family. He is known to have been a straightforward man, with total faith in the authority of church and state and no desire to tamper with this. His father was a minister, who passed his fondness for the Dutch Reformed Church on to Stuyvesant. Stuyvesant's mother's first husband had also been a minister. So it is hardly surprising that Stuyvesant's wife was the daughter of a minister as well. Stuyvesant himself was active in the church. He became a member of the church council in New Netherland from the moment he assumed his post in the colony. When the English took over New Amsterdam, in 1664, he even stayed on as a church elder.[22]

The last Dutch director of New Netherland started his career with the Dutch West India Company around 1632. At first sight his choice of a commercial profession does not seem in keeping with his religious background. Nevertheless, the two were not incompatible, as service in the Dutch West India Company provided an opportunity to work against Catholic Spain. Indeed, one of the Company's chief objectives was to pursue the conflict with Spain by damaging or capturing Spanish colonies wherever possible.

In 1647 Stuyvesant took up his new post as director-general of New Netherland. He had a reputation as a tough, intrepid leader who dug his heels in when his subordinates strayed off course. He was certainly no advocate of tolerating dissidents, in which regard he differed from the ruling political class in Amsterdam, who were somewhat more indulgent. Profoundly convinced that religious faith should be the guiding light in government, creating order and authority, Stuyvesant managed to hold fast to his beliefs throughout his term of office. Religious pluralism, he believed, would only further undermine the colony whose diverse communities and nationalities already made it lack cohesion: strict observance of Calvinism, clamping down on all other religions and rigorous enforcement of the Sabbath rest would bring the colony the peace and order that it needed.

Stuyvesant died in 1672, after a tumultuous life. A contemporary, Henricus Selyns, wrote a poem about him, which includes several punning lines on his name that would not have been out of place on his tombstone: "Do not raise up too much sand. For there lies Stuyvesant." His tombstone can no longer be seen in the Church of St. Mark's-in-the-Bowery, named after Stuyvesant's farm (*bouwerij*), although it does contain other memorials to Stuyvesant and his progeny. A bust of Stuyvesant stands in the church garden, while one of the stained-glass windows includes his portrait. Several memorial plaques to Stuyvesant and his descendants can also be found in the lobby.

Portrait of Petrus Stuyvesant
Attributed to Hendrick Couturier, ca. 1660
New York Historical Society, New York
Inv. no. 1909.2
Oil on panel, 59 x 45 cm

The Appointment of Peter Stuyvesant

One of the factors that delayed Stuyvesant's appointment process was the States General's slowness in issuing his letters of commission. All the director-general's appointments and job specifications had to be approved by the States General. The States General also gave other high-ranking Company officials, like the vice-director, a letter of commission. This obliged them to swear an oath of fealty to both the Dutch West India Company and the States General.

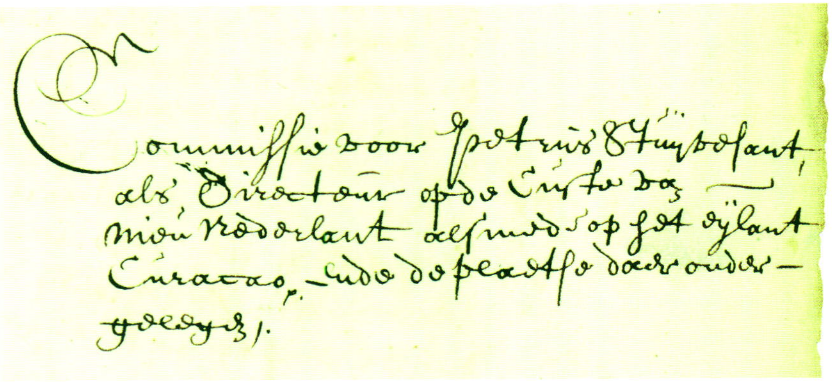
Commissie voor Petrus Stuyvesant, als Directeur op de Custe van Nieu Nederlant, alsmede op het eylant Curacao, ende de plaetsen daer onder gehoorende.

Commission Books of the States General, 1646
Nationaal Archief (National Archives of the Netherlands), The Hague
States General, 1.01.06, inv. no. 12227
Ink on paper, 36.5 x 23.5 cm

Stuyvesant was appointed director-general of New Netherland. In the years before his appointment other titles had been used in various periods to designate the highest official in the colony. During the colony's early years the title and function was that of commander. This later became director, a higher rank than commander. On Stuyvesant's appointment in 1647, the post was changed to director-general, since Stuyvesant also exercised authority over Curaçao.
In several letters and documents the title of governor is sometimes applied to Stuyvesant too. This was a lower rank than that of governor-general. The Dutch East India Company had one governor-general, based in Batavia (now Jakarta in Indonesia), while the Dutch West India Company employed a governor-general in Dutch Brazil. The office of governor-general never existed in New Netherland, which says something about the colony's importance to the Company. Stuyvesant valued his title greatly. On arriving in New Netherland he informed his people that he wished to be addressed as Lord General, an announcement that was not well received in some quarters.

Portrait of Petrus Stuyvesant
Stained Glass, Church of St. Mark's-in-the-Bowery
Donated to the church by the Society of Daughters of Holland Dames in 1903
Photo: M. Gosselink, 2008

one aim of this mission was to seek help in halting the expansion of the English colonies, which were increasingly encircling New Netherland, Stuyvesant did not like the way in which Van der Donck had arranged the delegation. The director-general was determined to make his influence felt, while Van der Donck and the members of the Board of Nine wished to feel free to speak their minds, even if this entailed criticizing the Company.

Enraged by Van der Donck's attempt to circumvent his command not to consult the entire population of New Amsterdam, Stuyvesant had the lawyer arrested on a charge of high treason. Things came to a head on 8 March 1649 when Stuyvesant summoned all the people of the community to the church to discuss a serious matter. Cornelis Melyn and Jochem Kuyter, banished by Stuyvesant in 1647, had managed to find support in the States General during their exile in the Republic and had returned to the colony in a position of much greater strength; Melyn even had a letter from Stadholder Prince Willem II in his possession.[23] The two men had been given permission to appeal against their sentence and to await the verdict in the colony. Now, in the church, Melyn handed a document bearing the States General's seal to a member of the Board of Nine, and requested that he read this aloud. Stuyvesant tried in vain to grab the document but could not save himself from suffering the humiliation of everyone in the church hearing what the government of the Dutch Republic had to say about him. The letter instructed Stuyvesant to obey the States General's commands and to return to the Republic to account for himself.

The Colonists and the States General

Stuyvesant released Van der Donck from custody, but excluded him from serving on the Board of Nine. Van der Donck immediately devoted his energies to collaborating with the Board of Nine on the compilation of a document that he would call the *Vertoogh van Nieu Nederland*, or the "Remonstrance of New Netherland." He intended this formal complaint to serve several purposes. In the first place he wanted it to encourage the Dutch government to make effective, permanent agreements with the English concerning the borders between the Dutch colony and the adjoining English territories.

Secondly, he peppered the *Vertoogh* with criticisms of the Company that targeted both the gentlemen directors in the Republic and the colonial administration. Van der Donck was perceptive in his opinion of Stuyvesant: he denounced the director-general for taking personal action against his "innocent adversaries" even more than his predecessors, and deplored his obstinacy during council meetings: Stuyvesant, he claimed, could not stand criticism and responded with outbursts of rage and foul language.

The *Vertoogh*, the full title of which is *Vertoogh van Nieu Nederland, Weghens de Ghelegentheydt, Vruchtbaerheydt, en Soberen Staet desselfs* (The Remonstrance of New Netherland, concerning its location, productiveness, and poor condition), also considered the colony's impoverished situation and what Van der Donck regarded as its imprudent administration: money had been squandered on expensive, unnecessary mills which had not been properly maintained; if this had been spent instead on sending people and livestock to the colony, it would have had a healthy economy, he asserted.

The real aim of the document was to propose that the States General remove the administration of New Netherland from the hands of the WIC and turn the territory into an independent colony, under the direct authority of the States General. When Van der Donck drew up the *Vertoogh*, he must have borne in mind the possibility of gaining support from Prince Willem II, who had plans to convert the colonial administration into a Colonial Council. The *Vertoogh* was also an exhortation to dispatch more emigrants, to accelerate the process of instituting an appropriate administrative system, to allow more economic liberties and to settle border disputes with neighboring colonies through effective agreements. Included in Van der Donck's plans was the suggestion that patroons be allowed to sit on the Council, which would have created a fine office for the *Vertoogh*'s author, since Van der Donck was patroon of Colendonck. Van der Donck and ten others signed the *Vertoogh*, including all the members of the Board of Nine.[24]

Naturally Stuyvesant was enraged by these suggestions and the accusations directed against him. He defended himself in a letter to the States General, in which he proposed that his secretary Cornelis van Tienhoven travel to the Republic to explain the true situation in the colony.

Van der Donck returned to the Republic in the summer of 1649 with the *Vertoogh* under his arm. At his side were two members of the Board of Nine, the trader Jacob Couwenhoven and the farmer Jan Evertsen Bout. Stuyvesant sent his confidant, Van Tienhoven. It was important for both parties to be seen in the Republic: if there was to be a new colonial administration, who would have the first seats in it.

The States General appointed a committee to examine affairs in New Netherland and assess the petition submitted by Van der Donck and his confederates. In April 1650 the committee produced a report which endorsed the view that the colony was poorly governed, both from the Republic and locally. However, it did not approve the proposal

The “Remonstrance of New Netherland,” 1650

The printed version of Van der Donck’s 1650 petition bears the name *Vertoogh van Nieu Nederland* (Remonstrance of New Netherland). The manuscript version is part of a document entitled “Remonstrantie van Nieu-Nederlandt ende de gelegenheden aldaer” (Remonstrance of New Netherland and the occurrences there) and dates from 28 July 1649.
One of Van der Donck’s goals with the *Vertoogh* was to reach firm agreements regarding the borders between the Dutch colony of New Netherland and the English colonies of Virginia and New England. To foster negotiations between the two countries, he produced a map with all the potential borders inked in, and described these borders in the accompanying text.
Although this manuscript map has not survived, it was engraved by Johannes Janssonius in 1650. The engraving shows not only the border areas but also the degrees of latitude in which the territory claimed by the Dutch was located: the region between the 38th and 42nd latitude, from Cape Hinlopen to Staten Hoeck, now Cape Cod. Less than a year later the map was improved and reissued under the title “Novi Belgii Novæque Angliæ” (see the illustration at the side on page 102).
Visscher made the map more attractive by including a view of New Amsterdam, taken from Blaeu’s map of 1650. Blaeu, in turn, had copied this view from the drawing by Augustijn Heerman (as ill. on p. 115), which Van der Donck had in his possession when his *Vertoogh* was published. Danckerts, Allard, Ottens and many others copied the Visscher map until the late eighteenth century.[25]

Remonstrantie
Nieu Nederlandt En
gelegentheden aldaer
Aende
Hooch Mogende Heer
Generael der Vereen
Landen.
Vande Gemeente in
28 July
1649

“Remonstrantie van Nieu Nederlandt ende gelegentheden aldaer” (Remonstrance of New Netherland and the occurrences there), 1649
Nationaal Archief (National Archives of the Netherlands), The Hague
States General, 1.01.07, inv. no. 12564.30A
Ink on paper, 32 x 21.5 x 1.5 cm

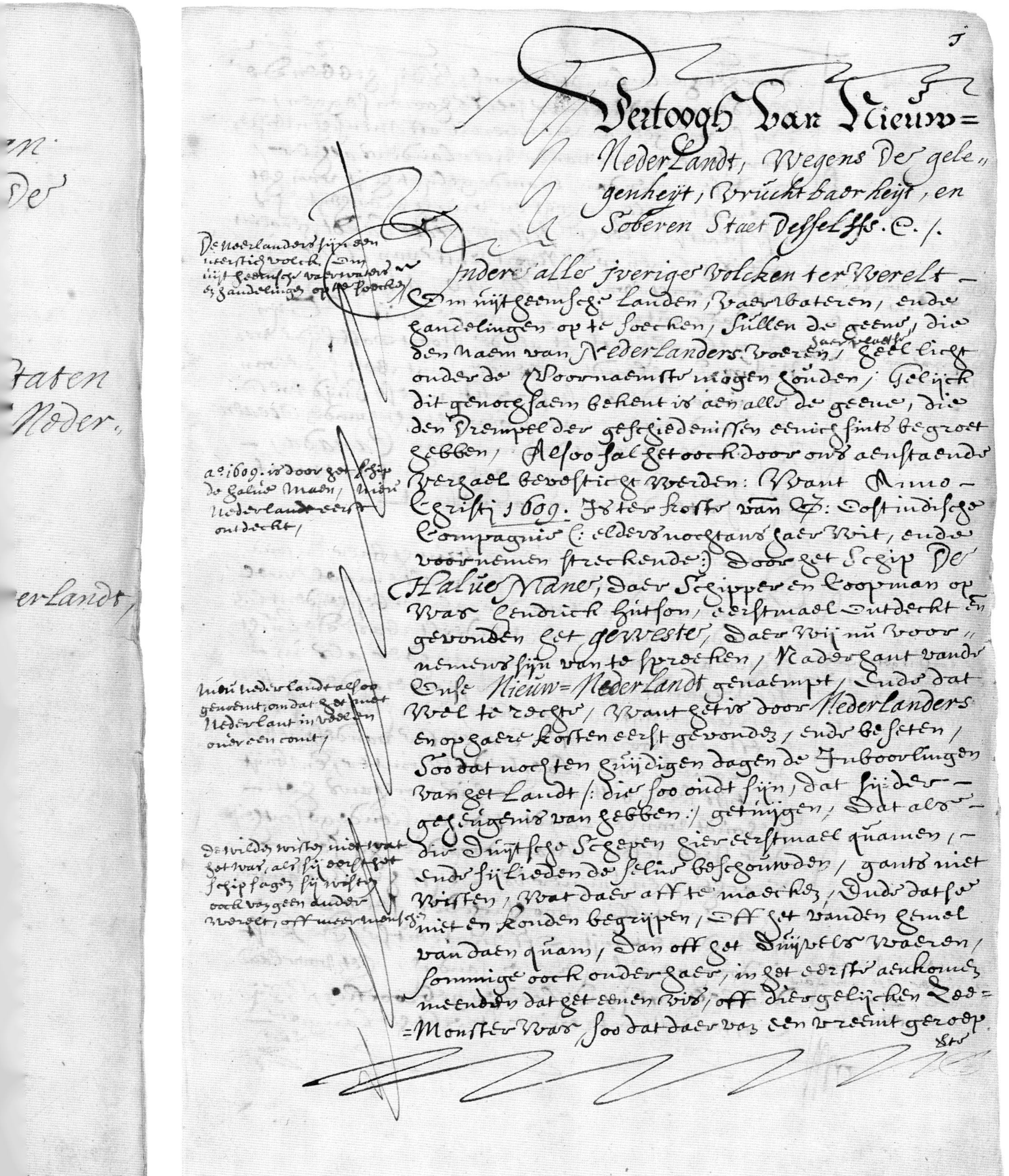

1

Vertoogh van Nieuw= Nederlandt, Wegens de gele= genheyt, Vruchtbaerheyt, en Soberen Staet desselffs. &c./

De Nederlanders sijn een ijverich volck, om uijt geensche vaerwateren en handelingen op te soecken

Onder alle ijverige Volcken ter Werelt – Om uijt geensche Landen, vaerwateren, ende handelingen op te soecken, sullen de geene, die den Naem van Nederlanders voeren, heel licht onder de voornaemste mogen houden, Gelijck dit genoechsaem bekent is aen alle de geene, die den Drempel der geschiedenissen eenichsints begroet hebben, Alsoo sal het oock door ons aenstaende verhael bevestiget worden: Want Anno Christi 1609. Is ter koste van de Oostindische Compagnie (: elders nochtans haer wit, ende voornemen streckende :) door het Schip De Halve Mane, daer Schipper en Koopman op was Hendrick Hutson, eerstmael ontdeckt en gevonden het gewest, daer wij nu voor= nemens sijn van te spreecken, Naderhant van de Onse Nieuw=Nederlandt genaempt, Ende dat wel te rechte, want het is door Nederlanders en op haere kosten eerst gevonden, ende beseten, Soodat noch ten huijdigen dage de Inboorlingen van het Landt (: die soo oudt sijn, dat sij der= gehuegenis van hebben :) getuijgen, Dat als de Duijtsche Schepen hier eerstmael quamen, ende sijluijden de selve beschouwden, gants niet wisten, wat daer aff te maecken, Ende dat se niet en konden begrijpen, Off het vanden hemel vandaen quam, dan off het Duijvels waeren, sommige oock onder haer, in het eerste aenkomen meenden dat het eenen vis, off diergelijcken Zee= =Monster was, soo dat daer van een vreemt gerucht

Ao. 1609. is door het Schip de halve Maen, Nieu Nederlant eerst ontdeckt,

Nieu Nederlandt alsoo genoemt, om dat het met Nederlant in veel en overeen comt,

de wilden wisten niet wat het was, als sij eerst het Schip sagen, sij wisten oock van geen ander wereldt, off meer menschen

NOVI BELGII NOVÆQUE ANGLIÆ NEC NON PARTIS VIRGINIÆ TABULA multis in locis emendata a Nicolao Joannis Visschero
NIEUW AMSTERDAM op t Eylant Manhattans
AMERICÆ SEPTENTRIONALIS PARS
NOVA BELGICA sive NIEUW NEDERLANDT
VIRGINIÆ PARS
MAR DE
Modus muniendi apud Mahikanenses
Maniere van Woonplaetsen ofte Dorpen der Mahicans ende andre Natien haer geburen
Charioquet
La Grand Riviere de Canada
Mont Royal
Groote Val
Rio St. Laurentius
Rio St. Laurens ali:
De Groote Rivier van Nieu Nederlandt
Tadoussac
Quebecq
Lacus Irocoisi: ensis ofte Meer der Irocoisen
IROCOISIA
Rio Irocoisiensis
Horikans
Mahikans
Mackwaas
Canomakers
Armeomecks
Sennecaas
Minnessinck ofte t'Landt van Bacham
Gacheos
Capitanasses
Matanac: kouses
Konekotays
Minquaas
Sasquesahanough
Tockwoghs
Kuscaraawaoks
t'Landt van Kats Kill
t'Hooge Landt van Esopus
Fort Orangie
RENSELAERS WYCK
Nawaas
Sequins
Conittekock
Makimanes
Quiripeys
Quyropey
Moricans
Pequatoos
Wapanoos
Nahicans
Waranawankongs
Wappinges
Waoranecks
Wecke
Pachami
Tappaans
Siwanoys
Manhattans
Nieuw Amsterdam
Sanhicans
t Lange Eylandt alias Matouwacs
Groote Rivier
Matovancons
Aquauachuques
Sauwanoos
Ermomex
Naraticons
Zuydt Rivier
Barndegat
Eyerhaven
Swanendael
Nieuw port May
Caep May
C. Cornelius
C. Hinlopen
Chesapeack Bay
Smyths Fales
Smyths Iles
C. Charle
Lacus
Milliaria Germanica communia

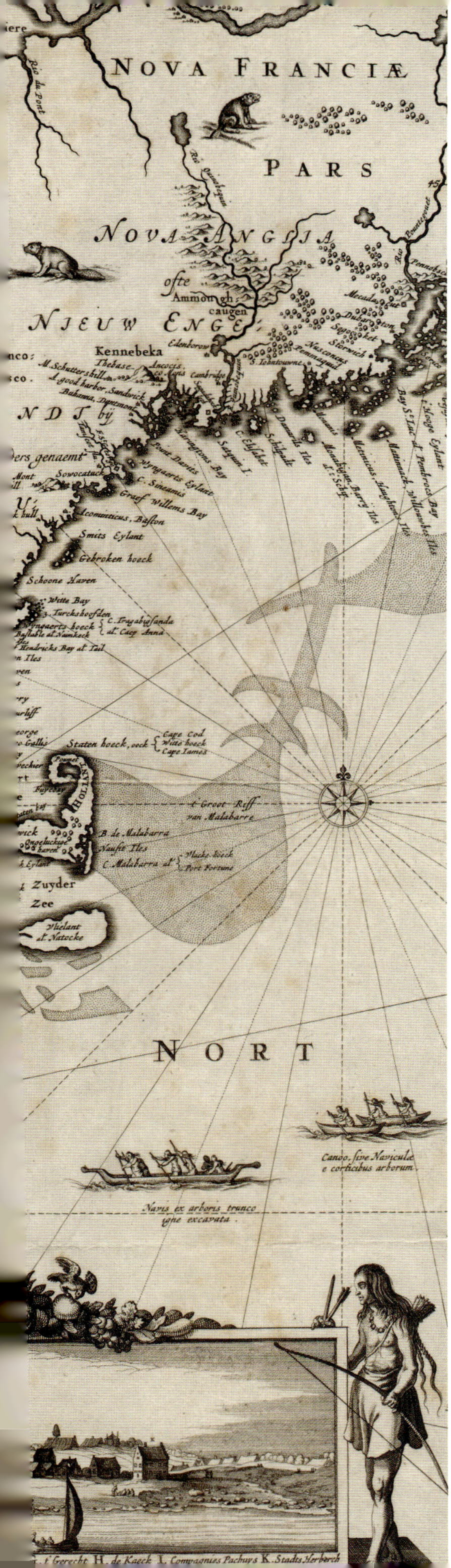

A Map from Van der Donck's *Vertoogh* Reused

One of the best known and most valued maps of New Netherland is this one by Nicolaes Visscher. Seventeenth-century printed maps are virtually never 100 percent original, for other cartographers always base them on manuscript maps or earlier printed works. This map is copied from a work with the same title by Joannes Janssonius, based in turn on a manuscript map appended to Van der Donck's *Vertoogh* that has not survived. Many elements from Blaeu's 1635 map (ill. on p. 93) can be recognized, including a few mistakes: Lake Champlain, for example, is bizarrely situated to the east of the Fresh (Connecticut) River. Nevertheless the map incorporates the latest geographical discoveries of the period, such as Lange Eiland (Long Island), which is no longer represented as an area broken up by a number of waterways but as a continuous island. The Hudson Highlands, the Catskill Mountains, the Mohawk River and several Mohawk villages have also been drawn in. Various Swedish and English names show that foreign settlers had infiltrated the Dutch colony. The map also includes several attractive details, such as the waterfall, which Van der Donck describes at length in the *Vertoogh*.

"Novi Belgii Novæque Angliæ"
(New Netherland New England)
Nicolaes I Visscher, 1656
Nationaal Archief (National Archives of the Netherlands), The Hague
4.VELH 568 D
Engraving, 46 x 55 cm

Van der Donck: A Passionate Lawyer

Much nonsense has been written about Van der Donck in history books.
The author of a slender volume from 1904 made one such an error when he described Van der Donck as "the earliest lawyer in New York," even though Lubbert van Dinclagen had been in the colony since 1633.[26]
Van Donck had only just finished his law studies at Leiden University when he left his fatherland in 1641 to start a new life elsewhere. In August of that year he arrived in the country where he would live, work and die. His first job was as *schout* (a kind of bailiff) on the Rensselaerswijck patroonship, where he worked for three years. In 1648 his name turns up as one of the Board of Nine, the advisory body created by Stuyvesant.
The following years would be important ones for Van der Donck and for New Netherland. With his *Vertoogh* (Remonstrance) he endeavored to right various wrongs and focus attention on the neglected colony. Although everything seemed to go well with his petition initially, Van der Donck eventually suffered defeat. Instead of Stuyvesant being required to travel to the Dutch Republic to explain his administrative methods, Van der Donck was charged to remain in the Republic, to prevent him from continuing to obstruct the new colonial administration. Ultimately Van der Donck did not achieve a great deal with all his work for the colony: the *Vertoogh* met with little or no success and Stuyvesant remained in his post.

Van der Donck made good use of his "house arrest" in the Republic. During this period he produced a second publication, the *Beschryvinge van Nieuw-Nederlant* (A Description of New Netherland) (ill. on p. 134). One is inclined to think, when reading the *Beschryvinge*, that the man genuinely loved New Netherland. Yet the book should not be regarded simply as a eulogy of the New World, for Van der Donck had a clear agenda when he wrote it: his summary of the land's countless riches was intended to encourage potential colonists to appreciate the wealth and beneficence of the territory, and the advantages they could enjoy there; after reading the *Beschryvinge* people were supposed to think: "What are we still doing here? Come on, let's go to New Netherland!"
Van der Donck did not return to his beloved America until 1653. He would not enjoy much more time there for he seems to have died at the age of 37, during an attack by Indians. His legacy is not only the *Vertoogh* and the *Beschrijvinge*, but also the name "Yonkers," for his patroonship became known as "Jonkheer's Land," or Young Squire's Land, which was subsequently corrupted to Yonkers.

Mr. Adriaen van der Donck, the Earliest Lawyer in New York.

A PAPER PRESENTED
AT THE TWENTY-SEVENTH ANNUAL MEETING
OF THE
New York State Bar Association,
HELD AT THE CITY OF ALBANY, N. Y., ON THE 19TH AND 20TH OF JANUARY, 1904, AND REPRINTED FROM THE TWENTY-SEVENTH ANNUAL REPORT OF THE PROCEEDINGS OF THE ASSOCIATION.

BY ALFRED L. BECKER,
OF THE BUFFALO, N. Y., BAR.

"Mr. Adriaen van der Donck, the Earliest Lawyer in New York"
Alfred L. Becker, 1904
Royal Library, The Hague
502 K 15
22.5 x 14.5 x 0.5 cm

that the Dutch West India Company be stripped of its administrative task: Stuyvesant was to remain in office but was commanded to travel to the Republic to account for his behavior.

The report favored the people of New Amsterdam: they were to be given a greater say in their government and the Council was to be overhauled, henceforth comprising a director and vice-director, a judge advocate, a councilor appointed by the States General and the WIC and two councilors chosen from the colonists. Another innovation was the introduction of a city council, the "municipal government," to be composed of a schout (bailiff), two burgomasters and five aldermen. Moreover, the *Vrijheden en Exemptieën* (Liberties and Exemptions) of 1640 were to be replaced by a new, more liberal version.

Everything seemed clear and settled. But the Amsterdam Chamber of the WIC fiercely resisted the new arrangements. The directors did not understand why Stuyvesant should be recalled; they deemed such an action totally unnecessary and claimed little was amiss in the colony anyway. Stuyvesant reacted similarly. When the delegation returned to New Amsterdam, and triumphantly presented the report and the States General's new rules to the director-general, he proved totally determined not to implement the slightest change until the report had been ratified. Ratification would not be immediate so Stuyvesant had gained some time. In the years 1650-1651 no changes were introduced. This impasse prompted the Board of Nine to write numerous letters of complaint to Van der Donck, who was still in the Republic. The lawyer was entrusted with ensuring that these letters found their way to the States General.

The Board of Nine's letters of complaint were intended to accelerate the process of administrative reorganization in the colony. However, they barely had an effect. The Amsterdam Chamber of the WIC simply refused to cooperate. It was not until April 1652 that the States General took up the issue once more and decided to recall Stuyvesant to the Republic to explain himself. Again the Amsterdam Chamber proved obstructive; its members were indignant for they had not been consulted when the government body had decided to send for the director. They deliberately hampered progress by writing Stuyvesant, expressly instructing him not to hasten to the Republic.

In the end Stuyvesant did not have to worry about any kind of trip: the decision to recall him to the Republic was rescinded when war between the Republic and England seemed imminent. The States General had other concerns. When the First Anglo-Dutch War actually broke out, in May 1652, Stuyvesant was required to remain at his post to counter possible attacks on the Dutch colony.

Nevertheless one change was made to the colony's administrative structure. On 2 February 1653 an important element in the 1650 plans became reality when the Board of Nine was transformed into a municipal administration with its own court. Several courts had already been installed elsewhere in the colony.[27] By this time, however, the Board of Nine's composition had been radically altered. At the end of 1650, Stuyvesant had not complied with the Board of Nine's recommendations but had appointed six new members who were more favorably disposed towards the WIC. Not one of the members of the Board of Nine who had formed the core of resistance to the Company from 1647 to late 1650 was still in office. This had created a new political situation, in which Stuyvesant and his Council had felt safe to propose, in September 1651, that the Board of Nine be remodeled as a municipal administration.

Peter Stuyvesant had managed to outmaneuver his adversary Van der Donck. The criticism of colonists and fellow administrators may have forced his predecessors to beat a retreat, but he was a leader who had stood firm.

1232

Augustijn Heerman

A Cartographer from Bohemia who Fought for the Colony

His given name was variously written as Augustinis, Augustin, Augustyn and Augustine and there are several versions of his family name: Heerman, Herrman and Herman. Augustijn Heerman, the first New Amsterdammer from Bohemia, was born in 1621 in the vicinity of Prague. Around 1627 his family left the area but it is not clear where they went.

When exactly Heerman arrived in New Netherland cannot be determined with any certainty either. Like Adriaen van der Donck, he put a great deal of effort into improving the government of New Netherland. He too was one of the Board of Nine, who jointly signed the *Vertoogh* (Remonstrance) drawn up by Van der Donck. This document attempted to address and improve several matters of importance in the colony. As an appendix to the document, Heerman made a drawing of a view of New Amsterdam (see illustration p. 115). Heerman first worked as a land surveyor for the WIC before becoming an agent for a trading house around 1644, after which he set up his own company.

Like so many New Amsterdammers, Heerman had a house in the city as well as property to the north. His city dwelling was on the corner of Heere Straet (Broad Way) and Heere Dwars Straet (Exchange Place).[28] Heerman's property lay just north of what is today Wall Street, then known as the Singel.

Around 1660 Heerman moved to the neighboring British colony of Maryland, founded in the 1630s by Lord Baltimore, who gave Heerman permission to buy a tract of land of about 8,000 hectares (20,000 acres). Heerman named his home Bohemia Manor. It is not known where he learned cartography. Possibly he acquired the skill in Amsterdam, where his fellow-countryman Johann Amos Comenius worked as a cartographer; or possibly in London, where another Bohemian, the draughtsman and engraver Wenceslaus Hollar, was then living.

He died in 1686 and is commemorated by Augustine Herman Highway, which runs right through the state of Maryland.[29]

Detail from Heerman's Map Showing Virginia and Maryland

Heerman's Map of Virginia and Maryland
"Virginia and Maryland as it is Planted and Inhabited this Present Year 1670, Surveyed and Exactly Drawne by the Only Labour & Endeavour of Augustim Herrman Bohemiensis"
Augustin Heerman, London, 1673
Library of Congress, Washington, D.C.
MSA SC 5339-1-172

Photo of Broadway between Wall Street and Exchange Place, where Augstijn Heerman lived

Pieter Henket, photographer
Born 1979 Geldrop
In New York since 1998

The Board of Nine's Letters of Complaint About Peter Stuyvesant

Thirteen letters of complaint about the colonial administration's policies written by the Board of Nine were collected and bound under the title: "Extracten en copien van de brieven memorien journaelen ende resolutien bij de gemeente van Nieuw Nederlant in den jaere 1650 ende 1651 aen Adriaen van der Donck gesonden dienende tot verificatie van de requeste volgens de ordre van haer Hoog Mogenden in dato 16 februari 1652" (Extracts and copies of the letters, memoranda, journals and resolutions of the community of New Netherland in the years 1650 and 1651 sent to Adriaen van der Donck serving in verification of the petition in accordance with the order of their High Mightinesses dated 16 February 1652).

Among the names on the letters are those of Jochem Pietersz. Kuyter, Augustijn Heerman and Jacob van Couwenhoven, all members of the Board of Nine. In the period 1650-1652 they sent these complaints to Adriaen van der Donck who was in the Dutch Republic at the time. Van der Donck forwarded the letters to the States Generals. However, to the Board of Nine's immense frustration, the States General ignored or barely responded to these missives. Back in the Republic there were far more important matters to get wound up about.

In 1650 Stadholder Willem II had tried to settle a conflict with the States General over troop reduction with an unsuccessful coup d'état. His death later that year proved beneficial to the Dutch West India Company: Willem had envisaged himself at the head of a colonial administration; his politics would have jeopardized the WIC's future but that threat had now been removed. The resulting power vacuum in the Republic caused the States General to ignore the letters from the North American colony. Over time the letters seem to grow increasingly peevish in tone. Various passages in them are underlined:

"To Adriaen van der Donck: … the vexation that exists in the poor community here can no longer be abided."

"From the vice director Dincklage to the noble directors of the Amsterdam Chamber on 8 September 1650: … here men goeth not the right way. Profit has become loss, and the common goods private, the assets have been consumed and dispersed without advancing the noble company and the land. I cannot help it, as Director Stuyvesant says it is not my concern."

"Extract from a statement by Joachim Peters Cuijter: … That Mister Stuyvesant had received many letters … that they would continue to write to the director and him with all their might and means, yea, until they bled."

"Augustin Hermans dated 20 September 1651: … will not only be threatened, plagued, hindered [and] affronted but also totally ruined."

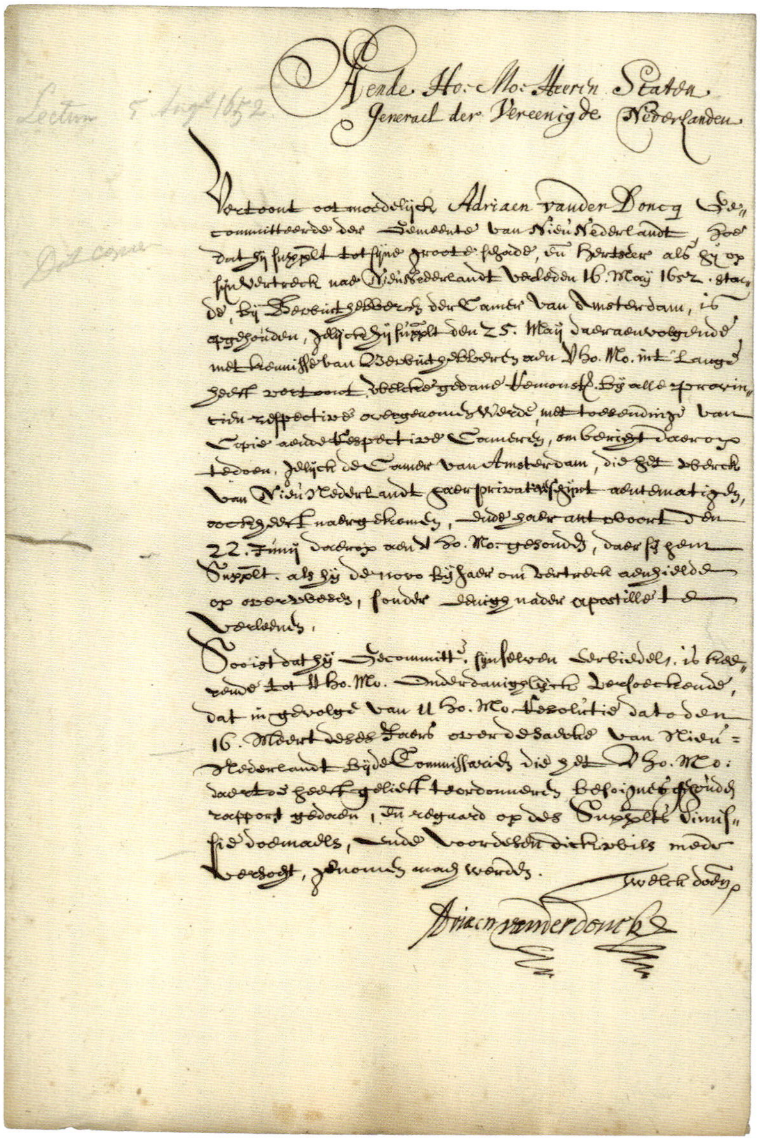

The Board of Nine's Letters of Complaint About Peter Stuyvesant
Nationaal Archief (National Archives of the Netherlands), The Hague
States General, 1.01.07, inv. no. 12564.36
Ink on paper, 21 x 32 cm

The States General Assembly Reacts to the Complaints

The States General in 1651
Dirck van Delen
Rijksmuseum, Amsterdam
Oil on copper, 52 × 68 cm

The interior of the Ridderzaal (Knights' Hall) in The Hague. The States General gathered in this thirteenth-century hall during the Great Assembly. The painting presents the States General's most important assembly in 1651, the year in which they debated constitutional relationships within the Dutch Republic from January through August. After Stadholder Willem II had died in November of the previous year, the States General decided not to appoint a successor from his family. They made this decision at the assembly depicted in the painting, which thus marked the beginning of the First Stadholderless Era. More than 300 delegates – the entire membership of the States General – attended the assembly.

In the same year, 1651, Van der Donck was living in the Republic. There he received the letters of complaint sent by the Board of Nine, which he was entrusted with forwarding to the States General. The letters initially prompted the States General to order that Stuyvesant be recalled from New Netherland to account for his actions. When the First Anglo-Dutch War broke out, however, this order was soon rescinded.

The painting shows flags and standards hanging from the ceiling and walls of the Ridderzaal. These trophies had been taken from forts and ships captured from the Republic's enemies.

[1] Jacobs, "The Hartford Treaty," pp. 74-79.
[2] De Vries, *Korte historiael ende journaels aenteyckeninge*, p. 174.
[3] Rink, *Holland on the Hudson*, pp. 119-121; Jacobs, *Een zegenrijk gewest*, pp. 116-117.
[4] Rink, *Holland on the Hudson*, pp. 112-114.
[5] Jacobs, "A Troubled Man," pp. 213-232.
[6] Jacobs, "A Troubled Man," pp. 213-232; De Vries, *Korte historiael ende journaels aenteycken inge*, pp. 174-176.
[7] Den Heijer, *De geschiedenis van de WIC*, p. 85; Rink, *Holland on the Hudson*, pp. 123-126.
[8] Jacobs, "A Troubled Man," pp. 213-232.
[9] O'Callaghan, *History of New Netherland*, p. 258.
[10] O'Callaghan, *History of New Netherland*, pp. 258-259.
[11] Schuyler van Rensselaer, *History of the City of New York in the Seventeenth Century*, I, p. 259.
[12] O'Callaghan, *History of New Netherland*, pp. 258-259 in the footnote, p. 258: "The supposition that the town of Gravesend, on Long Island, derived its name from the first settlers having sailed from Gravesend, in England, is altogether gratuitous. It was the fashion with all European powers who had possessions in the New World, to transfer the names of towns in the mother country, to their new settlements in America. The Dutch were observant of this custom as any other nation of which fact any person can satisfy himself by looking over a map of Holland."
[13] O'Callaghan, *History of New Netherland*, p. 287; Griswold??Schuyler van Rensselaer, *History of the City of New York in the Seventeenth Century*, I, p. 228.
[14] Schuyler van Rensselaer, *History of the City of New York in the Seventeenth Century*, I, p. 485.
[15] Zandvliet, "Een ouderwetse kaart van Nieuw Nederland," p. 59.
[16] Frijhoff, "Neglected Networks."
[17] Otto, *The Dutch-Munsee Encounter*, p. 152.
[18] Frijhoff, *Wegen van Evert Willemsz.*, pp. 735-725.
[19] De Vries, *Korte historiael ende journaels aenteyckeninge*, p. 271.
[20] Jacobs, *Een zegenrijk gewest*, pp. 138-140.
[21] Jaap Jacobs will publish a biographical sketch of Stuyvesant in 2009, *Petrus Stuyvesant. Een levensschets*, 2009 Bert Bakker Amsterdam; Jacobs, "Like Father, Like Son?"; Gehring, *Correspondence* 1647-1653, pp. xiii-xxx.
[22] Jacobs, *Een zegenrijk gewest*, p. 243.
[23] "To Petrus Stuyvesant, Director of New Netherland, the 19th of May 1648. Honorable, prudent and discreet, specially dear. You will receive by the bearers hereof, Joachim Pietersen Kuyter and Cornelis Melyn, the commands which the High and Mighty Lords States General have resolved to communicate to you, to the end that you allow these people to enjoy their property free and unmolested there ... we are disposed earnestly to admonish you hereby, in addition, expressly notifying that you shall have to allow said petitioners, peaceably and without objection to enjoy the effect of their High Mightinesses aforesaid resolution. And herewith, Honorable &c. Willem, Prince d'Orange" in: Shorto, *The Island at the Center of the World*, pp. 228-229.
[24] Jacobs, "Migration, Population, and Government in New Netherland." For the names and professions of the signatories, see Jameson, *Narratives*, pp. 289-290.
[25] Kupcík, "Die kartografische Tätigkeit von Augustin Herman," pp. 203-219, fig. 6.
[26] Jacobs, *Een zegenrijk gewest*, p. 482.
[27] Jacobs, *Een zegenrijk gewest*, pp. 146-157.
[28] Phelps Stokes, *The Iconography of Manhattan Island*.
[29] http://www.msa.md.gov/msa/speccol/sc2200/sc2269/html/cartographers.html; Kupcík, "Die kartografische Tätigkeit von Augustin Herman," pp. 203-219.

II

CHAPTER 4

A City for the Colony 1653-1660

By 1653 the principal seat of the colony has grown from a hamlet into a sizeable place with a population of 500 to 700. New Amsterdam acquires city rights and gradually evolves into a genuine town. The director-general and his councilors govern the colony as a whole. The city council, comprised of mayors, a *schout* (a kind of bailiff) and aldermen, make policy in New Amsterdam.

New municipal facilities are built, such as a marketplace and a pier. The existing town inn is converted into a town hall. Running these public institutions requires new officials, from dogcatchers to town criers.

The famous Castello map presents an image of the city around 1660; we can see how in the course of time houses, streets and windmills sprang up on the tip of Manhattan.

Drawn by the opportunities the colony has to offer, the inhabitants have to build up a new existence and cooperate with each other. Given the settlers great ethnical, cultural and religious diversity this is not always easy in a town like New Amsterdam. The question arises whether the townspeople find it more difficult to deal with the deviating customs of their neighbors or with authority in the colony.

How do the director-general and his council deal with all of these different people? In old Amsterdam in the Republic dissenters are granted a certain amount of tolerance. Does New Amsterdam compare to the mother city in this respect?

Finally, we take a look at agriculture and nature on Manhattan. Has the island been swallowed up by farms, pastures and fields in the meantime? The colony does not stop with Manhattan, for its hinterland too has much to offer the European pioneers.

Arms of New Amsterdam

This design for the arms of New Amsterdam was just a proposal. In this drawing we see the three vertically placed crosses which stand for the arms of the city of Amsterdam in the Republic. The famous Dutch lions have here been replaced by two beavers. The crown is decorated with the WIC's logo. The design was never realized, for the board of New Amsterdam did not approve it.

Arms of New Amsterdam, ca. 1653
New York Historical Society, New York
Inv. no. 45814
Watercolor, gouache and chalk, 35.6 x 45.7 cm

The Face of New Amsterdam

Municipal Facilities

In 1629 the colony counted about 250 to 350 inhabitants, the majority of whom lived in New Amsterdam. Twenty-five years later the population of New Netherland had swelled to between 2000 and 3500.[1] This increase called for a new vision of town and country planning and the public works of New Amsterdam. Defenses, roads and canals had to be maintained, firemen had to practice drills regularly and regulations were introduced prohibiting the disposal of waste in the canals. As the city expanded, the need for public institutions grew. An orphanage, a school and a weigh house were built. Civil servants had to steer new developments in the right direction and fill positions in official organs as the heads of orphanages, fire chiefs, warders, ushers and schoolmasters. With the establishment of new institutions, several new occupations emerged on Manhattan, such as dogcatcher and town crier.

There was plenty of work for all of these people. This also applied to the master builders and their workmen and craftsmen, because the fort had crumbled and the houses built in the 1620s were on the verge of collapse.

When Peter Stuyvesant arrived in New Amsterdam in 1647, he set out to improve the layout and the defense of the city. A comparison of the city view of 1648 (ill. on p. 115) with later ones reveals that the coastline was transformed from a muddy twisting line into a taut division between land and water. The sheet piling that Stuyvesant had ordered to be installed explains this change. Another difference between the early and later city views is the presence of a pier. Van der Donck said that this pier was one of the few good things Stuyvesant had done for the population. This is somewhat of an exaggeration because the director-general also tackled other projects, such as building the weigh house and later also the Latin School. The weigh house was supervised by the WIC rather than the city. The city council, however, did regularly demand that the proceeds from it would in part or fully benefit the municipal treasury.

On Mondays, the weekly market was held between the pier and the town inn, which served as the town hall as of 1653. When the quay underwent repair in 1656 the market was moved to the corner of today's Pearl Street and Whitehall Street. When work on the quay was completed, the market could be held on the square on the northern side of the fort, which came to be called Marckvelt (Market Square).[2] A covered meat market was also built there.

New Amsterdam was now a genuine town with all the proper provisions. There were canals, churches, schools and an orphanage. Can we then say that the New Amsterdam of the 1650s resembled Amsterdam, the mother city in the Republic? There is little sense in trying to discern the similarities between the two cities: New Amsterdam remained too small to warrant being juxtaposed with Amsterdam.

What are of interest are the names of a few locations. Amsterdam has a "Schreiers Hoeck Toren," a tower on the Oude Waal, the place where according to city lore families bade their loved ones farewell when they sailed to the East or West. New Amsterdam also had such a "schrijers hoeck" located on the waterfront, likewise was called the Waal. Other names found in both cities are the Singel, the Heeregracht, the Prinsegracht, the Tuijnstraet and the Hoogstraat.

The City in 1660

Thanks to a splendid city plan (ill. on pp. 122-123) called the Castello map after the villa of the De Medici family near Florence where it was long kept, we know approximately what New Amsterdam must have looked like in 1660, down to its gardens and trees. Such an elaborate map begs to be described in greater detail.

The map shows that there was no rectilinear design to the layout of the streets and structures in the colony's earliest years. The streets at the southern tip of Manhattan differ in length and breadth and thus cannot be compared to the later street pattern further north. Even though the tip of Manhattan has expanded through coastal accretion in the last centuries and no traces of the Dutch buildings have survived, the street plan still largely corresponds with the present layout.

Two roads immediately catch the eye: the horizontal Heere Straet, also known as the Brede Wegh or Wagen Wegh, and the vertical road with seven bastions, which functioned as the town rampart and was called the Singel (later in the seventeenth century Langs de Wal; presently Wall Street). Financed by the burghers, this town rampart marked the boundary between the densely built up southern tip and the northern section of Manhattan. This afforded the settlers a sound defense from outside attacks. Prior to its construction, the fort had served as a safe haven for the inhabitants but had become too small to accommodate all of them, and so the director-general and his councilors in collaboration with the city council had seen fit to build the rampart. The first one, a wooden palisade, dates from 1653 and was erected during the Anglo-Dutch War. In the map, however, stone bastions rather than wooden palisades are depicted.

Heerman's View of New Amsterdam

More than likely, this drawing, discovered in the Albertina Collection at the Austrian National Library in Vienna, was made by Augustijn Heerman, a Bohemian businessman from Prague.[3] After a career as a military officer and an agent for an Amsterdam commercial establishment, Heerman landed in New Amsterdam in 1643. There, in 1648, he was asked together with Van der Donck to serve on Stuyvesant's advisory Board of Nine. He made this drawing of New Amsterdam in that capacity and in the same year. The sketch was an important part of Van der Donck's *Vertoogh* (Remonstrance), the document intended to convince the States General that a new regime was badly needed in New Netherland.[4] Along with Van der Donck, Augustijn Heerman was one of the ten men to sign the *Vertoogh*.

By depicting the deplorable state of New Amsterdam, and perhaps exaggerating it a bit, the drawing supported the text in the *Vertoogh*. Just look at the dilapidated mill with two sails. Leaks in the roof had caused the mill to rot, and it was operated with two rather than four sails for fear that it would collapse under their weight. Van der Donck wrote that this had been the situation for close to five years.

On the left can be seen part of the fort and two striking buildings: the house of the director-general and the church, built in 1642. David Pietersz. de Vries recounts in his own, always somewhat intrepid way, how the church came to be: Kieft had boasted to De Vries about "his" new inn, one of the very few buildings in New Amsterdam to have been made entirely of stone. Thanks to these new accommodations, English merchants from Virginia and New England could spend the night in comfort. In turn, De Vries apparently admonished him "that while it was indeed convenient for the traveling man, the need for a church was much greater, for it would be a disgrace for us were the English to pass by and see the run-down shed where we worship".[5]

View of New Amsterdam
Attributed to Augustijn Heerman, ca. 1648
Österreichische Nationalbibliothek, Vienna
ÖNB/K, Albertina/vues 12.720/1
Watercolor on paper, 53 x 31.5 cm

De Vries was able to present matters in such a way that the city more or less had him to thank for the church. Van der Donck later complained in his *Vertoogh* that the church was erected inside the fort much against everyone's will. The church was for the community which, after all, had paid for it. So, why then did it have to be constructed within the fort walls? Van der Donck's criticism did not end there. He noted that the tall building obstructed the prevailing south-easterly wind, which was why the mill could not turn.

Heerman also depicted the sorry state of the fort. Intended to protect the settlers from harm, the complex more closely resembled a crumbling molehill. There was no foundation that could support even a single piece of artillery and the ramparts were unstable. In point of fact, Van der Donck was calling New Amsterdam a ruin and Heerman painted it as such. Van der Donck blamed various parties for the fort's ramshackle condition: the WIC had neglected the city by continually focusing on Brazil; the States General had dismissed it, preoccupied by the ongoing struggle against Spain; and Kieft had discounted it because of his hostile obsession with the Indians. An interesting detail in the drawing is the inclusion of Heerman's own house. C in the legend marks the "Compagnies Packhuys," or Company's Warehouse. The building to its right was almost certainly owned by Heerman between 1645 and 1651.[6]

NIEUW AMSTERDAM OFTE NUE NIEUW IORX

Vingboons' View of New Amsterdam

This watercolor by Johannes Vingboons presents the same scene in the drawing by Heerman from 1648. Vingboons, who never set foot outside the Republic, copied his maps from the ground plans, views and maps made by others.[7] Going on the title and in particular the words "Nieuw Iorx," Vingboons' view could be dated to 1664, the year in which New Amsterdam was taken over by the English and renamed New York. However, the situation depicted in Vingboons' watercolor is from around 1650.

A comparison of the two views reveals that the mill in Vingboons' watercolor has all four, rather than two, sails again. The red tiled roofs make a cheerful impression, and the step gables line up neatly. A dilapidated fort is nowhere to be seen, and the wooden houses are freshly painted. The facades, incidentally, recall those of houses in Waterland in present-day Noord Holland province, known as single-nave double fronted houses. This is not so surprising given that various colonists hailed from this region.[8] In reality, the condition of the fort will not have been as pristine as the watercolor would have us believe. After all, the almost entirely tumbledown fort would be rebuilt in 1654. Frightening is the low gallows with two pole, which was called "het Gerecht" (the court). Next to this is a long pole, which is often interpreted as a hoisting crane. It is also plausible that a smoldering firepot was hung from this pole as a beacon for incoming ships.[9]

"Nieuw Amsterdam ofte Nue Nieuw Iorx opt 'T Eylant Man" (New Amsterdam or New York on the Island of Manhattan)
Johannes Vingboons, third quarter of the seventeenth century
Nationaal Archief (National Archives of the Netherlands), The Hague
4.VELH 619-14
Watercolor on paper, 42 x 63 cm

"Nieuw Amsterdam op 't Eylant Manhatans"
(New Amsterdam on the Island of Manhattan)
Inset of the map "Novi Belgii Novæque Angliæ"
(New Netherland New England) by Nicolaes
Visscher, 1656
Nationaal Archief (National Archives
of the Netherlands), The Hague
4.VELH 568 D
Engraving, 46 x 55 cm

Emulators of Heerman's Drawing

Heerman's drawing did not serve as a model for Vingboons' watercolor alone. Many cartographers used his view of the city to add luster to their maps. Ironically Heerman's drawing, intended only to portray the plight of the settlers in the Dutch colony, continued to serve as a Romantic example for the depiction of old New York, an attractive and charming place to settle, until the second half of the eighteenth century. Here we see an inset in the map by Nicolaes Visscher illustrated on pages 102-103. There are a few minor deviations from Heerman's drawing: the mill has four rather than two sails and a tiny figure hangs from the gallows.

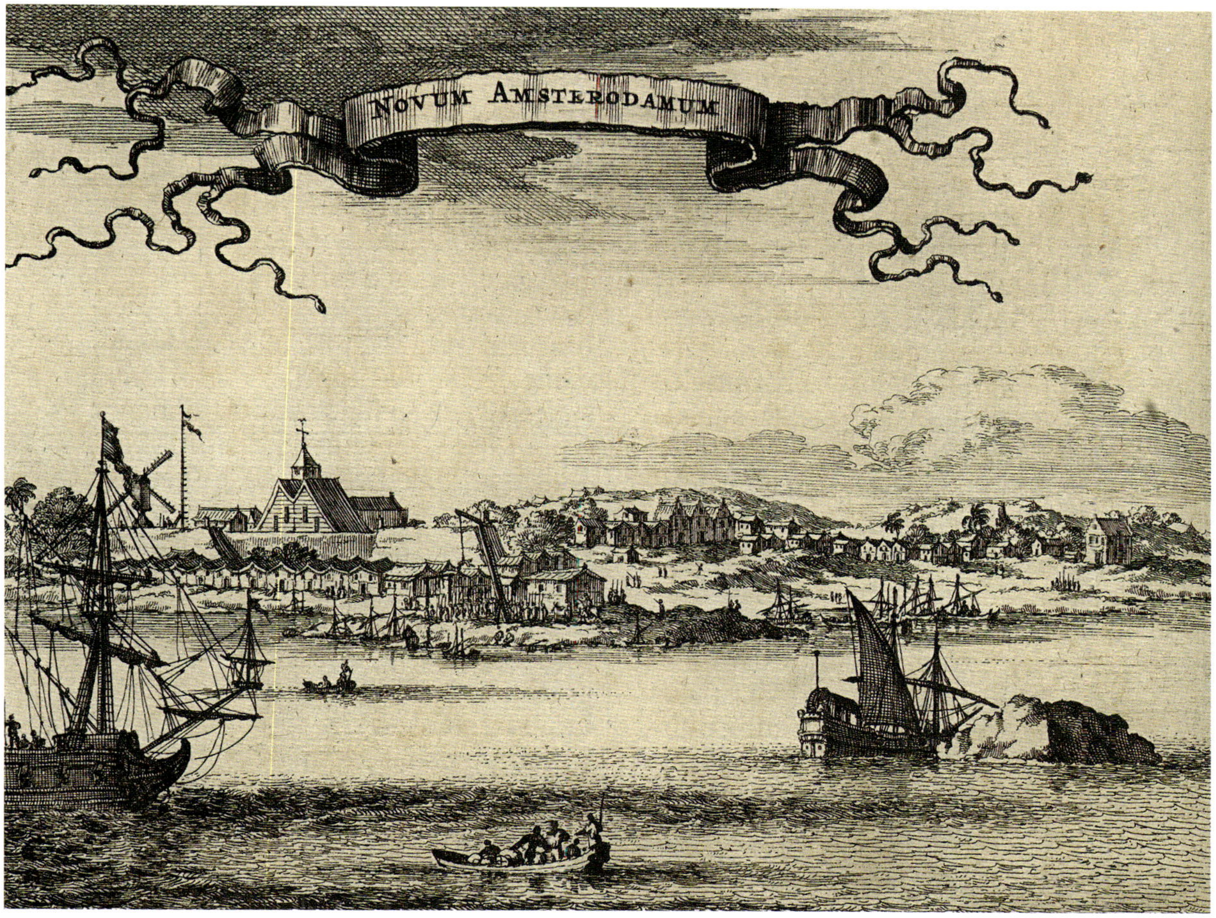

Nieuw Amsterdam around 1650
Detail of "Novum Amsterodamum"
(New Amsterdam) in: Arnoldus Montanus,
De nieuwe en onbekende weereld: of Beschryving van America en ..., (The new and unknown world: or a description of America and ...),
Amsterdam, 1671
Royal Library, The Hague
185 B 14
Engraving, 13.5 x 11 cm

WIC Buildings in Amsterdam and New Amsterdam

Warehouse of the WIC in Amsterdam
Royal Library, The Hague
496 D 8
Engraving, 13.5 x 11 cm

Warehouse of the WIC in Amsterdam
Photo: David Cohen de Lara, 2009

The warehouse of the Dutch West India Company (WIC) in Amsterdam: in 1641-1642 the Amsterdam Chamber decided to have this warehouse built on Rapenburg Island. For a while the building served as the headquarters of the WIC board. The warehouse still exists and is located at the 's Gravenhekje. Presently, the complex comprises offices and luxury apartments with a view of the city's inland waterways. Here, the Oudeschans flows into the IJ River.

Town Hall in New Amsterdam
In: Jasper Dankers and Petrus Sluyter, *Journal of a Voyage to New York*, 1679-80 (translated by Henry C. Murphy in 1867)
Royal Library, The Hague
676 C 160
Engraving

Town Hall in New Amsterdam
Samuel Hollyer, 1826-1919
New York Public Library, New York
ID: 800004

In its day, the Town Hall in New Amsterdam was a striking edifice. Like the warehouse in Amsterdam, it was built around 1642.[10] The Town Hall in New Amsterdam was initially a town inn. In 1653, upon acquiring city rights, the "Stadt Herberg" (town inn), which had been built by Stuyvesant's predecessor Kieft, was transformed into the administrative seat of the new city regents. Stuyvesant and his councilors convened there as of 1647.

Town Hall: Detail of the "Castello Map"
(see pp. 122-123)

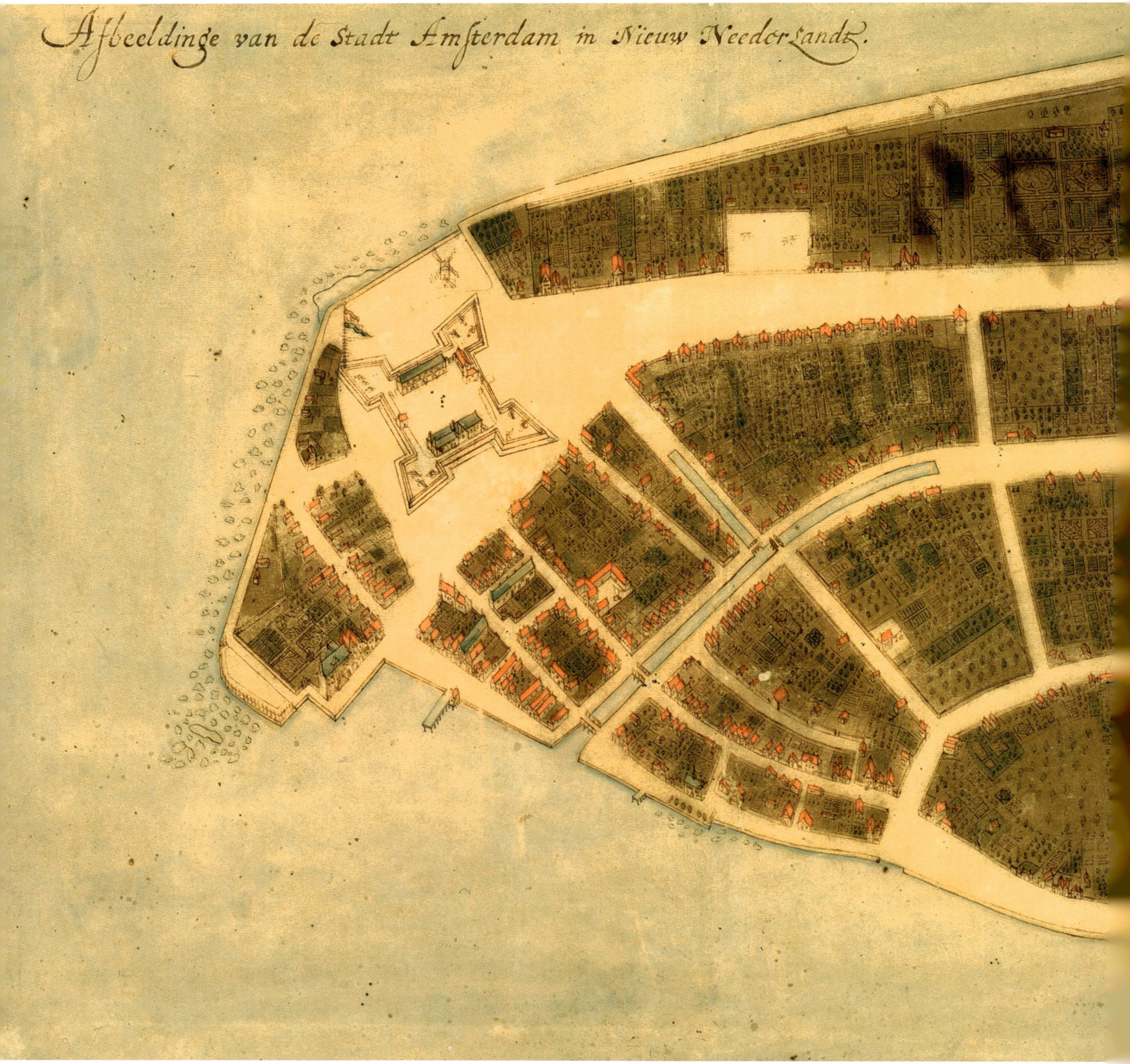
Afbeeldinge van de Stadt Amsterdam in Nieuw Neederlandt.

Illustrations of the City of Amsterdam in New Netherland

Johannes Vingboons made this map in the second half of the 1660s. He relied on a map by Jacques Cortelyou of 1660, which has not been preserved.
Given the situation, it is not surprising that in 1660 the director-general and the councilors commissioned Jacques Cortelyou to produce a detailed city plan.[11] The more inhabitants the city drew, the more land had to be parceled out among them. As time went by differences of opinion abounded and lawsuits were brought regarding where boundaries began and ended. In the early years this would not have been an issue as there was plenty of land to go around. However, in 1660 much of the land south of the embankment was occupied. Most people no longer had any clear idea of what was their own or their neighbor's property.
A plan had been devised earlier in 1655 to chart all the roads, streets, houses and plots. Stuyvesant hired land surveyors to make exact measurements. The first map with plots of land sketched in was completed in 1656. Four years later surveyor Jacques Cortelyou was asked to make a new "platte kaart" of the city.[12]
As mentioned above, the Cortelyou map was copied by the cartographer Johannes Vingboons. Vingboons' version, the Castello map, is not only the most famous plan of Manhattan but also the earliest preserved street plan of the city. Moreover, it is the only known map of the city from this period. And, in the twentieth century, it served as the example for all kinds of scale-models and maps. Using this map or a twentieth-century replica of it, quite a few New Yorkers have searched for landmarks in their neighborhood. But alas, except for the present street layout, there is little that recalls earlier times.
In recent years archeologists have demonstrated that various details in the Castello map do not agree with the data yielded by their investigations. For instance, finds indicating the foundations and quays along canals do not coincide with the markings on the map. Moreover, many of the demarcations of plots in the Castello map do not correspond with the findings of the archeological investigation. Accordingly, the Castello map is probably not an entirely faithful recording of the situation around 1660.

The Sille's List and Phelps Stokes' Observations

In 1660, Nicasius de Sille, the *schout* (bailiff) of New Amsterdam, compiled a list of several houses and their New Amsterdam owners: "Lijste van de opgenomen Huijsen op den 10 Julij 1660 Binnen dese stede Amsterdam in N:Nederland". This list can be seen as a "legend" of the Castello map.[13]
On the basis of the list and other archival material, in the beginning of the twentieth century Isaac Newton Phelps Stokes tried to link those houses in the city not mentioned by De Sille to other New Amsterdammers. He attempted to match up dozens of inhabitants whose names are known from the archives to all of the 342 buildings and dwellings in the Castello map. Phelps Stokes subsequently superimposed a grid based on the Castello map on the present New York plan to gain insight into how the modern situation compares with division of land in 1660.[14]
As appealing as it seems to follow Phelps Stokes, it is wiser not to do so. As mentioned above, the Castello map is not all that reliable. And neither is Phelps Stokes' investigation. On the basis of so-called "grondbrieven," or title deeds, he was able to date the construction of a house on a given plot. However, because many plots actually remained vacant for years on end his assumptions are not always accurate.

"Afbeeldinge van de Stadt Amsterdam in Nieuw Neederlandt" (Illustration of the City of Amsterdam in New Netherland)
The "Castello Map," Johannes Vingboons, third quarter of the seventeenth century, after Jacques Cortelyou
Biblioteca Medicea Laurenziana, Florence
Carte di Castello 18
Watercolor on paper, 52 x 66.4 cm

The Heere Straet or Brede Wegh

Would these people have actually sat together like this on the sidewalk of the Heere Straet? According to John Gadsby Chapman they did. The Heere Straet or Brede Wegh connected the fort with the Company's gardens, located in the upper right of the Castello map. The street was the beginning of a 240 kilometer long trade route that ran to Fort Orange at Beverwijck, present-day Albany.

Couple Conversing on the Heere Straet
John Gadsby Chapman, second half of the nineteenth century
New York Public Library, New York
ID: 805600

The Heere Straet: Detail of the Castello Map (see pp. 122-123)

The square to the north of the fort, at the beginning of the Brede Wegh, corresponds with today's Bowling Green. On the eastern side of the fort there was an open space, the Marckvelt, now Whitehall Street. Present-day Pearl Street is also recognizable in the map. Called Paerl Straat at the time, it was the most eastern street of New Amsterdam and home to the weigh house, several businesses and the homes of wealthy merchants.

The Brede Wegh ended in the square where Fort Amsterdam was located. With its tall flagpole, four pointed bastions and a church, barracks, warehouses and officers' dwellings in its inner court, the fort was by far the largest structure in the city. The bastion was built on the site where the National Museum of the American Indian is currently located. The first fort built in 1625 and completed in the 1630s was made of heaped earth. It had begun to crumble soon thereafter and was gradually transformed into the fort with the four bastions, as we know it from most of the illustrations of Manhattan in the Dutch period.[15]

The cartographer distinguished other buildings of significance by coloring their roofs blue. There are four of them. The first is a tall building to the left of the roadstead, Stuyvesant's house on what is now Whitehall Street. A decorative garden – the only one in New Amsterdam in the seventeenth century – can be seen at the back of this house in the Castello map. The other gardens were for growing vegetables. The largest one belonged to the Company, to the left of the Singel. To its right there appears to be an enclosed garden, which, in fact is the new cemetery. The old churchyard was located at the beginning of the Heere Straet.

The second blue-roofed building, the "Compagnies Pachuys," or the Company's warehouse (see also at letter "I" in Visscher's inset, p. 118), is directly opposite the roadstead. The third blue-roofed structure is located behind it and consists of five houses owned by the Company for employees and the storage of goods. The fourth blue-roofed building is situated further to the right and is surmounted by a tower, the "Stadt Huys" or Town Hall.

In 1660 New Amsterdam had all of three canals: the Begijn Gracht, the Prince Gracht and the Heere Gracht, which discharged into the ocean. At high tide the inhabitants could load and unload their ships in the canal. Four bridges connected the parts of town separated by the canals. Although there were two mills, we only see the public mill next to the fort.

Discovered in 1910, the Castello map is the only preserved map of Manhattan from the Dutch period.[16] Prior to its discovery various American historians posited that the Dutch administration had been organized so minimally that no map of the town existed at all. The first true map, it was believed, was the English "Duke's Plan" of 1664 (ill. on pp. 144-145). When the Castello map came to light, however, it became clear that the English map was nothing more than a rough copy of the Dutch one.[17]

Religion and Tolerance

How "Amsterdam" was New Amsterdam?

A new minister, Johannes Cornelisz. Backer, arrived in the colony almost at the same time as Stuyvesant in 1647. Normally the authorities in Amsterdam appointed the minister of New Amsterdam. This was not the case for Backer. He was en route from Curaçao and happened to make a stopover in New Amsterdam just when the position became vacant. The incumbent minister Everardus Bogardus, together with Kieft and the latter's other opponents, had been called back to the Dutch Republic. Backer arrived as a gift from the gods; the city now had a temporary replacement. The reverend would stay until the summer of 1649. Stuyvesant heaved a sigh of relief when he left, given that Backer had become involved in the anti-Stuyvesant Board of Nine. The relationship between the reverend and the director cannot be described as close. Stuyvesant, however, would get along much better with Backer's successor and the other ministers in New Netherland: in their aversion to Jews, Lutherans and Quakers they were of one mind.

With the diversity of people, cultures and languages, New Amsterdam had begun to resemble Amsterdam in the Republic. There, too, the population was anything but united and uniform. Naturally, the mores of Amsterdam were rooted in Protestantism, but there were so many other religious denominations. Amsterdam had several synagogues, a couple of Lutheran churches with German-speaking pastors, a Protestant Walloon church that held services in French, an Armenian church and two English churches. Professing Catholicism openly was forbidden; small Catholic home churches and several clandestine churches were tolerated.

There were just as many religions in New Amsterdam. Did the believers also have official churches there? And how did the colonial government allow them to adhere to their faith? Just how tolerant was New Amsterdam?

Neither Stuyvesant nor his councilors and colleagues in the city council were known for their flexibility in religious matters. The Calvinist body of beliefs provided Stuyvesant with more than just a footing or guideline for life. Uniformity and faith benefited the colony, while diver-

Stuyvesant's House
Samuel Hollyer, 1905-1914
New York Public Library, New York
ID: 805315

Stuyvesant's House

This is Peter Stuyvesant's house on Whitehall Street. This is the name given to the street by the English when they took over Manhattan and is a reference to the residence's white roof. Samuel Hollyer, who may have based this drawing on the Castello map, did not give the house a white roof. In the Castello map it is colored blue to indicate its importance.

Stuyvesant's House
Detail of the Castello Map (see pp. 122-123)

sity endangered the community. He considered his deep-seated faith as a guiding principle for sound governance, law, order and stability. He did everything in his power to maintain peace, in particular on Sunday. In 1663 he was bent on prosecuting some seven men for playing backgammon on Sunday.[18] The sale of alcohol was prohibited on this holy day of rest, which had to be observed always and by everyone. Stuyvesant was supported in this by his councilors and the town council of New Amsterdam.

In 1664 New Netherland counted 11 religious congregations with a total of six ministers. The congregations paid a part of the salary of their ministers. A classis, or umbrella governing body of pastors and elders, did not exist. Officially the clergymen resorted under the Amsterdam classis. Just as in the Dutch Republic, only the Reformed Church was allowed public worship. Likewise, freedom of conscience applied to both the colony and the Republic. Legally speaking the situation was alike. The difference between the Republic and New Netherland was the culture of permissiveness. While dissenters in certain cities in the Republic, such as in Amsterdam, were allowed to assemble in clandestine churches, this was not the case in New Amsterdam. For the most part this had to do with the scale of New Netherland and its capital. It was a modest community in which those at the helm – generally Calvinists – determined when and how to enforce the laws and how much leeway to give other religions.

The Lutheran congregation, which had arrived and grown with the Scandinavians and Germans, tried for years to recruit a pastor to come to New Netherland, but to no avail. The Quakers, a radical English sect, too, fought for freedom of religion. They attempted to proselytize, holding sermons and proclaiming their message. When this was noticed and communicated to Stuyvesant, he responded in no uncertain terms.

These Quakers in particular bore the brunt of his disapproval. As discussed below (p. 197), this had less to do with their faith than the fact that they accepted no authority other than God. The Quakers were actually permitted to hold services in family circles. Freedom of conscience was considered a precious commodity, also in the colony. As long as people did not excite displeasure with their views, non-public religious expressions were accepted. However, the Quakers provoked the authorities by refusing to acknowledge any kind of governing power, for which they were severely punished. They were fined, dismissed or banished. In some cases they were so ill-treated that the population and even Stuyvesant's own sister fiercely resisted the director-general's policy.

Action was also taken against Catholics, atheists and Mennonites, though less frequently and less harshly. The Jews who reached the colony from Brazil and the Dutch Republic experienced Stuyvesant's bigotry first hand, though this had more to do with his anti-Semitism than his religious intolerance.

The directors in the Republic naturally caught wind of the attendant persecution and excesses. While they agreed with Stuyvesant that New Netherland had to remain free of sects, they would prefer his measures to be less draconian. In this respect they were following the prevailing political-religious stance in Amsterdam. In point of fact, the administration in New Netherland was instructed in 1663 to permit the home sermons. The directors were made to understand that arrests were unwarranted as long as groups gathered for worship in a domestic setting. The officials were to close their eyes to the non-church assemblies even though they were forbidden by law.[19] Neither the right to public worship nor equality among all of the religious denominations existed in New Netherland. The various religions represented in the colony are discussed in greater detail in the third part of this book.

Joan Bleau's Map of Amsterdam in 1649
Nederlands Scheepvaartmuseum, Amsterdam

How Tolerant was Amsterdam?

For a host of reasons, in the first half of the seventeenth century the Dutch Republic was one of the most tolerant countries in Europe. Jews, Lutherans, Mennonites and Remonstrants were allowed to profess their religious beliefs. This openness did not spring from some lofty ideal that all people are equal and therefore entitled to the same freedom of religion. The Dutch authorities were simply afraid of adverse reactions should the practice of these religions be prohibited. These disowned religious groups could turn against the community and pose a threat to burghers and public safety. Moreover, the Dutch Republic was dependent on migrants for its economy and they just might stay away if Calvinism were to be forcefully imposed on the population. As a matter of course, Amsterdam, the nation's largest city, became a haven for religious refugees who had been persecuted in their own country. However, the Reformed Church remained the official faith. The city protected the church, allowing it to hold services and conduct other church-related tasks. In this way the Reformed Church acquired more power than all the other religious denominations. Followers of other religions were not permitted to worship publicly.

The Dutch Republic did not assume an unequivocal position with respect to other religions. A large group favored a more tolerant outlook, which held high freedom of conscience. They were opposed by Calvinist "hardliners," who believed that this tolerant stance paved the way for sects, and would lead only to misery and destruction. Stuyvesant belonged to the latter group.

The Population

"A hodgepodge of all kinds of backgrounds"

This is how Stuyvesant characterized the constellation of the population of New Amsterdam in 1661.[20] Earlier, in 1643, Director Kieft purportedly said to a French Jesuit who was passing through that some 18 languages were spoken in New Amsterdam, but it is not clear whether he meant only independent languages or dialects as well.[21] This comment does indicate that there was little homogeneity among the settlers. New Amsterdam measured up to Amsterdam as far as the diversity of its settlers was concerned. They hailed from the Netherlands, Flanders, France, Germany, England and Scandinavia. There were Poles and Bohemians from Eastern Europe and people from the more closely situated Caribbean islands lived and worked there. Then there was a large group of slaves and freed slaves, the majority of whom came from the west coast of Africa. In this respect, the colonial town differed from the mother city; after all, the Dutch Republic prohibited slavery. Because they lived and worked in the town, the Africans were part of colonial society, in contrast to the original inhabitants, the Indians. As a consequence, slaves and freed slaves were regularly Christened, particularly in the first decades of the colony's existence. Attempts to convert the Indians met with little if any success.

The population's diversity, thus, was indeed great. The question arises whether these groups led strictly separate lives. This appears not to have been the case, for a quarter of the marriages performed in the church of New Amsterdam were mixed: Swedish-English, Prussian-French, Dutch-French, white-black. Naturally, many colonists will have sought daily contact with fellow countrymen and there will have been groups who spoke each other's language and understood each other's culture. At the same time, the various groups merged, as the marriages attest.

How Amsterdam was New Amsterdam? Succinctly stated, Amsterdam and New Amsterdam compared fairly closely in terms of ethnic diversity, the mixing of population groups and the variety of languages spoken in the street. Most of the other towns in the Dutch Republic were less racially diverse, more uniform, more "Dutch." In these places primarily Dutch, albeit in a variety of dialects, was spoken. Neither Amsterdam nor New Amsterdam qualified as "typical" Dutch cities.

How Dutch was New Netherland? Well, it was Dutch territory and governed by a Calvinist elite, the majority of whom came from Holland and set the public cultural agenda. However, the lower echelons of society were anything but homogenous with respect to Dutch culture.
The various ethnic communities absorbed each other's customs. Minorities too small to manifest a specific identity were transformed or assimilated into the larger entity as solitary individuals.[22]

Agriculture and Nature

New Amsterdam did not end at the city wall built in 1653. Beyond it lay "bouweryen" or farming estates that supplied the ever-growing population with the fruits of the land. Not much is known about nature on the island itself. What we do know is that beavers were hardly, if ever, hunted on Manhattan, in contrast to the rest of the colony. Beavers live in channels and creeks, of which there were virtually none on the island. The land, however, was suitable for cultivating crops such as corn and tobacco.

To get an idea of agriculture and nature on Manhattan, certainly in the beginning of the settlement of New Amsterdam, an appeal can be made to sources describing the surrounding areas. One of the most extensive descriptions of the colony, including its natural resources and marvels, was written by Adriaen van der Donck. His *Beschryvinge van Nieuw-Nederlant* (A Description of New Netherland) is discussed at length in the following chapter. This book had a clear objective, namely to rouse the interest of potential emigrants to begin a new life on the other side of the ocean. With his "recruitment" pamphlet Van der Donck conjures up a good, if slightly idyllic and sometimes exaggerated, image of the wonders of nature of New Netherland and its potential for agriculture, cattle breeding and hunting.

Van der Donck describes how the entire colony was covered in forests. All kinds of wood was found there, most of it well suited for fashioning tools and equipment as well as structural elements for houses, mills and ships. And also useful to note: with that much wood there would never be a shortage of firewood. While there were forests everywhere, one should not imagine that the land was simply a vast uncultivated wilderness. On the contrary, thanks to the Indians' farming practices, namely the burning of tracts of forest which were then cultivated, the land had been excellently developed. The advantages of this method were manifold: the empty fields were good for hunting; the forests were thinned out; and the sections burned down to the ground were free of dead wood, branches and fallen trees.

The land was suitable for growing every imaginable type of grain: wheat, rye, barley, buckwheat and "Turckse terwe" (Turkish wheat) and corn. When it came to these products, the colony could even surpass

Flora and Fauna in the Colony

An Eagle
In: Jan Velten, *Wonderen der Natuur* (Wonders of Nature), ca. 1700
Royal Library, The Hague
AEL 204

Surely Van der Donck thought there was something for everyone when he described the mammals, fish and birds of New Netherland. All you had to do was raise your hand, and birds would fly to you, or so it seemed. Van der Donck wrote of the multitude of turkeys, pheasants, partridges, grouse and pigeons. There were so many migratory birds that they "fill the sky like clouds, and even when the sun shines they cast shadows on the ground". Their sheer numbers made them easy prey. The waterfowl included several edible varieties: geese and ducks, also found in abundance.
Naturally, he listed the uses of these animals: the many bears provided fur for muffs; the elk and deer were known for their tender meat. Animals of little use, such as wolves and snakes, did not bother anyone. Moreover, the colonist only had to dip his fishing net into the river and he would catch salmon, sturgeon, bass, unknown species the fishermen called "elft" (eleven), "twalift" (twelve) and "dertien" (thirteen), as well as carp, pike, trout, eel, haddock, herring, mackerel, ray, flatfish, flounder, lobster, crab, oysters, mussels, shrimp and turtle.
In 1647 two whales swam up the river, opening up new prospects for whaling.

And then there is the beaver, the reason why the Dutch were so keen to conduct trade with the people of New Netherland. Its beautiful fur was popular in the Dutch Republic and elsewhere as well. But not just beaver pelts! Raccoons, mink, wild cats, otters and foxes provided the best and most sumptuous furs. The writer devoted eight whole pages to these creatures, which were crucial for the profits of the colony. Indians ate beaver meat, an "extremely delicate food" that they rarely if ever sold to the Dutch. And that's too bad, because the tail in particular is most delectable.[23]

A Parrot and a Beaver
In: Jan Velten, *Wonderen der Natuur*
(Wonders of Nature) ca. 1700
Royal Library, The Hague
AEL 204

Scandinavia as a grain supplier. The colonists had brought along seeds and cuttings from the Dutch Republic for their own use. Now, growing alongside the indigenous varieties, were all kinds of European trees bearing apples, pears, cherries, apricots and peaches. Sometimes the trees were so laden with fruit "that they sometimes split or their branches broke off." In his *Beschryvinge van Nieuw-Nederlant* Van der Donck listed many delicacies: "plums, almonds, medlars, cornel, figs, all manner of currants and indigenous gooseberries, licorice, clove trees". Apparently olives thrived there as well. Also interesting are the lists of vegetables that grew there: "lettuce, cabbage, parsnip, yellow and red carrots, beets, endive, chicory, fennel, sorrel, dill, spinach, radish, black radish, parsley, chervil, cress, onion, chives."

Pumpkins, watermelons, cucumbers, peas, turnips and beans thrived well. Grapes grew in the wild. The author was of the opinion that an abundance of wine would be produced within the foreseeable future. Even when crops did not fare well, such as tobacco, Van der Donck made it seem as though this was no reason for not traveling to the colony, for the tobacco farmers would also soon reap the benefits of the land.

Having observed the landscape closely, Van der Donck was convinced of the potential wealth of iron ore and precious metals in the mountains. Almost immediately after settling the colony the Dutch began surveying for minerals and precious metals. Copper and mercury were found. Furthermore, there was an abundance of clay that could be used for pottery. And for the millers, Van der Donck points out that there was plenty of the kind of stones needed for making millstones. Alabaster, amber and rock crystal were other costly materials also found there.[24]

[1] Rink, *Holland on the Hudson*, pp. 144, 164.
[2] Phelps Stokes, *The Iconography of Manhattan Island*, p. 345.
[3] Kupcík, "Die kartografische Tätigkeit von Augustin Herman," pp. 203-219: Kupcík suggests that Heermann trained in London with his fellow-countryman Weceslaus Hollar. De Koning, "From Van der Donck to Visscher." http://web.archive.org/web/20030630211837/mercatorsworld.com/article.php3?i=75; Van Bracht and Schilder, *Origins of New York*, pp. 22-23 and pp. 36-38.
[4] De Koning, "Dating the Visscher," note 19: The *Vertoogh* was presented to the Commission of the States General. It included a "perfect map of the country in its situation" (now considered lost). Dutch State Archives, The Hague, States General inv.no.: I 2564-25.
[5] De Vries, *Korte historiael ende journaels aenteyckeninge*, p. 249.
[6] Kupcík, "Die kartografische Tätigkeit von Augustin Herman," pp. 203-219, fig. 5.
[7] Gosselink, *Land in Zicht*, pp. 24, 49.
[8] Van Bracht and Schilder, *The Origins of New York*, p. 43.
[9] De Koning, "Dating the Visscher."
[10] A few illustrations of the site of the Town Hall are found on the website http://beatl.barnard.columbia.edu/rothschild/1.htm.
[11] Van Bracht and Schilder, *The Origins of New York*, p. 52.
[12] Van Bracht and Schilder, *The Origins of New York*, pp. 45-54.
[13] Jacobs, *Een zegenrijk gewest*, p. 482.
[14] Phelps Stokes, *The Iconography of Manhattan Island*, reprint II, pp. 215-341.
[15] Temminck Groll, "New Amsterdam (New York)," p. 286, note without number.
[16] Wieder, *Monumenta Cartografica*, p. 89.
[17] Schilder, "Van New Amsterdam naar New York in kaarten," pp. 8-14.
[18] Goodfriend, "Struggle over the Sabbath," p. 218.
[19] Jacobs, *Een zegenrijk gewest*, p. 265.
[20] Jacobs, *Een zegenrijk gewest*, p. 103.
[21] Frijhoff, "Dutchness in Fact and Fiction," p. 341.
[22] For more on the Dutch identity of New Netherland, see: Frijhoff, "Dutchness in Fact and Fiction" and Cohen, "How Dutch were the Dutch of New Netherland," pp. 43-60.
[23] Jacobs, *Een zegenrijk gewest*, pp. 33-54.
[24] The passages from Van der Donck's *Beschryvinge* (A Description) in this chapter were taken from Jacobs, *Een zegenrijk gewest*, pp. 33-54; Van der Donck, "A Description of New Netherland."

II

CHAPTER 5

Years of Growth, Borders and Surrender

New Amsterdam is given its own city government with legal powers in 1653. This is not the only good news: ever more colonists are making the crossing to America. The West India Company had relinquished control of the fur trade in 1640, and the benefits of this decision are gradually being felt: New Netherland is becoming a true settlement colony.

In the meantime lobbying is being done to attract more people to the colony. For this purpose Van der Donck writes a pamphlet entitled *Beschryvinge van Nieuw-Nederlant (A Description of New Netherland)*.

Stuyvesant proves to be a true leader, resolute and firm. He successfully opposes the Swedes, who have penetrated the south of the colony, and manages to make clear agreements covering the borders between English and Dutch territory. The colony is at last able to thrive. And so it does – up to the invasion by the English in 1664. The taking of New Netherland is strategically important for the English in that they will then possess a large, continuous area in North America. The Peace of Breda in 1667 decrees that each country will keep the territory it has captured from the other. So New Amsterdam, rechristened New York, remains English and the Dutch retain the colony of Suriname, which they seized in 1667.

In 1673 New Netherland once more belongs to the Dutch for a few months, but in 1674 the curtain finally falls for this enclave.

An Enticing Pamphlet to Attract Colonists

With its lyrical quotations about the beauty and economic potential of the country, Van der Donck's *Beschrijvinge van Nieuw-Nederlant (A Description of New Netherland)*,[1] which appeared in 1655, is truly a hymn of praise to the colony. The *Description* is an expanded version of the *Vertoogh* (Remonstrance) that he published earlier. However, he left out the criticism of the administration that was in the *Vertoogh*. The document is based on Van der Donck's own experience of the colony, both in the countryside and with the inhabitants, the Indians.[2]

The pamphlet begins with a description of the coast before moving on, via the rivers, to the areas along their banks, which corresponded with where the Dutch were living. The coast was "clear and sandy" and good for anchoring. Beyond it were pastures where cattle and hogs could graze. Van der Donck had little to say about the remote hinterland, for the simple reason that not many Dutchmen had been there. Only "a few of our Dutch had been deep into the country," "up to seventy to eighty miles and more measuring from the sea." The Dutch had no sense at all of the total extent of the land. Sometimes they had to journey for all of 20 or more days to trade furs with the Indians living farthest from the coast, but how much farther the land extended was unknown.

The waters of New Netherland ranged from big rivers to small streams. The hinterland was full of creeks and channels, most of them easily navigable and "suitable for all kinds of milling" and the lakes were "well provided with fish." Van der Donck also had words of praise for the Fresh (Connecticut) River: "it is also in a very good position and is a navigable place with beautifully located estates, and a reasonable fur trade." The name Fresh River resulted from the fact that less seawater from high and

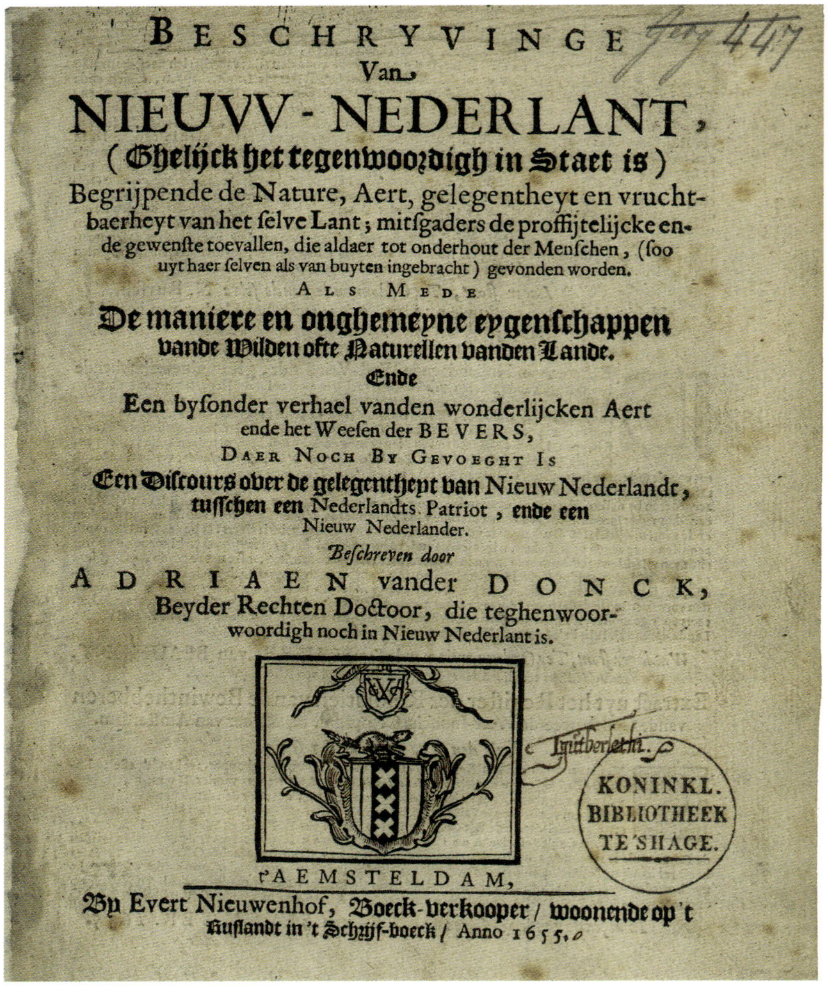
BESCHRYVINGE Van NIEUVV-NEDERLANT, (Ghelijck het tegenwoordigh in Staet is) Begrijpende de Nature, Aert, gelegentheyt en vruchtbaerheyt van het selve Lant; mitsgaders de proffijtelijcke ende gewenste toevallen, die aldaer tot onderhout der Menschen, (soo uyt haer selven als van buyten ingebracht) gevonden worden. ALS MEDE De maniere en onghemeyne eygenschappen vande Wilden ofte Naturellen vanden Lande. Ende Een bysonder verhael vanden wonderlijcken Aert ende het Weesen der BEVERS, DAER NOCH BY GEVOEGHT IS Een Discours over de gelegentheyt van Nieuw Nederlandt, tusschen een Nederlandts Patriot, ende een Nieuw Nederlander. Beschreven door ADRIAEN vander DONCK, Beyder Rechten Doctoor, die teghenwoordigh noch in Nieuw Nederlant is.

t'AEMSTELDAM, By Evert Nieuwenhof, Boeck-verkooper, woonende op 't Rusland in 't Schrijf-boeck, Anno 1655.

Beschryvinge van Nieuw-Nederlant (A Description of New Netherland), Adriaen van der Donck, 1655, second edition, 1656
Royal Library, The Hague
343 J 2

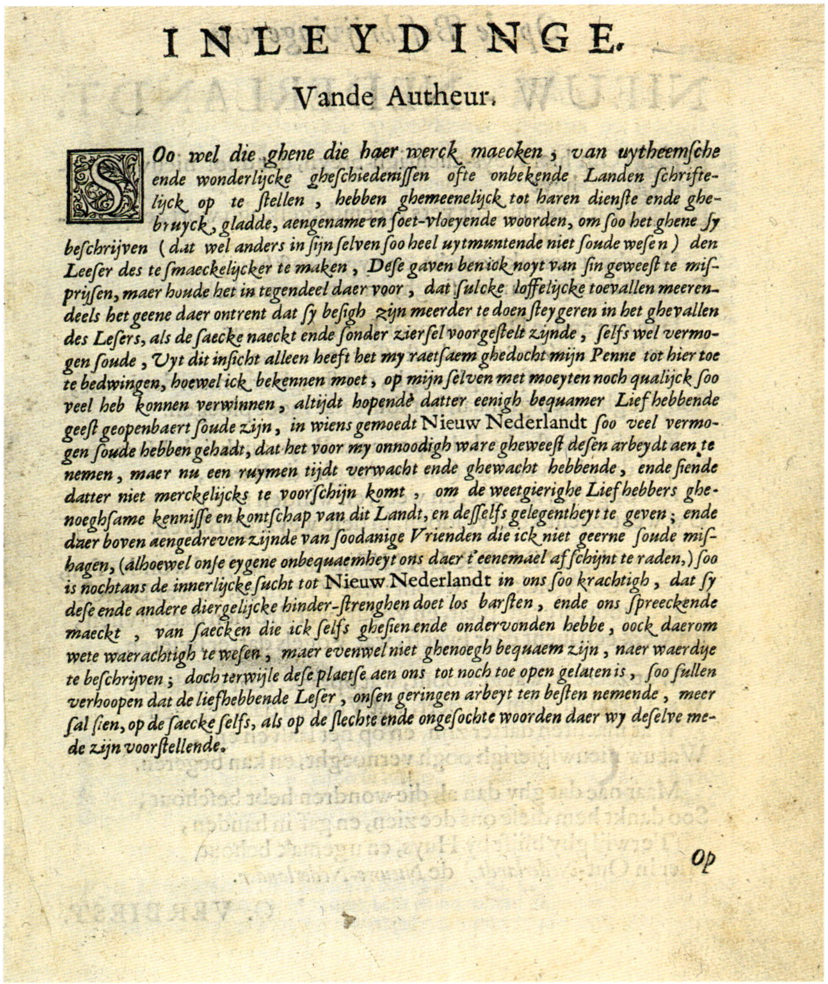
INLEYDINGE. Vande Autheur.

Soo wel die ghene die haer werck maecken, van uytheemsche ende wonderlijcke gheschiedenissen ofte onbekende Landen schriftelijck op te stellen, hebben ghemeenelijck tot haren dienste ende ghebruyck, gladde, aengename en soet-vloeyende woorden, om soo het ghene sy beschrijven (dat wel anders in sijn selven soo heel uytmuntende niet soude wesen) den Leeser des te smaeckelijcker te maken, Dese gaven ben ick noyt van sin geweest te misprijsen, maer houde het in tegendeel daer voor, dat sulcke loffelijcke toevallen meerendeels het geene daer ontrent dat sy besigh zijn meerder te doen steygeren in het ghevallen des Lesers, als de saecke naeckt ende sonder ziersel voorgestelt zijnde, selfs wel vermogen soude, Uyt dit insicht alleen heeft het my raetsaem ghedocht mijn Penne tot hier toe te bedwingen, hoewel ick bekennen moet, op mijn selven met moeyten noch qualijck soo veel heb konnen verwinnen, altijdt hopende datter eenigh bequamer Liefhebbende geest geopenbaert soude zijn, in wiens gemoedt Nieuw Nederlandt soo veel vermogen soude hebben gehadt, dat het voor my onnoodigh ware gheweest desen arbeydt aen te nemen, maer nu een ruymen tijdt verwacht ende ghewacht hebbende, ende siende datter niet merckelijcks te voorschijn komt, om de weetgierighe Liefhebbers ghenoeghsame kennisse en kontschap van dit Landt, en desselfs gelegentheyt te geven; ende daer boven aengedreven zijnde van soodanige Vrienden die ick niet geerne soude mishagen, (alhoewel onse eygene onbequaemheyt ons daer t'eenemael afschijnt te raden,) soo is nochtans de innerlijcke sucht tot Nieuw Nederlandt in ons soo krachtigh, dat sy dese ende andere diergelijcke hinder-strenghen doet los barsten, ende ons spreeckende maeckt, van saecken die ick selfs ghesien ende ondervonden hebbe, oock daerom wete waerachtigh te wesen, maer evenwel niet ghenoegh bequaem zijn, naer waerdye te beschrijven; doch terwijle dese plaetse aen ons tot noch toe open gelaten is, soo sullen verhoopen dat de liefhebbende Leser, onsen geringen arbeyt ten besten nemende, meer sal sien, op de saecke selfs, als op de slechte ende ongesochte woorden daer wy deselve mede zijn voorstellende.

Op

From: *Beschrijvinge van Nieuw-Nederlant*

low tides flowed into this river than into the South and the North River.
He accorded great honor to the North (Hudson) River. It was "the most famous and most populous of New Netherland" and was also known as "Rio de Montaigne," "Manhattes rieviere," "Groote Rivier" and the "grootte Mouritse reviere," after Prince Maurits.
The South (Delaware) River also receives plenty of attention. He compares it with the Amazon, not in extent but in "other excellent qualities."
Van der Donck adored the American summers. The climate was good: for the European colonists it was better than in West Africa or the Caribbean. He describes the air as "dry, pure and healthy," without "heavy vapors or stinking mists." If you had fallen ill somewhere else, here you would soon be cured. And if it did occasionally get very hot, the thunder and lightning would soon clear the air.

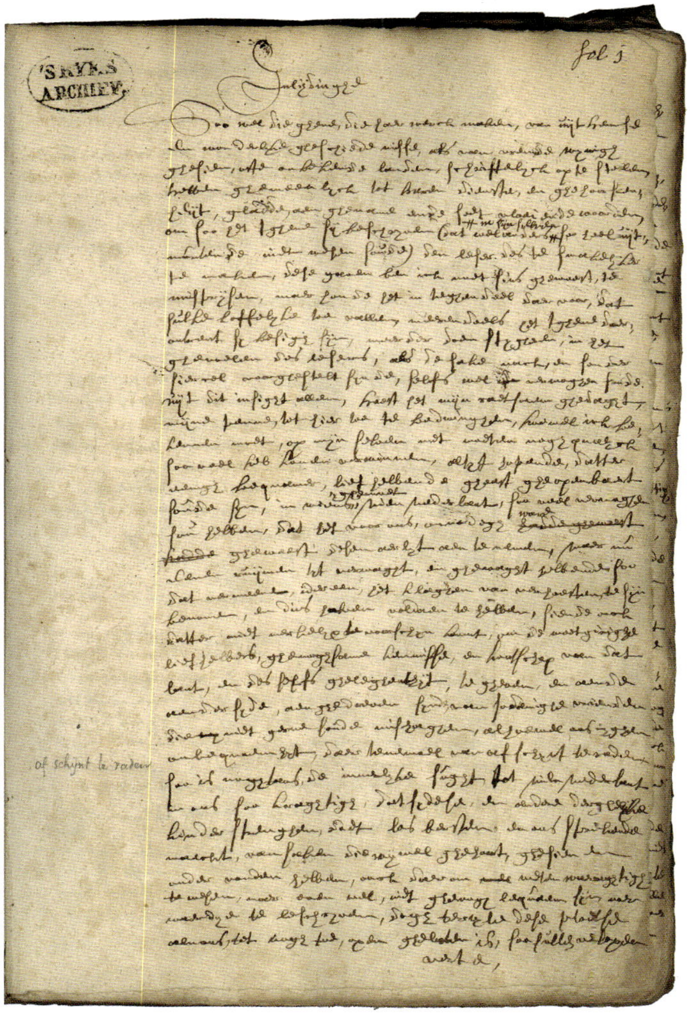

Manuscript version of *Beschrijvinge van Nieuw-Nederlant* (A Description of New Netherland), Adriaen van der Donck, 1655, second edition, 1656
Nationaal Archief (National Archives of the Netherlands), The Hague
States General, 1.01.07, inv. no. 9414
Ink on paper, 33 x 22 x 1.5 cm

Stuyvesant and the Borders of the Colony

New Amsterdam was now a city, with a charter. This marked the beginning of a productive and prosperous period for New Netherland. The population increased to an extent that Stuyvesant's predecessors could only have dreamed of. Good profits were being made on beaver pelts and the WIC was earning money by levying taxes on the skins and other exported goods. More houses were built and municipal services were organized. The city was finally beginning to flourish.

Yet Peter Stuyvesant faced a difficult task. He had to deal with the new administrative structure of the colony and with the reconstruction of the city that had suffered so much through the neglect of his predecessors, the shortage of money and the wars with the Indians. These internal problems were not his only concern. There was friction with the owners of the patroonship Rensselaerswijck near the town of Beverwijck on the upper reaches of the North (Hudson) River. A few years after the death of Kiliaen van Rensselaer, the administration of Rensselaerswijck was taken over by Brant Aertsz. van Slichtenhorst. From his appearance on the scene in 1648, Van Slichtenhorst was sure of himself, in any case sure enough not to give in to Stuyvesant over every dispute. And there were quite a few matters in which Van Slichtenhorst felt challenged by the central government of the colony.

For instance, Stuyvesant proclaimed a day of prayer, which was also to be observed in Rensselaerswijck, where such dictates were the last thing they needed. Another dispute concerned the use of the land in the immediate vicinity of Fort Orange. Van Slichtenhorst was of the opinion that this area belonged to the patroonship, and had houses built and the land cleared. Stuyvesant's view was very different, and he had his soldiers fetch wood and building materials from the area. He warned Van Slichtenhorst repeatedly and ordered him to keep the land around the fort free. In 1648 he gave orders to pull down all the houses within shooting range of the fort. The quarrels between the colonial government and the patroonship escalated. By the spring of 1652 Stuyvesant was left with no choice but to claim the area around the fort in the name of the Company. Van Slichtenhorst was arrested in April 1652 and imprisoned in New Amsterdam. Stuyvesant then made use of his absence to found the village of Beverwijck to the north of the fort and to install a court, with the result that the inhabitants of Rensselaerswijck suddenly came under the jurisdiction of the Company. This was a severe blow to Rensselaerswijck, which all at once lost its principal settlement.[3]

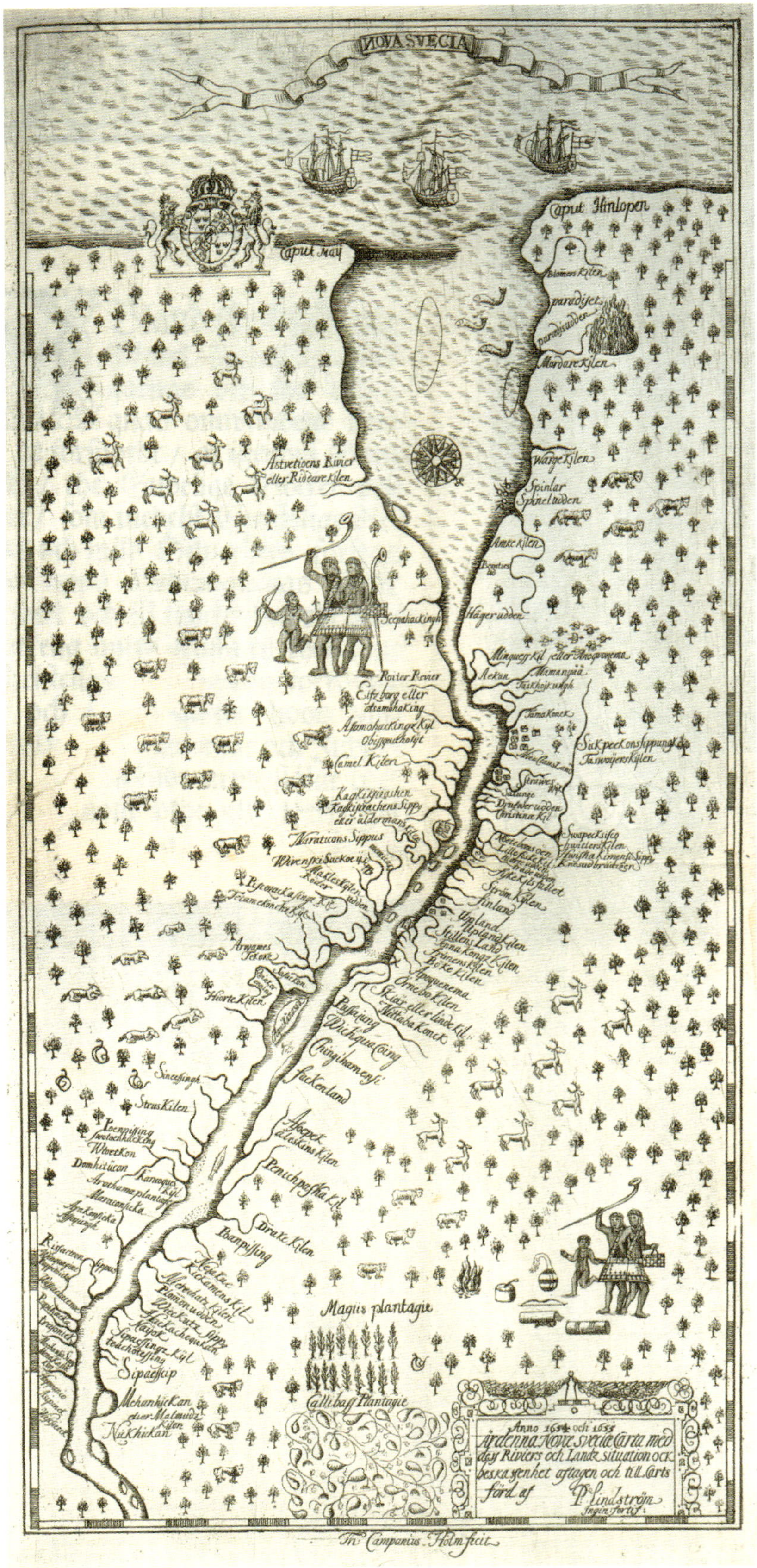

Nova Svecia (New Sweden)

The colony of New Sweden was founded in part by individuals who had earlier been involved in New Netherland on behalf of the Dutch Republic. Willem Usselincx, the Flemish merchant who had been unable to realize his dream of a great new Protestant state, apparently drew the attention of Peter Minuit, one of the first directors of New Amsterdam, to Swedish plans for a colony in North America.

Together with the Swedes and the former WIC director Samuel Blommaert, Minuit turned these plans into reality. The Swedes sent him to New Netherland and on 29 March 1638 he established a colony on the South (Delaware) River, next to the Dutch colony. Less than six weeks later the first Swedish fort was built. Minuit named it Christina, after the Swedish queen. Two ships brought Swedish colonists who were to populate the shores of the river.

In the following years the enclave expanded bit by bit, and in 1651 Stuyvesant decided to build Fort Casimir, some 12 kilometers south of Fort Christina. This enabled the Dutch to keep a closer eye on the Swedes. Less than three years later the Swedes captured the fort, whereupon the Dutch retaliated in 1655 and put an end to the Swedish colony.

Detail of the "Nova Scevia" Map

Map of Nova Svecia on the Delaware River
Th. Campanius Holm, 1696
New York Public Library, New York

This example reveals a director-general who could stand up to everyone and everything. Stuyvesant is often portrayed as power-mad, and unwilling to share his authority with others. Even though he was resolute in character and governed the colony from 1647 to 1664, his power was nevertheless limited. If his style of government is compared with that of his English colleagues, Stuyvesant's turns out to have been less authoritarian. This had to do with how the administration of the colony was organized. First, like his predecessors, Stuyvesant was subordinate to those in power in the Netherlands. Moreover, in every step in the decision-making process the director-general depended on the agreement of his fellow council members. Indeed, Stuyvesant almost always consulted his Board. Within the Board decisions were made by the democratic principle of a majority of votes. Remarkably, Stuyvesant's vote carried just as much weight as that of the other members. It was only when the votes were tied that Stuyvesant's vote counted for two. Cases are known of proposals from the director-general being voted down. These rules were imposed by the WIC and were an extension of the culture of collegiate administration in the Dutch Republic.[4]

Van der Donck Campaigns for Emigration

According to Van der Donck, New Netherland was almost the same as paradise. This is hardly surprising, since his pamphlet was written to attract people to the colony. The dominant theme is the persuasive description (see. p. 134) of how the colonists make use of the rich land. What was the climate like? What products came from the land? Were the rivers easily navigable? In short, what was in it for the colonists?[5]

With great attention to detail and the requisite exaggeration, Van der Donck described the beauty and fertility of the land. Whether or not because of his *Description*, New Netherland attracted more and more people, many of them settling in New Amsterdam.

Swedish Intruders

Meanwhile Dutch authority was coming apart at the seams on the borders of the colony. As early as 1637 the Swedes had founded a colony on the South (Delaware) River. The initiative came from none other than Pieter Minuit, the man who had been in on the founding of the Dutch colony in 1626. Now he had been commissioned by the Swedes to find a suitable location for the Swedish colony. He found it on the Delaware, where a few Swedish forts were built. The WIC, Minuit's former employer, had told him on several occasions that it would be better for all concerned if he and the Swedes were to leave. In the Company's view the Swedish trading post stood on Dutch territory. These warnings had no effect: the Swedes stayed put.

In June 1654 the Swedes took the Dutch Fort Casimir. The WIC resolved not to tolerate this and borrowed a substantial sum from the city of Amsterdam to charter the ship the *Waegh* (Weigh House) for a military operation. In 1655 Stuyvesant was able to send a large expedition to make short work of the Swedes. It was probably not just Stuyvesant's show of strength that persuaded the colony to surrender. The community had been seriously weakened by shortages of food.[6] First Fort Casimir fell into Dutch hands, and then the Swedish Fort Christina.

New Amstel City-Colony

The mission was successful, and the Swedes had to pack their bags. At least this applied to the colony's leaders and the soldiers; the Swedish citizens were allowed to stay. The Company, however, could not pay back the money it had borrowed from Amsterdam for the *Waegh* (Weigh House). After the fall of Dutch Brazil in 1654, the Company was as good as broke. Thus there was no alternative but to give the liberated area as a patroonship for Amsterdam to manage. In this way the city became the patroon of the city-colony, which was given the name of New Amstel. Amsterdam at once decided to send over 100 Dutch colonists to populate the territory. They were told to concentrate on agriculture. Amsterdam hoped to use its newly acquired city-colony to create a granary as a way of reducing its dependence on foreign imports.

Anglo-Dutch Borders

The problem of the Swedes had been solved, but that still left the English. They would not be so easy. In the border area between the two colonies there had been disputes for some time about smuggling and offering protection to each other's criminals. Stuyvesant did his best to maintain good relations with his English neighbors. It seemed to him a good idea to establish to the extent possible where the borders between the two territories lay. Once there could be no misunderstandings on this point, a great deal of vexation and conflict would be avoided.

In Hartford in September 1650 Stuyvesant reached an agreement with the English in which the exact borders were laid down. The Lange Eiland (Long Island) was split into two parts, with the eastern part coming under the English. The area around the Connecticut River also went to the English. Stuyvesant was satisfied with the outcome of the negotiations: for the first time he had managed to get the English colonists to recognize the borders of New Netherland. Determining where the borders lay did not mean, however, that there were no longer any English colonists living on Dutch territory. In addition

Niew Sweden.
Swanen
Dael.
Godins
Baij.
Cabo Maij
39 Graede
De Natien aende Zuydt Rivier
Sewapois.
kleyne Siconese
Naraticongk
Mantaes
Armewamex.
Momakaraongh
Rem kokes.
Minquaen toegenaemt Machaorikyus.
Atsayonok
Reckaweyjk
Matikongk
Sankikans.
Deese boven geschreeven natien hebben altesaamen vriendtschap ondermalcander, ende syn meest eenerlay volck en van een spraeck, uytghesondert de Machaoretyns, die soo ghenoemt syn van weegen haar spraeck, die Minquaens is, en wel soo veel geseyt syn als by ons onduytsche ofte Waellen.
Het leeven van deesen luyden is volcoomelyck vry haer waersegers ofte duyvels proekers en hebben niet ooven haer te seggen hare Sakima en heben niet te gebieden ende en hebben geen autorityt om iemandt te straffen aen den Hals.
De Huwelycke en hebben geen clem, meest heeft elck een vrouw, de ooverste meer ende licht verlaeten sy haer wyven, die dan van d'een tot d'ander voor hoer loopen nauwelyck sal iemandt een vrou houden, die twee oft dry kinderen ghehadt heeft, ordinari verstooten sy de vrouwe als die bevrucht sy, en hier door blyft het landt sooben van volck
Memkokes
Amakaronck
Mocroaukonck
Sewapois
Bossen

Map of New Netherland or New Sweden?

Queen Christina of Sweden, one of the greatest collectors of art and books of her day, would have acquired the atlas to which this map belongs around 1650. The atlas, appropriately known as the *Christina Atlas*, has been kept in the Vatican Library since 1689.

This map is an excellent example of how power and egos in Europe were linked to the colonies. It shows New Netherland, the area claimed by the Dutch. We see the Swanendael patroonship, to the left of the shore of the South (Delaware) River. In the mouth of the river we also see the name "Godins Baij," named after the WIC director Samuel Godijn, who founded the patroonship Swanendael in 1630 (see also p. 75). But the map, made by the Amsterdammer Vingboons, reflects the situation at the time when the Swedes had also settled on the South River. And so along the river we encounter various Swedish names, from Fort Christina to Fort Gottenburch.

The Dutch never accepted the Swedish colony on the South River. Yet clearly written at the top right are the words "Kaert vande Suyd Rivier in Niew Sweden." And at the top left are the words "Niew Sweden" again. How is that possible on a Dutch map?

Detail of the "Kaert vande Suyd Rivier in Niew Sweden"

It is likely that the cartographer Johannes Vingboons adapted the inscription when he heard that Queen Christina of Sweden had bought the atlas containing the map. Looking closely we can see that beneath the word "Sweden" something else was first written: "Nederlandt." A piece of paper was glued over it to conceal the fact that the Dutch also claimed the area, a seventeenth-century Wite-Out as it were, all for the greater glory of the royal purchaser of the atlas.

"Kaert vande Suyd Rivier in Niew Sweden" (Map of the South River in New Sweden)
Johannes Vingboons, third quarter of the seventeenth century
Christina Atlas, Biblioteca Apostolica Vaticana
Reg. Lat. 2105-26 (sign. 53)
Watercolor on paper, 47 x 69 cm

Map of the South River in New Netherland
Johannes Vingboons, third quarter of the seventeenth century
Library of Congress Geography and Map Division, Washington, D.C.
G3291.S12 coll .H3 Vault: Harr vol. 3, map 14
Watercolor on paper, 47 x 69 cm

Briefly Swedish: Now New Netherland Again

This map closely resembles the one in the Vatican, but here the territory is Dutch again, as attested by the inscription "Caerte vande Svydt Rivier in Niew Nederland" (Map of the South River in New Netherland). At the center once again is the South or Delaware River, which according to Van der Donck was comparable to the "glorious River Amazon, not so much in size as in other excellent qualities."[7] The fascinating anthropological observations about the local Indian tribes, at the lower left on each map, read as follows: "The marriages are not binding, most have one wife each, the Chief more, and they leave their wives lightly, who then go from one to another as whores. Hardly anyone will keep a woman who has had two or three children; normally they reject women if they have been impregnated and had children, and as a result the land stays soberly populated."

Agreement Between Amsterdam and the Colonists of New Amstel

In 1655 the Swedish colony was captured. The city of Amsterdam was given the territory to manage as reparation for the costs the WIC had incurred to hire the ship *Waegh* (Weigh House) with which Stuyvesant expelled the Swedes. Amsterdam named the new overseas city-colony "New Amstel."

The mother city had ambitious plans for this project. The regents of Amsterdam gathered to put down in black and white the rules for a colony with potential for growth. The main question was how to motivate people to cross the ocean. The answer was the pamphlet *Accoort tusschen de stad Amsterdam & Coloniers van Nieuw Nederlant* (Agreement between the city of Amsterdam and Colonists of New Netherland). It contained the articles that were important for the Amsterdammers and other Dutch citizens wishing to emigrate to New Amstel. The first article no doubt immediately reassured them: "The colonists going there will be taken across in suitable ships with their families, necessary household goods and other needed effects".

The first suitable ship was the *Prins Maurits* (Prince Maurits). In December 1656, 112 colonists set sail in it, only to arrive in 25 April 1657. Three ships soon followed, bringing another 55 people and materials. The passengers on the *Prins Maurits* had bad luck: on arrival in the colony the ship ran aground. It was quite an undertaking to transport all the passengers, their luggage and the other materials to the South (Delaware) River. After the inevitable delays and damage, work on building the new settlement could begin.

They tackled the job in high spirits. It soon became apparent, however, that there were too few competent farmers among the colonists. Agriculture got off to a poor start, and extra supplies from Amsterdam were needed to survive the first winter. The next year was even worse. Epidemics broke out. In 1658 no less than 100 colonists died. The winter was mercilessly severe and the settlers fought among themselves.[8]

After two hellish years New Amstel had yielded nothing other than a debt of 132,000 guilders. The regents wanted to get rid of it as soon as they could. But how? The Company was as good as bankrupt and could not afford to take over the colony. Yet it did see the necessity of a takeover; otherwise the English from the adjacent Virginia and Maryland would swallow up the land. The WIC consented and Amsterdam was to do its best to continue sending large numbers of colonists. New investment by Amsterdam was also part of the deal. And indeed soon there were several hundred inhabitants. New Amstel was growing, but for how long?[9]

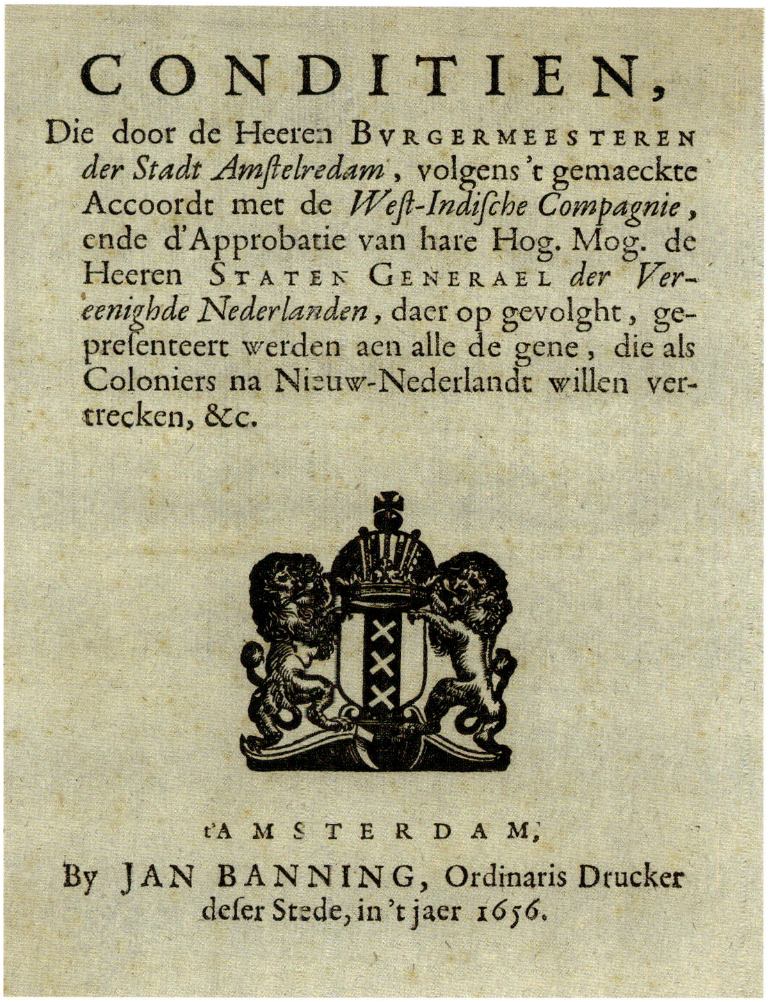

CONDITIEN,

Die door de Heeren BVRGERMEESTEREN *der Stadt Amſtelredam*, volgens 't gemaeckte Accoordt met de *Weſt-Indiſche Compagnie*, ende d'Approbatie van hare Hog. Mog. de Heeren STATEN GENERAEL *der Vereenighde Nederlanden*, daer op gevolght, gepreſenteert werden aen alle de gene, die als Coloniers na Nieuw-Nederlandt willen vertrecken, &c.

t'AMSTERDAM,

By JAN BANNING, Ordinaris Drucker deſer Stede, in 't jaer 1656.

Conditions of the mayors of Amsterdam to the colonists of New Netherland, Amsterdam 1656
Nationaal Archief (National Archives of the Netherlands), The Hague
Verspreide Westindische Stukken, 1.05.06, inv. no. 6
15.5 x 20 cm

A Proposal for a Colony

Pieter Cornelisz. Plockhoy of Zierikzee had high ideals. He dreamed of a Puritan, democratic state based on complete freedom. In his colony elections would be held every year to appoint a leader. There would certainly not be any slavery and definitely no state religion. He believed everyone should be free to follow his own brand of Christianity. When he learned that the city government of Amsterdam was seeking colonists for New Netherland, the idealist saw his chance. Plockhoy was granted permission by Amsterdam to found a colony on the South River in the vicinity of Swanendael, which had been established more than 30 years earlier by patroon Samuel Godijn. In May 1663 Plockhoy set sail for North America with 41 other Mennonite idealists. They landed near the Whorekill area on the South River. Unfortunately for Plockhoy and his group, in 1664 the English put paid to their plans. After the peaceful surrender of New Amsterdam, the outlying areas were treated less gently. The settlement was destroyed. Sir Robert Carr brutally drove the group away, and some inhabitants were sold into slavery.[10] Nothing more was heard of Plockhoy.

The Dutch Surrender

New Amsterdam had passed into English hands without a drop of blood being shed. For the colonies on the South River, both that of Plokhoy and New Amstel, the English takeover would be less peaceful. In 1664 both settlements were razed to the ground in a ruthless operation led by the English army officer Sir Robert Carr.[11] With this pamphlet the directors of the WIC wanted to draw attention to the suffering of the colonists in New Netherland because of the brutal actions of the English. Through such petitions the Company asked for military aid from the mother country and for a response to the English aggression.

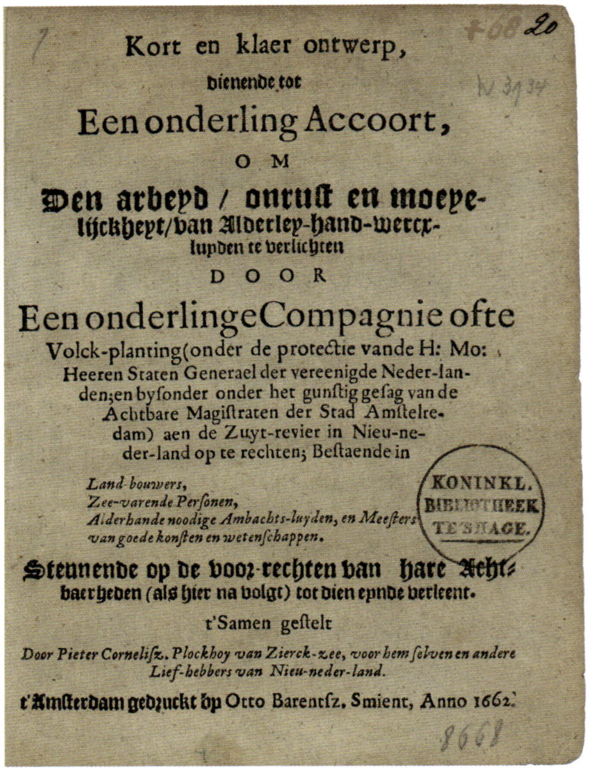

Kort en klaer ontwerp,
dienende tot
Een onderling Accoort,
OM
Den arbeyd / onrust en moeyelijckheyt/van Alderley-hand-wercxluyden te verlichten
DOOR
Een onderlinge Compagnie ofte
Volck-planting (onder de protectie vande H: Mo: Heeren Staten Generael der vereenigde Neder-landen; en bysonder onder het gunstig gesag van de Achtbare Magistraten der Stad Amstelredam) aen de Zuyt-revier in Nieu-nederland op te rechten; Bestaende in

Land-bouwers,
Zee-varende Personen,
Alderhande noodige Ambachts-luyden, en Meesters van goede konsten en wetenschappen.

Steunende op de voor-rechten van hare Achtbaerheden (als hier na volgt) tot dien eynde verleent.
t'Samen gestelt
Door Pieter Cornelisz. Plockhoy van Zierck-zee, voor hem selven en andere Lief-hebbers van Nieu-neder-land.
t'Amsterdam gedruckt by Otto Barentsz. Smient, Anno 1662.

Kort en klaer ontwerp..., (Brief and clear design...)
Pieter Cornelisz. Plockhoy, 6 June 1662
Royal Library, The Hague
Pflt 8668
18 x 14 x 0.5 cm

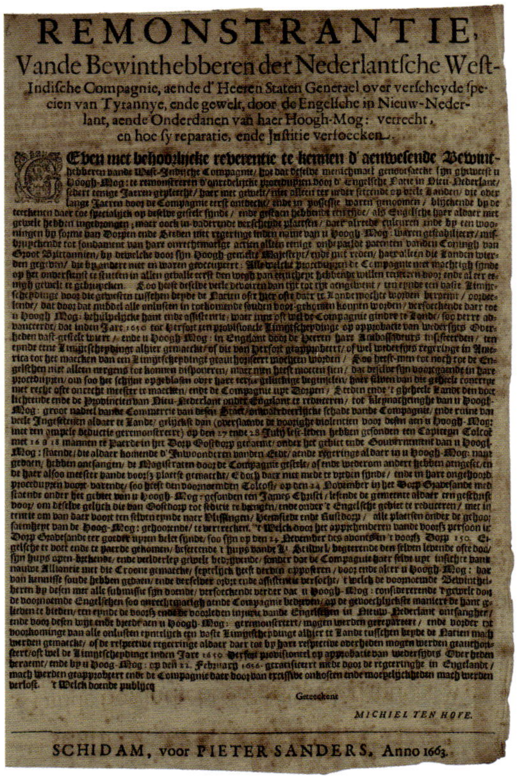

REMONSTRANTIE,
Vande Bewinthebberen der Nederlantsche West-Indische Compagnie, aende d'Heeren Staten Generael over verscheyde specien van Tyrannye, ende gewelt, door de Engelsche in Nieuw-Nederlant, aende Onderdanen van haer Hoogh-Mog: verrecht, en hoe sy reparatie, ende Justitie versoecken.

Geteeckent
MICHIEL TEN HOVE.

SCHIDAM, voor PIETER SANDERS, Anno 1663.

Pamphlet denouncing English violence, 1664
Royal Library, The Hague
Pflt 8844
18 x 14 x 0.5 cm

to the English inhabitants of New Amsterdam, various villages with English inhabitants dotted New Netherland, particularly Long Island.[12]

Peace returned after the new agreements were made and the borders established. But in Europe there was a threat of conflict between the Dutch Republic and England. In May 1652 the First Anglo-Dutch War broke out. The consequence for Stuyvesant was that he was not recalled to Holland, as we saw on page 105.

The war was waged entirely at sea, and mainly in European waters. While the Dutch were successful in the first year of the war, they were unable to fight on for a few years longer. The English gradually gained the upper hand, but they too were near the end of their rope. The English commander, Oliver Cromwell, realized that the two Protestant nations were completely draining each other's resources. Cromwell took the initiative in opening negotiations. As early as the summer of 1653 the main obstacles had been overcome and the path to a peace agreement smoothed. It was signed in the spring of 1654. The war was over, but in both the colonies and Europe the rivalry continued to simmer beneath the surface.

New Amsterdam – New York – New Orange

The English Everywhere

In the meantime the English had not been idle. In the first half of the seventeenth century their possessions in North America had been substantially extended. There were English colonies along the coast from the present states of North Carolina to Maine. To the south of New Netherland lay Virginia, founded as early as 1607. The colony, with Jamestown as its capital, was named after Queen Elizabeth I, the "Virgin Queen". Between New Netherland and Virginia was the Catholic-oriented Maryland, a colony established by Lord Baltimore around 1634 that took its name from the wife of King Charles I of England.

The Pilgrim Fathers, English Puritans who had left England because of religious persecution, founded the Plymouth Colony in 1620. Nine years later the Massachusetts Bay Colony was established to the north of New Netherland by like-minded settlers. From there, around 1633 the Puritans moved to the vicinity of the Dutch settlement on the Connecticut River, where they founded Hartford and laid the basis for the colony of Connecticut. New England became the collective name of the territories Connecticut, Massachusetts, Maine, New Hampshire, Rhode Island and New Haven, which was later abandoned.

Not all the leaders of these colonies intended to maintain close ties with the mother country. Some of them had fled precisely in order to create a new, more or less autonomous society. England naturally took a different view: Virginia and New England were 100 percent English. Between these two English areas lay New Netherland, the Dutch colony, which was almost completely surrounded by English possessions. The Dutch Republic was England's main opponent, and New Netherland was a thorn in the side of the English.

Curbing Dutch Power

New Amsterdam had enjoyed a relatively prosperous and productive decade by the time plans were made in England to capture the city and the surrounding colony. One of the first steps paving the way was the Navigation Act of 1651, which struck at the heart of Dutch shipping. Non-English ships were forbidden to transport cargoes from outside Europe to England and Dutch ships were not allowed to unload goods from Europe in England. The aim was to give the best possible protection to English trade overseas. A new version of the 1651 Act was passed in 1660. The English colonies were forbidden to trade goods like tobacco, sugar and cotton directly with non-English customers. In this way the mother country hoped to ensure that in the future trade in these products would take place via England itself. This made England the principal staple in Europe and now there was nothing to prevent the English from becoming the leading world power.

One obstacle was left: the conquest of New Amsterdam. For the traders on the island it was still simple to evade the navigation laws and bring in goods from the English colonies. Conversely, the English traders could use New Amsterdam as a staging post. To prevent that, England believed that the Dutch enclave had to be captured.

King Charles II, who had just been put in power by the restoration of the monarchy, was a great believer in the new laws and the protectionist policy. Just as in 1651, when the First Anglo-Dutch War broke out as a result of this policy, now the consequence would again be war. The Duke of York, the brother of King Charles II, took on the role of adversary and was given the task of capturing the Dutch colony in North America. He hoped that this show of strength would persuade the surrounding English colonies, which he believed bore too little respect to the English crown, to fall into line. If New Netherland was taken, England would be lord and master of almost the entire east coast of North America, from New England to Carolina.

LONGE · ISLELAND ·
Passage
Passage Place
A · DESCRIPTION · OF THE
TOWNE · OF · MANNADOS
OR · NEW · AMSTERDAM
lying in Latitude 40 : and 40
1664
Governours Garden
Hudsons · River
This Scale of Five Hondred yeardes is for the Towne
50
100
200
300
400
500
THE · MAINE · LAND

"The Duke's Plan"

In the nineteenth century "The Duke's Plan" was named after the Duke of York, who took the city in 1664. On the left we see the cartouche still bearing the name "Mannados or New Amsterdam," but the flags on the ships in the bay clearly indicate an English presence. Yet the map shows a situation that is still entirely Dutch, given the inscription in the cartouche: "A descriptor of the Towne. Of Mannados: Or. New Amsterdam: as it was in September 1661 … Anno Domini: 1664." No one knows who made the map. But the inscription reveals that the cartographer worked from a now lost Dutch map of Manhattan of 1661. Is that why the city in the map is not yet named New York? After all, Fort Amsterdam has already been renamed Fort James; and the North River is called the Hudson River, which was also known until the early nineteenth century as "The North."[13]

Map of New York, 1664
British Library, London
Maps.K.Top.CXXI.35

The Conditions of Surrender

ARTYKELEN,
Van 't overgaen van
NIEUW-NEDERLANDT.
Op den 27. Augusti, Oude-Stijl, Anno 1664.

Symon Gilde van Rarop, Schipper op 't Schip de Gideon, komende van de Menates, of Nieuw-Amsterdam in Nieuw-Nederlandt, rapporteert dat Nieuw-Nederlandt, met accoort, sonder eenighe tegenweer, den 8. September Nieuwe-Stijl, aen de Engelsen is overgegeven, op Conditien als volght:

[illegible]

Was onderteeckent

J. d. Decker.
N. Verlet.
Sam. Megapolensis.
Cornelis Steenwijck.
O. Stevensz. Cortlant.
Jacque Cousseau.

Robbert Carr.
George Cartwright.
John Winthrop.
Sam. Willes.
Tho. Clarcks.
John Phinchon.

Ick stae dese Artijkelen toe (en getekent)

RICHARDT NICOLLS.

Artykelen, Van 't overgaen van Nieuw-Nederlandt. Op den 27. Augusti, Oude-Stijl, Anno 1664 (The conditions of the surrender of New Netherland. On 27 August, old style, in the year 1664)
Royal Library, The Hague
Pflt 8867

Nieu Amsterdam, een stedeken in Noord Amerikaes Nieu Hollant op het eilant Manhattan: namaels Nieu jork genaemt toen het geraekte in 't gebiet der Engelschen (New Amsterdam, a town in New Holland in North America on Manhattan Island: later named New York when it came under the territory of the English)
Peter Schenk and Carel Allard, 1673
New York Public Library, New York
ID: 1650614

In 24 articles this pamphlet sets out the stipulations applying to the transfer into English hands of the colony of New Amsterdam. The conditions of surrender proposed by the English were not all bad. For example, the judiciary were allowed to stay in office for as long as their term under the Dutch system, after which new magistrates would be appointed. As for the law of succession, Dutch law would continue to apply, even though it differed from English law. In the case of the civil code there would be a change: English civil law would apply after the surrender.[14]

Here we see the surrender of Peter Stuyvesant through the eyes of a twentieth-century draftsman. There are numerous prints and drawings of Stuyvesant having to give up his city to the English. Favorite scenes include the moments preceding the official surrender, such as the inhabitants' pleas to Stuyvesant to spare the city and their lives and hand over New Amsterdam without bloodshed. Another favorite is the image of Stuyvesant furiously tearing up the piece of paper with the conditions of surrender.

The Surrender of Petrus Stuyvesant
Henry Alexander Ogden, 1856-1936
New York Public Library, New York
ID: 800032

The End of New Amsterdam

James Stuart, the Duke of York, was granted permission by his brother King Charles II to attack the Dutch colony. If James succeeded, he stood to gain a great deal of income from the tax on products from the North American coast. Richard Nicolls was in command of the ships fitted out for the operation. The fleet consisted of three frigates, which sailed from Plymouth harbor in 1664. After the planned conquest, Nicolls would have to keep the whole area under control without these ships, which carried 300 soldiers. This would be no easy feat, thus Nicolls decided that it would be better if the conquest transpired without bloodshed. Only then would there be a chance that the inhabitants would not resist and that they might cooperate more easily after the victory. That was the plan. Would it work?

Not if it was up to Stuyvesant. He was not going to give up his city and country for any price. But it was not up to the director-general alone. There was the Board, which had to be consulted, and, much more importantly, there were the people. When Nicolls' frigates lay at anchor in the city's roadstead, it was the New Amsterdammers who in the end decided what their future was to be. Stuyvesant called for resistance against the intruders, but he stood alone. The colonists had absolutely no desire to fight. They foresaw that it would be impossible to defeat the English, even if there were not that many of them. The defenses of Fort Amsterdam were in too poor a state.

Nicolls had meanwhile informed the inhabitants of Manhattan of his conditions: they had two days in which to surrender, otherwise he would take the city. There were between 2000 and 2500 citizens, and they did not support Stuyvesant's resistance. Thus Manhattan fell into English hands without a shot being fired. On 7 September a meeting was held at Stuyvesant's farm to discuss the conditions of the surrender; the document was signed the next day, on 8 September 1664.[15]

Nicolls would be the first governor of the English city. Fort Amsterdam became Fort James. New Netherland became the Province of New York and New Amsterdam became New York City. Beverwijck was also given a name connected with the Duke of York, namely Albany, after the region in Scotland from which James derived his second title, Duke of Albany. The duke himself was to be governor of the Hudson's Bay Company for some 20 years, though without playing an active role.

War and Peace

The Second Anglo-Dutch War, which lasted until 1667, was not fought solely in Europe and New Netherland. In addition to New Amsterdam, the English captured other WIC possessions: the island of Curaçao and several trading posts on the coast of West Africa. The Dutch Republic responded by sending Admiral Michiel de Ruyter to Africa to recapture the trading posts, in which he was highly successful. At sea the English and the Dutch seized each other's ships, with the English scoring by far the most victories. In the year after the conquest of New Amsterdam the English still had substantial successes, and many Dutch ships were sunk or fell into English hands.

The tide turned when Michiel de Ruyter won ever more sea battles and the French king Louis XIV sided with the Dutch. Both nations became exhausted, above all financially. Once more it was the English king who took the initiative in opening peace negotiations. During this period De Ruyter sailed up the Thames and captured the English flagship the *Royal Charles* at Chatham. This daring exploit strengthened the Republic's bargaining position at the peace talks.

The peace was finally concluded on 31 July 1667 in the city of Breda in Brabant. The Dutch were delighted by the outcome: first of all, there would be a relaxation of the English navigation acts, which had long been a thorn in the side of the Dutch companies and excluded them from many commercial activities. In addition, the parties agreed that the German hinterland should belong to the Dutch trade area. As for the captured colonies, for the time being the status quo was maintained: Suriname remained a Dutch possession, and New Amsterdam continued to be English.

The Peace of Breda, 1667

Peace Treaty agreed at Breda between the States General and the king of England, 1667 July 31.

1
Original Treaty of Peace between His Royal Majesty of Great Britain Special Ambassadors on one side and the High Powers plenipotentiaries agreed and sig[ned?] in Breda on 31 July 1667 and here for the Assembly the further separate Articles and acts displayed on 4 August 1667 (Origineel Tractaet van Vreede tusschen Sijne Coninklijke Majesteit van Groot Brittannien Extraordinaris Ambassadeurs ter eenre ende hare Hoog Mogenden plenipotentiarissen tot Breda geslooten ende get[ekend?] op den 31en juli 1667 ende alhier ter Vergaderinge nevens de verdere separate Articulen ende actes geexhibeert op den 4en augustus 1667)

2
Act of Ratification by the king of England of what is stipulated in Art. 3 of the Peace of Breda, covering the return of the territories which the English and the Dutch had captured from each other since 20 May 1667, 1667 August 8

The Second Anglo-Dutch War ended with the Peace of Breda, whereby New York remained in English hands and the Republic kept the colony of Suriname, which it had taken from the English in 1667. These are the official final documents of the Peace of Breda concluded on 31 July 1667. England and the Netherlands were not the only interested parties. Four countries were involved in the negotiations and the resulting agreement: the Dutch Republic, England, France and Denmark. They decided to which countries a number of overseas possessions should be allocated.

The Peace Treaty was signed in the Great Hall of the castle in Breda. The English king, Charles II, knew the castle well. Sixteen years earlier, in 1651, he had fled his country when the republican Oliver Cromwell came into power. He stayed in Europe for nine years. It was not until after Cromwell's death in 1658, which brought about a political crisis, that there was again talk of Charles returning to England. At that point he was staying at Breda Castle, as that was where his sister Mary Stuart, the widow of Stadholder Willem II, was living. From Breda, on 4 April 1660, he accepted the conditions attached by the English to the restored monarchy. He was then free to return and restore the crown to its former glory.
A few years later war broke out between the English and the Dutch, which was initiated by Charles II and ended by the Peace of Breda in 1667.

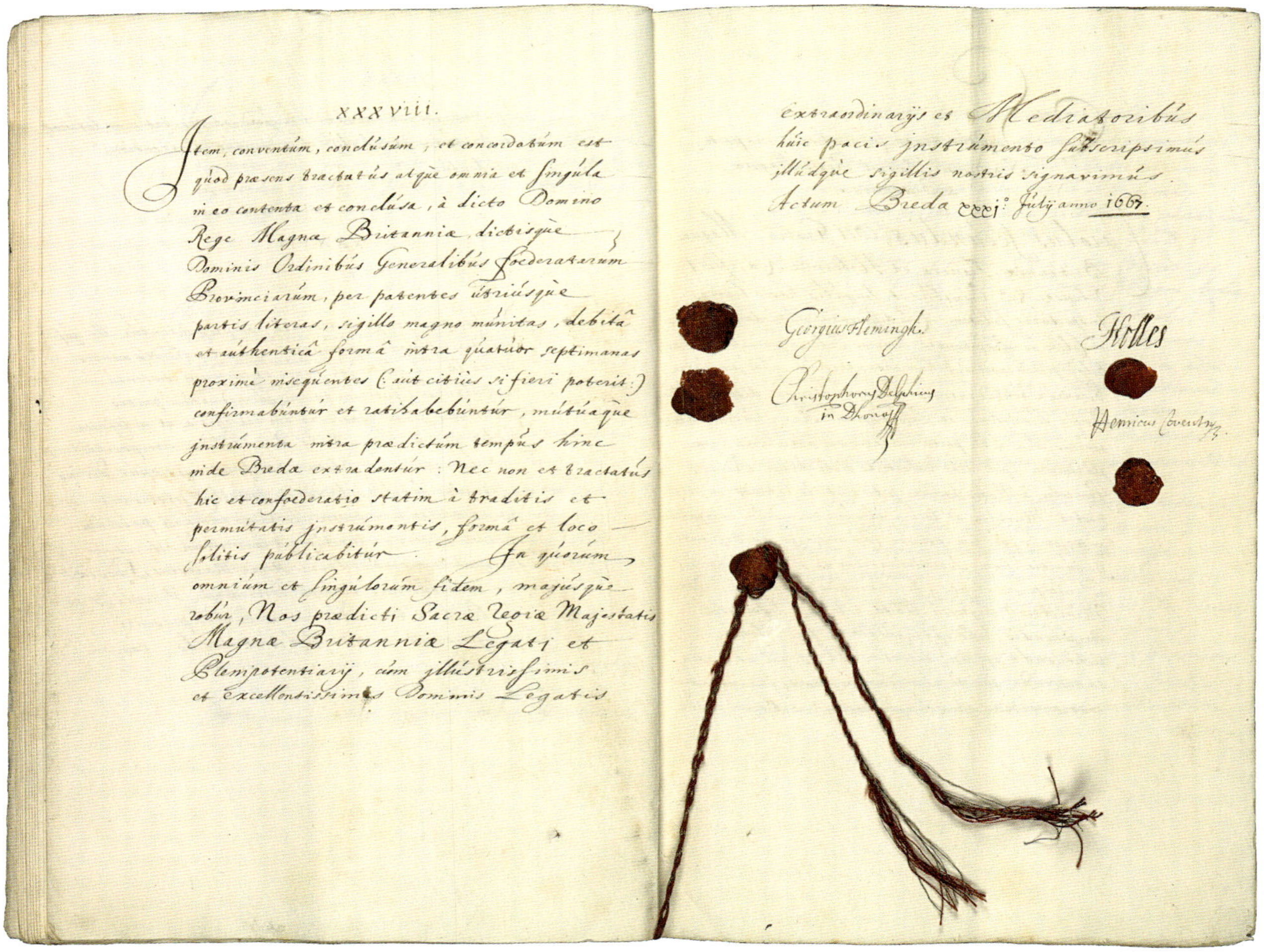

1
Peace Treaty, 1667
Nationaal Archief (National Archives of the Netherlands), The Hague
States General, 1.01.08, inv. no. 12589.127
37 x 24.5 cm

Signing of the Peace Treaty of Breda
In: Marcus Willemsz. Doornick, *Kort en bondigh verhael van 't geene in den oorlogh, tusschen den Koningh van Engeland ... der vrije Vereenigde Nederlanden* (Brief and concise account of the war between the king of England ...the free United Netherlands), Amsterdam, 1667
Royal Library, The Hague
3107 C 28

Exhibitum 9. 7bris 1667

Nos Carolus Secundus Dei gratiâ Magnæ Britanniæ, Franciæ, et Hiberniæ Rex, Fidei Defensor, &c. notum testatumq. facimus omnibus et singulis, quorum interest aut quomodo libet interesse poterit. Quandoquidem in Tractatu Pacis inter Nos et Celsos ac Præpotentes Dominos Ordines Generales Foederati Belgij die 21/31 Julij An.o 1667. in Urbe Bredâ conclusæ, Articulo tertio conventum est, ut utraq. Pars cum plenario jure summi imperij, proprietatis et possessionis, omnes ejusmodi Terras, Insulas, Urbes, Munimenta, Loca ac Colonias teneat et possideat in posterum, quotquot durante hoc bello, aut ante hoc bellum, ullis retro temporibus, vi et armis, aut quoquomodo ab alterâ Parte occupavit aut retinuit, eum prorsus in modum, quo ea 10/20 Maij proxime elapsi occupaverat et possedit, nullis eorundem locorum exceptis: Et quandoquidem porrò ad evitandam omnem Litis et contentionum materiam, quæ oriri interdum solet ex causâ Restitutionum, articulo sexto itidem conventum est, ut si alterutra Pars post dictum diem 10/20 Maij proxime elapsum, aliquas Terras, Insulas, Urbes, Munimenta, Colonias, aliaq. Loca ab alterâ Parte interceperit et occupaverit, omnia et singula horum absque ullâ loci temporisq. distinctione, in eodem planè statu confestim restituantur, quo tunc temporis reperientur, quandocunq. de instauratâ Pace in ijs Locis constiterit: Hisce jubemus ac mandamus Omnibus Nostris Gubernatoribus, Officialibus, Præfectis, Militibusq. tam mari quam terrâ, cujuscunq. demum qualitatis et conditionis

fuerint

2

Memorandum of Ratification, 1667
Nationaal Archief (National Archives of the Netherlands), The Hague
States General, 1.01.08, inv. no. 12589.131
35 x 23.8 cm, seal diam. 14.5 cm

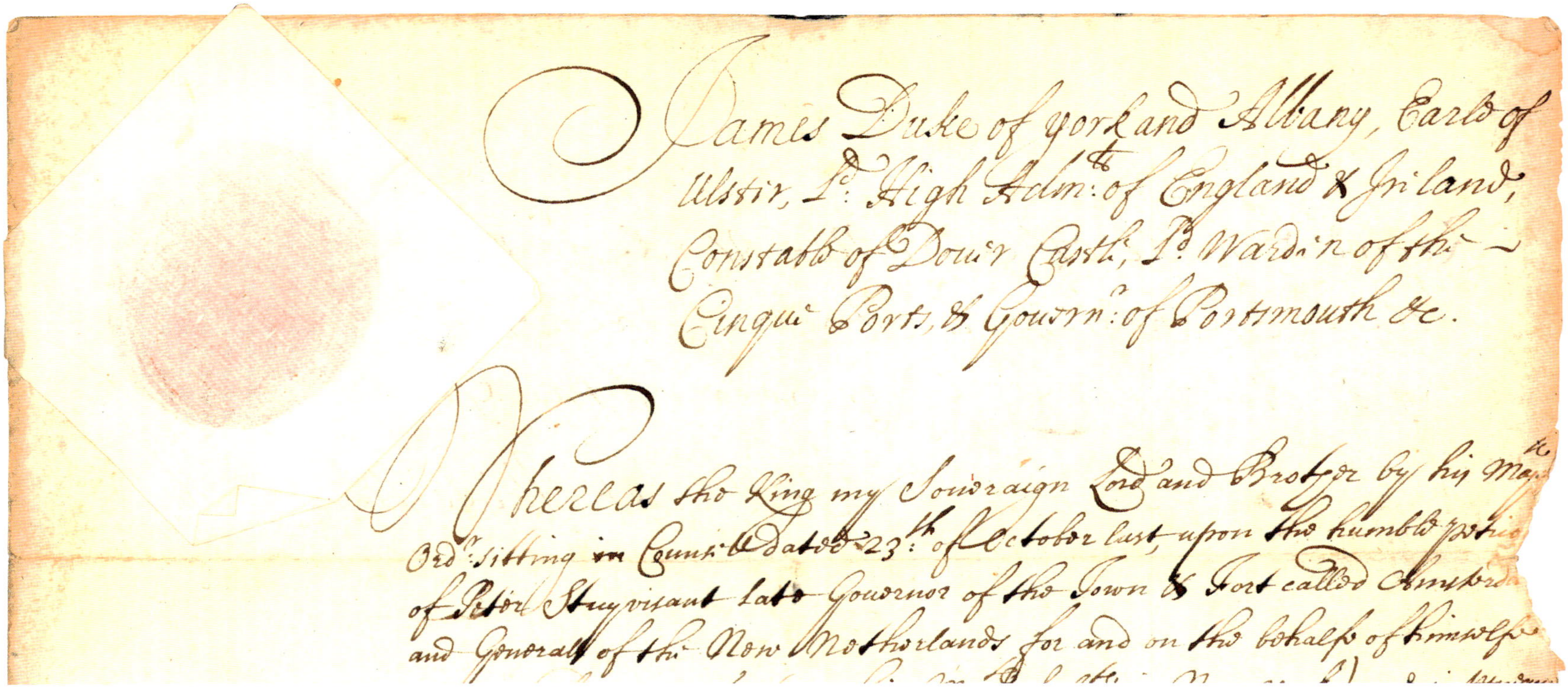
James Duke of York and Albany, Earle of
Ulster, Ld. High Adm.ll of England & Ireland,
Constable of Dover Castle, Ld. Warden of the
Cinque Ports, & Governr: of Portsmouth &c.

Whereas the King my Soveraign Lord and Brother by his Ma.tie
Ord.r sitting in Councill dated 23th of October last, upon the humble petition
of Peter Stuyvesant late Governor of the Town & Fort called Amsterd.
and Generall of the New Netherlands for and on the behalfe of himselfe

Pass from His Highness of Great Britain, 1667
Collectie Antiquariaat Forum BV, 't Goy-Houten, the Netherlands
Ink on paper, 33.5 x 23 cm

Stuyvesant Can Return Safely to New York

Now that New Amsterdam had become New York, what would Peter Stuyvesant do? Sail back to Holland? Or stay in the country where he had been in charge for more than 15 years, but where an English governor now gave the orders? He had to pay a visit to The Hague anyway to report on the English takeover. Stuyvesant made the journey in 1665. It cannot have been a pleasant time for him: he will have had to listen to complaints about his administration and the defeat he had suffered. With his work done, Stuyvesant asked the States General for permission to return to his farm on Manhattan. It was granted and at the end of 1666 he was free to leave.

The former director-general would have been aware that the return journey to New York was not without its risks. This is why he stopped off in London and asked King Charles II for a passé partout. If English ships stopped Stuyvesant's vessel, the royal passport would provide him with a safe passage.

Charles had the passport drawn up by his brother James, the Duke of York. Stuyvesant also had a request for him. Together with a number of Amsterdam businessmen, he wanted to establish a trading company to supply the Dutch inhabitants of New York with clothing and other goods from Holland. Authorization from the duke was required in order to engage in trade between the Dutch Republic and New York. Stuyvesant's wish was granted. For a period of one year he was permitted to set up a shipping venture between his fatherland and the English colony, using three ships. This was a special concession, because in principle the English did not allow ships into the harbor.

The letter, which is signed by James and bears his seal, gave Stuyvesant permission to send one of the three ships, namely the *Nieuw Jorck* captained by Pieter Reijersz. van der Beets, to New York. A year later James was to rescind permission and Stuyvesant had to cease the trade.

1673, New York Dutch Again for a Year

After the Peace of Breda the States General no longer concerned itself with the people living in the former colony. Later, however, the Dutch Republic was forced to take an interest again, if only for a short time. Despite the Peace of 1667, not long afterwards war broke out again, and once more there was fighting in several places. In December 1672 a Swedish fleet commanded by Cornelis Evertsen the Younger went to sea in search of English ships returning from Asia. For eight months Evertsen scanned the ocean looking for prey. The island of St. Helena was captured so that it could be used as an operational base.

According to the orders he had been given in Zeeland, at the end of his mission Evertsen was to sail to Suriname to discharge goods. Once that was done, Evertsen would have completed his mission and be due to return to his home base. But he was not ready for that yet. After he joined an Amsterdam squadron commanded by Jacob Binckes, in mid-1673 they set sail together for the coast of Virginia. The fleet, now numbering 21 ships, sailed north towards New York.

On his arrival there Evertsen learned from a few Dutchmen who had come aboard that the city could easily be taken. They said that the fort was poorly defended, that the English governor Lovelace was away and that anything was better than living under the yoke of the English. At least, so we are told. It is quite possible that Evertsen later exaggerated what the Dutch said in order to justify his plans to attack. He decided to inform the inhabitants of New York immediately about the impending takeover. Attempts by an English delegation to persuade Evertsen to change his mind were to no avail. He saw his chance, and without an order to do so he retook Fort James.[16]

The inhabitants were spared, and there was no looting or plundering during the recapture. Immediately afterwards Evertsen put the city's defenses in order and appointed a committee to draw up a war plan. New York was to have yet another name: New Orange, and the fort was also renamed Willem Hendrick.[17]

The governor-general of the Dutch colony was Anthony Colve, who had earlier been the captain of the flagship of Evertsen's fleet. Colve was given 120 men, deemed necessary for enforcing the new situation. Evertsen arranged for the replacement of the village authorities in the colony. Men of Dutch origins took the places of the English administrators. Meanwhile the province of Zeeland, Evertsen's patron, knew nothing about his actions. It was not until October 1673 that the first reports about the recapture reached the Netherlands. They caused consternation. The Dutch government was shocked. This had never been the intention: Evertsen's task had been to fight only at sea. And now all of a sudden he had retaken the whole of New Netherland!

Were the Dutch excited about this unexpected victory? Not really. The year before had been the "year of disasters." War had broken out not only with the English but also with the French king Louis XIV, who had invaded the eastern provinces of the Dutch Republic with the help of German troops. Three provinces had fallen into their hands. A last-ditch effort had been needed to prevent the country being annexed by France. An appeal was even made to Spain, the old enemy. The Spanish king promised to offer help to halt the French advance, but only on condition that the Dutch made peace with England. Moreover, the Spanish thought it important that the recently recaptured territories should be given up immediately. They included New Netherland and St. Helena. This was bad news for the colonists in New Netherland, who had been hoping that the situation would remain unchanged. It was also a blow to those in the mother country who were campaigning for the colony to be retained.

There were secret negotiations with Spain and England intended to lead to the return of the territories. In the spring of 1674 a peace proposal was presented to the English king Charles II. Only the States General knew about this; the individual provinces were still in the dark. Charles II agreed to the proposal.

During the same period the States General received a letter from New Netherland. It was a cry for help. The administration of the colony asked the national government for assistance: the Dutch colony had to be retained at all costs. But the letter disappeared into the archives. The individuals addressed were much too busy with the peace negotiations. With the Treaty of Westminster in 1674 the Dutch colony passed into English hands for good.

ONE
PEARL ST
MOORE ST

Cornelis Steenwijck

An Extremely Wealthy Slave Trader

Cornelis Steenwijck, who lived on the corner of Brugh Straat (Bridge Street) and Marckvelt (Whitehall Street),[18] was one of the most prosperous New Amsterdammers of his time. When precisely he arrived in New Amsterdam is uncertain, but it must have been around 1650. He began as an agent for a trading company but when his contract expired he set up his own business, buying and selling slaves. His wealth gave him entry to the highest circles in the city. He was one of the richest men in Manhattan, as evidenced by the fact that when his wife was pregnant he sailed back to the Dutch Republic with her, to seek the best natal care.

His name appears frequently in municipal registers, and he held important posts. In fact in 1664 he became burgomaster. After the Dutch briefly recaptured New York from the British in 1673, Steenwijck was made a councilor, responsible for the appointment of burgomasters and aldermen. The British too put great trust in him, for after they finally secured control of the city in 1674, Steenwijck was given an important position in the city government, at a time when he was the second richest man in the colony. He served as mayor of New York from 1668 to 1670/2 and from 1682 to 1683/4.

It is not known who painted this portrait. Until recently it was attributed to Hendrick Couturier, a painter trained in Leiden. In 1660 Couturier moved from Holland to Delaware and then to New York. Evidently Steenwijck was very proud of his home and had a cartouche with a view of New York added to his portrait. Some sources suggest that the picture was made on the occasion of Steenwijck's visit to the Dutch Republic around 1667, in which case the artist was probably either the Haarlem painter Jan van Goosen or Jan van Goter.[19]

Potrait of Cornelis Steenwijck
Anonymous, 1668
New York Historical Society, New York
1882.172
Oil on canvas, 81.3 x 63.5 cm

Photo of Pearl Street between Moore Street and MacDonald Avenue, where Cornelis Steenwijck lived

Winka Dubbeldam, architect
Born 1966 Strijen
In New York since 1990

New Amsterdam Recently Renamed New York and Now Retaken by the Dutch on 24 August 1673

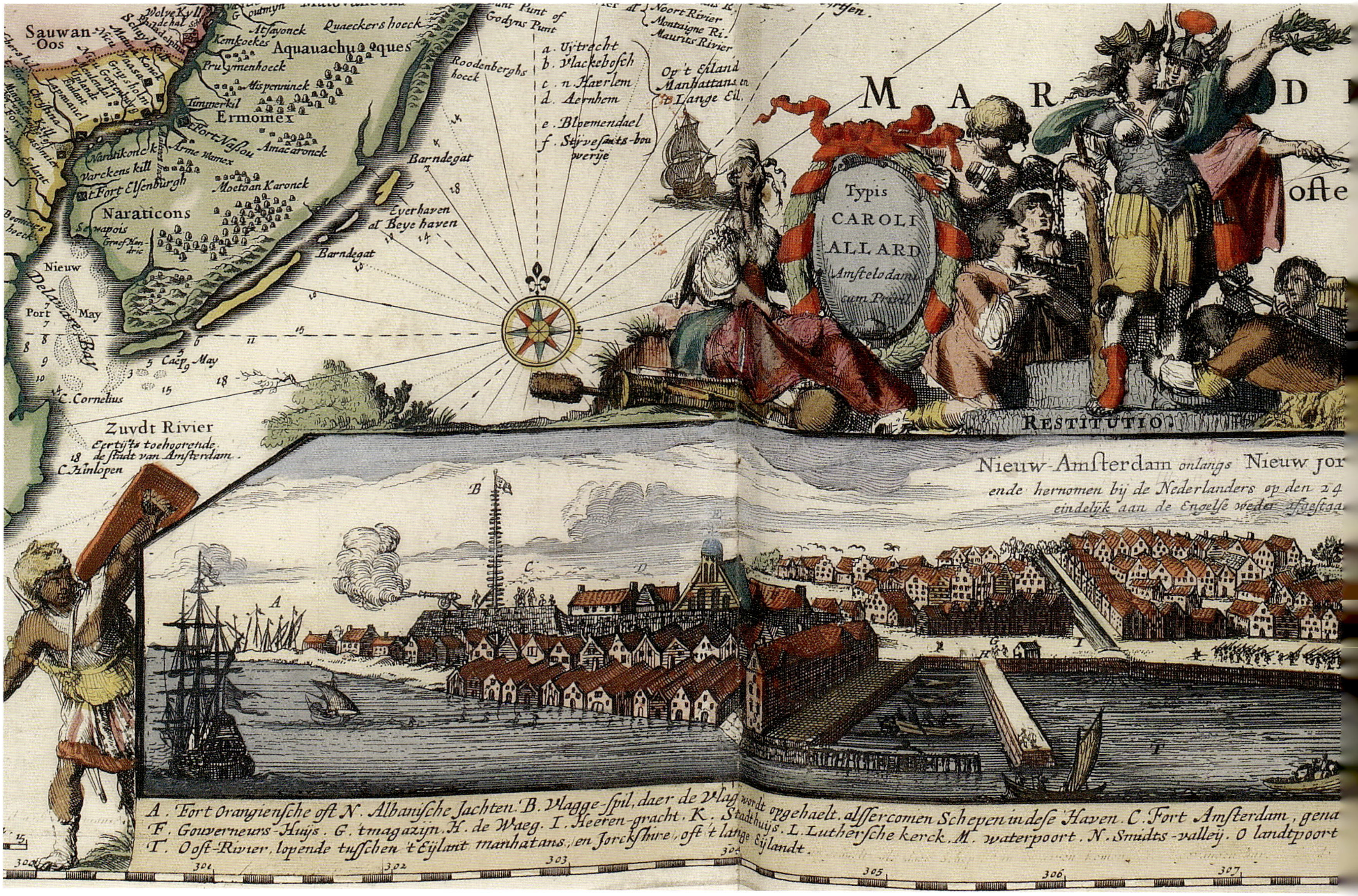

Maps can sometimes be seen as staking a claim. Just as the English recorded the taking of New Amsterdam in 1664 with their "Duke's Plan," the Dutch in turn did the same in 1673 with the map by Carolus Allard entitled Totius Neobelgii Nova Et Accuratissima Tabula. The map is embellished with an inset at the lower right. Upon closer scrutiny, the capture seems to unfold before our eyes. Troops march on the quay. At the far left, near the fort, a cannon is being fired. The city is depicted from the east, so that the eastern side of Wall Street is clearly visible.

Above the inset is a scene with all manner of figures in which Victoria, or Victory, is central. She stretches out her arm with the laurel wreath. Indians offer her gifts; one man throws himself at her feet and grips her left leg. The word "Restitutio," under Victoria's feet, is crucial: it indicates that authority has been restored in New Netherland. Indeed, things looked rosy for the Dutch for a while. But in the end the city and the surrounding colony remained in Dutch hands for only a year. With the Treaty of Westminster the English got New York back: on 11 October 1674 the new English governor Edmond Andros was installed.[20] This marked the end of close to 50 years of Dutch domination of Manhattan.

A *Fort Orange or N. Albany Yachts*

B *Flagpole, where the flag is raised when ships enter the harbor*

C *Fort Amsterdam, named Fort James by the English*

D *Prison*

E *Reformed Church*

F *Governor's House*

G *Storehouse*

H *Weigh House*

I *Herengracht*

K *Town Hall*

L *Lutheran Church*

M *Water Gate*

N *Smiths' Valley*

O *Land Gate*

P *Road to Fresh Water*

Q *Windmill*

R *Bastions*

S *Stuyvesant's House*

T *East River, running between Manhattan Island and Yorkshire or Long Island*

Inset of a map entitled *Totius Neobelgii Nova et Accuratissima Tabula*
Hugo Allard, 1674
New York Public Library, New York
ID: 54735

[1] For passages from Van der Donck's *Beschryvinge* in this chapter, use has been made of Jacobs, *Een zegenrijk gewest*, pp. 33-54; Van der Donck, A *Description of New Netherland*.
[2] Van Bracht and Schilder, *The Origins of New York*, p. 20.
[3] Jacobs, *Een zegenrijk gewest*, pp. 127-128; Jacobs, "Dutch Proprietary Manors in America," pp. 18-19.
[4] Jacobs, "Between Repression and Approval," p. 56; Jacobs, "Incompetente autocraten?," p. 11.
[5] Gehring, "A Description of New Netherland."
[6] Craig, "Chronology of Colonial Swedes."
[7] Jacobs, *Een zegenrijk gewest*, p. 35.
[8] Hart, "De stadskolonie Nieuwer-Amstel," pp. 89-94.
[9] Jacobs, *Een zegenrijk gewest*, pp. 129-132.
[10] O'Callaghan, *The documentary history of New Netherland*, II, p. 538; Jacobs, *Een zegenrijk gewest*, p. 101.
[11] O'Callaghan, *The documentary history of New Netherland*, II, p. 538.
[12] Jacobs, "The Hartford Treaty," pp. 74-79.
[13] Cohen, *Manhattan in Maps*, p. 43.
[14] Jacobs, *Een zegenrijk gewest*, p. 165.
[15] Rink, *Holland on the Hudson*, p. 263.
[16] De Waard, *De Zeeuwsche expeditie*, pp. xxvi-xlvii.
[17] Shomette and Haslach, *Raid on America*, p. 170.
[18] According to Phelps Stokes, *The Iconography of Manhattan Island*.
[19] Frijhoff, *Going Dutch*, p. 33; Jacobs, *Een zegenrijk gewest*, p. 278.
[20] Cohen, *Manhattan in Maps*, pp. 46-47.

THE INHABITANTS

III

CHAPTER 1

The Americans

Various tribes of Native Americans live in the region where New Netherland arose. For obvious reasons these "Americans" will be discussed first. They represent an important exception in the colony for they are the only original inhabitants; the other ones come from all corners of the earth.

Focusing specifically on the Indians on Manhattan, there is yet another key difference with the rest of the seventeenth-century inhabitants of the island. As of the middle of the seventeenth century, the Manhattan Indians no longer live on the island, while the Dutch, Germans, Angolans, Jews and other ethnic groups are still found there. Illness, wars and a lack of land ultimately drive the Manhattans out of their native habitat. The colonists' arrival is the direct cause of this.

The complex bond that arises between the Indians and the colonists in New Netherland is explored on the basis of seventeenth-century European sources – which virtually never present the Indian side's point of view. The relationships are anything but straightforward. Some groups have more fundamental ties with the Europeans than others. The greater the number of contacts and instances of trade, the stronger the mutual interdependence: the Europeans want beaver pelts, and the Indians want European merchandise.

As time passes, however, this mutual dependence becomes more one-sided. The colony's economy no longer depends solely on the fur trade. The Indians' habituation to the European presence goes hand in hand with violence and conflicts over areas that are inhabited or used communally. In the end, some groups accept Dutch supremacy, if only because they are fed up with the wars or are too few to continue fighting. Some tribes become allies, others remain hostile...

Map of New Netherland, Virginia and New England
Johannes Vingboons, third quarter of the seventeenth century
Library of Congress, Geography and Map Division, Washington, D.C.
G3291.S12 coll .H3 Vault: Harr vol. 2, map 7
Watercolor on paper, 48 x 69 cm

The Land of the Indians

The maker of this map, Johannes Vingboons, frequently produced maps based on the material provided by others – he never set foot outside the Netherlands, and may never have gone beyond Amsterdam. Thus he must have used material, such as original maps, that is drawings by sailors and WIC servants working in situ. Vingboons processed these authentic maps into more decorative ones that were not used at sea or on the work floor. He mapped half of the world, namely that of the VOC and WIC.

This map covers New Netherland, Virginia and New England and a part of today's Canada. New Netherland is indicated in yellow, Virginia and New England in green and Canada is colored purple.

The map that served as the model for the one on display probably originated between 1630 and 1635. The Hudson and Delaware Rivers were being extensively investigated by the Dutch at that time: large-scale mapping expeditions took place primarily under the leadership of Pieter Minuit. What is striking in this map is that all of the English names are indicated in red ink, while those of the Indian villages and the Dutch place names are in black.

The Arrival of the Europeans

Indians and the *Halve Maen* (Half Moon)

On his trip in 1609 Hudson met Manhattans, Wappingers and Mahicans[1] For them his visit heralded the beginning of a new era, the starting shot for intercultural relations. Henry Hudson's *Halve Maen* (Half Moon) was probably the very first European ship that the Native Americans living near the Hudson River had ever seen. While it is true that various intrepid Europeans had explored the coasts in the area already in the sixteenth century, there were few if any encounters between the various parties.

When the Indians saw the European ships, they interpreted them as sea monsters or unusually large fish.[2] According to various sources, initially the Indians did not consider the ships and their crews as human but rather as creatures with supernatural powers. The earliest meetings with Europeans were actually perceived as spiritual experiences. For the Indians who became acquainted with Hudson and his crew it was therefore important to receive the strangers hospitably – and with the necessary caution. After all, it was not immediately clear what Hudson and his men were after.

Both Robert Juet, one of Hudson's crewmembers, and Johannes de Laet wrote about the encounters between the Indians and Hudson's men. Generally speaking they talk about friendly introductions, with the exchanging of gifts being one of the most important cultural expressions of the Indians. By giving goods to one another, the world was kept in balance, or so they believed. Moreover, this was meant to take place with due ceremony. In their animistic worldview, the Indians saw the white men as apparitions from the spirit world, which allowed the Indians to acquire certain powers through gifts. The European items could also have a spiritual value. And so the exchange of gifts for both parties was a crucial aspect of the encounter, even if the underlying reasons and the significance of the gifts differed.

Skirmishes sometimes took place on Hudson's trip without any clear cause. Juet writes about a few crewmembers who had sailed up the river in a sloop. When they came back they were being hotly pursued by two canoes, and showered with arrows! The weather had turned, and it had begun to rain whereby the crew's muskets had become wet and therefore unusable. The Indians gained the advantage and an arrow pierced one of the men's throats. Juet does not say what preceded this situation. From other fragments about the journey, though, it becomes clear that in their fear and distrust the Europeans all too readily reached for their weapons, which might also be what happened in the above incident.[3]

Fur in Exchange for Wampum, Axes and Knives

In Hudson's wake Dutch merchants came to the land of the Indians. There were regular encounters between both peoples in the years 1610-1623 through which they continued to learn more from and about one another. For instance, the Dutch came to understand the great value the Indians attached to wampum. They treated these shell beads with utmost care and respect. Wampum was exchanged only on special occasions, for instance at marriage ceremonies, the making of important decisions and the closing of agreements.

The fur traders attached a different meaning to the strings of shell beads. For them, the strings of wampum were a medium of exchange and in time they also began using them as such. Wampum became an essential link in the commercial money circuit in New Netherland. The shortage of silver coinage meant that the Dutch merchants became accustomed to paying for the beaver pelts with shell beads. At a certain moment transactions among the Dutch were also conducted with wampum. Later wampum even penetrated into New England as a means of payment, so that the English and the Dutch could more easily continue to buy each other's products. In addition to wampum, called *sewant* by the Dutch, beaver pelts and later tobacco as well were also common means of payment.[4]

In turn, the Indians became familiar with European consumer items such as axes, cauldrons, boors and knives. As the years passed by and the encounters became less special, the objects themselves and the ceremonial exchange of the gifts lost their spiritual connotation. In the early years, the objects were sometimes used in ways other than what they were produced for. Spearheads and ornaments, for instance, were made from copper cauldrons. Later the items were more frequently used the way the Europeans meant them to be. And so both parties gradually became accustomed to each other's customs and objects.

Initially primarily the Mahicans, who lived upstream along the Hudson River, worked together with the European fur buyers. Before long, though, other groups in the surrounding area got wind of the Dutch trading ships. They too were curious about the Europeans wares. They began to hunt beaver more frequently and amassed large numbers of pelts.

The peoples who most frequently came into contact with the New Netherlanders belonged to the Munsee, the Algonquins, the Mahicans, the Iroquois, the Lenape and the Susquehannocks. The Munsee group

Hudson Being Welcomed

Indians meeting Hudson
Library of Congress, Prints and Photographs Division, Washington, D.C.

Hudson sailed up the North (Hudson) River on 11 September 1609. Quite soon the first Indians came forward to meet him. A few Munsee Indians set foot on the *Halve Maen* (Half Moon), while other contacts took place along the riverbanks. The captain and his crew were welcomed with green tobacco, hemp and dried berries. In return the Indians were given knives and other articles.

Sewant, or Wampum, in a European Collection

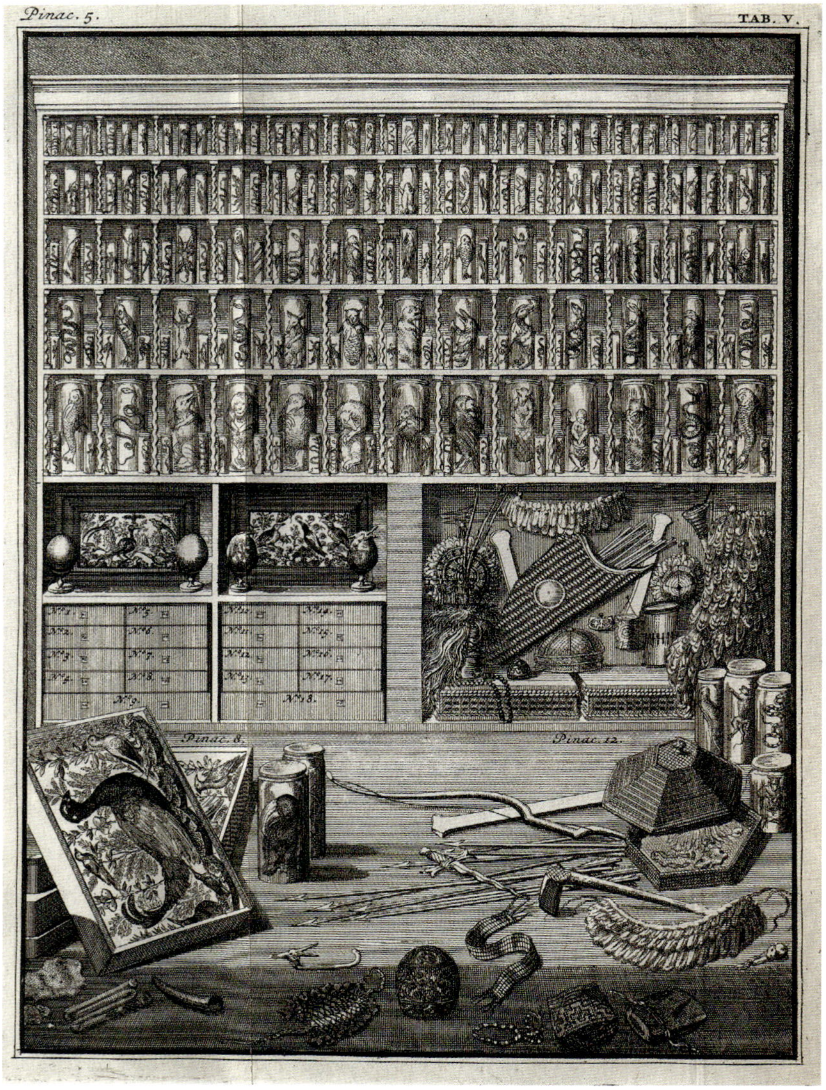

The collection of Levinus Vincent
In: *Wondertooneel der natuure* (Wondrous Theater of Nature), 1706
Amsterdam City Archives
Inv. no. 15030, 96915
Engraving

This print presents some of the objects in the collection of Levinus Vincent, a merchant who had amassed a considerable fortune with a business in damask. He earned enough, in any case, to build up an impressive collection of art and rarities, a hobby only the rich could afford. Vincent's collection was greatly admired; even Czar Peter the Great took time to visit it. The collection consisted of paintings and drawings, as well as objects from nature, such as shells, animals, specimens and insects. In the foreground of this print can be seen a string of sewant, or wampum, along with several other Indian artifacts from the new world.

was large, and its most important subgroups were the Manhattans, Esopus, Hackensacks, Tappans, Raritans, Wappingers, Weckquasgeeks, and Canarsees. The Munsee lived in the immediate vicinity of Manhattan, Staten Island and the southern tip of Long Island. Their northeasternmost neighbors were the Algonquins, who lived on the Lange Eiland Zeestraat (Long Island Sound) and in the valley of the Connecticut River. To the north, between the Hudson and the Connecticut Rivers lived the Mahicans. To the west of the Hudson River lived the neighbors of the Mahicans, namely the Mohawks, Oneidas, Onondagas, Cayugas and Senecas, who were all part of the Iroquois League. Then there were still two groups of Indians who lived further south: the Lenape Indians east of the Delaware, after which they were also later called, and the Susquehannocks to the west of the Delaware.

Other Indian groups also found their way to the ships. With a certain regularity the purveyors of fur trekked to the Hudson River, visiting the ships lying at anchor there during the trading season. Negotiations took place on board, those of the Indians accompanied by a delegate from the group. This function of middleman was new in Indian society and originated entirely thanks to the arrival of the foreign traders.[5]

The Indians Are Forced to Share their Land

When Captain Adriaen Jorisz. Thienpont of the *Eendracht* (Unity) dropped anchor in the North (Hudson) River in the spring of 1624 (see p. 53), the Dutch were cordially welcomed, as always, by the Indians. Only now they saw that there were many more white people on board than usual. After a few days it became clear that these Dutchmen had come to stay. The life of the Indians was about to change irrevocably. If at first the Dutch had simply been their trading partners, now they were going to have to actually share their land with these foreigners.

The WIC instructed Director Willem Verhulst to maintain good relations with the Native Americans. Should colonists behave badly to the Indians, they would be tried for their actions. The Indians had to have faith that justice would prevail, regardless of background. According to the instructions, the colonists were to take over the Indians' land through contracts. Under no circumstances were they to be chased out against their will or by means of violence.[6] In the eyes of the Company this was the proper way to establish ties with a new people and acquire land. In exchange for the right to live on and work their land, the Indians received goods from the Dutchmen.
The Indians granted the colonists users rights to ever more areas around Manhattan: Noten (Governors) Island, part of Lange Eiland, or Long Island, Staten Eiland (Staten Island), land along the banks of the Hudson and the bay of the Delaware. But matters would not long be limited to simply taking over the land. As the years passed and more Dutch arrived, they also increasingly assumed positions of authority with respect to the Indians.[7] And, perhaps more important still in the eyes of the Indians, they claimed the "acquired" lands. Around 1630, when the WIC made it possible for investors to develop patroonships for which vast tracts of land were cultivated, the Indians lost more and more land to the colonists. In retrospect, in this instance too there was never a question of users rights; the patroons considered themselves the owners of the ground.

Disagreements about ownership ensued. The Indians did not view the "purchase contracts" as granting exclusive and permanent rights to the land: the concept of land ownership was entirely foreign to them. After reaching an agreement with the colonists they continued to use and often live on the land themselves, which suggests that with the "sale" they had in no way relinquished their own rights.[8]

Nevertheless, most of the Indians accepted the new relationship, for they had become dependent on the European products. Moreover they certainly understood that the Dutch were a powerful party, after all they had firearms. Because there still was enough land for everyone and trade continued to flow fairly smoothly, the Indians did not feel threatened by the newcomers. Without actually understanding each other's cultures, both groups gradually got used to each other's presence. In general, with the exception of a few incidents, this was a peaceful period.

Both cultures influenced one another. Some Indians changed the way they dressed. Animal hides were replaced by European duffels, wool blankets that served as clothing during the day and bedding at night. Later stockings, shoes and shirts came to be worn. In turn, the Dutch adopted agricultural practices from the Indians. Primarily the way in which corn was cultivated was taken from the local tribes.[9] This reciprocal influence was not limited to adopting each other's customs or using European articles. At times the contact went further: there are instances of Indian women living with white men and bearing their children. This occurred primarily in the early period. In 1638 sexual relations between Indians and colonists were forbidden by the colonial administration and in the next few years several sentences were handed out. Later, mixed cohabitation would be less problematic, even though it remained morally reprehensible in the eyes of most of the colonists.[10]

New Amsterdam at[que] New York
Aldert Meyer, ca. 1700
In: Carolus Allard, *Orbis habitabilis Oppida et Vestitus*, ca. 1700
Royal Library, The Hague
374 A 19
Engraving, 22.2 x 27.8 cm

Beaver Skins and the Skins of Otters

In this Indian scene, a man and a woman discuss the beaver held up in the seated men's left hand. With his right hand he holds another animal against the ground. The man wears a fur cap, the woman perhaps fur leggings. They don't look like Indians, but the artist seems to have been unconcerned about this. This print is not about the people of the new world, but rather the bounty of the land.
To ensure that everyone would get the message, the artist depicted yet another two animals to either side of the man and the woman. New Netherland and its surroundings abounded in animals that provide fur and skins, the print tells us. And this was true: beavers, otters, raccoons, mink, foxes, weasels, deer, lynx and squirrels all lived there.

Internal Wars over Fur and Land

The colonists practiced professions such as farmer, soldier or craftsman. However, in the first decades most of the newcomers to New Netherland were there to buy fur and sell it to the WIC and later to private enterprises. While some did this exclusively, the majority traded other products in addition to fur or alongside their regular profession also ran small businesses in fur. Per year close to 7000 beaver and otter pelts were sent to the Dutch Republic. A particularly good year was 1635, when more than 16,000 were shipped over. It is plausible that beaver, the most intensively hunted animal, began to decline. The number of Indians, too, decreased. Accordingly, there were ever fewer hunters to provide the coveted furs. And so after the middle of the seventeenth century the supply of fur also dwindled. The Indians were spurred to find other products that might prove interesting to the Europeans. They offered them food, which came in handy when the colonists were suffering times of scarcity, but also services, such as guiding them through unknown territory, interpreting during negotiations and providing information about the land and the inhabitants. For the Dutch it was vital to acquire intelligence about the tribes collaborating with the French and English. Finally, ever more land was bought from the Indians.[11]

The scarcity of fur and land naturally heightened competition. Groups of Indians fought each other to be able to continue trading with the Europeans; by now they were dependent on the new products and vied for the commercial activities. As a result mutual relationships became unbalanced. This competition extended beyond New Netherland. A demand for fur – and the ensuing strife – was present in the adjoining colonies inhabited by the French and English. The rivaling parties became caught up in a long-lasting and bloody war. A sweeping intertribal struggle arose for the first time, which became known as the "Beaver Wars," even though the shortage of fur and beaver was not the only cause of it. Bit by bit the Iroquois gained the upper hand in this war. Their growing power was partly related to the fact that from the early 1640s they had begun to obtain firearms, in contrast to some of the other groups. This not only made them stronger in actual battle, but more successful as hunters. Moreover, the weapons allowed them to commandeer pelts from groups without firearms.[12]

For the Indians it was imperative that the Europeans maintain their neutrality and stay out of the fray. But this went haywire now and then, for instance in 1626, when a few "Swannekens," as the Dutch were called, assisted the Mahicans in an attack on the Mohawks (see also pp. 67-69).

Indians in the Eyes of the Dutch

According to European Sources

Our knowledge of the customs and practices, the clothing and the food of the Indians in the New Netherland period depends largely on western sources, such as the writings by Juet and De Laet mentioned above. There are other sources as well: letters, journals and descriptions of the land. What follows is a selection of various seventeenth-century texts with accounts of the Indians and their customs.

Courtesy of Juet and Hudson, we have detailed descriptions of the groups of Indians they came into contact with. For instance, they recorded that the Indians were well clothed and wore loose deer hides. Some were dressed in cloaks of feathers, and others in various kinds of fur. They smoked green tobacco from red copper tobacco pipes and ate very tasty baked corn. Hudson reported that he and his crew were most cordially received in a village counting 57 men and women. The house they were brought to was round and built of wood. Corn and grain were stored in the dome-like attic.[13]

Johannes de Laet describes primarily how the Sankikans or Sanhikans – a group belonging to the Delaware Indians – lived. He addresses their language and includes some of their words in his book, like numbers, the names of body parts, of animals and weather conditions. De Laet calls them barbarians because they did not believe in a God but worshipped the devil. He also describes how their society was not run by an organized administration or a ruler. Only the "sackmos," or "sachems," assumed leadership as the head of the family. De Laet characterized the Sankikans as a suspicious people quick to take revenge, though also hospitable and helpful if treated humanely. They asked for only a small gift in exchange for some service and were used to long journeys on foot. In general De Laet had a positive image of the Indians, even though he never met any himself.[14]

Reverend Megapolensis gives an extensive description of the Indians in the little book *Een kort ontwerp van de Mahakuase indianen* (A Short Account of the Mohawk Indians) of 1644, in which he primarily outlines the customs and practices of the Mohawks, who lived to the west of Fort Orange and belonged to the Iroquois League. Megapolensis wrote his *Kort Ontwerp* (A Short Account) not long after his arrival at Rensselaerswijck, where he was to preach for a period of six years. He regularly came into contact with the Mohawks living in the surroundings of Rensselaerswijck. The Dutch called the Mohawks "Maquas," or "Mahakobaasen." In contrast to other chroniclers who steadfastly

Mohawks and Mahicans

Detail of the map by Hessel Gerritsz., ca. 1616 (see p. 51)

This detail of the map on page 51 shows the borderland between the Maquaas and the Mahicans. The map dates to 1616, seven years after Hudson sailed up the North River. The small Dutch Fort Nassau, quite visible in the map, lay on a little island in the river. It was later replaced by Fort Orange. The stronghold of Beverwijck (Albany) was built somewhat more to the north.

In 1616 Mahicans were living on both sides of the North (Hudson) River, both to the north and south of it. Around 1628 the Mohawks, who in 1616 were still living somewhat more to the west, drove them out of the west bank. As a result Fort Orange came to be located between the two tribes and the North (Hudson) River began to function as a natural boundary.

The Mohawk Sychnecta
1764
Amsterdam City Archives
Inv. no. 10094, 10007836
Etching

One century after the Dutch Republic had been forced to relinquish dominion of New Netherland, Amsterdam citizens were given the opportunity to gape at this Indian. The Mohawk, called Sychnecta, was exhibited in the inn of Blauw Jan on the Kloveniersburgwal in Amsterdam in the fall of 1764. In the inn's courtyard was a kind of zoo where in addition to all kinds of exotic birds and wild animals, people were also sometimes on view. Sychnecta returned to his native country in the summer of 1765. According to the inscription he is dressed as a warrior. We immediately notice his bow and arrow. In his right hand he holds an object that functions as a pipe and as a tomahawk. If it snowed – after all, he did winter in Amsterdam – Synechta would be able to wear his snowshoes, shown near his feet at the left.

used the term "savages" when referring to the Indians, Megapolensis stuck to "Indians."

Megapolensis' frustration in his attempts to master the Indian languages is striking. He was amazed by the many verb forms, which according to him could be used interchangeably without any structural connection. When discussing their usage with a clerk of the Company, who knew the Mohawks well, the latter noted that they changed their language every two or three years, which struck Megapolensis as odd.[15] He was not the only one struggling with the many Indian languages. Only a few colonists ever mastered even one or more of them.

Interpreters were generally used during negotiations. Indians who had learned Dutch offered their services in this respect. There were also young Indians who had been kidnapped and taken to England, France or the Dutch Republic. Once there they became fluent in the merchants' language. Nicolaes van Wassenaer tells the story of two boys who as early as 1613 had been taken to Amsterdam by Adriaen Block and Hendrick Christiaensz. Perhaps they were brought to the Republic so that they could learn Dutch and become interpreters. The boys were called Orson and Valentine, names derived from a romance then popular in Europe. Orson and Valentine were two brothers who grew up independently, the one in a civilized world, the other in the wild. When they met up again as adults, the savage Orson naturally became cultivated once more. This may have been what the Dutchmen had in mind when they introduced these boys to the ways of the western world. The experiment though ended rather differently. Back on his native soil Orson took revenge on his kidnapper. Disguised as merchants, members of Orson's tribe boarded Christiaensz.'s ship and murdered the captain and many of his crewmembers.[16]

For the Indians, smoking a pipe was an essential ritual performed at important gatherings. De Rasière gives an amusing account of a meeting between the chief, the sachem, and a stranger who had come to visit him: they do not talk, but "drink a pipe of tobacco". Only after this ritual has taken place will the sachem ask the stranger why he has come. The stranger must give answer before all the tribe members. The sachem does not first address the stranger, but rather the group that has gathered. If they agree with him they sigh in assent, and if not they remain silent.[17]

In his *Beschrijvinge van Nieuw-Nederlant* (Description of New Netherland) Van der Donck devotes a great deal of attention to the Indians and their way of life. Clothing, appearance, physique, illnesses, the division of domestic roles, housing, language, organization, food, the preparation of meals and the time when they were eaten, hunting and faith are all addressed. Van der Donck's extensive descriptions afford a fairly reliable picture of the life of the Indians in New Netherland. He was trying to sketch a favorable image of the country in order to entice as many people as possible in the Dutch Republic to undertake the crossing. He never lost sight of the fact that his reader was best benefited by practical information on the goings-on in the area. Naturally part of this was the potential usefulness of the local population. With respect to the Indians' work ethic, though, Van der Donck was sad to disappoint the aspiring colonist: Indians were in no way suitable for hard labor, he stated baldly.

In general the Dutch were not impressed by the character of the Indians, who were often portrayed in a negative light.[18] They were considered naive, thievish and vindictive. Ironically, several journals mention the fact that as long as the Indians were well treated, they reacted in a friendly manner. The admiration that filters through certain passages at times is usually related to their physical prowess. Van der Donck, for example, was impressed by the Indians who could go without food for three or four days. Megapolensis was struck by the strength the women showed right after giving birth. Even when it was cold, they stood up and washed themselves and their newborn in the snow. They certainly did not lie down for fear of dying. The women went straight back to work, from which it would appear that Dutch women bellyached too much, said Megapolensis. He, and others, praised the Indians' boundless hospitality. Particularly noteworthy is his comment at the end of the *Korte ontwerp* (A Short Account) that though cruel in nature, in his view, the Indians committed far fewer murders than Christians.

The Dutch writers do not always make clear which Indian groups they are describing. As a result a general image has arisen that often does not agree with reality. Naturally there were practices common to both the Mohicans and the Mohawks, but there were also differences, minor though they might be. What the Dutch also failed to understand were the differences within groups. They assumed that the groups they distinguished were different tribes, which was only sometimes the case. The names the Indians called themselves were basically associated with the place where they lived, the name of the village head or something else with which the group identified.[19]

It was noted above that the Dutch generally had little interest in the Indians, focussing mainly on the trading possibilities.[20] Having said this, there were also certainly a few colonists who were morecurious about the Native Americans, for instance David Pietersz. de Vries. His journal (see also p. 86) abounds with reports of his encounters with the Indians. At times he evidences an eye for detail in their cultural

A Reliable Image?

More often than not these types of "ethnic"' prints are unreliable. The "savages" and "naturals" were often either rendered incorrectly or romanticized. The draftsmen – who had never actually seen a Native American firsthand or visited America – were not averse to copying one another. The customs and practical attributes of different tribes were mixed up. There are also instances of more reliable depictions, for instance when the draftsman concerned had been to the place in question, or had recourse to authentic material without making mistakes in interpretation.

A Family on the Move
Anonymous, 1671
New York Public Library, New York
ID: 806881

Detail of "Nova Svecia" (New Sweden) (see p. 136)

Shown here is a detail of a map depicting the Swedish colony along the South (Delaware) River made by Th. Campanius Holm. He was the grandson of the Swedish minister John Campanius, who lived in the colony for six years in order to conduct services in the Swedish community and bring Christianity to the Lenape Indians. Campanius became so fluent in their language that he was even able to translate the Lutheran catechism for them. His notes on the life of the Lenape were published together with the Indian catechism in 1696.

This engraving is a more abstract version of the image above. We see a Delaware family in full regalia. The man and the woman hold a pipe almost as tall as they are. Slung across their chests is a band of wampum. The child also wears a similar band.

A Delaware Family
Th. Campanius Holm, 1696
New York Public Library, New York
ID: 433864

habits. More surprising though is that on various occasions De Vries stands up for the Indians, finding the colonial administration's way of trading with the local inhabitants reprehensible. Interesting too is the passage in which he describes an encounter with the Indians who had destroyed the patroonship of Swanendael, which he shared with Samuel Godijn. He visited them and asked what lay behind their attack. They answered that the colonists had become enraged when one of them had made a pipe from a sign that had been hung up by one of the colonists. The Indians had been offended by the colonists' reaction and taken revenge on the settlement. De Vries concluded his account by comparing the temperament of the Indians to the Italians, who after all, according to De Vries, were just a vindictive.[21]

It is paradoxal that precisely De Vries continues to write positively about the Native Americans, while they were responsible for destroying his enterprises on not just one, but on two occasions! The first time Swanendael had to pay for it, and during "Kieft's War" his farm on Staten Island was reduced to ash. Even though De Vries was subject to violence at the agency of the Indians, he bears them no ill will in his journal. On the contrary, he was proud to have been called a "good ruler" by an Indian who showed affection by patting him.[22]

Fascinating is the way in which the writers, as well as the colonists, classify the various Indian groups into either "useful" or "useless" people, which all too quickly led to them being labeled "good" or "bad" people. This simplification led to snap decisions with great consequences. In the period preceding Kieft's War this unsubtle distinction caused some groups to be subject to acts of senseless violence. Sometimes only because they were "useless" for the colonists, for instance because they could not provide any fur.[23]

Indian and Christianity

When Director Willem Verhulst received his instructions in 1625 for the governing and shaping of the colony, it was made clear to him that he would also be held responsible for disseminating Christianity. In the very first years this was the concern of Bastiaen Jansz. Krol, a lay missionary who preached and was authorized to baptize people. Later the pastors of the municipality were charged with the task of "selling" Protestantism.

The Indians could be taught civilized manners and the proper faith if they were to be accepted into a respectable society, wrote the Calvinist De Laet in his *Nieuwe Wereldt* (New World) of 1625.[24] With regard to acquiring the "proper religion" (Protestantism) he would be proved wrong. The cultural divide between the colonists and the Indians was too great for any large-scale Christianization. While some groups of Indians did live among the colonists, they were not part of colonial society. Contact between the two peoples was limited to short-lived negotiations on fur skins.

Reverend Michaëlius, who had heard in the Republic that converting Indians to Christianity would be easy given their "geseggelijckheyd," or docility, and good character, wrote the opposite in 1628: "when we want to speak to them of God, it seems like a dream to them". Understanding that it would be difficult to spread the faith among the Indians he devised a rigorous plan: some Indians had to part with their children. If they were to receive a Christian education, these young Christians could then later spread the faith among their own people. The plan was never implemented: the Indians had no intention of ever giving up their children.[25]

The attempts to convert them to the "true faith" failed. Most of the pastors also abandoned the idea.[26] While Indians believed in a myriad of ghosts and powers, the Dutch made do with faith in a single god. Yet individuals sometimes talked about the subject among themselves. Interesting in this respect is the account of a disagreement between a Dutch captain and a Mohican chief about faith. According to the Indians, the Devil was responsible for Death. The captain said that God was the one who controlled Death. The Indians were baffled by the idea of a God who stood for good nevertheless allowing something as bad as Death.[27]

Indians on Noten (Governors) Island

Village of the Minqua Indians (Susquehannocks)
Detail of the map by Hessel Gerritsz., ca. 1616 (see p. 51)

How reliable are these kinds of drawings? And what are they based on? Mapmakers in the Dutch Republic did not have a great deal of material at hand that could serve as a model. Around 1600 the illustrations by the engraver and publisher Theodoor de Bry constituted virtually the only visual source on the Indians, showing their dwellings and their vessels. De Bry relied on a series of drawings by John White. While traveling in America in 1585, this Englishman had made 70 drawings of the Indians, depicting them in their natural setting. These drawings afforded a reliable image of the Indians fishing, hunting and canoeing. De Bry adopted White's drawings fairly faithfully, though he nevertheless gave his own twist to the Indians, rendering them in classic poses and with European facial features; in addition, the artist who hand-colored the engravings gave all the Indians blond hair.[28] De Bry drew a village relying on White's drawings. This village recurs in a simplified form as a detail in the map by Hessel Gerritsz. from 1616. We see four small, enclosed villages in the area of the Minquas, or Susquahannock Indians. It is possible that Gerritsz. also used De Bry's village as his model.

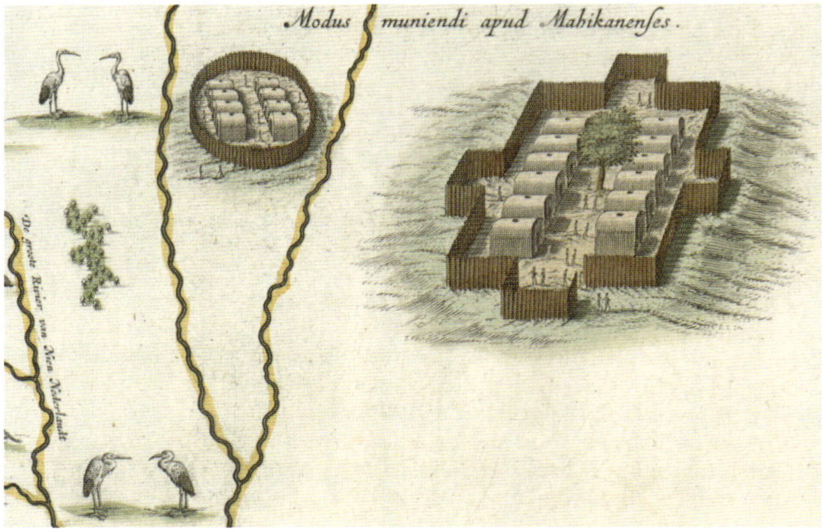

This detail in Blaeu's map also presents a circular village. Written in Latin next to it is "Modus muniendi apud Mahikanenses" or "Maniere van Woonplaetsen ofte Dorpen der Mahicans ende andre Natien haer geburen," Types of dwellings or villages of the Mahicans and other, neighboring, nations.

Mahican Villages
Detail of "Nova Belgica et Anglia Nova"
(New Netherland and New England) (see pp. 92-93)
Willem Jansz. Blaeu, 1635

Wars Between Indians and Colonists

Not long after Willem Kieft was appointed the new director of New Netherland, tensions between the Indians and the Europeans mounted. These were related to different interpretations of the "sales contracts" and the colonists' attitude of superiority vis-à-vis the Indians. However, a lack of knowledge about their respective cultures also played a role. Incident upon incident piled up and mutual irritations were met with increasingly harsh measures. The consequence of all this was a bitter two-year war, which has come down in history as "Kieft's War."

"Kieft's War"

The Company had invested vast sums of money constructing forts in the areas where conflicts had arisen either between the tribes or between the Indians and the colonists. In Europe it was not unusual to request a contribution from the inhabitants in such regions for the maintenance of the forts and the soldiers who protected them. Kieft believed he could exact a comparable contribution from the Indians who according to him also profited from the expensive safety measures. Kieft asked for payment in beaver pelts, wampum and corn. With the corn he could prevent the colonists from starving. The Indians were flabbergasted: why should they pay for something they made absolutely no use of? The colonists were ungrateful; after all, had they not offered them protection in times of trouble and given them land for cultivation? Conversely they had received hardly any protection from outside hostilities. They flatly refused to pay even a single kernel of corn. Kieft was not to be thwarted and resolved to punish them.

Kieft also wanted to make it clear to a group of Raritan Indians just who was in charge of the colony. In 1639 they had attacked a sloop with three colonists on board, and there were casualties. Kieft was not a man who did things by halves. He offered a reward of ten strings of wampum to anyone bringing him the head of a Raritan Indian, and would give double that for the head of one of the killers.[29] Secretary Van Tienhoven was dispatched with a group of close to 70 soldiers to apprehend the Raritans. Punishment could be avoided only if the Indians agreed to pay compensation. Before Van Tienhoven could begin negotiations, some of his men had already taken up arms. In the years that followed the Indians avenged the deaths on their side in a series of reprisals.

Deaths also regularly occurred on farms. For example, as mentioned above, the farm of David Pietersz. de Vries was burned to the ground in 1641 and all of his men were murdered. De Vries blamed Kieft. The incident had begun with the theft of De Vries' pigs. A couple of Indians were charged with the crime and duly punished. On 16 July 1640 De Vries noted in his journal that Secretary Van Tienhoven had flogged their chief. De Vries observed dryly that it is impossible to "make friends with the inhabitants" in this way![30] In reality though Company employees had stolen the pigs. According to De Vries, while the Indians did in fact steel cattle fairly regularly, this time they were quite understandably enraged by the unjust punishment and vented their anger on De Vries' people.[31] He laid the murder of his staff at Kieft's feet: "...the innocent savages were blamed. Although they are clever enough, if no harm is done to them, they will do no harm to you. And so it came to pass that I lost my fledgling colony on Staten Island because of the policy of Commander Kieft...."[32]

Such practices did not make it easy for the colonists to keep their farms running. Hostilities increased on both sides and finally culminated in "Kieft's War." The war was sparked off by the death of the wheelwright Claes Cornelisz. Swits, an old man who was murdered by a young Wickquasgeck Indian. His motive was revenge for the murder of his uncle, which had taken place 15 years earlier. The young Indian had sworn to avenge his death and old Claes was the victim. Kieft ordered the sachem of a neighboring tribe to help find the young killer. He refused and told Kieft that he was sorry only one Christian had died and not 20![33]

Kieft set up a Council of Twelve Men that would act as the responsible organ for the entire community. The Twelve were meant to advise him regarding retaliation. In this way he would gain the support of the community for his actions. They advised Kieft to wait. Only six months later, in January 1642, did they indicate that the time was ripe to avenge the death of the old man. Kieft, however, was not yet ready to follow their advice. In the meantime, hostilities between the Indians and the colonists remained unabated, albeit they took place on a smaller scale. In February 1643 the conflict assumed disastrous proportions. In Pavonia 80 Wappingers were killed in an attack launched by soldiers and colonists, and was sanctioned by Kieft. The majority was slaughtered in their sleep.[34] The bloodbath would go down in history as the "Massacre of Pavonia." This was the last straw. The Indians closed ranks and in the following months raided the colonists' houses, burned their property and killed the farmers.

Kieft called a new council into being, the Council of Eight Men this time. The members agreed that the war against the Indians had to be resumed, but that the tribe on Staten Island would be exempted, as there had never been any problems with it. No genuine solution was at hand, however: peace was closed with a few tribes, while the fighting went on with others.

"Unus Americanus ex Virginia. Ætat: 23" (An American from Virginia, aged 23)
Wenceslaus Hollar, 1645
Rijksmuseum, Amsterdam
Inv. no. RP-P-OB-11.592
Etching

A 23-Year-Old Indian

This print portrays a young Indian man adorned with a headdress, earrings, and a wampum necklace. He also sports a cockscomb, today a symbol of punk culture. The Indian is thought to be a certain "Jaques," a warrior taken prisoner by colonists and subsequently given by Director Kieft to two WIC soldiers, Peter Cock and Peter Ebel. In 1644 the soldiers took Jaques to Amsterdam, where he was put on display as a curiosity. From a contract dated 3 September 1644, now in the Amsterdam City Archives, it emerges that special arrangements were made for exhibiting the man to the public. Wenceslaus Hollar, the maker of this print, will have seen the Indian in Antwerp, where he drew him from life in 1645.[35]

The print does not make clear the identity of his tribe. To figure this out, we must have recourse to the description of "een mahakuaes Indiaen," or a Mohawk, by Reverend Johannes Megapolensis in his little book *Kort Ontwerp* (A Short Account) from 1664. Megapolensis described the lifestyle of the Mohawks, delving into their language, religious beliefs and appearance. About the hairstyle of the Mohawks, he noted that they wear a long lock of hair, sometimes on one side, sometimes on both sides of their heads. On top of their heads was a strip of hair standing straight up, extending from their forehead to the back of their neck, and resembling a cockscomb. The hair to either side of this strip was shaved off.[36]

Kieft had decided to hire the Englishman John Underhill. A few years earlier, this soldier had gained experience butchering Indians in New England during the Pequot War. He commanded a raid in the north. An Indian village was surrounded and set on fire. Hundreds died.

The question was how to proceed? The colonists were on the verge of despair. Many of them had been enticed by the attractive conditions of 1640 to come to the colony and build a new life. They were part of the circuit of fur traders or were farming the land, which according to the free rules of the *Vrijheden en Exemptieën* (Liberties and Exemptions) of 1640 had been made available to them. These people had something to lose and that loss came ever closer as a result of the ongoing wars with Indians. More and more colonists turned against Kieft. After all, he had dragged them into this senseless war, they believed, even though many of them had initially supported Kieft. Only now they were losing income. The traders were dependent on the Indians for fur and the farmers could not cultivate their fields or tend their cattle if they felt unsafe.

The Council of Eight wrote a letter of complaint to the States General and asked for immediate help from the Republic. The request was sent on to the WIC, which in turn deposited the letter at the Amsterdam Chamber. The directors responded that the Company had no more money for any assistance whatsoever. Everardus Bogardus, the minister of New Amsterdam, also turned against Kieft, fulminating from his pulpit against the slaughter of the Indians. According to the sources, Kieft reacted to this attack by disrupting Bogardus' services with drumming and gunshots. Finally, in 1644 peace was concluded between the Indians and the colonists.

Historians disagree about Kieft's role in all of this.[37] Should he be considered the instigator of the war with the Indians, or was he "only" one of the parties aiming for it? Given that he twice set up an advisory organ to council him he obviously did not dare make a number of important decisions on his own and wanted support from the people. The fact remains that during Kieft's directorship the relations between the colonists and the Indians were seriously disrupted, as were those between the colonial administration and the colonists.

Typical of Kieft's lack of diplomacy and understanding of Native American culture is the way in which he tried to end the war. When during the peace negotiations the chiefs attempted to explain that exchanging gifts was crucial for mutual acceptance and the balance necessary for entering into a renewed relationship, Kieft flatly refused to participate. Instead, he demanded that the Indians obey Dutch law. Despite this disconcerting situation, the Dutch and the Indian leaders closed peace in 1645. They never really trusted one another again though.[38]

Pleas For and Against the War

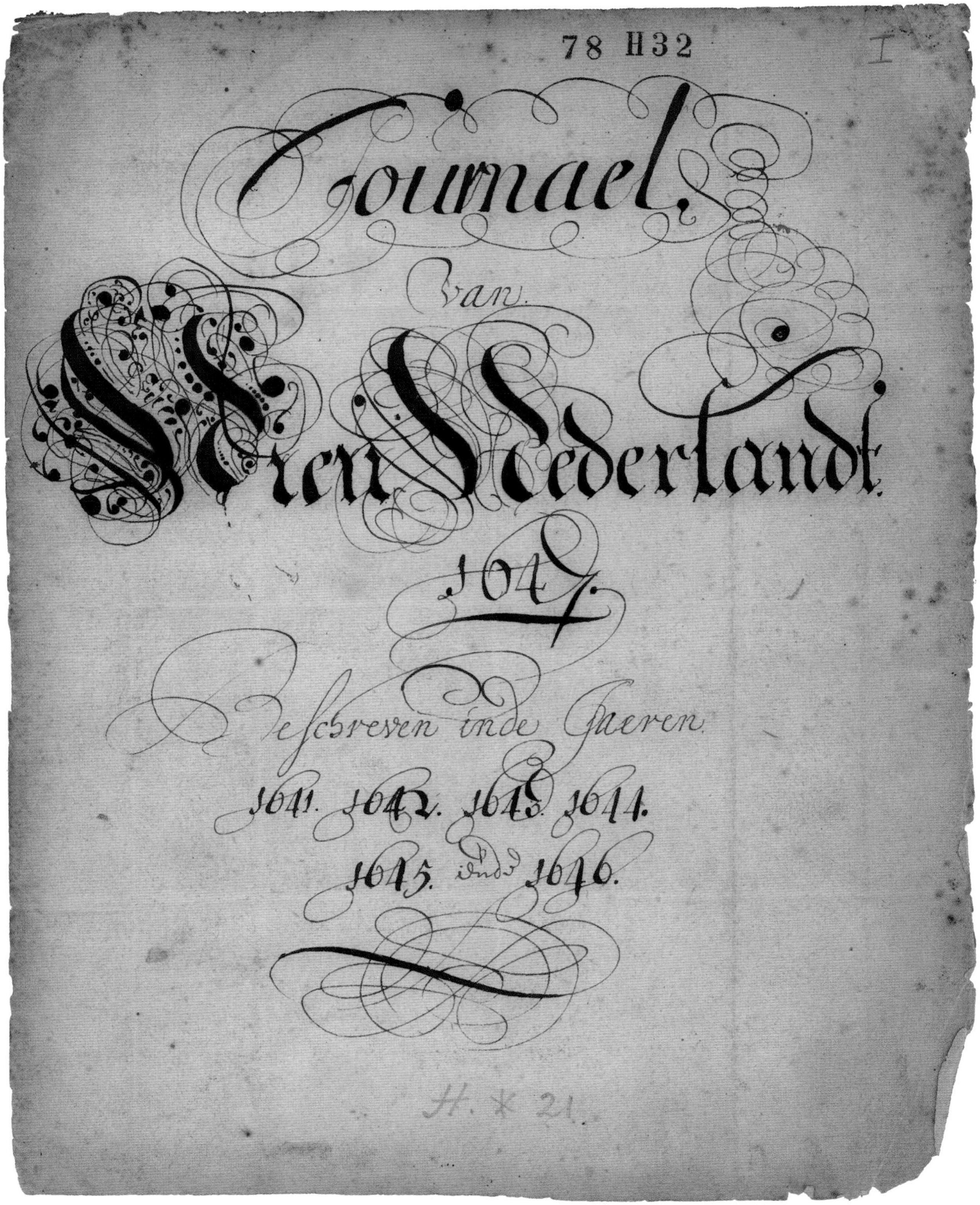

Journael van Nieu Nederlandt
(Journal of New Netherland), 1647
Royal Library, The Hague
78 H 32
Manuscript, pen and ink, 17 x 21 cm

After Kieft's War, advocates and adversaries of it took up their pens to add weight to their pleas: some were intent on justifying the war (in retrospect), while others wanted to demonstrate that Kieft had made the wrong choices, to the detriment of the colony's position relative to before the war.

One of the documents underwriting the war is the 39 page long *Journael van Nieu Nederlandt* (Journal of New Netherland) by an anonymous author. It has been suggested that it was written by Cornelis van Tienhoven, the secretary in New Netherland from 1638 to 1649 and the prop and stay of Director Willem Kieft. The author sympathizes with Kieft, who just like him had nothing good to say about the Indians. The document is a unique, yet biased account of the years 1641-1646, which attempts to explain and sanction the actions against the Indians.

The document begins with the obvious statement that New Netherland's name derives from the fact that it is visited and inhabited by free Dutchmen. The first chapter sketches a picture of the colony's geography, flora and fauna.

The second chapter addresses the inhabitants of New Nederland. Striking is that the Indians are not discussed here as the original inhabitants of the land, but rather in the first section, with the flora and fauna, where they are by and large not portrayed in a friendly light. The author states that the colony had grown and flourished only in recent years. Even the arrival of the English is described as a positive phenomenon, for according to the author they came to New Netherland to experience freedom and to escape from the uncooperative government in neighboring New England. The English and Dutch exerted themselves in creating the new society, farmsteads popped up everywhere and there was work for everybody, the author proclaims. There wasn't a cloud in the sky, that is, until the Indians destroyed everything that had been so carefully built up.

The third part recounts how the war with the Indians in New Netherland broke out and what transpired. While it reads like boys' book, it is also full of horrific details. The journal is a report written by a person who sided with Kieft. The layout is a plea, as it were, for the war against the Indians. One of the key arguments forwarded is that the war was widely supported by the people, that Kieft was spurred on to it by the community. This part, naturally, exculpates him for his role as the agitator, for the people themselves wanted the war. A written request to attack the Indians had even been submitted on two occasions.

Therefore, the story can be understood as testimony to promote Kieft's interests in the suit that was brought against him. The account tries to impress upon the reader that all of the aggression came from the side of the Indians and that ultimately there was no choice but to slaughter them. Kieft is painted as kind, humane: he conferred cordially with the sachems, he assisted the victims caught up in a tribal war. No mention is made of the tax the Indians were forced to pay Kieft or the fact that the director had punished those who refused to pay it by killing them. So, too, the fact that the murder of the old man was an act of revenge by a young Indian, who 15 years earlier had been witness to the death of his uncle, is never broached. Some caution is warranted, however, given that we do not what was written in the missing pages.

In closing, the author mentions that according to the reports of the Indians they suffered 500 or even 700 casualties. That bloodbath was the work of the Englishman John Underhill, hired by the Dutch to attack the Indians in the north. The author notes that after the massacre the troops first headed to Stamford, where the English met them. The next day the soldiers marched on to Manhattan, where they were welcomed with a celebration.

Stuyvesant, the Peach War and the Esopus Wars

When Stuyvesant was running New Netherland, from 1647 to 1664, times of peace and war alternated. The indirect reasons for the wars that took place in this period were the Dutch supremacy, the fact that steadily more land was annexed and the economic interdependence. Only one more aspect came to play a role: while the Dutch grew in numbers, the Indian population was being decimated by illness and war. For the Indians this was a life-threatening situation. Tribal chiefs gathered regularly to discuss how to best deal with the situation. Some groups decided to accept Dutch authority and stop engaging in war. Others found it more difficult to renounce their freedom and self-governance and thought that the colonists should be driven out, or in any case change their tune.

In 1655 the moment had arrived. According to the stories, the so-called Peach War began with the theft of a few peaches. An inhabitant of New Amsterdam, Hendrick van Dijk, caught an Indian man or woman in the act of stealing fruit from his orchard and beat the thieft to death. News of the murder spread like wildfire among the Indians. They decided to take revenge. With close to 80 canoes they sailed to Manhattan in search of Van Dijk. While they did find him, they were unable to kill him. At the same time another group was looking for a colonist who had traded with their enemies, contrary to the agreement. At the end of the night the Indians decided to leave. Having arrived at the beach they were attacked by soldiers under the command of Cornelis van Tienhoven. Sixty Indians met their death. Retaliation was swift: in the next three days 28 farms on Staten Island, in the patroonship of Pavonia, and elsewhere along the North (Hudson) River were burned to the ground. Crops were destroyed and 40 colonists were killed. A significant number of white women and children were kidnapped by Wappingers, Wickquasgeck, Hackinsacks and Esopus Indians.[39]

Once order had been restored, the Indians offered to release the hostages in exchange for gunpowder and munition. Stuyvesant accepted and negotiations followed. The first group of hostages to be released had been with the Hackinsacks. During the negotiations the Indians ran the show. Only when they were certain there would be no Dutch attacks were the hostages released. Finally, except for a few children, everyone was freed around March 1656.[40]

After the Peach War, Stuyvesant showed greater lenience than Kieft with respect to violent encounters. He elected to maintain peace with his neighbors. When acts of aggression occurred Stuyvesant did not counter them with military actions, as was previously the case. In fact, he did everything in his power to avoid conflicts. For instance,

A Broadside Against Kieft

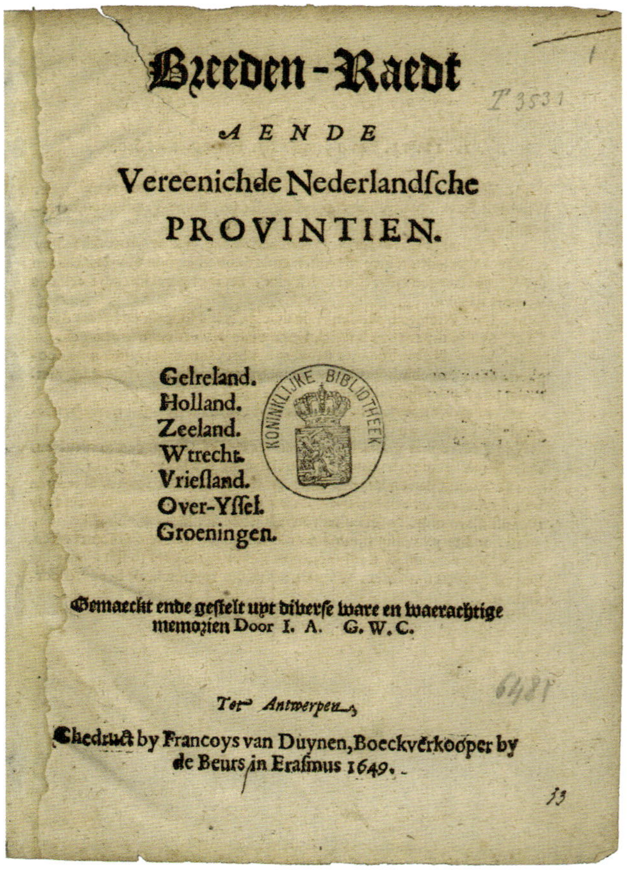

Breeden-Raedt

AENDE

Vereenichde Nederlandsche

PROVINTIEN.

Gelreland.
Holland.
Zeeland.
Wtrecht.
Vriesland.
Over-Yssel.
Groeningen.

Gemaeckt ende gestelt upt diverse ware en waerachtige memorien Door I. A. G. W. C.

Tot Antwerpen,

Ghedruckt by Francoys van Duynen, Boeckverkooper by de Beurs in Erasmus 1649.

Breeden-Raedt (Broad Advice), 1649
Royal Library, The Hague
Pflt 6481
14 x 19 cm

The pamphlet *Breeden-Raedt* (Broad Advice) from 1649 may be considered as the rebuttal to the *Journael* (Journal). The document is also by an unknown author, alternately identified as Cornelis Melijn or Jochem Pietersz. Kuyter, who were among Kieft's fiercest adversaries. The *Breeden-Raedt* made mincemeat out of Kieft and his secretary Van Tienhoven. What is surprising is the significant role allotted Van Tienhoven, who was still secretary when the *Breeden-Raedt* appeared. For instance, the secretary is credited as being: "...the main cause of the situation".

The massacre in Pavonia is described so horrifically in the *Breeden-Raedt* that the reader has little choice but to loathe Kieft and his minions. It should be noted, though, that here too there may be some exaggeration for the sake of propaganda: "between 25 and 26 February 1643, at night in Pavonia more than 80 savages were massacred by 80 soldiers, among them infants who were torn from their mother's breasts, and hacked to pieces in the presence of their parents, and the pieces thrown into the fire and in the water, and other sucklings, being bound to wooden boards, were cut, stabbed, and pierced and miserably massacred in a manner that would move even a heart of stone."[41]

Stuyvesant and the Indians

Stuyvesant in New Amsterdam, Anonymous
New York Public Library, Mid-Manhattan Picture Collection, New York
ID: 800002

This print presents a meeting between New Amsterdammers and Indians. In the middle is Peter Stuyvesant, recognizable by his wooden leg. For reasons of safety Stuyvesant and his councilors decreed that the Indians could only visit Manhattan during the day and were not allowed to overnight there.
Moreover, the Indians were prohibited from drinking alcohol. Innkeepers would be punished for selling liquor to them.

Sometimes the authorities even banished colonists who infringed upon this rule from the colony, for instance the barkeeper Sander Toursen and his wife when they sold brandy to two Indians in 1656. Usually this punishment was not carried out if the guilty party showed sufficient remorse. Drunken Indians, however, were locked up until they divulged the name of the person who filled their glasses.[42]

he bought tracts of land, which had been bought earlier, for a second time. He did ask the Indians to move off them though.[43]

In the years that followed fewer and fewer Indians visited Manhattan. Those who lived in the immediate vicinity of the island left the colonists in peace. The Indians on Long Island sided increasingly with the Dutch in these years, even becoming allies. A few other groups in the area followed their lead. Stuyvesant must have welcomed their support. Certainly in 1659, when war broke out with the tribe living near the Esopus River close to present-day Kingston. The Esopus Indians did not have particularly close ties with the colonists. Growing numbers of Europeans were moving into their neighborhood; a few Dutch families had found their way to the village of Wiltwijck. The starting shot for the Esopus Wars was fired on 21 September 1659. A group of young inebriated Indians aggravated the colonists living in the area. While they were sleeping off their drunkenness armed colonists ambushed the Indians, killing and wounding a number of them. The farmers were made to pay the very next day. Somewhat later the hamlet was surrounded by 500 Esopus braves. In the years that followed Stuyvesant's soldiers from New Amsterdam and the Esopus Indians clashed regularly, with hostages being taken on both sides. In the end Stuyvesant involved other groups of Indians to end the war. The parties only reached a peace agreement in May 1664. Finally, the entire region of New Netherland was virtually pacified. Stuyvesant, however, would only be able to enjoy his success for a few months, for in September the region passed into English hands![44]

Consequences of the European Invasion

The history of Dutch Manhattan and New Netherland is characterized by a number of – at times protracted – conflicts between the original inhabitants and the newcomers. The consequences of the wars were by no means small: countless people died or fled the torn regions. Yet the European bullets were not the most important reason for the disappearance of the Indians. In his description of the country in 1655, Van der Donck mentions various European diseases to which the Indians had no resistance: smallpox, measles and influenza. Even though the Indians were strong and only a few evidenced physical ailments according to Van der Donck, the diseases brought by the colonists proved fatal to them. Van der Donck estimated that in the middle of the seventeenth century only ten percent of the original Indians were left as a result.[45]
Wars or diseases, trade continued. This was profitable for both parties. Initially the colonists were the most dependent on their trading partners. The existence and success of the colony relied on the supply of fur. Without beaver pelts the economy would crash. Peace with the various tribes living on and around Manhattan only benefited the white society. Nevertheless the colonial administration did not succeed in maintaining the peace. Differences in culture, in religion, the struggle for dominion in the area and the different perception of the sale of land or ownership all contributed to the irritations and hostilities back and forth, time and again.

The tribes frequently differed as to how to deal with the colonists. Because of this, as well as competition, tribal wars ensued. Occasionally, flouting Company directives, the Dutch got involved in the internal strife and took sides, which sometimes led to substantial shifts of power. The same applied to the English and the Dutch supply of arms to certain groups of Indians. Trade in arms was lucrative for the Europeans: the weapons yielded large numbers of beaver pelts and simultaneously stimulated the fur trade. For the Indians who received arms in exchange for fur, the transaction was equally favorable. But the groups without them were at a serious disadvantage in battle and fell behind. They lost power and prestige vis-à-vis the groups with arms.

In the end the Indians lost out; the European presence proved too dominant for the Indians to retain a lasting position of power. They lost their traditions, some left, others adapted. But by then the eighteenth century was at hand.

[1] Waldman, *Atlas of the North American Indian*, p. 81.
[2] Otto, *The Dutch-Munsee Encounter*, p. 33.
[3] Otto, *The Dutch-Munsee Encounter*, pp. 33-39, pp. 44-47.
[4] Jacobs, *Een zegenrijk gewest*, pp. 175-177.
[5] Otto, *The Dutch-Munsee Encounter*, p. 54.
[6] Jacobs, *Een zegenrijk gewest*, p. 110.
[7] Frijhoff, *Wegen van Evert Willemsz.*, p. 782.
[8] Otto, *The Dutch-Munsee Encounter*, p. 97.
[9] Jacobs, *Een zegenrijk gewest*, p. 43.
[10] Jacobs, *Een zegenrijk gewest*, p. 50; Van Wassenaer, *Historisch verhael*, Feb. 1624; Jacobs, *Een zegenrijk gewest*, pp. 330-331.
[11] Otto, *The Dutch-Munsee Encounter*, p. 99; Jacobs, *Een zegenrijk gewest*, p. 181.
[12] Otto, *The Dutch-Munsee Encounter*, p. 91; Waldman, *Atlas of the North American Indian*, pp. 93-94.
[13] Otto, *The Dutch-Munsee Encounter*, pp. 38-40.
[14] De Laet, *Nieuwe Wereld*, 1625, Virginia, Chapter 11.
[15] Jameson, *Narratives*, pp. 172-173.
[16] Otto, *The Dutch-Munsee Encounter*, p. 56, p. 61, pp. 64-65. Upon their return to the Dutch Republic, Block and Christiaensz. left behind one member of their crew, Jacob Eelkens, for the first time. It has been suggested that they did this to convince the Mohicans that nothing would happen to the two boys and that they would return safe and sound. Van Wassenaer, *Historisch Verhael*, December 1624 and April 1625. Meuwese, '"For the peace and well-being of the country," p. 77; Wieder, *New York*, p. 8; Hart, *The prehistory*, p. 19.
[17] Jameson, *Narratives*, p. 109.
[18] Jacobs, *Een zegenrijk gewest*, p. 54.
[19] Otto, *The Dutch-Munsee Encounter*, pp. 62-63.
[20] Goodfriend, "Writing/Righting Dutch Colonial History," pp. 5-28.
[21] De Vries, *Korte historiael ende journaels aenteyckeninge*, p. 156.
[22] De Vries, *Korte historiael ende journaels aenteyckeninge*, p. 252.
[23] Otto, *The Dutch-Munsee Encounter*, p. 66.
[24] De Laet, *Nieuwe Wereld*, 1625, Virginia, Chapter 11.
[25] Jacobs, *Een zegenrijk gewest*, p. 273.
[26] Rothschild, "De sociale afstand tussen Nederlandse kolonisten en inheemse Amerikanen," pp. 189-190.
[27] Van Wassenaar, *Historisch Verhael*, February 1624 and November 1626 (in: Jameson, *Narratives*, p. 87).
[28] Van Groesen, *The representations of the overseas world*, p. 275.
[29] Rink, *The Dutch-Munsee Encounter*, p. 218; Schulte Nordholt, "Nederlanders in Nieuw-Nederland," p. 60.
[30] De Vries, *Korte historiael ende journaels aenteyckeninge*, p. 246.
[31] De Vries, *Korte historiael ende journaels aenteyckeninge*, p. 248: "On the first of September the savages and Raritans murdered my people on Staten Island. The Dutch told an Indian, who serves our people, that they would fight the Indians because they had killed Dutchmen. Indians assaulted us viciously because of pigs, which Dutchmen had accused them of stealing, when, in fact, they were not to blame. The [theft] had been committed by servants of the Company who had sailed to the South River and arrived on Staten Island where they first chopped some wood and fetched some water and then stole the pigs. The innocent savages were blamed immediately. Although they clever enough, if no harm is done to them, they will do no harm to you. And so I lost my fledgling colony on Staten Island, thanks to the policy of Commander Kieft, who wanted to seek revenge on the savages for what they had done to his people."
(Den eersten September wierden mijn Volck op 't Staten-Eylandt dood-geslagen, vande Wilde en vande Raritans, ende spraken teghens een Wild die ons Volck diende, men soude nu komen vechten teghens haer om ons Volck, ende hadden wy haer voor desen qualijck komen trackteeren om Verckens, datmen haer te last leyde ghenomen te hebben daerse geen schuld toe hadde, 't welck by de Companies Dienders wierde gedaen, alsose naer de Zuyd-Rivier zeylden, quamen dan eerst aen het Staten-Eylandt wat Hout hacken ende Water halen, dan stalense met een de Verckens, ende men leyde de schuld al op de onnoosele wilden, en al-hoe-wel sy slim genoeg zijn, maer doet haer geen quaed sy sullen u oock geen quaed doen, ende soo raeckte ick het begin van mijn Colonie quyt op het Saten-yland, door beleyt vande Commandeur Kieft, die het geen op de Wilden wilde verhalen dat sijn Volck gedaen hadde).
[32] De Vries, *Korte historiael ende journaels aenteyckeninge*, p. 248.
[33] Shorto, *The Island at the Center of the World*, p. 112; Jameson, *Narratives*, pp. 274-275 and p. 213.
[34] Jacobs, *Een zegenrijk gewest*, pp. 133-136; Frijhoff, *Wegen van Evert Willemsz.*, pp. 718-719; Schulte Nordholt, "Nederlanders in Nieuw-Nederland," pp. 38-94.
[35] With thanks to Simon James Turner and George R. Hamell for access to their unpublished article, "Jaques: A Munsee from New Netherland, 1644"; Otto, *The Dutch-Munsee Encounter*, p. 119.
[36] Otto, *The Dutch-Munsee Encounter*, p. 119.
[37] Frijhoff, *Wegen van Evert Willemsz.*, pp. 713-738; Frijhoff, "Neglected Networks: Director Willem Kieft," pp. 198-200; Schulte Nordholt, "Nederlanders in Nieuw-Nederland," pp. 38-94.
[38] Otto, *The Dutch-Munsee Encounter*, pp. 125-126.
[39] Otto, *The Dutch-Munsee Encounter*, p. 143.
[40] Otto, *The Dutch-Munsee Encounter*, pp. 143-147.
[41] *Breeden-raedt aende Vereenichde Nederlandsche provintien*, p. 18.
[42] Gehring, *New York Historical Manuscripts Dutch*; Gehring, *Council Minutes, 1655-1656*, pp. 294-295: 173; Jacobs, *Een zegenrijk gewest*, p. 328.
[43] Otto, *The Dutch-Munsee Encounter*, p. 148.
[44] Otto, *The Dutch-Munsee Encounter*, pp. 148-155.
[45] Jacobs, *Een zegenrijk gewest*, p. 50.

III

CHAPTER 2

The Europeans

Of the broad spectrum of newcomers in New Netherland, the group from Europe is the largest and most varied. For the sake of clarity, the European community is divided here into four groups: first the Walloons and the Dutch; then the Germans, Eastern Europeans, French and Scandinavians; next the English and Scottish; and finally the Jews from Eastern Europe and Dutch-Brazil.

As diverse as the colonists are so too their reasons for bidding their fatherland farewell and making the great crossing to a new, virgin territory. Naturally, among them are fortune hunters and adventurers, as well as emigrants longing for a life free of the fear of being persecuted for their religious beliefs. Some arrive in the colony by chance and decide to stay; others view emigration to a new land from the start as an opportunity to build a new life with their entire families. What are their expectations and earliest experiences? How do they get along with each other? How do they make a living and what are their occupations?

In this chapter, these and other questions are answered when possible on the basis of nationalities and ethnic groups. In our view, such a division by country of origin is permissible, as long as we bear in mind that the concept of "nationality" is later in date and does not always reflect language or culture in the seventeenth century. Finally, it should be noted that the following enumeration is not complete.

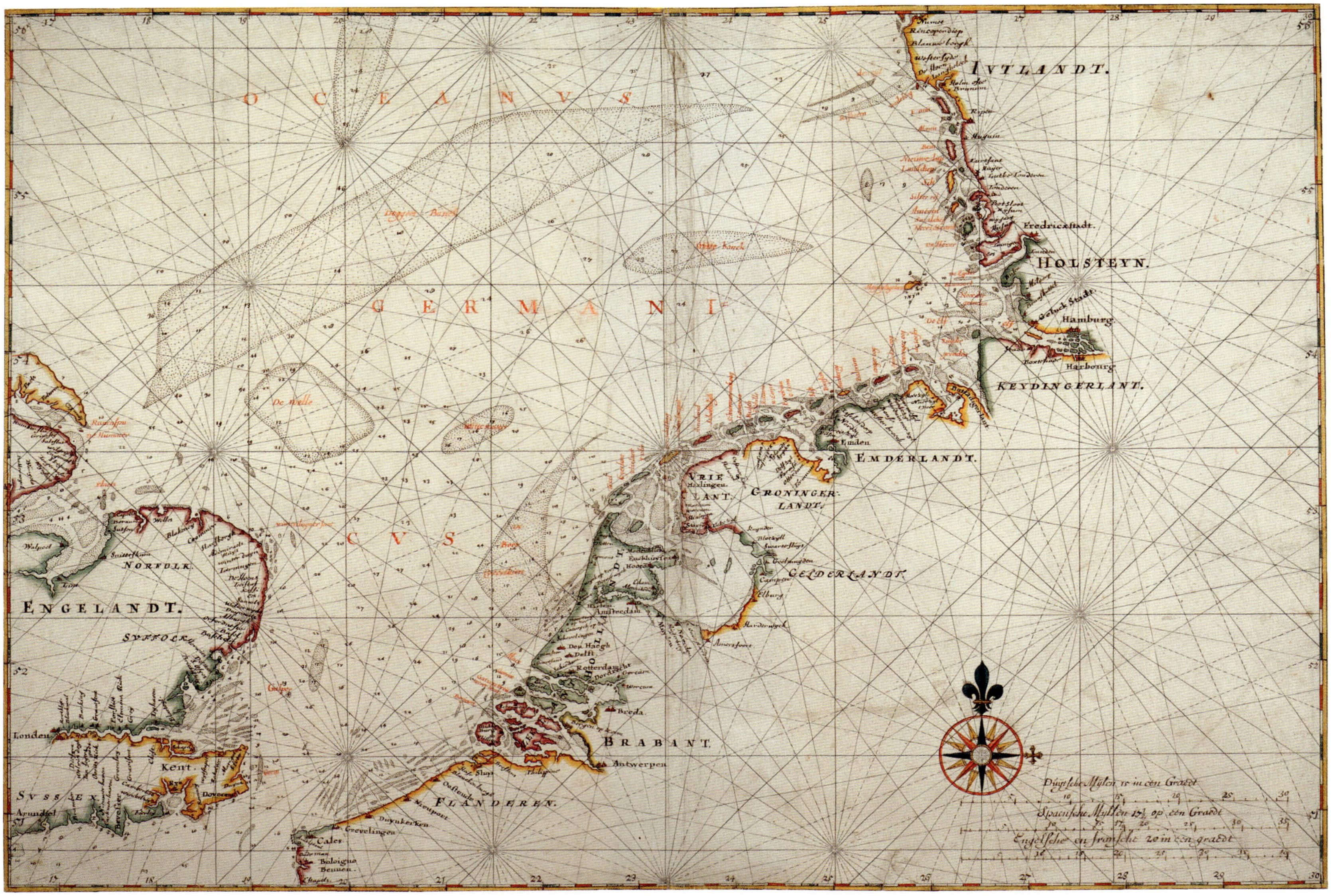

The Dutch Republic and Surrounding Countries
Johannes Vingboons, third quarter of the seventeenth century
Nationaal Archief (National Archives of the Netherlands), The Hague
4.VELH 619-001
Watercolor on paper, 48.5 x 69 cm

Countries along the North Sea Coast

This map does not present the division of Northwestern Europe as we know it today. Where are the borders of France, Germany and Belgium? Where did the Netherlands' end? The mapmaker's aim was to chart the North Sea and its coastal regions. Unintentionally, this map provides an interesting picture of the area where most of the first inhabitants of New Amsterdam came from. This was not just from the Dutch Republic, but also from all over Northwestern Europe. The names of several provinces of the Republic can be discerned: Brabant, Gelderland, Friesland and Groningen. The Republic had seven provinces in total: Friesland, Gelre (Gelderland), Holland, Overijssel, Stad en Lande (Groningen), Utrecht and Zeeland. As of 1568, these regions were in revolt against Spain, a conflict that would last 80 years. In 1588 they united as the Republic of the Seven United Netherlands, which explains the plural form of the country name "the Netherlands" in English as well as in other European languages (les Pays Bas, die Niederlände, and so forth). That the Republic was also referred to as "Holland" already from that time has to do with that province's dominant position. Even now, the country's two names are synonymous in everyday parlance.

The Walloons and the Dutch

The First Colonists: 30 Walloon Families

"The ship with the families to New Netherland lay at Plymouth. Receiving a favorable wind, it wished to set out to sea, but was visited by the plague, 11 had already died and 20 lay ill, being from the Walloon families who were to be transported yonder to the colony: the merchant's mate had also taken ill, but was now recovering."[1] There they were, 30 families from the southeast of present-day Belgium, marooned on board a ship in the English port of Plymouth, among them victims – dead and dying – of the plague, waiting to cross the ocean to America.

The Dutch colonization of New Netherland did not actually begin with the Dutch, but with Walloons. As we saw on page 55, in the spring of 1624 the first five or six Walloon families arrived on the *Eendracht* (Unity). Soon thereafter, the colonization ship *Nieu Nederlandt* (New Netherland), with Captain Cornelis Jacobsz. May at the helm, bore the 30 Walloon families across the ocean. On the orders of the directors, upon their arrival the families were dispersed over four locations. The largest group was brought to Fort Orange on the upper reaches of the North (Hudson) River, where Beverwijck (presently Albany) would later be established.[2]

How did it come about that Walloon, rather than Dutch families, were the first to inhabit New Netherland? The Protestant Walloons had abandoned their houses and villages, fleeing from the Spanish inquisition, which tolerated no other church than the Catholic. Many sought refuge in the north, some ending up in the Dutch Republic and settling in Leiden and Amsterdam, where they could practice their religion. The Walloons who went on to New Netherland set sail from Amsterdam. Among them were the Walloon couple Catalina Trico and Joris Rapalje (see also p. 183), who married at the last moment in the Walloon church.

Trial Journeys

The Walloons' reasons for seeking safety in the Republic is patently clear, but what motives did the Walloon families have for traveling to New Netherland? Hardly any sources provide an answer to this question, but the desire to share a new life with fellow believers may well have played a role. Just how fervent their wish to start a new life elsewhere was emerges from an earlier attempt by several families to emigrate to the New World. The leader of this group was Jesse de Forest, from the Wallonian town of Avesnes, who had established himself as a linen weaver in Leiden in 1615. In 1621 he drafted an appeal to emigrate to Virginia with a group of compatriots, which was signed by the heads of 56 Walloon families. Because the English had laid claim to this territory, the petition was submitted to King James I of England via the English ambassador to the Republic, Sir Dudley Carleton. The English Virginia Company, to which the petition was forwarded, had no objections to the coming of the Walloons, but the king refused them permission.[3]

Two years later, though, De Forest was successful. He received permission from the States General to travel to the New World. Under the flag of the WIC, with a few Walloon men he would make the crossing to Guyana to size up the possibilities for establishing a colony. Once there, De Forest decided to stay on: the other Walloons returned. De Forest would die there in 1624. Guyana was dismissed as a future colony: its climate was unhealthy and the Walloons found the conditions for settling there unfavorable.[4] New Netherland, thus, was their second choice. In January 1624 an advance guard with just a few Walloon families set sail to New Netherland on the *Eendracht* (Unity), with Captain Adriaen Jorisz. Thienpont at the helm.

Agreements between the Walloons and the WIC

From the contract that the WIC and the Walloons concluded in 1624, the Company appears to have tried to create a solid basis with the colonists for the newly-to-be established colony.[5] The "Provisionele Ordere," outlined the rights and duties of both the Company and the colonists, describing the conditions under which the families would be brought to the colony, what requirements would be attached to their stay and what privileges they could expect. With respect to the Walloon colonists, the "architects" of the "Provisionele Ordere" were interested in farmers who could provide agricultural products to the fur traders. The WIC-appointed director of the colony would allocate land to the Walloons, decide the locations for their housing and convene a council of colonists.

In addition, the director would have a decisive say in matters relating to trade, the cultivation of crops and religion. As to the latter, the same guidelines were followed in the Republic. Freedom of conscience with respect to a personal interpretation of religion would prevail, but for public manifestations the inhabitants were to abide by the catechism of the Synod of Dordrecht, which was adopted by the Reformed Church in 1618-1619.[6] For the Walloons, who were Calvinists, this was a perfectly acceptable regulation. For the Company, the matter of religion did not play a significant role in the first years of the colony and no church was founded. Even so, the Dutch lay minister Bastiaen Jansz. Krol was sent there and was empowered to preach, and perform marriages and baptisms. The first official clergyman, Jonas Michaëlius, would only set foot in the colony in 1628.

Catalina Trico

Mother of Sarah, the First Protestant Child Born on Manhattan

Catalina Trico and Joris Rapalje were members of a group of Walloons (French-speaking Protestants from what is today southern Belgium) who set out for New Netherland in 1624. They wanted to be married before they embarked on their voyage. There was generally a wait of three weeks between the posting of the marriage banns and the wedding ceremony, but in this case the church moved to assist the young couple; two weeks after the announcement, the wedding ceremony took place in Amsterdam's Waalse Kerk (Walloon Church) and a few days later, on 24 January 1624, they set off for America.[7]

The 18-year-old Catalina's half-sister acted as her witness. Presumably Joris (one year older than his bride) had no relatives in Amsterdam, for he had no witness. Joris had a Wallonian background, as Catalina probably did, although the church register states that she came from Paris. It would seem that apart from her half-sister the couple had no relatives in Amsterdam, and they probably had little to lose by quitting the city.[8]

Catalina and Joris settled with some eight other families close to Fort Orange. Their first years there were full of hardship. The pioneer life was one of constant labor. The farmers tended their grain crops and traded in furs with the Indians who lived nearby. In 1625 the couple's first daughter, Sarah, was born. She has gone down in history as "the first-born Christian daughter of New Netherland."[9] Eleven more siblings followed. Sarah herself had eight children. A rough estimate would suggest that today over a million Americans are descendants of Joris and Catalina.[10]

In 1626 the settlement near Fort Orange was temporarily closed and the WIC obliged the Walloons to settle in New Amsterdam. Catalina and Joris moved into a house on Paerlstraat (Pearl Street), close to Fort Amsterdam after probably living in a shack beside what is today the East River. Their circumstances slowly improved. In 1637 Joris bought two estates in present-day Brooklyn. The ever-growing family remained in Manhattan.[11] In 1654 they sold the house on Pearl Street to Hendrick Hendrickszoon Obe; it is not clear where the family moved next[12]

Photo of Pearl Street seen from Whitehall Street, where Catalina Trico lived

Fransisco de Miranda, lawyer
Born in Curaçao
In New York since 2008

Some of Catalina and Joris' Descendants
John Durand, 1768
New York Historical Society, New York
Inv. no. 1946.201
Oil on canvas, 128.9 x 101.6 cm

From the archives, it appears that Joris undertook many different activities, ranging from innkeeper to tradesman to farmer.[13] He was socially active and became one of the twelve councilors who advised and supported Kieft during the war against the Indians.[14]

Catalina witnessed the rise and the dissolution of New Amsterdam. At the time of the British takeover in 1664 her husband Joris had just died, but she survived him by many years, living to the age of at least 80, at which point she recounted for the benefit of the British governor of New York what life had been like in her early years in the Dutch colony at Fort Orange.[15] She ended her days surrounded by her family of 145 individuals. She had her own small house with a small garden, and enjoyed a contented old age.[16]

The Dutch on Manhattan

Could the Dutch on Manhattan have looked like this? Howard Pyle, the nineteenth-century artist who depicted this couple near houses along the waterfront, thought so. The houses have step gables. The man at the left on the stairs before his home is smoking a Gouda pipe, and the ladies wear Dutch lace collars. In the background we see the masts of two ships and the cross on the roof of a church. There is nothing to indicate that this is Manhattan, it could just as easily be a village in Holland.

Dutch Couple
Howard Pyle, 1893
In: *Harper's Magazine*, New York, 1893
New York Public Library, New York
ID: 805610

Colonists were not to practice métiers that yielded a profit. This applied in particular to most of the activities in the weaving industry, at which the Walloons excelled. The colonists were obliged to contribute physically to the infrastructure of the colony, such as the building of forts, roads and other public facilities. For all intents and purposes, the Walloons were in the service of the WIC. Lastly, Walloons were not allowed to leave New Netherland before the end of their six-year contract period.[17]

So much for the duties and restrictions, but were there any privileges? The voyage would be free of charge for the Walloons. As there were not yet any shopkeepers who sold clothing and the farms would yield little in the beginning period, the Company would provide the basic necessities of life for two years. Thereafter, clothing and food would be supplied at a "reasonable price" and interest free. A significant privilege was that the allocated plots became their property. Anyone discovering a gold, copper or silver mine would be rewarded. In addition, the colonists were permitted to conduct trade with the Indians and to set animal traps. All otter and beaver pelts, though, had to be sold at fixed prices to the Company; after all, it had the monopoly on the fur trade. The promise to the Walloons with respect to the beaver trade was the WIC's most important concession to the colonists. By allowing trade with the Indians the colonists could make a profit and thus improve their personal situation. Obeying the "Provisionele Ordere," they were to deal "getrouwelijck," or properly, with the indigenous population.[18]

Spread Out Over the Colony and Back Again

From the instructions Director Willem Verhulst received in 1625, it emerges that he had to establish a council. Besides him, this organ would be comprised of two WIC officers and two colonists: the Walloon François Vesaert and an Englishman from Canterbury, Jan Lampo. Several months after its foundation, the council was expanded to include nine members: "Willem vander Hulst, Adriaen Jorissz Thien pont, Joost vanden Boogaert, Daniel van Cryeckenbeeck, Gerrit Fongersz, Piere Minuyt, Cryn Fredericxsz, the captains who come there from time to time, colonist Johan Lampo and Franchoys Fezard".[19]

While the establishment of the new council was vital for the colonists who settled in New Amsterdam, it would mean little to those who had spread throughout New Netherland. And this applied to the majority of the Walloons. Upon their arrival in the colony, the colonists were divided into four groups. A couple of families moved on to an area along the South (Delaware) River where Fort Wilhelmus was founded. Two families and six single men were sent to a trading post on the Fresh (Connecticut) River. The third settlement would be on Noten (Governors) Island, where a fort was built as well. The largest group comprised about eight families, including the young Walloon couple Catalina Trico and Joris Rapalje. This group was brought to a location just south of present-day Albany on the North (Hudson) River, where Fort Orange would be raised.[20]

Thanks to Catalina Trico we can gain some insight into the living conditions of the early Walloons. Aside from her testimony, little to nothing is known about the earliest existence of the colonists in these four places. Even though not all of Trico's stories can be substantiated, her accounts dating from 1684-1685 and 1688 are nevertheless important sources for this earliest period.[21]

According to Trico, upon reaching the colony, the Walloons were forced to live temporarily on small ships. They worked on their new houses and sowed grain that they had brought from the Republic. Cordial relations were maintained with the Indians. As a token of friendship, they gave the new inhabitants beaver pelts. They got along well, traded easily and left each other in peace. On the basis of Trico's observations it would seem that the Walloons experienced a difficult though relatively successful time, free of danger and with the Company's support in the form of clothing, food and compensation for expenses incurred. On the whole, the plots of land were fertile and trade with the Indians was not disappointing.

For the Company, however, this first year was unsatisfactory. Due to the steep colonization costs, profits from the beaver trade fell short of the high expectations. The WIC took measures by equalizing the price of beaver pelts throughout the entire colony with the asking price at the four trade posts. The Walloons considered the introduction of this new regulation as a breach of contract. In their view there was no use in bothering with this trade; after all, they would no longer be able to make a profit from it. The colonists did not earn any money from farming, and relied on the trade in beaver pelts. Now that they were cut out as the link between the suppliers and the buyers, they would be forced to hunt for beaver themselves.[22]

Clearly the Company was wrestling with the soaring costs of the colonization. The obligation of providing the colonists with the basic necessities in the first two years began to present problems for the WIC. For the Amsterdam Chamber, the discouraging profits, the mounting expenses, the inability to guarantee protection against Indian attacks and the unverifiability of illicit trade by colonists were all good reasons for closing down the four posts as settlement areas and transferring all

Promenading on Pearl Street

The New Amsterdam Paerlstraat, or Pearl Street, owes its name to the many oysters that were found in the water around Manhattan. Presently Pearl Street runs from Battery Park to Brooklyn Bridge. In the Dutch period Paerlstraat was located along the coast. The southern tip of Manhattan has become broader through land reclamation, which caused the shoreline to shift.

Promenade on Pearl Street
Lewis Jesse Bridgman, 1888
New York Public Library, New York
ID: 805607

The Heere Gracht: Now Broad Street

This print represents the mouth of the Heere Gracht flowing into the river. A bridge connected the Brugh Straet – for us the street at the right – with the Stadthuyslaan.

Heere Gracht
Samuel Holleyer
New York Historical Society, New York
Collection PR020, Box no. 2
ID: 800461
11 x 17 cm

of the inhabitants of New Netherland to New Amsterdam. This was a bitter disappointment for the Walloons. They had just settled into and organized their homes and farmlands and were now being forced to start all over. The Walloons from the South (Delaware) River were the first to arrive in New Amsterdam in the beginning of 1626, and the colonists from Fort Orange, the group to which Trico belonged, the last.[23]

All of the Walloon families were now living in New Amsterdam. The impossibility of hunting for beaver on Manhattan soon became clear to them. Their hope of earning something in the colony came to naught. The Walloons were at the mercy of small-scale farming around New Amsterdam, and there was no profit to be made there. Fortunately, they could at least subsist on it, or so it seemed initially. The ground proved less fertile than in the places where they had lived earlier. The harvests were meager. And, after two years the Company would stop distributing free clothing and food. How were the Walloons going to survive?

All in all, life in this small colonial community was rough going. Director Verhulst did not possess the skills needed to make a success of this difficult start-up phase. The Company could not invest the trust and courage in the Walloons that would allow them to persevere. On the contrary, the attitude of the director and the councilors towards the Walloons was uncompromising and authoritarian.[24] According to the "Provisionele Ordere" the Walloon men were required to assist the Company with various activities. The board deemed their efforts inadequate and problems ensued. In 1628 the Dutch minister Michaëlius also spoke out angrily about the Walloon's recalcitrance: " ... saying that they had not come to work, that they would have preferred to stay at home to do work".[25]

The relocation of the four smaller settlements to the main one of New Amsterdam had worked out unfavorably for the Walloons. Frustrated, the colonists had no interest in doing the work the Company demanded of them. There was only one way out, and that was to return to Europe the moment their contract expired. And this is exactly what many Walloons did. They had been deceived with false promises, presented with a prospect of life that failed to live up to reality. Accordingly, upon their return to the Republic several Walloons filed suit against the WIC.[26] Whether the failure of this grand scheme can be blamed solely on the WIC is debatable. Perhaps the Walloons themselves had been somewhat naïve about the opportunities in the New World.

The Dutch: Where Did They Come From, Where Did They Go?

Even though numerous Walloon families left, for a long time the Walloons nonetheless represented the largest section of the population.[27] Yet even as more Dutchmen than Walloons came to live in the settlement, it never assumed the character of an average Dutch community. Its composition was too heterogeneous for that, as will be discussed below. After all, many individual colonists traveled from all kinds of places throughout the Republic and elsewhere in Europe to the colony. Only after 1640 did more couples and families begin to emigrate there. And only then did stronger social connections and mutual affinities unfold.

The motives of the individual colonists who made the crossing on their own in the early years are difficult to recover. At that time work was widely available in the Republic, much of it better paid than in the colony. These men spent time in the colony as passers-by, temporary workers for the Company, such as soldiers, seamen and craftsmen. They did not intend to settle permanently in the colony. A few of them may have considered sending for their families, should their new life agree with them. However, as work became scarcer in the Republic, the emigration of skilled laborers began to rise. The colony's population grew especially in its last 15 years, reaching 7000 to 8000 people in 1664. This last period witnessed the arrival of the "classic" emigrant families. Collectively or independently, farming families decided to leave hearth and home behind and embark on a new life.[28]

From the Company's bookkeeping it emerges that far fewer single men emigrated to the colony in the years prior to 1664. In contrast, there was a substantial increase of single women. No less than six percent consisted of "maagden," or unmarried women, and a few "widwe," or widows.[29]

The newcomers usually arrived in New Amsterdam in the summer after a voyage lasting two and a half months on average. They must have been deeply relieved when the long journey was behind them and they were finally on terra firma again. Aside from the cramped cabins, the lack of privacy if you slept between-decks, the scarcity of fresh food and water, illness and unexpected death, there was always the possibility that the ship could end up at the bottom of the ocean due to storms or wars. The crossing, moreover, was not cheap. For the first colonists it was free of charge, but later, accommodation in the saloon cost one guilder per day. For a day in the cabin you paid 12 stuivers and if you slept between-decks you were out 8 stuivers. In later years the crossing became more expensive.[30]

People with relatives and acquaintances in New Netherland knew exactly where their final destination lay. Those without had a multitude of choices. They could stay in New Amsterdam, which had by far the most diversions and people. Or, they could travel on to the second town in the colony, Beverwijck, where close to 1000 colonists were living around 1664.[31] They could also choose from among some 20 villages, most of which counted between 100 and 200 inhabitants, such as Nieuw-Amersfoort (Flatlands), Breuckelen (Brooklyn), Midwout or Vlackebos (Flatbush) and Nieuw Haarlem (Harlem).

The Immigrants: Their Motives and Occupations

In 1661, Stuyvesant wrote that the population of New Netherland generally consisted of "a hodgepodge (with few exceptions) of all kinds of backgrounds."[32] In his book *Een zegenrijk gewest* Jaap Jacobs successfully unraveled and specified this "hodgepodge." He distinguished the following six immigrant groups.[33]

Farmers, Burghers and Company Men

The first group consists of men who were employed by the Company: soldiers, seamen and functionaries. Often, a soldier or sailor's motive for going to New Netherland was not prompted by a specific choice. They simply applied to the Company and in most instances had to wait and see whether they would end up in Brazil, Africa or America. These mostly young men only stayed for a while. Occasionally attempts were made to "retrain" the soldiers into genuine colonists, but to no avail: the soldiers were not schooled as craftsmen or farmers. When not needed on board ship, seamen were actually equipped to perform other tasks: they cooked or supplied provisions for the crew. In addition to sailors and soldiers, there were other occupations, such as surgeon, steward, carpenter, officer in charge of the weapons, and ship rigger. They were made to work on the land after the journey from the Republic. Some opted for a life on ships and worked on smaller vessels navigating the inland waterways.

Soldiers and sailors formed by far the largest group of people working for the WIC. Furthermore there were administrators of all ranks: the director, the vice-director, the fiscal, council members, the secretary, clerks and the supercargo. What is striking is that the higher officials often stayed on in New Netherland at the end of their contracts, sometimes entering into a new one. This applied particularly to those men who spent a part of their time working for the Company and the rest of the time on their own estates. They had invested in that land by purchasing plots and wanted to stay in order to expand their property. Numerous other occupations were also practiced in the service of the Company. Colonists were needed to keep local institutions going, such as barbers, midwives, schoolmasters, clergymen and surgeons. Furthermore, there were officials who were employed in workshops, offices and construction sites: foremen, messengers, clerks, customs officers, tax collectors, crew masters and slave overseers. They were responsible for the day-to-day management of craftsmen and workmen.

Merchants

Jacobs' second immigrant group consists of merchants. Sometimes they operated as independent entrepreneurs, or as agents in the hire of a trading house. The group of merchants expanded particularly after the Company deregulated the beaver trade. That moment also witnessed the emergence of the first private shipping companies that organized the trade traffic between the colony and the Republic. Then there were the shopkeepers and venders. They were referred to as "Scottish" merchants, but had nothing to do with Scotland. Often these peddlers were perceived as elusive figures that ruined the trade with the Indians for others. The usually brief duration of their stay in the colony limited their expenses and they could thus sell their wares for low prices. Stuyvesant once proposed giving them permission to trade only if they had been living in the colony for three years. The Amsterdam Chamber took a dim view of this: no one was to be kept in the colony against his or her will.

Farmers and Independent Craftsmen

The third group of immigrants consisted of people who came to New Netherland on their own steam. They can be divided into farmers and craftsmen and were in no one's employ. In his Beschrijvinge (p. 134), Adriaen van der Donck – who was eager to see his beloved America populated with farmers from the Republic – held up the prospect that they would be reaping fine harvests and making a profit already in their third year. Things didn't move quite so quickly. In addition to the cost of the crossing, the farmers needed a substantial starting capital of 2000 guilders in order to set up a "bouwerij," or farm. Such an investment was a considerable risk, one that not everyone dared to take. As of 1650 the Company went to some lengths to stimulate the migration of farmers. Financial support from the Company made it much easier for farmers to venture the crossing. The spring of 1650 witnessed the emigration to the colony of 200 people, who were independent farmers and farmhands who received partial assistance from the WIC. If they ultimately decided to pack it in and return to the Republic, they would have to pay double the travel expenses.

Other farmers headed to the colony because of the rising taxes in the Republic, or because they did not own enough land to divide among their sons. They left their native soil with the idea of building a new life for themselves. They established new farms and purchased land. Most landowners will not have been inclined to return to the Republic. This was different for their farmhands, contract laborers who had little to leave behind.

Workmen

Farmhands, land laborers and maidservants formed the fourth group of immigrants. They were unschooled, indentured laborers who signed a contract in order to work somewhere for a few years with no idea of what the future would bring. Of the contracts signed in Amsterdam, 251 have been preserved. Under what conditions did these – often young – people leave for America? Eighty percent were men, the majority of who ended up as farmhands. Others had previously worked as assistants to tailors, cobblers, bakers or brewers and now wanted to practice this trade elsewhere. Twenty percent were women who found work as maidservants. These girls and young women had to be careful: if they married while under contract, they could count on having to repay the cost of the crossing to New Netherland. Most contracts ran for three to six years. The younger the laborers, the longer they were required to stay in the colony and the lower their wages were. The workmen who earned the least pocketed 30 to 40 guilders a year. Then again their crossing, and room and board were paid for.

Some Dutch laborers were recruited in the region from where the master, commissioner or patron originally hailed. Others were brought in via middlemen or captains who sailed to the colony. Naturally, sometimes a prospective maidservant or workman regretted the signature or cross he or she had put on paper maybe just an hour before. At times the grand adventure proved to be a terrible letdown and all the servants or maid wanted was to return home on the next best ship. This was a blow for the Dutch employers in the colony, because labor was scarce and expensive.

Orphans

The fifth group of immigrants comprised Amsterdam orphans. Because the annual support of the orphans cost Amsterdam a substantial amount of money, around 1650 the municipality decided to cutback on their care. A plan was drawn up to send 300 to 400 children to New Netherland. A large-scale investigation was conducted among orphans. Account was taken of the youngsters' suitability and they were asked whether they wanted to emigrate. But just how objective was this process? After all, the city was eager to have as many children as possible end up on the list. In fact, a selection procedure did take place and not every child was considered eligible for emigration: the boys and girls had to be at least eight years old and in good health. Of the hundreds of orphans in Amsterdam, ultimately only a few dozen made the journey across the ocean.

Several months later the burgomasters of Amsterdam offered the colony many more children for the crossing. This will have sooner been related to municipal cutbacks than to the children's willingness. The city council took measures for the transport to America. However, when the boat was just about to set sail, the responsible officials did not dare allow the children to board ship. Just prior to this, in the run-up to the First English War, several Dutch ships had been captured by the English and it would have been unconscionable if that were to happen to a ship carrying children. Still, a few years later, in 1654, the crossing went ahead and the first few dozen Amsterdam orphans emigrated to New Netherland. A second group of orphans was sent in 1655 and a third one in 1659. Only healthy and older children, who had personally consented to the journey, set sail. They were cared for and trained in the colony.

Religious Refugees

The sixth category that Jacobs distinguishes included people who had emigrated to the colony for religious reasons. The Walloons, discussed above, were the most important exponents of this. Individual Dutchmen also left their fatherland for religious reasons, such as Mennonites and Catholics. In 1663, Pieter Cornelisz. Plockhoy, for example, fled with a few dozen fellow-believers to the South (Delaware) River, where he founded a small settlement. A year later the English obliterated his colony. Nothing was ever heard again of most of the inhabitants; they were reportedly sold as slaves in Virginia (see also p. 142).[34]

M A N A T V S
Gelegen op de Noot
Riuier
Staten Eylant.
Hoogen Hoeck
Sant Punt

Manatus: An Island for Everyone

This map is the earliest known registration of the colonization pattern on Manhattan and surroundings.[35] Made around 1665, it nevertheless shows the situation of the island of Manhattan in 1639. This is evidenced by the comment in legend numbers 2 to 6: "five raided Company farms, which are empty, three of which are now, in the year 1639, inhabited again." We do not know why and when the farms were raided. In 1639 New Amsterdam could not yet be called a town: it consisted of a handful of farms dispersed over the entire island. Nor was there any concentration of houses or a village center to speak of.

Of interest are the plantations owned by people who played an important or notable role in the history of New Amsterdam. For example, at Number 10 is "The plantation of Twiller," property of Wouter van Twiller, who was director of the colony from 1633 to 1637. He also owned Number 20, a farm on a small island (Wards Island) located "in 't Hellegat," the narrow passage in the present East River. At Number 18 is the farm of Cornelis van Tienhoven, who served as secretary for many years under both Kieft and Stuyvesant. Number 22 is the farm of Anthony "The Turk." The farm of Jonas Bronck, to which the borough of the Bronx owes its name, was located at the easternmost point of the Bronx (legend no. 43). At the time this map was made, his farm was in the early stage of construction, given the mention in the legend "building begun." Finally, at "F" we read "the quarters of the black Company slaves."

Manhattan, located on the North River
Johannes Vingboons, third quarter of the seventeenth century
Library of Congress, Geography and Map Division, Washington, D.C.
G3291.S12 coll .H3 Vault: Harr vol. 3, map 12
Watercolor on paper, 45 x 67 cm

Portrait of Peter Minuit
Anonymous
Library of Congress, Washington, D.C.
Inv. no.: LC-USZ62-33018

Pieter Minuit: A German Walloon

Pieter Minuit is a good example of a seventeenth-century European who cannot easily be pigeonholed in a single modern nationality. Born in Wezel (in present day Germany) to Walloon parents, Minuit was a merchant hired by a Dutch company, the WIC, to work in New Netherland. When the Company dismissed him after several years, he effortlessly switched allegiance to Swedish employers. By doing this was he being unfaithful to his fatherland? If so, we must ask ourselves what his fatherland was? Was it Wallonia, where his parents were from and which in Minuit's time belonged to Spain? Or was the region where he was born in 1585 his fatherland? In the seventeenth century, Minuet's birthplace was ruled variously by Brandenburgers, Spaniards, the Dutch and the French. During the Eighty Years' War with Spain, many Protestants fled from Wezel and surroundings to the Republic, where they found a safe haven. Whether they ever felt like Dutchmen though is a moot point.

Germans, Eastern Europeans, French and Scandinavians

Via Amsterdam to New Amsterdam

Other immigrants came from all over Europe: Switzerland, France, Poland, Bohemia, Germany, Denmark, Sweden, Finland, and England. In principle they could be divided into groups just like Dutch, indicated above. However, no orphans or farming families will have come from these countries. Foreign businessmen, craftsmen and contract workers traveled via the international labor market from Amsterdam to the colony. Drawn by rumors of Amsterdam being a prosperous city with a great demand for labor, they traveled to the Republic. And indeed, especially in the first half of the seventeenth century, work there often abounded. You could sign on as sailor, soldier or servant in the VOC or the WIC, and then it was a matter of waiting to see where you would end up.

From various sources it emerges that the soldiers who worked for the WIC in New Netherland were often of German extraction. Many Germans, as well as other Europeans, had escaped from the horrors of the Thirty Years' War. French Huguenots also left their country behind hoping to find a place where they could live and work free from persecution for their religious beliefs.[36]

Even though there was a relatively great demand for personnel, these job seekers did not always have an easy time finding gainful employment. The young men generally had to settle for work that paid poorly. The availability of work was primarily linked to the periods in which the VOC and WIC ships were about to set sail. Furthermore, men were deployed for military operations at sea; in times of war the Admiralty was a good employer.

Before it came to this, most of the job seekers lodged for a while with the proprietor of a pension, known as a "gasterijhouder" or "zielverkoper." They ate and slept there until the pension keeper was able to link them up with an employer, usually one of the two Companies. They were required to hand over their first salary to the so-called labor sub-contractor, the "zielverkoper." In Dutch, this appellation plays on the word "ziel," or soul, but in fact it is a corruption of the word "ceel," or warrant. Because the first salary of a soldier often did not cover his expenses with the proprietor of the pension, a "transportceel," an agreement, was signed entitling the proprietor to part of the prospective wages. The sailors or soldiers could only look on in misery at how little of their paltry wages remained in those first months. They earned eight to nine guilders per month, while the more highly ranked midshipmen received slightly more: ten guilders per month.[37]

In addition to soldiers and sailors, unschooled laborers also found their way to New Netherland. In the eyes of the colonial administration, they were a rough lot and as such were viewed with some ambivalence. Every director of New Netherland was, of course, delighted with every additional inhabitant: the quicker the land became populated, the better. But, at the same time, it was feared that people who were not Dutch would soon become "a burden on the church poor relief." And, indeed, the poorest migrants often came from outside the Republic.

Laborers were not the only people to land in New Netherland via Amsterdam. For example, Director Pieter Minuit hailed from the German town of Wezel, and his brother-in-law, one of the first shopkeepers in Manhattan, was also German. Also of interest is the man from Heidelberg specialized in wine growing who wanted to use his expertise to cultivate wine in the colony. Parenthetically, already very early on, before the existence of New Amsterdam, trading was conducted not solely by the Dutch. Hendrick Christiaensz., for instance, the captain who explored the waterways of New Netherland around 1613, came from Cleves in Germany.[38]

Not to be overlooked is Augustijn Heerman, the businessman from Bohemia, who as a member of the Board of Nine was devoted to creating a better administration in the colony and who can be considered the first cartographer to reside in New Netherland (see also p. 107). Then there were the German soldier Jacob Leisler from Frankfurt, who came to the colony as a midshipmen and rose to become one of the most influential merchants of New Amsterdam, and Storm Albertsz. van der Zee, son of a Norwegian couple. Storm owed his name to the weather circumstances during the journey on which he was born. His parents were en route to Rensselaerswijck where Albert Andriesz. Bradt, Storm's father, would go to work on the patroonship. Nicknamed Norman, Albert set up a sawmill in the vicinity of Beverwijck on the creek that is now called Normanskill.[39] Last but not least, there was of course Jonas Bronck from Sweden or Denmark, who leased a corn and tobacco plantation on Manhattan and himself set up a farm north of Manhattan, after which the Bronx was named.[40]

In addition to these colonists, who quite often had come to the colony on their own, there were dozens of Swedes and Fins living in New Netherland. In the years 1638-1655 the region along the Delaware River was annexed by the Swedes and populated by Scandinavians. After the takeover of the Swedish Colony by Stuyvesant, in 1655 the majority of this community decided to stay.[41]

The German-Lutheran Community

In the course of time so many colonists of German descent had flocked to the colony that a substantial Lutheran community had grown up. They formed the first non-Reformed congregation, which in 1654 tried to arrange for its own minister to come over to New Netherland. The Reformed clergymen of the colony did everything in their power to prevent this. Even though the Lutherans were close to their own Calvinist creed, they feared that with the arrival of a Lutheran minister the Reformed Church's standing and congregation would diminish. And if the Lutherans were to be successful, other congregations would follow their example. Total chaos would break out and in no time New Amsterdam would be a den of heathens. The Amsterdam Chamber followed the advice of the Reformed clergymen. Henceforth, the director was to immediately refuse any new requests to bring spiritual shepherds of other churches to the colony.

So everything stayed the same; everyone was free to worship as they wished in the privacy of their homes, but public gatherings other than Reformed services were strictly forbidden. The Lutherans were disappointed and carried on with their crusade. Against regulations they arranged for Reverend Johannes Ernestus Gutwasser to come to the colony in 1657. A conflict ensued. The board asked Gutwasser to leave; he flatly refused! First he postponed his return voyage and then he went into hiding. This was perceived as undermining colonial authority, compelling Director-General Stuyvesant and his councilors to have the good reverend deported. The Lutherans lost out. Their second preacher would only arrive in New Netherland when it was no longer Dutch.[42]

Jonas Bronck

How the Bronx Got its Name

The Swedish sea captain Jonas Bronck is said to have sailed from Amsterdam to New Amsterdam in the company of his Dutch wife Teuntje Jeuriaens, plus a few house servants and farm workers.

He gave his new farm across the river from the northern end of Manhattan the biblical name of Emmaus. The land stretching beyond his farm still bears his name: Bronck's land.

Bronck was probably a Lutheran, judging by many of the books among his possessions. The fact that all his books were in Danish suggests that he came from Denmark. His wife was a Calvinist and her books too are listed as being in the couple's extensive library. Between them they owned over 60 volumes.[43]

Bronck cultivated new land on Manhattan, across what is today the East River from his existing farm. His shrewd method of developing the new ground was to send for two tenant farmers from the Dutch Republic, Pieter Andriessen and Lourens Duyts, advancing them their fares to the New World on the understanding that the men would clear virgin land to grow their own corn and tobacco for three and a half years, after which Bronck would take the land back for his own use. By this agreement they repaid him the cost of their Atlantic crossing.[44]

In autumn of 1641 a young Wickquasgeck native murdered an elderly colonist in revenge for the robbery and murder 15 years before of the Indian's uncle, as described on page 171. Kieft, the West India

Bronck's Farm is no. 43.
Detail of the "Manatus Map," Johannes Vingboons (see pp. 190-191)

Map of England
Johannes Vingboons, third quarter of the seventeenth century
Nationaal Archief (National Archives of the Netherlands), The Hague
4.VELH 619-002
Watercolor on paper, 48 x 69 cm

The English

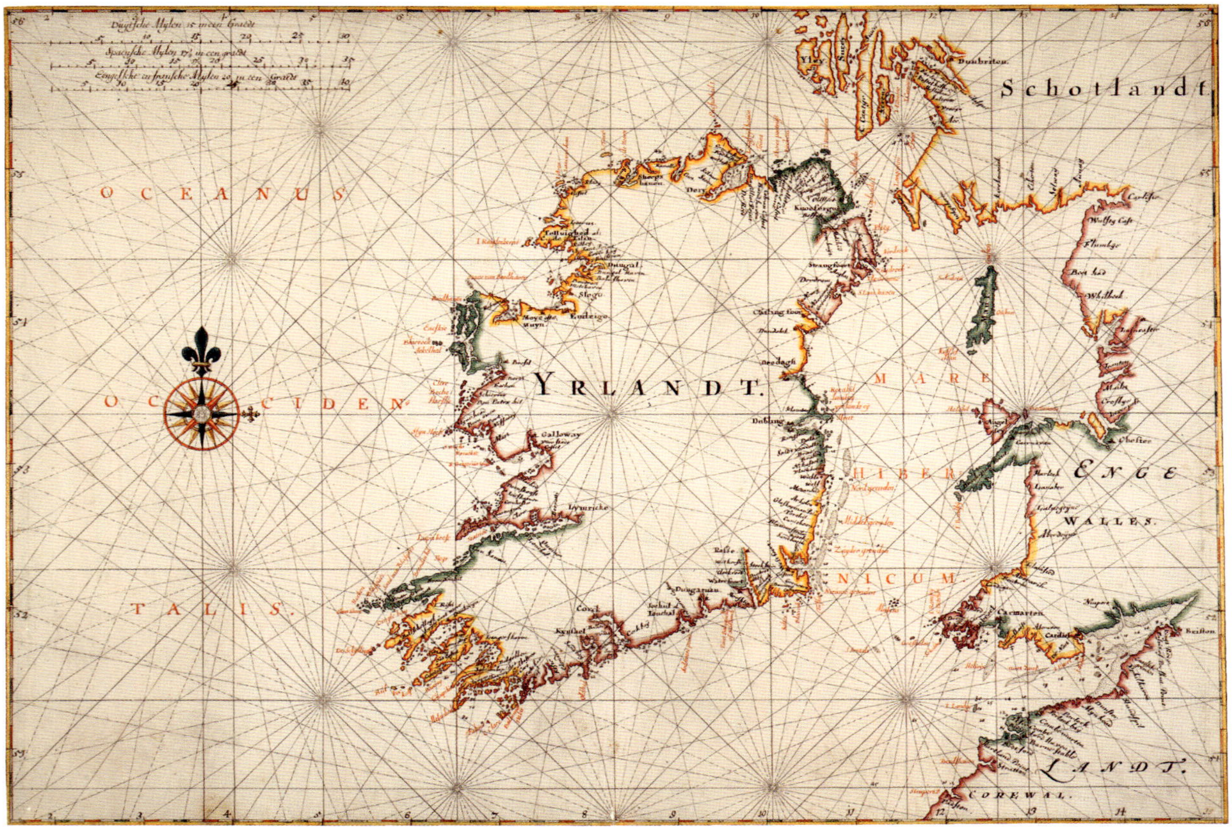

The government in the New Netherland colony was involved with the English in two ways. The English colonies of Virginia and New England had been neighbors for 50 years. Sometimes they were allies, sometimes as enemies. But quite a few English people lived in the Dutch Colony. In the second half of New Netherland's existence, the number of English colonists increased due to an influx of religious refugees grouped primarily on Lange Eiland (Long Island), like Lady Moody for instance (see p. 91).

Map of Ireland
Johannes Vingboons, third quarter of the seventeenth century
Nationaal Archief (National Archives of the Netherlands), The Hague
4.VELH 619-003
Watercolor on paper, 48 x 69 cm

English Pilgrims and Quakers

Just before the establishment of the WIC, in February 1620, a large group of colonists, consisting of 400 families, had requested permission from the States General to go to New Netherland. They were English-speaking Pilgrims, partly from the Republic and partly from England. Persecution in England caused many Pilgrims to flee to Amsterdam already in 1608. From there they had moved on to Leiden. Now, under the guidance of a Dutch-speaking English minister, they wanted to make the crossing to America. In their petition they begged for the protection of two warships.[46] The States General refused to commit to this, probably to avoid problems with England. In addition, trouble with the Indians was feared.[47] The Puritans nevertheless found another way of traveling to America. Via Southampton, where they met up with the second group of Pilgrim Fathers, they sailed with the *Mayflower* to a region north of New Netherland. There, in New England, in 1620, work was begun on the settlement called New Plymouth. In 1629, New England experienced a second emigration wave of Puritans from England, who founded the Massachusetts Bay Colony.

The letter from Secretary De Rasière to Samuel Blommaert is described on page 70. It contains not only an account of New Netherland, but also the earliest description of New Plymouth. De Rasière also mentions the deeply religious Pilgrim William Bradford, the founder of the English colony. Bradford saw a huge difference between the profligate conduct of the Dutch and his own incorruptible, faithful colony. It was generally thought that the English colony was more homogeneous and run more tightly than the Dutch one.

Ultimately, more people would migrate to New England than to New Netherland for religious reasons.[48] A large group of English believers who sought refuge in the Dutch colony was the Quakers. This radical group had come into being as a result of the English civil war. They rejected every single form of authority other than God. They did not accept any form of human rule, which in the eyes of the Dutch colonial government made the Quakers impossible citizens, let alone people they could talk to. Stuyvesant, as well as councilors, simply loathed them and will have taken insult when the first ship with Quakers arrived from London in 1657 and did not fire salutes, as was customary.

This act of public disrespect would be followed by many more. Against the law, the Quakers organized conventicles, that is secret or non-authorized religious meetings. As a consequence the Quakers were reprimanded and fined, which they flatly ignored. The Quakers were punished not so much for their beliefs, but rather their blatant refusal to submit to colonial authority. The cat and mouse game between the authorities and the Quakers degenerated when the reprimands turned into severe punishments and ended up in whippings. Eventually, the population had had enough of the unprecedentedly harsh discipline that was being meted out.[49]

The villagers and magistrates of Vlissingen (Flushing) on Lange Eiland (Long Island) submitted a petition to Stuyvesant on 27 December 1657. The authorities of the colony had drafted an ordinance forbidding the village to admit Quakers. The inhabitants and the magistrates asked Stuyvesant to be more accommodating. The petition, which was signed by some 30 people and went down in history as the "Flushing Remonstrance," was not honored.

The Quakers were not the only English colonists who were active in New Netherland. Lange Eiland (Long Island) in particular counted many dissenters, including Anabaptists: "many Puritans, independents, many atheists and various other lost souls".[50] They lived in almost entirely English-language villages, but under Dutch jurisdiction: Middelburgh (Newtown), Heemstede (Hempstead), Vlissingen (Flushing), 's-Gravesande (Gravesend), Oostdorp (Westchester) and Rustdorp (Jamaica).[51]

The Jewish Community

Twenty-Three Portuguese Jews

In the 1650s groups of Jews arrived in New Amsterdam. Twenty-three of them were refuges from Pernambuco in Brazil. Under Portuguese rule the Jewish community had lived there as converted neo-Christians. As of 1630, when the Dutch took Pernambuco from the Portuguese, they could again practice their religion more freely; in any case, they were no longer persecuted. This changed in 1654 when the Brazilian coastal region fell back into Portuguese hands. A large part of the Jewish community subsequently decided to leave Brazil. Under Dutch rule they had experienced freedom of conscience. Moreover, the Dutch had turned a blind eye to their religious practices, which was unthinkable under the Portuguese. And so they left the country together with the Dutch. They did not set a direct course for Amsterdam: the voyage led from Pernambuco, via Spanish Jamaica and Spanish Cuba ultimately to New Netherland.

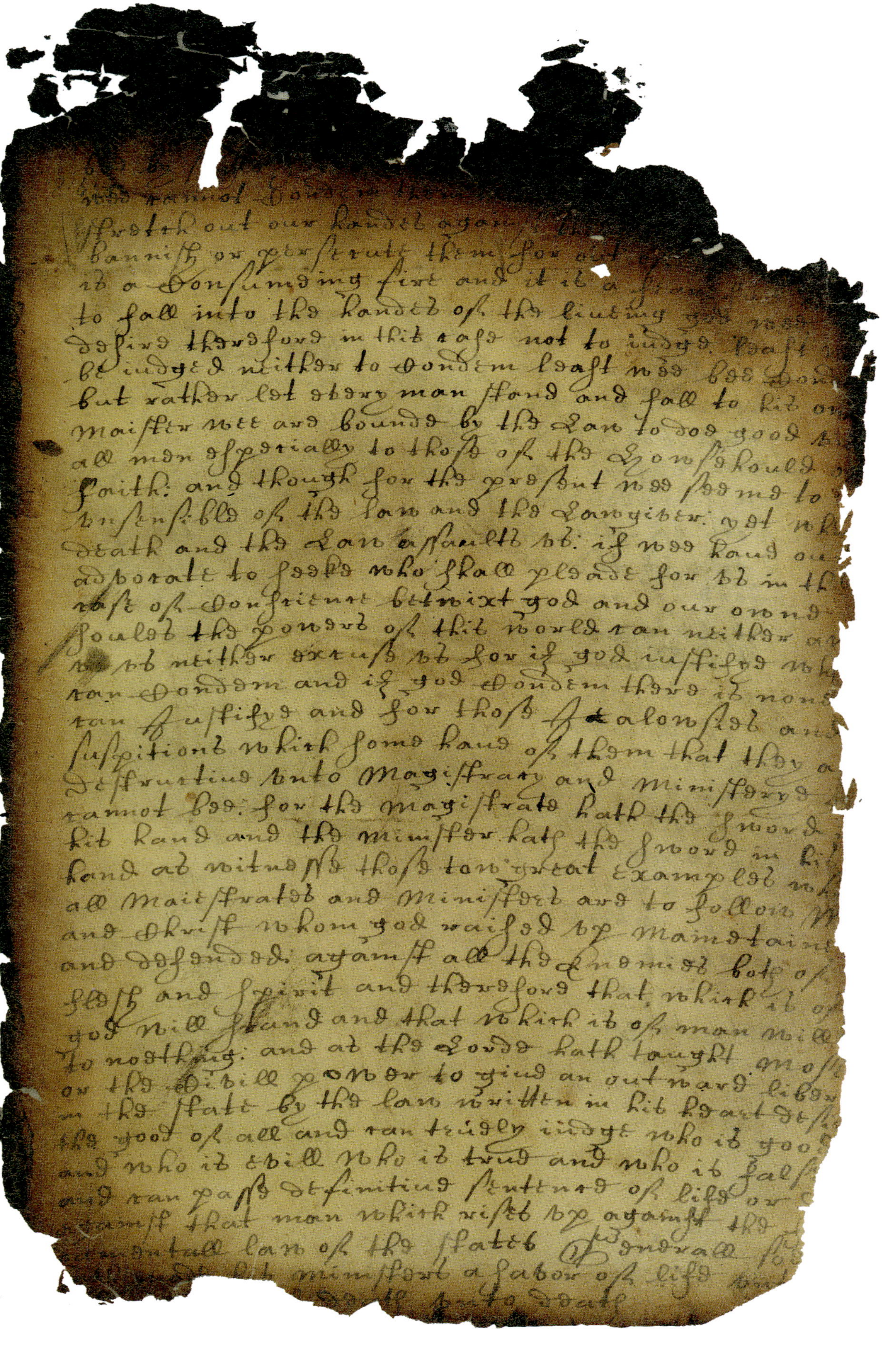

wee cannot condemn them
stretch out our handes against them to
bannish or persecute them for out of Christ God
is a consuming fire and it is a fearful thing
to fall into the handes of the living God wee
desire therefore in this case not to iudge least
be iudged neither to condem least wee bee con
but rather let every man stand and fall to his ow
Maister wee are bounde by the Law to doe good u
all men especially to those of the Houshould o
faith: and though for the present wee seeme to
unsensible of the law and the Lawgiver: yet wh
death and the Law assaults us: if wee have ou
advocate to seeke who shall pleade for us in th
case of conscience betwixt God and our owne
soules the powers of this world can neither at
us neither excuse us for if God iustifye who
can condemn and if God condem there is none
can iustifye and for those iealousies and
suspitions which some have of them that they a
destructive unto Magistracy and ministerye
cannot bee: for the magistrate hath the sword in
his hand and the minister hath the sword in his
hand as witnesse those two great examples wh
all Maistrates and Ministers are to follow M
and Christ whom God raised up Maintaine
and defended against all the enemies both of
flesh and spirit and therefore that which is of
God will stand and that which is of man will
to nothing: and as the Lorde hath taught Moses
or the civill power to give an outward liberty
in the state by the law written in his heart desi
the good of all and can truely iudge who is good
and who is evill who is true and who is false
and can pass definitive sentence of life or
against that man which rises up against the
fundamentall law of the States Generall so
his ministers a savor of life
unto death

The "Flushing Remonstrance," 1657
New York State Archives, Albany, NY
Inv. no. series A1809, Dutch Colonial
Council Minutes, vol. 8, pp. 626-627

The "Flushing Remonstrance," 1657

In Flushing or Flishing, a contamination of the Zeeland name Vlissingen, some 30 townspeople and magistrates signed the "Flushing Remonstrance," taking a stand for the Quakers in the village.
Stuyvesant and his councilors had several of the signers arrested, and placed those who persisted on a harsh diet of bread and water. Moreover, he also replaced members of the village council with individuals who would not tolerate such kinds of petitions. Six years later, in 1663, Stuyvesant was finally instructed in a letter from the directors back in the Republic to cease his religious persecution and to turn a blind eye to the sermons and gatherings of other denominations, as was customary in the Republic.[52]
For some Americans the "Flushing Remonstrance" of 1657 is considered the foundation of "the freedom of religion" right that is included in the Bill of Rights. The document (a copy from the same year of the original petition) was severely damaged in a fire in 1911. Fortunately, the entire text is still legible:

Right Honorable
You have been pleased to send unto us a certain prohibition or command that we should not receive or entertain any of those people called Quakers because they are supposed to be, by some, seducers of the people. For our part we cannot condemn them in this case, neither can we stretch out our hands against them, for out of Christ God is a consuming fire, and it is a fearful thing to fall into the hands of the living God.
Wee desire therefore in this case not to judge least we be judged, neither to condemn least we be condemned, but rather let every man stand or fall to his own Master. [...]
The law of love, peace and liberty in the states extending to Jews, Turks and Egyptians, as they are considered sons of Adam, which is the glory of the outward state of Holland, soe love, peace and liberty, extending to all in Christ Jesus, condemns hatred, war and bondage. And because our Saviour sayeth it is impossible but that offences will come, but woe unto him by whom they cometh, our desire is not to offend one of his little ones, in whatsoever form, name or title he appears in, whether Presbyterian, Independent, Baptist or Quaker, but shall be glad to see anything of God in any of them, desiring to doe unto all men as we desire all men should doe unto us, which is the true law both of Church and State; for our Saviour sayeth this is the law and the prophets.
Therefore if any of these said persons come in love unto us, we cannot in conscience lay violent hands upon them, but give them free egresse and regresse unto our Town, and houses, as God shall persuade our consciences, for we are bounde by the law of God and man to doe good unto all men and evil to noe man. And this is according to the patent and charter of our Towne, given unto us in the name of the States General, which we are not willing to infringe, and violate, but shall houlde to our patent and shall remaine, your humble subjects, the inhabitants of Vlishing.
Written this 27th of December in the year 1657, by mee.
Edward Hart, Clericus

Quakers in Flushing
Charles Etienne Pierre Motte, 1825
New York Public Library, New York
ID: 53896
18.7 x 28 cm

A nineteenth-century print shows us a Quaker assembly in Flushing in 1672. People have gathered under an oak tree. They are listening to a sermon given by George Fox, an Englishman who traveled throughout Europe and America to spread his faith. He also preached in England, for which he was imprisoned on several occasions.

The First Jews in New Amsterdam

It is often assumed that the first Jews in North America were 23 Jews from Brazil who arrived on the *St. Catherine*. However, other Jews had most likely arrived there long before them.[53] Other sources state that the 23 were the first Jews on Manhattan, but this, too, is incorrect. Another ship arrived just before the *St. Catherine*, namely the *Peereboom* (Pear Tree), which dropped anchor before the island on 22 August 1654.[54]

The *Peereboom* had left Amsterdam in July 1654. On board were the merchants Jacob Barsimon, Asser Levy and Solomon Pietersen. The ship subsequently sailed to New Netherland via London, where the fourth Jewish passenger probably embarked. They were not fugitives, but were traveling to the Dutch settlement of their own volition. The Amsterdam Jews had travel documents and did not experience any problems upon arrival. In so far as is known, these were the first Jews to call in at Manhattan. Solomon Pietersen and Asser Levy witnessed the arrival of the *St. Catherine* with the Jewish refugees from Brazil.[55]

In that same year, or in the spring of 1655, another group of Jews arrived on Manhattan. They were from the Dutch Republic and they, too, were probably in possession of the necessary travel documents. It is assumed that the papers were arranged by the Amsterdam parnassim, the religious and social leaders of the Jewish community in the city. This group of newcomers included several Jews who had first traveled to the Republic from Brazil and subsequently sailed from Amsterdam to New Amsterdam. Perhaps their choice to go to New Amsterdam was influenced by the shareholders of the WIC, which may have also been the case for the Jewish merchants who had arrived earlier on the Peereboom.[56] What would have motivated the Jews from Amsterdam to leave the Republic in those years? Many of them were originally from Eastern Europe, which often was ravaged by epidemics and pogroms. In fact, in 1648 the Jewish population in Amsterdam rose thanks to the migration from Eastern Europe. In addition, they will have been spurred on by trade opportunities in the colony as well as the healthy climate.[57]

Stuyvesant and his council do not seem to have objected to the arrival of a modest number of Jews to the Republic. However, this did not apply to the group of Brazilian Jews. On 22 and 25 September 1654, thus just after the Brazilian group had come onshore, Stuyvesant penned two angry missives to the directors of the WIC. He felt that New Netherland was not an appropriate destination for these people, because their poverty would place too great a burden on the city.[58] In March 1655 the councilors (Stuyvesant was then in the Caribbean) had given the mayors and aldermen of New Amsterdam to understand that the Jews had to leave the city as soon as possible. The council did not raise a single objection to this.[59] Not much later, Johannes Megapolensis, a minister in New Amsterdam, wrote a letter to the classis of Amsterdam, in which he mentioned the Jews who had come from the Republic a year earlier to conduct trade. Later, he wrote, other Jews had arrived, poor but healthy. Next Megapolensis expressed his displeasure at having to spend several hundreds of guilders on these newcomers from Brazil. They had already appealed to him for help on several occasions. They were depending on him, because they could not expect anything from the other Jewish merchants, Megapolensis claimed.

Furthermore, the Reverend believed that the Jews were after nothing else than Christian property. And, they interfered with the other merchants. He strongly advocated making the "ungodly" leave as soon as possible. They only created confusion in a colony that was already riddled with problems from the Catholics, Quakers, Mennonites and Lutherans. If the Jews were admitted, they just might form a ghetto.[60]

The Jews Resist

Pending further orders from the Amsterdam Chamber, Stuyvesant and the councilors tried to prevent the Jews from gaining a firm foothold. He stopped them from buying land, running an office or serving in the civil guard of New Amsterdam. They were also forbidden to trade with the Indians. Finally, the director-general and the councilors imposed additional taxes on the Jews. None of these measures were taken to restrict the Jews in their religious beliefs. The director-general and his councilors simply raised these obstacles because they were Jewish. It they protested to the board, they were told that they were free to go. Stuyvesant's policy was aimed at making life so difficult for the Jews that they would eventually leave of their own accord.[61]

For example, the Jewish community had asked Petrus Stuyvesant for a cemetery. His answer was no and the matter was never raised again. For the time being, no official Jewish community was established. The Jews will have practiced their religion within the family circle; later this was officially permitted. Abraham de Lucena, one of the last Dutch Jews to arrive in the colony, owned a "sefer Torah," which had been given to him by the Amsterdam community. He will hardly have used it, for not long after his arrival De Lucena left New Amsterdam and returned the scroll to the donors.[62]

When a Jewish man was interested in buying a certain house, Stuyvesant hastened to declare the purchase nul and void and put the dwelling up for sale at public auction. Jacob Cohen wanted to set up a bakery and was willing to buy the property behind closed doors; even so, he was not granted permission. When a group of Jewish colonists wished to show their loyalty to the city by joining the militia, they were refused.[63]

We know that Abraham de Lucena was dragged before the court by bailiff Cornelis van Tienhoven in 1655. A shopkeeper, De Lucena had kept his store open during the sermon and made a few sales, which was not permitted. No slack was cut for the Jews in New Amsterdam.

The Jewish New Amsterdammers appealed to leaders of the Jewish community back in Amsterdam. In turn, in January 1655 they drafted a petition to the Amsterdam administrators requesting that the Jews of New Netherland be allowed to move freely and conduct trade with Jewish merchants in the Republic. They argued that the Brazilian group had suffered greatly and proven its loyalty to the Republic. The colony was better off using such inhabitants rather than the English or French. Furthermore, they emphasized that the Jews who hailed from the Republic were respectable citizens.[64]

On 26 April 1655 the directors informed the director-general and the councilors that – though they understood their objections – it was unreasonable to deny the Jews access to New Netherland. The Jews had already suffered great losses in Brazil. And, it appeared that now a number of them had accrued substantial debts to the WIC during the Brazilian-Dutch period of Pernambuco. By admitting them to the colony and letting them maintain commercial relations with the Jews from Amsterdam, they would be able to earn back the money that they still owed the Company.[65] The poor Jews from New Netherland had to be taken care of by both the wealthy Jews and the colonial authorities, so that they would not be a burden to the community. Furthermore, the Jews in New Amsterdam had to have the same rights as the other free burghers. It had to be possible for them to conduct trade outside of the colony, to own real estate, to practice their religion in private, and to operate shops, albeit respecting certain hours.[66]

Now that there was formal permission, the group began to set up commercial enterprises. Isaac Israel and David de Ferera tried their luck in trade on the South (Delaware) River. In March 1655 Joseph da Costa, a shareholder in the Company, became an agent for for the Amsterdam company that shipped goods manufactured by the Verbrugge family business, which engaged in trade between New Netherland and Amsterdam. Various Jewish merchants imported and exported fur, cattle, butter, cheese, tobacco, fabric and lumber. David de Ferera bought tobacco in Maryland, south of New Netherland.[67]

Thus, Stuyvesant and the councilors received orders from the authorities to accept the Jews into their community. Dutiful as he was, the director-general complied with his superiors' demands. Gradually the colonial authorities adopted a somewhat more tolerant attitude. In 1656 the community was given a cemetery and trade on the South (Delaware) River, which initially was forbidden, was allowed. Nevertheless, anti-Semitism had done its work. Many Jews, among whom Abraham de Lucena, David de Ferera and Salvador d'Andrada, returned to the Republic after a problematic sojourn of close to two years.[68]

When the English took over the colony, most of the Jewish colonists had by then moved on to other areas. The city now counted a mere 50 Jewish inhabitants. Hardly any of those who had arrived in 1654-1655 were still in New Amsterdam. Nevertheless, a few Jews die achieve a reasonable to high standard of living: five of the twenty wealthiest men in the colony were Jews. Of those who had come to the new land on the *Peereboom* (Pear Tree) only Asser Levy was left.[69]

CITY OF NEW YORK

Asser Levy

The Kosher Butcher on the Hoogstraat, or High Street

Asser Levy, Jacob Barsimon and Solomon Pieterse were among the first Jews to settle in Manhattan. Levy probably arrived in the colony on 20 August 1654, most likely on the ship the *Peereboom* (Pear Tree).[70] He was the only Jew among all those who went to New Amsterdam in that period who spent the remainder of his life in the city. He had probably come to Amsterdam from Vilnius, the capital of today's Lithuania. Jews who fled the pogroms in Eastern Europe found comparative freedom in the Dutch Republic.

It is not known whether Levy was already married to Miriam at the time of his departure for New Amsterdam. Nor is much known about her background; while she may have come from a prominent Sephardic family living in Amsterdam it seems more likely that she was from a German Ashkenazi famil.[71] The couple had no children.

Asser Levy stood up for his rights in a conflict with Peter Stuyvesant and his councilors when the town council forbad Jews from standing guard together with the members of the militia, who felt an aversion for the people the Dutch referred to as "the Jewish Nation."[72] Levy was the first to protest against this regulation. He demanded the right to keep watch together with his fellow citizens, rather than pay a special tax imposed upon Jews in lieu of performing guard duty. His petition was rejected.

Levy earned his living as a kosher butcher and was the first Manhattan Jew to speculate in property.[73] Although not one of the city's wealthiest inhabitants, he was certainly not a poor man. He owned a house in the Hoogstraat, or High Street.[74]

While little is known about Asser Levy's life, his opposition to Peter Stuyvesant made him one of the most famous characters in the story of New Amsterdam. In New York City his name is commemorated by the street called Asser Levy Place, a bathhouse, a park in Brooklyn and a school.

Photo taken in front of the Asser Levy Bath House, named after the Kosher Butcher Levy

Koos van den Akker, fashion designer
Born 1939 The Hague
In New York since 1968

Fleeing Portugal and Portuguese Brazil

The Brazilian Sugar Mill "Engenho Real"
Frans Post, ca. 1650
Museum Boijmans van Beuningen, Rotterdam
Inv. no. 2116

Olinda, Brazil
Johannes Vingboons, third quarter of the seventeenth century
Nationaal Archief (National Archives of the Netherlands), The Hague
4.VELH 619-080
Watercolor on paper, 40.5 x 58.5 cm

Under threat of the Inquisition, at the end of the sixteenth century Jewish inhabitants of Spain were forced to convert to Christianity or leave the country. Tens of thousands of them fled to neighboring Portugal. Ultimately, this escape was but a temporary reprieve for the Inquisition eventually spread into Portugal. In the hope of finding greater religious freedom many migrated to the Dutch Republic, France or – sometimes via the Republic – to a new Portuguese colony, Brazil.

After its "discovery" by the Portuguese in 1500, Brazil, and the province of Pernambuco in particular, rapidly developed into the largest sugar exporter in the world. The Jewish immigrants soon became part of the "white" community, albeit not as Jews, but as neo-Christians. Like many of their forefathers, they had officially converted to Christianity, but continued to worship in secrecy. They were called "converses," converts, Marranos.

From the time the WIC was established in 1621, the Dutch wanted to take over Brazil. They knew that the Portuguese colony annually produced and shipped no less than five million guilders worth of sugar to Europe.[75] Hence, the productive sugar refineries were their motivation to attack the Portuguese in the *capitania* (province) of Pernambuco in 1623 and 1625. After two failed attempts, the surprise attack of the cities of Recife and Olinda in 1630 was successful. A few years later the entire province of Pernambuco was under Dutch control. Finally the Dutch could profit from the hundreds of sugar mills they had coveted for so long. In turn, the Jews could profit from the more tolerant attitude towards other religions that was introduced by the Dutch. Freedom of conscience prevailed, allowing the neo-Christians to once again practice their Jewish faith. It also meant that synagogues could be built. Sephardic Jews who arrived in Brazil from the Republic worked together with the neo-Christians to build houses of prayer. In 1637, the Kahal Zur Israel Synagogue was founded on the Jodenstraat (Jewish Street) in Recife, the first synagogue in the Americas.[76] The first rabbi in America was the originally Portuguese Jew Isaac Aboab da Fonseca, who had emigrated from Amsterdam to Recife.

The First Rabbi of South America, Isaak Aboab da Fonseca
A. Nagtegael, 1685-1686
Jewish Historical Museum, Amsterdam
01214

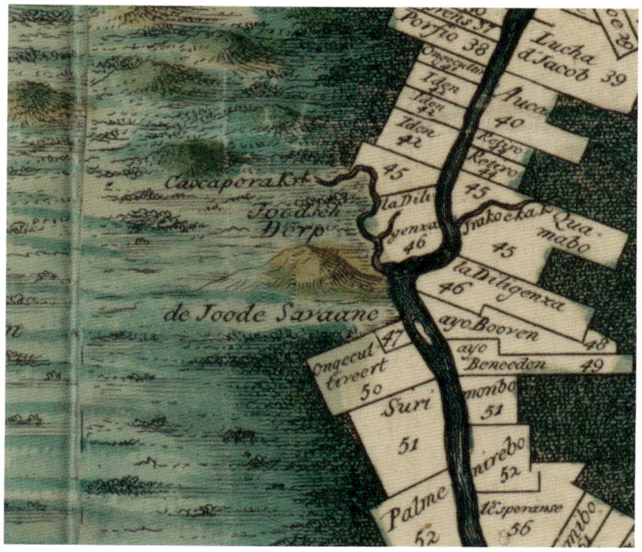

Detail of a Map of Suriname, The Jewish Savanna
Rijksmuseum, Amsterdam
Inv. no.: NG-478

The heyday of Dutch-Brazil began in 1636, the year when Governor-General Johan Maurits arrived in Brazil to stimulate its economy. That success was short-lived. An economic crisis in 1644 and ongoing Portuguese attacks on the sugar mills of Pernambuco obliged the WIC to give up the colony in 1654 and leave Brazil. Anticipating that the Inquisition would be reinstated under Portuguese rule, most of the Jews elected to leave Brazil.

Dutch and English trading posts and colonies were popular destinations: many of them fled to the Dutch settlements on the coast of Guyana and the Dutch-owned Curaçao. In Guyana the new colonists were offered attractive tax benefits. Others landed in English Suriname, in the village Jewish Savanna on a tributary of the Suriname River, where the Jewish refugees were offered land to settle on and cultivate.[77]

Upon the take-over of Dutch-Brazil, the Portuguese gave the Dutch and Jewish inhabitants three months to organize their departure. The Portuguese commander promised there would be no reprisals and that everyone would be treated with respect and courtesy. Moreover, they were allowed to keep any possessions that could be transported. These were very reasonable provisions for a take-over. The Portuguese commander, Francisco Barreto, ordered 16 ships, including several Dutch ones, to be made ready to sail.[78]

Twenty-three Jews boarded one of the Dutch ships, the *Valck* (Falcon). Under Captain Jon Craeck, the *Valck* set sail from Brazil on 24 February 1654 and because of unfavorable winds ended up in Jamaica, Spanish territory. His passengers probably remained on the island until the end of April, when they headed to Cuba, possibly again with the *Valck*. There, the 23 Jews boarded a French ship, the *St. Catherine* on which they sailed to New Amsterdam.[79] They were the second group of Jewish immigrants to settle in New Amsterdam; they arrived there utterly destitute.

[1] Wieder, *De Stichting van New York*, p. 121.
[2] Wieder, *De Stichting van New York*, pp. 4-5.
[3] Rink, *Holland on the Hudson*, p. 75; De Forest, "A Walloon family in America," pp. 13-28.
[4] Condon, *New York Beginnings*, pp. 90-91; Zabriskie and Kenney, "The Founding of New Amsterdam," p. 15.
[5] Wieder, *De Stichting van New York*, pp. 111-118.
[6] Rink, *Holland on the Hudson*, pp. 76-78.
[7] Zabriskie, "The Founding Families of New Netherland, No. 4," p. 7.
[8] Zabriskie, "The Founding Families of New Netherland, No. 4," p. 7.
[9] Shorto, *The Island at the Center of the World*, p. 41.
[10] Condon, *New York Beginnings*, p. 93.
[11] Zabriskie, "Founding Families of New Netherland, No. 4," part III, p. 11.
[12] Zabriskie, "Founding Families of New Netherland, No. 4," part III, p. 11.
[13] Zabriskie, "Founding Families of New Netherland, No. 4," part III, p. 11.
[14] Shorto, *The Island at the Center of the World*, p. 145.
[15] Shorto, *The Island at the Center of the World*, p. 337; Jameson, *Narratives*, p. 75.
[16] Schuyler van Rensselaer, *History of the City of New York in the Seventeenth Century*, II, p. 229.
[17] Wieder, *De Stichting van New York*, p. 116.
[18] Jacobs, *Een zegenrijk gewest*, p. 114.
[19] Wieder, *De Stichting van New York*, p. 135 ff, p. 118: "Nadere instructie voor Willem Verhulst 25 April 1625" [Van Rappard document D], p. 137.
[20] Zabriskie and Kenney, "Founding Families of New Netherland," p. 11.
[21] O' Callaghan, *Documentary history of the state of New York III*, pp. 49-51; Bachman, *Peltries or Plantations*, p. 82, note 23.
[22] Bachman, *Peltries or Plantations*, p. 86.
[23] Zabriskie and Kenney, "The Founding of New Amsterdam," p. 14.
[24] Jacobs, *Een zegenrijk gewest*, p. 118.
[25] Eekhof, *Jonas Michaëlius*, p.103.
[26] Zabriskie and Kenney, "The Founding of New Amsterdam," p. 7.
[27] Rink, *Holland on the Hudson*, p. 144.
[28] Jacobs, *Een zegenrijk gewest*, p. 89.
[29] Rink, *Holland on the Hudson*, pp. 165-168.
[30] Jacobs, *Een zegenrijk gewest*, p. 67.
[31] Jacobs, *Een zegenrijk gewest*, p. 69.
[32] Jacobs, *Een zegenrijk gewest*, p. 103.
[33] Jacobs, *Een zegenrijk gewest*, pp. 72-103.
[34] Jacobs, *Een zegenrijk gewest*, p. 101.
[35] Van Bracht and Schilder, *The Origins of New York*, p. 12.
[36] Van Ruymbeke, "The Walloon and Huguenot Elements," pp. 41-54.
[37] Jacobs, *Een zegenrijk gewest*, pp. 72-74.
[38] Jacobs, *Een zegenrijk gewest*, p. 44.
[39] Jacobs, *Een zegenrijk gewest*, pp. 86-87, note 91 on p. 421.
[40] Jacobs, *Een zegenrijk gewest*, pp. 75, 89-90.
[41] Louhi, *The Delaware Finns*; Craig, *Chronology of Colonial Swedes* in www.colonialswedes.org/Publications, Volume 2, Number 5 (Fall 2001).
[42] Jacobs, *Een zegenrijk gewest*, pp. 255-260.
[43] Schuyler van Rensselaer, *History of the City of New York in the Seventeenth Century*, I, p. 161; Jacobs, Een zegenrijk gewest, pp. 90, 255, 351.
[44] Van Laer, *Council Minutes*, 1638-1649, I: 141
[45] Schuyler van Rensselaer, *History of the City of New York in the Seventeenth Century*, I, p. 181.
[46] NA 1.01.07 (States General) 5484, Ingekomen stukken / Lias Admiraliteiten 1620, 12-2: "As it happens, a certain English minister is living in Leiden who has a fine command of the Dutch language and who is inclined to undertake the voyage there in due course. He assures the suppliants that more than 400 families, both from here and from England, would go there with him. This, provided they are shielded and safeguarded in the new country under the authority and protection of Your Royal Excellency and the Honorable Gentlemen of the States General from all violence perpetrated by other potentates so that they can propagate the one true Christian faith and teach the Word to the savages of that land and convert them to Christianity and thus - through the grace of God and to the great praise of the Dutch government - can there populate a new government entirely in compliance with the orders and command of Your Royal Excellency and the Honorable Gentlemen of the States General." (...T'is nu soo dat tot Leijden is woonachtich seecker Engels Predicant, doch geverseert in de Nederlantsche taele wel genegen soude sijn, hem aldaer metter woon te begeven de supplianten verseeckerend dat hij middel weet tot over de vierhondert huijsgesinnen die met hem derwaerts soo vuijt dese landen als Engellant soude vertrecken, mits datse door de authoriteijt, ende onder de bescherminge van Uwe Princelijcke Ex:cie ende Ho: Mo: Heeren Staeten Generael in de deselve landen voor alle gewelt van andere Potentaten souden beschermt & bewaert sijn, omme aldaer voorts te planten, de ware suijvere Christelijcke Religie, ende de wilden des selven lants totte waere leere te onderrichten ende totten Christes geloove te brengen ende alsoo door de genade des Heeren tot grooten loff deser lander Regieringe aldaer te peupleren eene nieuwe Regieringe alles opte ordre ende bevelen van uwe Pr: Ex.tie ende Ho: Mo: Heeren Staeten Tgenerael...).
[47] RGP Grote Serie no. 176 ; Resolutiën Staten-Generaal 2655, p. 390, 26-2-1620, printed in O'Callaghan, Documents I, p. 23-24.
[48] Jacobs, *Een zegenrijk gewest*, p. 100.
[49] Jacobs, *Een zegenrijk gewest*, pp. 262-263.
[50] Jacobs, *Een zegenrijk gewest*, p. 265.
[51] Jacobs, "Migration, Population, and Government in New Netherland."
[52] Jacobs, *Een zegenrijk gewest*, p. 265.
[53] Friedman, *Jews and the American Slave Trade*, p. 103: "There may have been Marranos among the Spanish settlers of St. Augustine in Florida in 1565, or Santa Fe, New Mexico when it was established in 1610. The names Torres, Rodriguez, and Abraham, favored by Crypto-Christians, are fairly common among Spanish settlers in the Southwest."
[54] Hershkowitz, "By Chance or Choice: Jews in New Amsterdam 1654."
[55] Hershkowitz, "By Chance or Choice: Jews in New Amsterdam 1654."
[56] Hershkowitz, "New Amsterdam's Twenty-Three Jews," pp. 176–177.
[57] Israel, *The Dutch Republic*, p. 658.
[58] Hershkowitz, "By Chance or Choice: Jews in New Amsterdam 1654," p. 9.
[59] Jacobs, *New Netherland: A Dutch Colony in Seventeenth-Century America*, p. 374; Friedman, *Jews and the American Slave Trade*, p. 105.
[60] Corwin, *Ecclesiastical Records*, 1: pp. 335-336.
[61] Jacobs, *Een zegenrijk gewest*, p. 318.
[62] Hershkowitz, "By Chance or Choice: Jews in New Amsterdam 1654," p. 9.
[63] Gehring, *Council Minutes*, 1655-1656, pp. 261-262; Gehring, *Correspondence*, 1654-1658, p. 93; Gehring, *Laws and Writs of Appeal*, pp. 50-51
[64] Oppenheim, "Jacob Barsimon," pp. 39, 40.
[65] Jacobs, *New Netherland: A Dutch Colony in Seventeenth-Century America*, pp. 374-377.
[66] Hershkowitz,"By Chance or Choice: Jews in New Amsterdam 1654," p. 9; Williams, "'Abominable Religion,'" p. 90.
[67] Hershkowitz, "New Amsterdam's Twenty-Three Jews," p. 176.
[68] Hershkowitz, "By Chance or Choice: Jews in New Amsterdam 1654," p. 10.
[69] Hershkowitz, "Original Inventories of Early New York Jews (1682–1763)," p. 244; Shorto, *The Island at the Center of the World*, p. 300; Friedman, *Jews and the American Slave Trade*, p. 105; Hershkowitz, "New Amsterdam's Twenty-Three Jews," pp. 179–180; Hershkowitz, "By Chance or Choice: Jews in New Amsterdam 1654", p. 10.
[70] Hershkowitz, *Chance or Choice*, p. 1.
[71] Hershkowitz, "New Amsterdam's Twenty-Three Jews'," p. 174.
[72] Shorto, *The Island at the Center of the World*, p. 311.
[73] Hershkowitz, *Original Inventories of Early New York Jews*, p. 3.
[74] Phelps Stokes, *The Iconography of Manhattan Island*.
[75] Den Heijer, *De geschiedenis van de WIC*, p. 35.
[76] Wiznitzer, "The Synagogue and Cemetery of the Jewish Community", pp.127-130.
[77] Den Heijer, *De geschiedenis van de WIC*, p. 91.
[78] Hershkowitz, "By Chance or Choice: Jews in New Amsterdam 1654," p. 3.
[79] Hershkowitz, "By Chance or Choice: Jews in New Amsterdam 1654," p. 3.

III

CHAPTER 3

The Africans

Numerous New Netherlanders do not come to the colony of their own free will: they are the Africans. Almost every newcomer among the first generations of Africans arrives in the colony as a slave. The resulting African community is almost as diverse as the European one. They come from various areas on Africa's west coast: the present Ghana, Congo, Angola and São Tomé.
The slaves of New Amsterdam are mostly seized from Spanish and Portuguese ships. The WIC, which becomes involved in the slave trade as of the 1630s, does not set out specifically to transport slaves to New Netherland. The reason for this is that African slaves fetch much higher prices in the Caribbean and Spanish America. Moreover, New Netherland is not organized for large-scale plantation agriculture, as are South and Central America, where indeed slavery is considered much more necessary.
The first free black communities in North America come into existence during the Dutch period. This chapter describes how they are formed, which developments precede them, and how the slaves and free black population live together with the other inhabitants of the colony.

Slaves and their Names

Garcia d'Angola, Paulo d'Angola, Lucie d'Angola, Anthony van Angola, Laurens van Angola and Catalina van Angola; these were the inhabitants of New Amsterdam, with names betraying their country of origin and just how "voluntarily" they came to the new colony.

African names were too difficult for the European slaveholders, so after they were bought the slaves were given a European name. No one was concerned about the fact that this was a violation of their original identity. The new name usually consisted of a European first name and a surname indicating the country of origin, such as Simon Congo. There were also slaves with the surname San Thomé, from the Portuguese island where many slaves, particularly Angolans, worked on the sugar plantations.

The particles "d'" and "van," the Portuguese and Dutch variants, alternate in these names. D'Angola was gradually corrupted and became Van Angola.

The first names also reflect the international nature of the trade: Garcia, Paulo, Anthony and Laurens.

The Portuguese influence on the names of the slaves slowly diminished, and they were increasingly given Dutch last names. Sometimes the slave took on the family name of the owner. This explains why there are still African Americans with surnames like Van Buren and De Vries (DeFreese). There were also cases in which the owner chose the first name of a newborn child. When Emanuel Neger had his twins baptized, they were named Adam and Eve.[1]

The City of Luanda in Angola
Johannes Vingboons, third quarter of the seventeenth century
Nationaal Archief (National Archives of the Netherlands), The Hague
4.VELH 619-063
Watercolor on paper, 44.5 x 63 cm

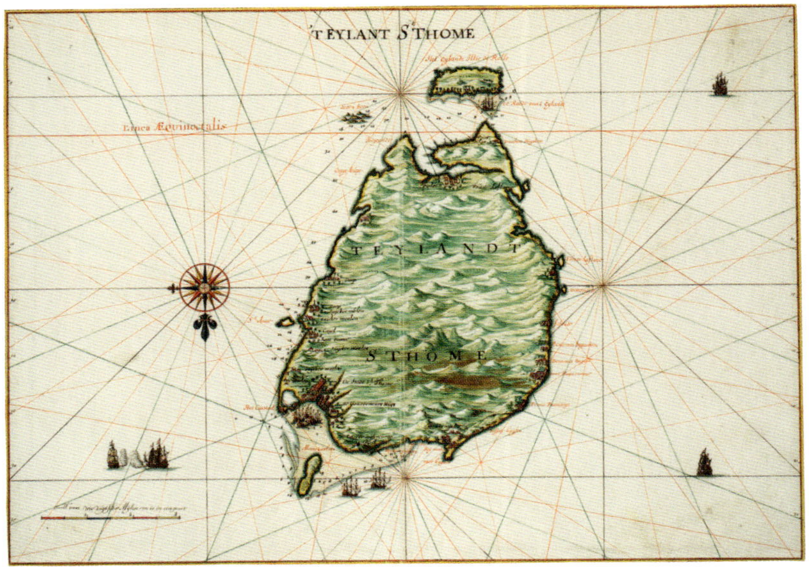

Slave Island São Tomé
Johannes Vingboons, third quarter of the seventeenth century
Nationaal Archief (National Archives of the Netherlands), The Hague
4.VELH 619-102
Watercolor on paper, 44.5 x 61 cm

The First New Amsterdammers from Africa

Numbers and Origins

The first slaves arrived fairly soon after the founding of New Amsterdam, probably as early as 1626. In 1630, six years after the coming of the first colonists, about 300 Europeans and at most 20 Africans were living in the settlement and the immediate surroundings. By 1639 this figure had risen to about 100 Africans. Towards the middle of the seventeenth century the black men and women of New Amsterdam made up ten percent of the total population. An unknown proportion of them consisted of free inhabitants. It is estimated that towards the end of the Dutch administration there were 500 to 600 slaves and free inhabitants of African origin in New Netherland. In the city of New Amsterdam there were 300 to 400 black inhabitants of whom probably less than 100 were free.[2]

Sometimes the surnames of the slaves tell us where they came from. This is obvious in the cases of Garcia and Paulo d'Angola, Simon Congo and Pieter San Thomé. With Manuel de Gerrit de Reus (Manuel Gerrit the Giant), Manuel de Groot and Cleyn Manuel (Big Manuel and Little Manuel), it is the name Manuel that indicates they were Africans who acquired their European name from the Portuguese and Spanish. The name of Anthony Portugis, who was later called Anthony de Portugees by the Dutch, suggests a similar background. It gets trickier with Jan Creoly and Jan Francisco. Did the latter Jan work previously on the Rio Francisco in Brazil, for instance, or did the Spanish give him that name? The same applies to Jan Fort Oranje. This Jan may have come from Fort Oranje (Fort Orange) in Dutch Brazil or from a fort with the same name at the Dutch trading post Sekondi on the coast of West Africa.

Why Slaves?

Part of the slave population had thus landed in New Netherland more or less "by chance," but that did not mean they could avoid being put to work as slaves. There were two reasons for this. The first is obvious: like other European overseas powers and African rulers, the Dutch made use of slaves as cheap labor. The second reason had to do with the chronic shortage of manpower in the new colony. Slaves were used in particular for digging and hauling for the construction of the fort and of roads; for building houses; for chopping wood; and for clearing land.[3]

As mentioned above, in the early years there were only a few dozen slaves in the colony. Accordingly, their share in the building of New Amsterdam was limited. In the 1630s the number of slaves gradually grew. As of 1637 the WIC took an active part in the Atlantic slave trade, concentrating on acquiring slaves for the sugar plantations in Dutch Brazil. In the early 1630s the first private investors prepared to cultivate and populate large tracts of land in New Netherland came forward. The WIC leased the land out in the hope that the colony would become more densely populated. To make it more attractive for the financiers, the patroons were allowed to have slaves and the Company even promised in the *Vryheden en Exemptiën* (Charter of Liberties and Exemptions) that it would try to supply the patroons with slaves. There is no evidence, however, that the Company succeeded in doing so.[4]

There was always work to be done in New Netherland and there was always a shortage of manpower. Yet, in contrast to other Dutch colonies such as Dutch Brazil, Suriname or on the Caribbean islands, this did not lead to a large slave economy. The chief reason for this was that in New Netherland there was no large-scale plantation agriculture, whereas there was in the other colonies. To be sure, there were tobacco plantations, but the climate in this region was too cold to cultivate high quality tobacco. While towards the end of Dutch rule the value of tobacco exports approached that of beaver pelts, the profits they brought probably remained small. This is why the patroons and the farmers had to achieve a substantial turnover before they could afford slaves. A slave was an expensive purchase and thus a valuable possession. In the 1650s a slave cost between 140 and 375 guilders. Later the demand for slaves in New Netherland increased and prices rose. In 1664 a slave cost some 600 guilders.[5]

As New Amsterdam had not developed into an important market for the slave traders, the best slaves were not taken there. At least, that is what the slave owners in New Netherland thought. According to them, the high-value slaves were put on sale at the Curaçao market.

As noted, high profits had to be made in order to own slaves, and for a long time that was not the situation in New Netherland. Slave labor was deployed mainly for the Company, which did not have the means to bring large numbers of slaves from West Africa to New Netherland. Nonetheless, it was the Company that "employed" the most slaves. For farmers and colonists with other businesses, it was not common to own slaves. In 1655 only 12 percent of private individuals owned a slave. Later in the seventeenth century the proportion of slave owners rose to 41 percent. Most of them used slave labor for work in the fields or domestic tasks.[6]

SQUARE NORTH
BROADWAY
DOWNTOWN

Manuel de Groot and Manuel de Gerrit de Reus

From Slaves to Landowners

The first slaves arrived in Manhattan in 1626. There were 11 of them and most had Portuguese names, such as Paulo d'Angola, Simon Congo, Anthony Portugis, John Francisco and Garcia d'Angola. Three were called Manuel, and to tell them apart the Dutch named them Manuel Groot (Big Manuel), Manuel Minuit (Little Manuel) and Manuel de Gerrit de Reus (Giant Manuel).[7] who probably belonged to Gerrit de Reux, a colonial settler in the 1620s and 1630s. This Manuel is sometimes confused with Manuel Groot, or Big Manuel, who was later simply called De Groot. As a result, the extraordinary story of the unsuccessful execution of Manuel de Gerrit de Reus (Giant Manuel) is sometimes mistakenly attributed to Big Manuel.

When in 1641 the slave Jan Premero was murdered, eight slaves, including Giant Manuel, made a group confession to the murder. They drew lots to decide which of the eight would be hanged and Giant Manuel was left with the short straw. The gallows was prepared. A double noose was placed around Manuel's neck. He climbed the steps and the hangman pushed him off the edge. But both nooses broke, Manuel fell safely to the ground. The crowd called for mercy: this had to be a sign from God. Manuel was set free.[8]

The first slaves were given their own plots to farm in 1643, during the war against the Indians. The 130 acres of the black community's fields and grazing land lay about a mile to the north of New Amsterdam.

In 1644 Manuel de Gerrit de Reus was granted about 12 acres while Manuel de Groot was given eight.[9] and was still living there 20 years later. His widow Christina inherited the property, as recorded in a 1667 document signed by the new British governor. Richard Nicolls.

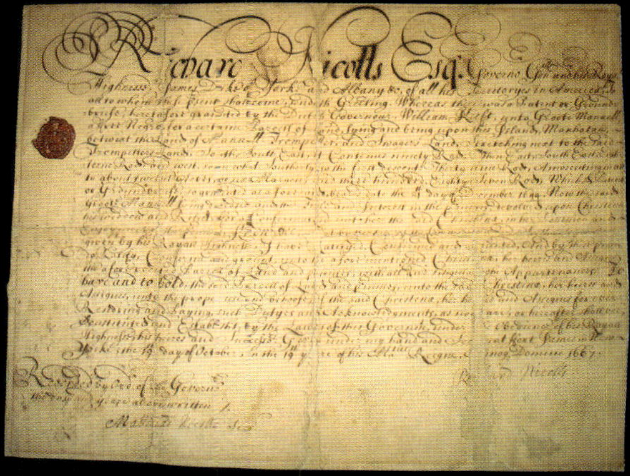

Christina Inherits the Property of Manuel de Groot, 1667
Mark E. Mitchell Collection of African American History
Free Man Institute, Gambrills, Maryland

The text of the document reads as follows:

"... Whereas there was a Patent or Groundbriefe, heretofore graunted by the Dutch Governour, William Kieft, unto Groote Manuell, a Free Negro, for a certaine Parcell of Land, lying and being upon this Island Manhatan, betwixt the Lands of Manuell Trompetter, and Swagers Land [...] graunted as aforesaid, beares date the 21th day of December 1644. Now the said Groote Manuell, being deceased, and the Title and Interest in the premises, devolved upon Christina his widdow and Relict; [...] To have and to hold, the said Parcell of Land and premisses, unto the said Christina, her heires and Assignes, unto the proper use and behoofe, of the said Christina, her heires and Assignes for ever: Rendering and Paying, such Dutyes and Acknowledgments, as now are, or hereafter shall bee, Constituted and Established, by the Lawes of this Governm't, under the Obedience of his Royall Highness, his heires and Successors: Given under my hand & Seale, at Fort James in New Yorke, the 19th day of October, in the 19th yeare of his Ma'ties. Reigne, Anno. Domini 1667. Richard Nicolls

Recorded by Ord. Of the Governo'r. the Day and yeare above written.
Matthias Nicolls Secr'y"

Photo of Washington Park Square, where Manuel de Groot lived

Frank Ligtvoet, born 1954 Rotterdam
Nanne Dekking, born 1960 The Hague,
Joshua 2004 and Rosa Marie 2006
In New York since 1996

Merchants, Slaves and Tobacco

This is one of the few images depicting slaves in New Amsterdam.[10] On the left is a woman with a basket, on the right a merchant holding tobacco leaves. On the ground lie tobacco leaves rolled together. The man and woman are portrayed in an almost identical fashion in another image, but then as planters on Barbados and with a different background. The publisher of the print kept the foreground and changed the background, probably to save time or money during production. Several slaves have been added in the version shown here.

Detail of "Nieu Amsterdam" (New Amsterdam), ca. 1640

"Nieu Amsterdam" (New Amsterdam), ca. 1640
New York Public Library, New York
ID: 54671
Engraving, 18.8 x 24.9 cm

Beads for People

A WIC order book, with an example of the blue beads that the factor of the Elmina trading post ordered from his home base in Amsterdam pasted into it, as if to say: "Another large shipment of these blue glass beads, please."
These beads were used for making payments to local slave traders who supplied slaves from the hinterlands of Africa. Yet beads and mirrors were not the goods used most often for barter. Trading was usually done with cowrie shells and textiles such as Indian silk and cotton. Other articles were used as payment, such as pearls, cutlery, iron, lead and alcohol. The Dutch ships generally had barter goods on board worth 25,000 to 60,000 guilders when they sailed for Africa's west coat to stock up on slaves.[11]
In the interior Africans were actively engaged in recruiting slaves. This was done in various ways. At times they enticed people to the coast under false pretences. Some slave dealers stole or bought people who had already been enslaved by others. People were taken as slaves during tribal wars. The African buyers took them to the coast for sale to European slave traders.

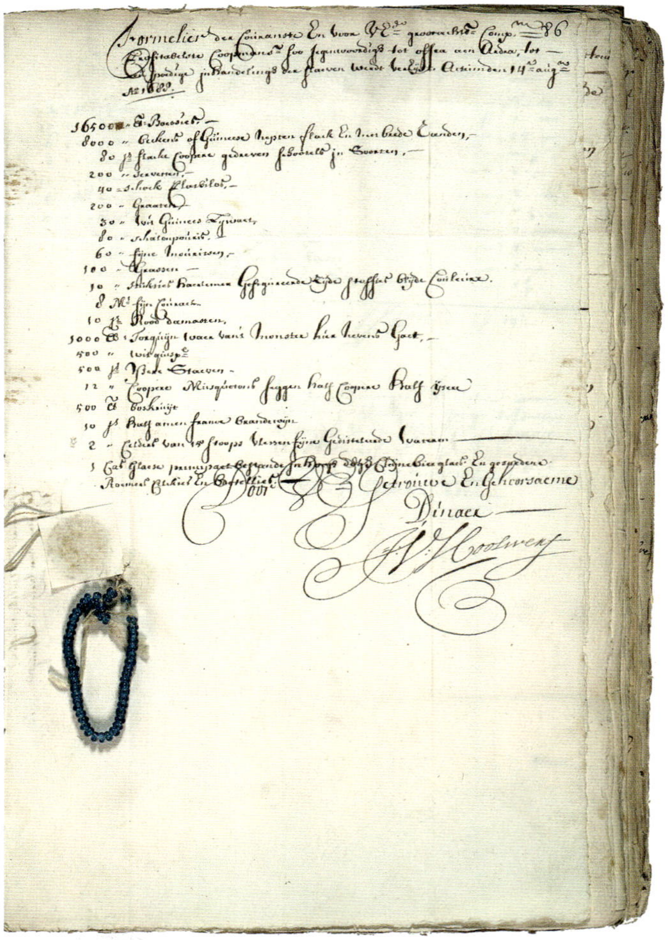

WIC order book, 1639
Nationaal Archief (National Archives of the Netherlands), The Hague
WIC, 1.05.01.02, inv. no. 180
Ink on paper, 32.5 x 20 cm

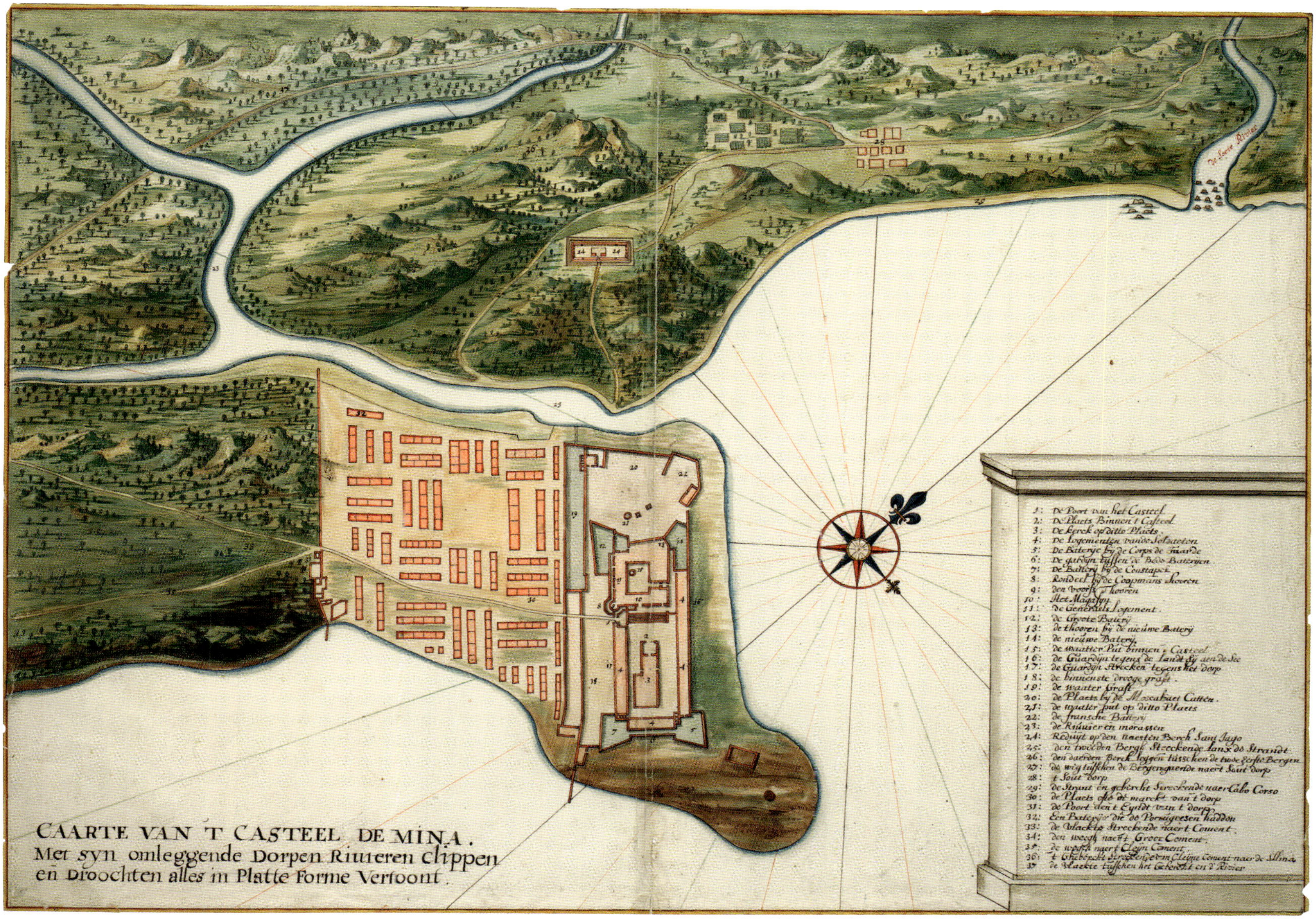

Map of Elmina, Ghana
Johannes Vingboons, third quarter of the seventeenth century
Nationaal Archief (National Archives of the Netherlands), The Hague
4.VELH 619-077
Watercolor on paper, 44.5 x 62 cm

On arrival at the coast the slaves were locked up in a "depot" in a fort. This fort is clearly visible in this map of seventeenth-century Elmina in Ghana. Elmina was the largest slave depot the Dutch had. The fort was captured from the Portuguese in 1637 and handed over to the English in 1872. Even today there are still many reminders of the Dutch period: a cemetery, some houses, and Ghanaians named Deveer, Zwennes and Van Dyke.[12]

The slave ships could anchor right by the fort. The slaves were rowed from the fort to the ships in small sloops. The little door that has come to be known as "the point of no return" is notorious. Once through it, there was no way back. The long wait began while still on board. Not waiting for the two-month long voyage, but rather until the ship was fully loaded. That process could take weeks, even months. The ship sailed back and forth along the coast until the hold was full. After all, hundreds of people had to be collected. The shackled slaves sat crammed together in the dark. To dispel the worst smells the people were sprinkled with vinegar. By the time they had made it to the other side of the ocean, on average 16 percent of the slaves had died through malnutrition and illness.[13]

View of Elmina, Ghana
Johannes Vingboons, third quarter of the seventeenth century
Nationaal Archief (National Archives of the Netherlands), The Hague
4.VELH 619-075
Watercolor on paper, 42.5 x 53 cm

From our point of view, this whole process is both inhuman and incomprehensible, but until the beginning of the nineteenth century millions of people were shipped in this way from the west coast of Africa to other parts of the world.

The WIC transported close to 273,000 slaves. The total number of slaves taken to America by Dutch shippers was about 530,000, between five and six percent of the total number of people shipped from Africa to the Americas.[14] The New Netherland colony played but a relatively modest role in the slave trade: during the approximately 50 years of Dutch control, “only” about 600 slaves were brought in, half of them a few days before the takeover by the English.

The Islands and Mainlands of the West Indies
Johannes Vingboons, third quarter of the seventeenth century
Library of Congress, Geography and Map Division, Washington, D.C.
G3291.S12 coll .H3 Vault: Harr vol. 1, map 1
Paper, 48 x 69 cm

The slaves who ended up in New Netherland were not generally brought to the New World by Dutch slave ships, as was the case with Curaçao and later Suriname. As a rule they were captured by the Dutch from Portuguese and Spanish slave ships in the Caribbean. Sometimes they were Africans who had been born in South or Central America or long worked in the Atlantic area. A few had earlier worked as free men. At any rate some of the slaves had long left their native district in Africa before they arrived in New Netherland. As a result of their time spent in South America or the Caribbean islands, they had often adopted customs that were current in those regions, and had become familiar with other languages and religions.[15]

Slaves in New Netherland

Although the Dutch Republic played a substantial role in the international slave trade of the seventeenth century, this was much less so when New Netherland was being developed. The first slaves came to Manhattan via the Caribbean. They had been captured from Spanish and Portuguese slave ships. It was not until 1654 that the first consignment of slaves coming directly from Africa arrived. After that only few more attempts were made to organize a direct slave trade with Africa. In August 1664, a few days before the English takeover of Manhattan, the *Gideon* arrived with 290 slaves from Angola on board. In a single go this virtually doubled the number of slaves.[16] The slaves' tasks included woodcutting, clearing land, burning lime and working the land. They also transported the stones needed to build the church in the fort. This was the church in which slaves too and free blacks would baptize their children and solemnize their marriages. The Company slaves lived in "the quarter of the black Company slaves", as indicated by the letter "F" in the legend.

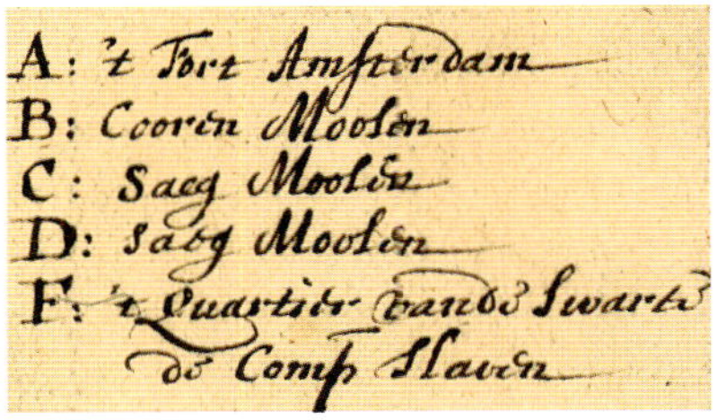

Detail of the "Manatus Map' (see pp. 190-191)

Integration in the Early Society of Manhattan

The men and women of African origin in a sense integrated into the colonial society. They adopted Dutch names and celebrated Dutch holidays. The most important step in assimilating was participation in the church community. In itself it is not surprising that the Africans turned to the Protestant Church. Part of the African population in Manhattan came from Portuguese and Spanish colonies, where they had already come into contact with Christianity. In the church at New Amsterdam their marriages were registered and their newborn baptized. The first known baptism of a black child was that of Barent Jan. His father was Pieter St. Anthony. The name of the mother is not given, but the witnesses include three blacks: Dominco Anthony, Jan Francoys and Susanna D'Angola.[17]

The baptismal registers reveal that quite a few children from the black community were baptized in the church. Were these the children of slaves or of free inhabitants of the city? This is not immediately apparent from the registers. In 1655 the baptisms suddenly stopped. A possible explanation is found in a letter of 1660 by Reverend Henricus Selijns. In contrast to his predecessors, particularly Everardus Bogardus, he did not consider requests for baptisms from black parents. He was of the opinion that they had to demonstrate that they understood the faith properly and that they were true believers in Protestantism. This was not usually the case. He feared that as a result the parents would not be able to raise their offspring in the Protestant faith. According to Article 35 of the Synod of 1629, Selijns was right about that. The Synod stated that the children of unbaptized heathens should themselves not be baptized without careful and extensive initiation in the fundamentals of Christianity, and that of course was impossible if they had only just been born.

Selijns had a second argument for being sparing with baptisms. Many parents wanted their children to become free. They tried to accomplish this by having them baptized; after all, Christians could not be slaves. Besides the theological arguments, another factor was the hardening of the attitudes of Europeans to other ethnic groups in the second half of the seventeenth century, not only in the Dutch colonies but elsewhere as well. The non-baptizing of black children was an element in this.[18]

People were married as well as baptized in the church. The first documented black marriage was that of Lucie D'Angola and Anthony van Angola. Lucie was the widow of Laurens van Angola and Anthony was the widower of Catalina van Angola. They married in 1641. In the next ten years more followed. Given their relative freedom of movement, the slaves in New Netherland were able to find a marriage partner for themselves, although it is likely that the slave owner's permission had to be obtained before the marriage was solemnized. Despite the baptisms and marriages, there were hardly any Africans who were official members of the church. The standards for knowledge of the faith were set too high for that. Only Susanna Negrin is known to have been admitted as a member before 1660.[19]

Half Citizens

Slaves with Rights

Legally speaking, the slaves in New Netherland had a right of ownership, which was inconceivable in many other colonies. Another privilege rarely found elsewhere was the protection of slaves against abuse by their masters. The fact that private individuals owned slaves did not mean that they could chastise their property at will. They were required to obtain permission from the city government if they wanted to punish their slaves. The most notable legislation that was favorable to slaves and free blacks, as compared to the position in other colonies, had to do with the administration of justice. The testimony of slaves was declared valid in law, and slaves were allowed to institute legal proceedings against others, whether slave or free. In a number of cases it appears that in determining the sentence no distinction was made between blacks and whites.[20]

Some slaves even obtained their freedom. Due to population increase, grants of freedom, buying out and escape from the English colonies, the black community – including indentured and freed slaves – grew considerably. In the middle of the seventeenth century the free black farmers owned plots of land near the area that is now Washington Square Park. Usually they had some cattle, a couple of goats or sheep and a garden. The amount of land they owned varied between seven and twelve acres. The area was known as "the black quarter" and lay about a mile north of New Amsterdam. It was there that the first free black community of African origin in North America arose.[21]

As we have seen, slavery in New Netherland, compared with slavery elsewhere, was relatively mild, if slavery can ever be mild. While some slaves were freed – either by his owner, or by the Company – most black inhabitants of the colony remained slaves and others continued to be brought in. The white community did not fully accept the blacks. In their eyes their black neighbors were no more than second-class citizens.

Second-Class Citizens and Half Freedom

Freedom or no freedom, a black man or woman was held in low regard by the white population. The nastiest jobs, such as that of executioner, were given to the black New Netherlanders. White criminals were sometimes punished by being made to work with Company slaves. An ordinance issued in 1642 laid down that whoever drew his knife to wound another had to pay 50 guilders at once or be put to work for three months with blacks in chains.[22]

Whites were forbidden to have sexual relations with Indians or black inhabitants. Those caught were punished. A white sergeant guilty of having an affair with a black woman was demoted to the rank of private. Other white men found themselves in prison or were condemned to forced labor beside slaves. Even though in law no distinction was made between white and black, it is clear from various sources that black people were not regarded as equals. Even when they were free, they remained in the underclass of this colonial society. Although the black community managed to earn a decent living from farming, lack of respect, money, education and training prevented them from working their way up and being seen as fully accepted members of society.[23]

Friends of the Black Population: Van der Donck and Bogardus

We have seen that neither the slave nor the free black man was considered an equal citizen of the colony. While almost none of the white citizens would have thought differently, this does not mean that there were no white colonists who stood up for the slaves or the free blacks.

One of them was Minister Everardus Bogardus. The minister, who had earlier worked for the WIC in Africa, encouraged black men and women to take part in the church services and to observe religious holidays. From September 1639, when the baptismal registers were begun, to August 1647, when Bogardus left New Amsterdam, he baptized 39 children of African origin. This is a substantial number given that there were about 100 Africans in the colony in 1639. It is not clear what his reasons for baptizing the children were. Was it really to make Christians of them? Whatever the case may have been, Bogardus certainly did stand up for the black community. In 1636, for instance, he asked the authorities via Director Van Twiller to send a schoolmaster “who could teach and improve both the Dutch and blacks in the knowledge of Jesus Christ.”[24] The present New York Collegiate School for Boys is convinced that the history of this institution can be traced back directly to the school where these pupils were taught.

The lawyer Adriaen van der Donck also took up the cause of the black families. In 1649 in his *Vertoogh van Nieu Nederland* (Remonstrance of New Netherland) he supported the freeing of the children of free parents. He argued that it was against the law for a child of a free Christian mother to remain a slave.

Stuyvesant and the Black Community

Peter Stuyvesant was the director not only of New Netherland, but also of the Caribbean island of Curaçao, which developed after the fall of Dutch Brazil into a transit port for slaves bound for Spanish America. From the 1650s the WIC followed a new, tougher policy towards the slaves. This was evident not only in New Netherland but elsewhere. The effect of the new policy was most noticeable in the church, where fewer and fewer slaves and free Africans were able to take part. In addition, from 1652 the Company allowed the colonists to import slaves directly into New Netherland.

In 1654 the merchants of Amsterdam prepared the ship *Witte Paert* (White Horse) to sail to Africa and from there transport slaves directly to New Netherland. A year later the ship brought a considerable number of slaves from the Gulf of Guinea. To prevent them from being sold outside the colony, Stuyvesant put an export tax of ten percent on each slave. Stuyvesant himself owned slaves on his farm; in fact, he was the biggest private slaveholder in New Netherland. This, though, says nothing about his attitude as a slave owner. There are various instances of his showing consideration to his slaves. When Stuyvesant sold a slave in 1664, he urged the buyer to also take the woman with whom the slave had a relationship, so that the couple could stay together. Sometimes he agreed to free slaves. In 1662 three elderly female slaves were given their freedom on condition that each in turn should do housekeeping work for him.[25]

Under the English Regime

In 1664 the English captured New Netherland. Stuyvesant’s last official act was to reach an agreement with the English that reconfirmed the ownership rights of slaves under the new regime. The English quickly granted harbor privileges and warehouse priorities to companies engaged in the slave trade. Not long thereafter, in 1665, the English wanted to know what the status was of the free blacks and the land they owned. Stuyvesant confirmed the legitimate status of the black farmers’ land, consisting of some 30 farms.[26]

African Burial Ground

The first freed slaves had been given a piece of land on the "common wagon road" north of New Amsterdam to clear and cultivate. The settlement made up partly of free black farmers and landowners and partly of slaves had developed there, not far from Stuyvesant's farm. Between the settlement and New Amsterdam, slightly north of where the New York Town Hall now stands, there was a small burial ground, where interments took place until well into the eighteenth century. This burial ground was one of the first black institutions.

In 1991 the graveyard, which became well known later as the African Burial Ground, was discovered during construction work. Archeological research was carried out, but it became surrounded in controversy. Many members of the black community in New York thought that the excavations were not being done with sufficient care or reverence. The remains of over 400 men, women and children have been found; slightly less than half were children. It is estimated that from the end of the seventeenth to the end of the eighteenth century, when the burial ground was closed, between 10,000 and 19,000 people were buried here. Some of their graves still lie under streets and buildings.[27]

Two Moors
Rembrandt van Rijn, 1661
Mauritshuis, The Hague
Oil on canvas, 77.8 x 64.4 cm
Inv. no. 685

[1] Berlin and Harris, *Slavery in New York*, p. 52; Jacobs, "Van Angola naar Manhattan," p. 72.
[2] Jacobs, *New Netherland: A Dutch Colony in Seventeenth-Century America*, p. 313.
[3] Wagman, "Corporate Slavery in New Netherland," pp. 34-35.
[4] *Vryheden en exemptien*, art. 30.
[5] Jacobs, "Van Angola naar Manhattan," p. 70.
[6] Jacobs, "Van Angola naar Manhattan," p. 70.
[7] Harris, *In the Shadow of Slavery*, pp. 18-19.
[8] Jacobs, "Van Angola naar Manhattan," p. 69.
[9] Gehring, Council Minutes 1638-1649., pp. 97-100; Dodson et al., *The Black New Yorkers*, p. 23.
[10] Phelps Stokes, *The Iconography of Manhattan Island*, pp. 140-142; http://www.nypl.org/research/chss/spe/art/print/exhibits/drydrunk/travel.htm, website consulted on 10 January 2009.
[11] Emmer, *De Nederlandse slavenhandel*, pp. 76-77.
[12] Gosselink, *Land in Zicht*, p. 13.
[13] Jacobs, "Van Angola naar Manhattan," p. 45; Emmer, *De Nederlandse slavenhandel*, p. 83.
[14] Jacobs, "Van Angola naar Manhattan", pp. 15-16 gives 5 percent for the Dutch share, whereby the WIC and privately-held ships transported close to 550,000 slaves in the seventeenth and eighteenth century.
[15] Thornton and Heywood, *Central Africans*.
[16] Swan, "Slaves and Slaveholding in Dutch New York," pp. 67-68; Jacobs, "Van Angola naar Manhattan," p. 70.
[17] Evans and Wright, *Records of the Reformed Dutch Church in New Amsterdam and New York*, p. 10.
[18] Frijhoff, *Fulfilling God's Mission*, pp. 539-546.
[19] Swan, "Slaves and Slaveholding," p. 58.
[20] Jacobs, "Van Angola naar Manhattan," pp. 72-75.
[21] Berlin and Harris, *Slavery in New York*, pp. 45-47.
[22] Van Laer, *Council Minutes*, 1638-1649, p. 151.
[23] Jacobs, *Een zegenrijk gewest*, p. 232.
[24] NA 1.05.01.01 inv. no. 051 doc. 028; Frijhoff, *Fulfilling God's Mission*, pp. 542-543.
[25] Jacobs, "Van Angola naar Manhattan," pp. 70 and 72.
[26] Berlin and Harris, *Slavery in New York*, pp. 53-56.
[27] Frohne, *The African Burial Ground in New York City*; Cantwell and di Zerega Wall, *Unearthing Gotham*, pp. 277-204.

Modern

Algra, A., and H. Algra. "Dispereert niet". *Twintig eeuwen historie van de Nederlanden*, I and V. 8th ed. Franeker, 1978.

Bachman, Van Cleaf. *Peltries or Plantation: The Economic Policies of the Dutch West India Company in New Netherland, 1623-1639*. Baltimore, 1969.

Berlin, Ira and Leslie M. Harris, ed. *Slavery in New York*. New York, 2005.

Bogardus, W. B. *"Dear Cousin". A Charted Genealogy of the Descendants of Anneke Jans Bogardus (1605-1663) to the 5th Generation*. Wilmington, 1996.

Bracht, J. van, and G. Schilder. *The Origins of New York*. Zurich, 1988.

Brake, W. te, and W. Klooster, ed. *Power and the city in the Netherlandic world*. Leiden, 2006.

Bruijn, J. R. et al. *Dutch-Asiatic Shipping in the 17th and 18th centuries II Outward-bound voyages from the Netherlands to Asia and the Cape (1595-1794)*. The Hague, 1979.

Cantwell, Anne-Marie, Diane di Zerega Wall. *Unearthing Gotham: The Archaeology of New York City*. New Haven, 2001.

Cohen, D. S., "How Dutch were the Dutch of New Netherland." *New York History Quarterly Journal of New York State Historical Association*, 62 (1981), pp. 43-60.

Cohen, Paul E., and Robert T. Augustyn. *Manhattan in Maps, 1527-1995*. New York, 1997.

Condon, Thomas J. *New York Beginnings: The Commercial Origins of New Netherland*. New York, 1968.

Craig, Peter Stebbins. "Chronology of Colonial Swedes on the Delaware 1638-1713." *Swedish Colonial News* 2 (2001) 5, pp. 12-15.

Daalder, Remmelt, Andrea Kieskamp and Dirk J. Tang, ed. *Slaven en Schepen. Enkele reis, bestemming onbekend*. Amsterdam, 2001.

Dodson, Howard, Christopher G. Moore and Roberta Yancy, ed. *The Black New Yorkers: The Schomberg Illustrated Chronology*. 2d ed. New York, 2000.

Eekhof, Albert. *Bastiaen Jansz. Krol, krankenbezoeker, kommies en kommandeur van Nieuw-Nederland*. The Hague, 1910.

Eekhof, Albert. *Jonas Michaëlius. Founder of the Church in New Netherland*. Leiden, 1926.

Emmer, P. C. *De Nederlandse slavenhandel 1500-1850*. 3d ed. Amsterdam, 2007.

Forest, Mrs. Robert W. de. *A Walloon family in America; Lockwood de Forest and his forbears 1500-1848*. Boston and New York, 1914.

Frijhoff, Willem. *Wegen van Evert Willemsz. Een Hollands Weeskind op zoek naar zichzelf*. Nijmegen, 1995.

Frijhoff, Willem. "Neglected Networks: Director Willem Kieft (1602-1647) and his Dutch Relatives." In Joyce D. Goodfriend, ed. *Revisiting New Netherland*. Leiden and Boston, 2005.

Frijhoff, Willem. *Fullfilling God's Mission: The Two Worlds of Dominie Everardus Bogardus, 1607-1647*. Leiden, 2007.

Frijhoff, Willem. "Dutchness in Fact and Fiction." In Joyce D. Goodfriend, ed. *Going Dutch: The Dutch Presence in America 1609-2009*. Leiden and Boston, 2008.

Frohne, Andrea E. *The African Burial Ground in New York City: Manifesting and Representing Spirituality of Space*. Ph.D. dissertation, Binghamton University, State University of New York, 2002.

Friedman, Saul S. *Jews and the American Slave Trade*. New Brunswick and London, 1998.

Gaastra, F. S. *De geschiedenis van de VOC*. Haarlem, 1982.

Gehring, Charles T. "Peter Minuit's Purchase of Manhattan Island - New Evidence." *de Halve Maen* 55 (1980-1981) 1, pp. 6-7, 17.

Goldman, Shalom, ed. *Hebrew and the Bible in America*. Hanover, New Hampshire, 1993.

Goodfriend, Joyce D. "Writing/Righting Dutch Colonial History." *New York History* 80 (January 1999), pp. 5-28.

Goodfriend, Joyce D., ed. *Revisiting New Netherland*. Leiden and Boston, 2005.

Goodfriend, Joyce D. "Struggle over the Sabbath." In W. te Brake and W. Klooster, ed. *Power and the city in the Netherlandic world*. Leiden, 2006.

Goodfriend, Joyce D., ed. *Going Dutch: The Dutch Presence in America 1609-2009*. Leiden and Boston, 2008.

Gosselink, Martine. *Land in Zicht. Vingboons tekent de wereld van de 17e eeuw*. Zwolle, 2007.

Griswold van Rensselaer, Mariana. *History of the City of New York in the Seventeenth Century*, I *New Amsterdam*. New York, 1909.

Groesen, M. van. *The representations of the overseas world in the De Bry collection of voyages (1590-1634)*. Leiden and Boston, 2008.

Hart, Simon. "De stadskolonie Nieuwer-Amstel aan de Delaware-river in Noord-Amerika." *Maandblad Amstelodamum* 38 (1951), pp. 89-94.

Harris, Leslie M. *In the Shadow of Slavery: African Americans in New York City, 1626-1863*. Chicago, 2003.

Heijer, Henk den. *De geschiedenis van de WIC*. 2d ed. Zutphen, 2002.

Hershkowitz, Leo. "New Amsterdam's Twenty-Three Jews — Myth or Reality." In Shalom Goldman, ed. *Hebrew and the Bible in America*. Hanover, New Hampshire, 1993, pp. 172–173.

Hershkowitz, Leo. "Original Inventories of Early New York Jews (1682–1763)." *American Jewish History* 90 (September 2002), pp. 239-322.

Hershkowitz, Leo. "By Chance or Choice: Jews in New Amsterdam 1654." *The American Jewish Archives Journal* 57 (2005) 1, pp. 1-13.

Israel, Jonathan I. *Dutch Primacy in World Trade, 1585-1740*. Oxford, 1989.

Israel, Jonathan I. *The Dutch Republic. Its Rise, Greatness, and Fall 1477-1806*. Oxford, 1995.

Jacobs, Jaap. "The Hartford Treaty: A European Perspective on a New World Conflict." *de Halve Maen* 68 (1995), pp. 74-79.

Jacobs, Jaap. "Between Repression and Approval: Connivance and Tolerance in the Dutch Republic and in New Netherland." *de Halve Maen* 71 (1998) 3, pp. 51-58.

Jacobs, Jaap. *Een zegenrijk gewest. Nieuw-Nederland in de zeventiende eeuw*. Amsterdam, 1999.

Jacobs, Jaap. "Van Angola naar Manhattan. Slavernij in Nieuw-Nederland in de zeventiende eeuw." In Daalder, Remmelt, Andrea Kieskamp and Dirk J. Tang, ed. *Slaven en Schepen. Enkele reis, bestemming onbekend*. Amsterdam, 2001, pp. 69-75.

Jacobs, Jaap. "A Troubled Man: Director Wouter van Twiller and the Affairs of New Netherland in 1635." *New York History* 85 (2004), pp. 213-232.

Jacobs, Jaap. *New Netherland: A Dutch Colony in Seventeenth-Century America*. Leiden, 2005.

Jacobs, Jaap. "Incompetente autocraten? Bestuurlijke verhoudingen in de zeventiende-eeuwse Nederlandse Atlantische Wereld." *De zeventiende eeuw. Cultuur in de Nederlanden in interdisciplinair perspectief* 21 (2005), pp. 64-78.

Jacobs, Jaap. "'To Favor this New and Growing City of New Amsterdam with a Court of Justice.' The Relations between Rulers and Ruled in New Amsterdam." In George Harinck and Hans Krabbendam, ed. *Amsterdam - New York: Transatlantic Relations and Urban Identities Since 1653*. Amsterdam, 2005, pp. 17-29.

Jacobs, Jaap. "Like Father, Like Son? The early Years of Petrus Stuyvesant." In Joyce D. Goodfriend, ed. *Revisiting New Netherland*. Leiden and Boston, 2005, pp. 205-242.

Jacobs, Jaap. "Dutch Proprietary Manors in America: The Patroonships in New Netherland." In Lou Roper and Bertrand Van Ruymbeke, ed. *Constructing Early Modern Empires: Proprietary Ventures in the Atlantic World*. Leiden, 2007, pp. 301-326.

Jacobs, Jaap. "Migration, Population, and Government in New Netherland." In Hans Krabbendam, Cornelis A. van Minnen and Giles Scott-Smith, ed. *Four Centuries of Dutch-American Relations*. Amsterdam and Albany, forthcoming 2009.

Jameson, J. Franklin. *Narratives of New Netherland, 1609-1664*. New York, 1953.

Kammen, Michael. *Colonial New York: A History*. New York, 1975.

Koning, Joep de. "Dating the Visscher, or Prototype, View of New Amsterdam." *de Halve Maen* 2 (1999) 3, pp. 47.

Kupcík, Ivan. "Die kartografische Tätigkeit von Augustin Herman (ca. 1621-1686) – Realität und Fiktion." In *Mappae Antiquae Liber Amicorum Günter Schilder*. 't Goy-Houten, 2007, pp. 203-219.

Louhi, E. A. *The Delaware Finns or the First Permanent Settlements in Pennsylvania, Delaware, West New Jersey and Eastern Part of Maryland*. New York, 1925. Reprint Baltimore, 2001.

Meuwese, Mark P. *"For the peace and well-being of the country": Intercultural Mediators and Dutch-Indian Relations in New Netherland and Dutch Brazil, 1600-1664*. Ph.D. dissertation, Notre Dame University, Indiana, 2003.

Munroe, John A. *Colonial Delaware: A History*. Millwood, ca.1978.

Nierop, L. van. "Rensselaerswijck 1629-1704." *Tijdschrift voor Geschiedenis* 60 (1949), pp. 1-39 and 187-219.

O'Callaghan, E. B. *History of New Netherland; or, New York under the Dutch*. New York 1846-1848.

Oppenheim, Samuel. "More About Jacob Barsimon, the First Jewish Settler in New York." *Publications of the American Jewish Historical Society* 29 (1925), pp. 39-44.

Otto, Paul. *The Dutch-Munsee Encounter in America: The Struggle for Sovereignty in the Hudson Valley*. New York, 2006.

Phelps Stokes, Isaac Newton. *The Iconography of Manhattan Island 1498-1909*. New York 1915–1928. Reprint New York, 1967.

Rink, Oliver A. *Holland on the Hudson: An Economic and Social History of Dutch New York*. London and Ithaca, 1986.

Rink, Oliver A. "1629 A Year of Decision for New Netherland." *de Halve Maen* 72 (1999) 4, pp. 84 and 88.

Rothschild, Nan A. "De sociale afstand tussen Nederlandse kolonisten en inheemse Amerikanen." In A. van Dongen, ed. *One man's trash is another man's treasure*. Rotterdam, 1995. pp. 189-190.

Roever, N. de. *Kiliaen van Rensselaer en zijne kolonie Rensselaerswijck*. [S.L.], 1890.

Roper, Lou, and Bertrand van Ruymbeke, ed. *Constructing Early Modern Empires: Proprietary Ventures in the Atlantic World*. Leiden, 2007.

Ruymbeke, Bertrand Van. "The Walloon and Huguenot Elements in New Netherland and Seventeenth-Century New York: Identity, History and Memory." In Joyce D. Goodfriend, ed. *Revisiting New Netherland*. Leiden and Boston, 2005, pp. 41-54.

Schilder, G. "Van Nieuw-Amsterdam naar New York in kaarten. Nederlanders aan de Hudson." *Geografie, vaktijdschrift voor geografen* I (1992) 1, pp. 8-14.

Schulte Nordholt, J. W. "Nederlanders in Nieuw-Nederland. De oorlog van Kieft." *Bijdragen en Mededelingen van het Historisch Genootschap* 80 (1966), p. 60.

Shomette, D. and R. Haslach. *Raid on America: The Dutch Naval Campaign of 1672-1674*. Columbia, 1988.

Shorto, Russell. *Nieuw Amsterdam. Eiland in het hart van de wereld*. Amsterdam, 2004.

Shorto, Russell. *The Island at the Center of the World: The Untold Story of Dutch Manhattan and the Founding of New York*. 2d ed. London, 2005.

Spinoza Catella Jessurun, J. *Kiliaen van Rensselaer van 1623 tot 1636*. The Hague, 1917.

Swan, R. "Slaves and Slaveholding in Dutch New York, 1628-1664." *Journal of the Afro-American Historical and Genealogical Society* 17 (1998), pp. 51-58.

Temminck Groll, C. "Nieuw-Amsterdam (New York)." In idem, *The Dutch Overseas. An Architectural Survey*, Zwolle, 2002.

Thornton, John, and Linda Heywood. *Central Africans, Atlantic Creoles, and the Foundation of the Americas, 1585-1660*. Cambridge, 2007.

Venema, J. Beverwijck. *A Dutch Village on the American Frontier, 1652-1664*. Hilversum and New York, 2003.

Vrijman, L. C. *Kaapvaart en zeerooverij. Uit de geschiedenis der vrije nering in de Lage Landen*. Amsterdam, 1938.

Wagman, Morton. "Corporate Slavery in New Netherland." *Journal of Negro History* 65 (1980), pp. 34-35.

Waldman, Carl. *Atlas of the North American Indian*. New York, 1985.

Weslager, C. A. "Did Minuit Buy Manhattan Island from the Indians?" *de Halve Maen* 43 (1968) 3, pp. 5-6.

Wieder, F. C. "Onderzoek naar de oudste kaarten van de omgeving van New York." *Tijdschrift van het Koninklijk Nederlandsch Aardrijkskundig Genootschap*, 2d series, 35 (1918) 2, pp. 235-260.

Wieder, F. C. *Monumenta cartographica. Reproductions of unique and rare maps, plans and views in the actual size of the originals. Accompanied by cartographical monographs*, I. The Hague, 1925.

Wieder, F. C. *De Stichting van New York in juli 1625. Reconstructies en nieuwe gegevens ontleend aan de Van Rappard documenten*. The Hague, 1925.

Williams, James Homer. "'Abominable Religion' and Dutch (In)tolerance: The Jews and Petrus Stuyvesant." *de Halve Maen* 71 (1998) 4, pp. 85-90.

Wiznitzer, Arnold. "The Synagogue and Cemetery of the Jewish Community in Recife, Brazil (1630–1654)." *Publications of the American Jewish Historical Society (1893-1961)* 43 (1953), pp. 127-30.

Zabriskie, George Olin and Alice P. Kenney. "The Founding of New Amsterdam: Fact and Fiction." *de Halve Maen* 51 (1977) 4, pp. 11-12, 15-16.

Zabriskie, George Olin and Alice P. Kenney. "The Founding of New Amsterdam: Fact and Fiction." *de Halve Maen* 51(1976) 3, pp. 11-14.

Zabriskie, George Olin. "The Founding Families of New Netherland, No. 4 – The Rapalje-Rapelje Family," Part I. *de Halve Maen* 46 (1972) 4, p. 7.

Zabriskie, George Olin. "The Founding Families of New Netherland, No. 4 - The Rapalje-Rapelje Family," Part II. *de Halve Maen* 47 (1972) 1, pp. 7-8, 16.

Zabriskie, George Olin. "The Founding Families of New Netherland, No. 4 - The Rapalje-Rapelje Family," Part III. *de Halve Maen* 47 (1972) 2, pp. 11-12.

Zabriskie, George Olin. "Anneke Jans in Fact and Fiction." *The New York Genealogical and Biographical Record* 104 (1973) pp. 65-72, 157-164.

Zandvliet, Kees. *Mapping for Money: Maps, Plans and Topographic Paintings and their Role in Dutch Overseas Expansion During the 16th and 17th centuries*. Amsterdam, 1998.

Zandvliet, Kees. "Een ouderwetse kaart van Nieuw Nederland door Cornelis Doetsz. en Willem Jansz. Blaeu." *Caert Thresoor* I (1982) 4, pp. 57-60.

Websites

Chadwick, Ian. "Hudson's Background and Early Years": http://www.ianchadwick.com/hudson/hudson_00.htm, visited on 4 February 2009.

Koning, Joep de. "From Van der Donck to Visscher": http://web.archive.org/web/20030630211837/mercatorsworld.com/article.php3?i=75, visisted on 4 February 2009.

Charting the Chesapeake – Cartographers: http://www.msa.md.gov/msa/speccol/sc2200/sc2269/html/cartographers.html , visited on 4 February 2009.

New York Public Library. "Travel and Discovery": http://www.nypl.org/research/chss/spe/art/print/exhibits/drydrunk/travel.htm, visited on 10 January 2009.

Archives

Nationaal Archief (National Archives of the Netherlands), 1.11.01.01 [Aanwinsten] inv. no. 256 Dagboek Buchelius, ca. 1636.

Nationaal Archief (National Archives of the Netherlands), 1.01.07 [Staten-Generaal] 5484, Ingekomen stukken / Lias Admiraliteiten 1620, 12-2.

Nationaal Archief (National Archives of the Netherlands), 1.01.07 [Staten-Generaal] 5484, Ingekomen stukken / Lias Admiraliteiten 1620, 11-4.

Nationaal Archief (National Archives of the Netherlands), 1.05.01.01 [West-Indische Compagnie] inv. no. 051 doc. 028.

Nationaal Archief (National Archives of the Netherlands), *De Vryheden en Exemptiën* of 1650: Staten-Generaal, LWI, inv. no. 5755, ingekomen 1640, C.1047 ff.

Nationaal Archief (National Archives of the Netherlands), *De Vryheden en Exemptiën* of 1650: Staten-Generaal, Loketkas WIC, inv. no. 12564.30A.

Contemporary References

Breeden-Raedt aende Vereenichde Nederlandsche Provintien: Gelreland, Holland, Zeeland, Utrecht, Vriesland, Over-Yssel, Groeningen, gemaeckt ende gestelt uyt diverse waerachtige memorien door I.A.G.W.C. Antwerp,1649.

Laet, Johannes de. *Nieuwe wereldt ofte Beschrijvinghe van West-Indien*. Leiden, 1625.

Laet, Johannes de. *Beschryvinge van West-Indie*. 2d ed. Leiden, 1630.

Meteren, Emanuel van. *Belgische ofte Nederlantsche oorlogen ende gheschiedenissen: beginnende van t'iaer 1598 tot 1611 mede vervatende enighe haerder gebueren handelinghe*. [S.L.], 1611.

Wassenaer, Nicolaes à. *t'Achste deel of t' vervolch van het Historisch verhael aller gedencwaerdiger geschiedenißen, die [...] van octobri des jaers 1624. tot april, des jaers 1625*. voorgevallen syn. By dec 1624 en april 1625. Amsterdam, 1625.

Primary References

Asher, G. M., ed. *Henry Hudson the Navigator: The Original Documents in Which His Career is Recorded*. New York, 1860.

Corwin, E. T., ed. *Ecclesiastical Records. State of New York*, I. Albany, 1901-1916.

Dam, Pieter van. *Beschrijvinge van de Oostindische Compagnie*, I. The Hague, 1927.

Donck, Adriaen van der. *A Description of New Netherland*. Charles T. Gehring and William A. Starna, eds. Lincoln, 2008.

Edwards, Philip, ed. *Last Voyages: Cavendish, Hudson, Ralegh. The Original Narratives*. Oxford, 1988.

Engelbrecht, W. A., and P. J. van Herwerden. *De ontdekkingsreis van Jacob Le Maire en Willem Cornelisz. Schouten in de jaren 1615-1617*, II. The Hague, 1945.

Evans, Th. G., and T. A. Wright, eds. *Records of the Reformed Dutch Church in New Amsterdam and New York. Baptisms from 25 December 1639 to 29 December 1800*. Upper Saddle River, 1968.

Gehring, Charles T., ed. *Council Minutes, 1655-1656*. New York, 1995.

Gehring, Charles T., ed. *Correspondence, 1647-1653*. New York, 2000.

Gehring, Charles T., ed. *Correspondence, 1654-1658*. New York, 2003.

Gehring, Charles T., ed. *Laws and Writs of Appeal, 1647-1663*, New York. 1991.

Hart, Simon, ed. *The prehistory of the New Netherland Company. Amsterdam notarial records of the first Dutch voyages to the Hudson*. Amsterdam, 1959.

Juet, Robert. "The third Voyage of Master Henry Hudson... written by Robert Juet of Lime-house 1626." In S. P. L'Honoré Naber, ed. *Henry Hudson's Reize onder Nederlandsche vlag van Amsterdam naar Nova Zembla, Amerika en terug naar Dartmouth in Engeland, 1609. Volgens het journaal van Robert Juet*. The Hague, 1921.

L'Honoré Naber, S. P., ed. *Henry Hudson's Reize onder Nederlandsche vlag van Amsterdam naar Nova Zembla, Amerika en terug naar Dartmouth in Engeland, 1609. Volgens het journaal van Robert Juet*. The Hague, 1921.

Laer, Arnold J. F. van, ed. *Council Minutes, 1638-1649. New York Historical Manuscripts: Dutch*. I. Baltimore, 1974.

Laer, Arnold J. F. van, ed. *Council Minutes, 1638-1649. New York Historical Manuscripts: Dutch*. IV. Baltimore, 1974.

Laer, Arnold J. F. van, ed. *Documents Relating to New Netherland 1624-1626 in the Henry E. Huntington Library*. San Marino, 1924.

O'Callaghan, E. B., ed. *Documentary history of the state of New York*, II. Albany, 1849-1851.

O'Callaghan, E. B., ed. *Documentary history of the state of New York*, III. Albany, 1849-1851.

O'Callaghan, E. B. et al., ed. *Documents relative to the colonial history of the state of New York*, I. New York, 1969.

Sainsbury, W. N., ed. *Calendar of State Papers: Colonial Series, 1574-1660*. Vaduz, 1964.

Vries, David Pietersz. de, *Korte historiael ende journaels aenteyckeninge van verscheyden voyagiens in de vier deelen des wereldts-ronde, als Europa, Africa, Asia ende Amerika gedaen'*. H. T. Colenbrander, ed. The Hague, 1911.

Waard, C. de, ed. *De Zeeuwsche expeditie naar de West onder Cornelis Evertsen de Jonge 1672-1674*. The Hague, 1928.

Acknowledgments

A special word of thanks is due Jaap Jacobs, who edited the contents of this book with the greatest precision. His knowledge of New Netherland was of inestimable value. I am more than grateful to Johanneke Braam and Menno Leenstra for their supplementary research and for continuing to suggest new angles. Editor-in-chief Paul Brood must be thanked for his critical eye. Without the exceptional efforts of Emiliet Albers, a great deal of wonderful visual material would not have been exhibited. I am indebted to Gijs Boink for verifying the accuracy of the spelling of the quotations from the archival as well as the contemporary sources. Dirk Tang, I hope you will continue to share your wise counsel with me for a long time to come. To the entire staff of Nieuw Amsterdam Publishers, all I can say is bravo. Thank you for your commitment and drive. Adriaan, I am grateful for all your advice as first reader and for so much more. Finally, Astrid Hertog and Irene Gerrits, making this book with you was both an honor and a pleasure.

Martine Gosselink

Credits

This book is published in conjunction with the exhibition *New Amsterdam, The Island at the Center of the World. The Exhibition*, in the South Street Seaport Museum in New York City.

Author: Martine Gosselink
Research assistants: Johanneke Braam and Menno Leenstra
Contents editor: Jaap Jacobs
Editors: Paul Brood and Astrid Hertog
Photographic editor: Emiliet Albers
Final editor: Paul Brood
Index: Gerben de Vries
Translators: Jennifer Kilian and Katy Kist, assisted by Donald Gardner, Michèle Hendricks, John Rudge and Wendie Shaffer

For their help, we gratefully acknowledge the following individuals and institutions: Louisa Balk, Martine Bartels, Madeleine van den Berg, Gijs Boink, Netherlands Consulate General in New York, Marieke van Delft, Irene Gerrits, Angela Haines, Tom Hennes, Gerard Jongerius, Anneke Leene, Joe Macdonald, Optical Techniques Department of the Royal Library in The Hague, Julia Schleppe, Russell Shorto, Saskia Smit, Dirk Tang, Gert Tetteroo, Maartje Ubbels, Eefje van der Weijden, Antiquariaat Forum, 't GoyHouten, Amsterdam City Archive, Amsterdam, Amsterdam Historical Museum, Amsterdam, Biblioteca Apostolica Vaticana, Vatican City, Biblioteca Medicea Laurenziana, Florence, City Hall, New York City, Library of Congress, Washington, D.C., Maryland State Archives, Annapolis, Mauritshuis, The Hague, Museum Boymans Van Beuningen, Rotterdam, National Gallery of Art, Washington DC, National Maritime Museum, Amsterdam, New York Historical Society, New York City, New York State Archives, Albany, Österreichische Nationalbibliothek, Vienna, private collection of Mr. Schimmelpenninck van der Oije, Rijksmuseum, Amsterdam, Royal Library, The Hague, The British Library Board, London, The Freeman Institute, Maryland, The New York Public Library, New York City.

Design: Philip Stroomberg, Ingrid Scheinhardt

Photography: Richard Koek (pp. 3, 4, 10, 34, 44, 59, 60, 80, 90, 91, 106, 152, 158, 182, 194, 202, 210)
David Cohen de Lara (pp. 54, 76, 120)
MDCdeWeerdt (p. 48)
Martine Gosselink (p. 98)
Illustrations: Bibian Harmsen (p. 38)

Cover illustration: "Nieuwamsterdam ofte Nue New Iorx opt' t.Eylant Man," Johannes Vingboons, circa 1665, Dutch National Archive Collection
Nieuw Amsterdam Uitgevers was unable to reach everyone holding the rights to the images included in this publication and kindly requests that anyone with such rights contact the publisher.

ISBN 9789046804483
NUR 680 general history

www.nieuwamsterdam.nl
www.nationaalarchief.nl

The publication and the exhibition were made possible in part thanks to support from:

The Reed Foundation
Robert Sterling Clark Foundation